INSTRUCTOR'S RESOURCE MANUAL
BUSINESS COMMUNICATIONS
LEHMAN, HIMSTREET, BATY   11TH ED.

DEBBIE DuFRENE
Stephen F. Austin State University

CAROL LEHMAN
Mississippi State University

SOUTH-WESTERN College Publishing

An International Thomson Publishing Company

EC72KX
Copyright © 1996
by South-Western College Publishing
Cincinnati, Ohio

I Ⓣ P
International Thomson Publishing
South-Western College Publishing is an ITP Company. The ITP trademark is used under license.

ISBN: 0-538-84781-6

1 2 3 4 5 6 7 8 9 0 PN 4 3 2 1 0 9 8 7 6 5

Printed in the United States of America

Acquisitions Editor: Randy G. Haubner
Developmental Editor: Alice C. Denny
Freelance Developmental Editor: Mary Lea Ginn
Production Editor: Crystal Chapin
Cover Designer: Craig LaGesse Ramsdell
Cover Photo: copyright Chuck Keeler
Marketing Manager: Stephen E. Momper

CONTENTS

SECTION A
INSTRUCTOR'S RESOURCE MANUAL

SECTION B
GRAMMAR TESTS   B–1

SECTION C
TRANSPARENCY MASTERS

SECTION A
INSTRUCTOR'S RESOURCE MANUAL

INSTRUCTOR'S RESOURCE MANUAL

TEACHING BUSINESS COMMUNICATION EFFECTIVELY

The eleventh edition of *Business Communications* has been prepared using a new pedagogical device, the Integrated Learning System. The text and supplements are organized around the learning objectives presented at the beginning of each chapter. Numbered icons identify the objectives and appear next to the material throughout the text, *Instructor's Resource Manual*, *Test Bank*, and *Study Guide* where each objective is fulfilled. When students need further review to meet a certain objective, they can quickly identify the relevant material by simply looking for the icon. This integrated structure creates a comprehensive teaching and testing system.

SUPPLEMENTARY ITEMS

All supplementary materials were prepared under the direct supervision of author Carol Lehman to guarantee full integration with the text. These supplements are available to instructors at educational institutions where *Business Communications,* 11e has been adopted. For additional information about the supplements, talk with your ITP Higher Education sales representative or call South-Western Faculty Support at 800–423–0563. Faculty Support may also be reached by fax at 415–592–9081 or through e-mail/Internet at review@swpco.com.

Study Guide to Accompany Business Communications (ISBN: 0-538-84779-4). Additional opportunities to reinforce the principles presented in this textbook may be found in *Study Guide*, 11e. This study guide includes review questions that can be used to check the student's understanding of each chapter in the textbook. It also contains practical applications in which students must solve business-writing problems. Lastly, the *Study Guide* contains a comprehensive review of major grammatical principles with exercises and solutions.

Multicolor Transparencies and PowerPoint® Screens. Also available with this edition is a set of 100 multicolor transparencies (ISBN: 0-538-85018-3). This package is keyed to the text and includes numerous figures from the text, key communication concepts, activities that reinforce concepts, and solutions to selected end-of-chapter activities.

The transparencies (and transparency masters) are also available electronically on a PowerPoint® presentation disk (ISBN: 0-538-85292-5). Simply load the files pertaining to a specific lecture and display them as needed. You will need a personal computer and LCD technology to use the presentation disk in lieu of transparencies. Use your own copy of PowerPoint® to further customize your presentation.

Test Bank and Computerized Test Bank. For the eleventh edition, the *Test Bank* (ISBN: 0-538-85291-7) includes approximately 1,000 test questions. As part of the Integrated Learning System, each test bank chapter includes a correlation table that classifies each questions according to type—factual or application oriented—and learning objective. True/false, multiple choice, and short answer items, arranged by learning objective, are available for each chapter. Page references from the text are included.

South-Western's automated testing program, *MicroExam 4.0* (ISBN: 0-538-84786-7), contains all questions from the printed test bank, with a pull-down menu that allows you to edit, add, delete, or randomly mix questions for customized tests. *MicroExam 4.0* will run on MS-DOS® computers with a minimum of 640K memory, a 3.5" disk drive and a hard drive.

Videos. Videos (ISBN: 0-538-84782-4, 0-538-84783-2, 0-538-84784-0) have been carefully prepared to correspond with the major concepts presented in each of the six parts of *Business Communicaitons*. Students "go inside" real companies and meet real business executives to learn effective communication strategies. Each video ends with "Business Tips," a focused review of the major principles the executive explained. Teaching/learning materials are available to help you integrate these videotapes in your classroom. A full-page discussion of each tape appears in the appropriate place within the text.

RATIONALE FOR TEXT SEQUENCE

The *Student Foreword*, "Effective Communication Skills: Key Ingredient to Career Success," helps students understand the link between career success and effective oral and written communication.

Part 1: Communication Foundations and Oral Communication

Part 1 consists of (1) Interpersonal Communication and Listening, (2) Organizational Setting for Business Communication, and (3) Public Speaking and Oral Reporting. Because communication activities occur within interpersonal and organizational spheres, we placed these chapters first to establish a working framework. Because speaking and listening are pervasive activities, most reviewers felt attention should be given to them early in the course.

Part 2: Analyzing Critical Factors Influencing Communication Effectiveness

Included in Part 2 are (4) Intercultural Communication, (5) Business Communication Technology, and (6) Ethical and Legal Guidelines. These three chapters provide additional dimensions that build a sound foundation for writing. If you prefer students to begin writing earlier, you can easily adapt the sequence of this flexible text to meet your students' specific needs. In addition, these three concepts—international, technology, and ethics/legal—have been integrated throughout the text and end-of-chapter exercises.

Part 3: The Writing Process

Part 3 covers (7) Organizing and Composing Messages, and (8) Revising and Proofreading Messages. These chapters focus on the process of writing—determining the purpose and the channel, envisioning the audience, adapting the message, organizing the message, writing the first draft, and revising and proofreading. We believe these two chapters, combined with the extensive Appendix B on grammar and mechanics, provide the best preparation for writing of all major business communication textbooks.

Part 4: Communicating Through Letters and Memorandums

Part 4 includes (9) Writing About the Pleasant and the Routine, (10) Writing About the Unpleasant, (11) Writing to Persuade, and (12) Writing Special Letters. Memorandums are integrated into the letter-writing chapters with the idea that memorandums, although generally direct, differ from letters primarily only in format.

Chapter 11 now focuses on promoting services and persuading readers to accept an idea. Several creative examples involve persuading supervisors to approve changes in work procedures and citizens to support worthwhile community projects.

Part 5: Communicating About Work and Jobs

Included in Part 5 are (13) Preparing Resumes and Application Letters and (14) Job Interviews, Employment Messages, and Performance Appraisals. Two factors directed our thinking in placing job search in this position. First, resumes and application letters build on the prior section on letter writing and provide a transition from letters to reports. Second, students have an opportunity to prepare their application materials just before the height of campus employment interviews in many schools if they take the course in the spring.

Part 6: Communicating Through Reports

Part 6 includes (15) The Report Process and Research Methods, (16) Managing Data and Using Graphics, (17) Organizing and Writing Short Reports and Proposals, and (18) Writing a Formal Report. Reports build on previous writing methods; in schools that offer two courses, reports often fall naturally in the second course. Also, many courses are planned to proceed only through short reports and omit the long, formal report.

Appendix A, Document Format and Layout Guide, and Appendix B, Grammar Review and

Exercises, can be incorporated formally into class activity or can be used for student reference.

Semester Program

A three-semester-hour course usually will be scheduled for approximately 45 classroom hours plus a final examination period. A four-semester-hour course usually will be scheduled for 60 classroom hours plus a final examination period. Differences in classroom activity will vary not only on the total course hours but also on the number of times a class meets each week. One-hour classes (50 minutes) seem to restrict classroom activities; in our opinion, two longer periods (75 minutes) provide better opportunities for both student and teacher to work effectively.

In a one-semester course that includes oral communication, teaching public speaking and oral reporting in a block by itself is probably not productive. If you can find an additional available classroom, you can divide the class into two groups—half to each room for speaking tasks. Half the students in each group can make three-to five-minute presentations in a single period. Those not speaking constitute the audience. Videotaping will allow the instructor to evaluate all presentations. Thus, four classroom periods will enable all students to appear before an audience twice. Also, topics in Chapters 4–6 can be used as subjects for oral reports, thus covering this material without the need for lecture. Time is then freed for an additional oral presentation.

In our opinion, oral communication deserves at least this much attention in any course. Students can learn something from one speaking experience, but that learning applied to a second effort can pay significant dividends. More will be said about oral communication in the discussion of Chapter 3.

If a minimum of 10 percent of the course is devoted to oral communication, total course time in percentages might be as follows:

Organization and interpersonal theory	10
Oral communication	10
Factors influencing communication	10
Usage and writing review	10
Letter writing	25
Job search (including interviews)	10
Reports	25

Such a percentage distribution devotes about 70 percent of classroom time to written communication. However, inductive and deductive planning, the logic of reports, and word usage and style—topics included in written communication—carry over into other forms of communication.

Quarter Program

In a quarter program, choices will need to be made about the topics to include in the course. If all chapters of the book are selected for inclusion, mere superficial coverage will be possible. Covering fewer concepts well is preferable. For instance, the course might focus on written communication, excluding coverage of Chapters 1–4, and Chapters 13–14. In many cases, the long, formal report is omitted.

Two-Term Program

Two-course programs, usually in schools on the quarter system, place emphasis in the first course on letter and memorandum writing. The course includes a thorough review of usage, style, and mechanics, as well. From the text, this first course would include the following:

Part 1: Communication Foundations. Chapters 1, 2, and, perhaps, 3 would be covered.

Part 2: Factors Affecting Communication Effectiveness. Overview of selected portions of Chapters 4–6.

Part 3: The Writing Process. Chapters 7 and 8, along with considerable work from the organized grammar review in Appendix B, provide the base for the study of letters and memorandums.

Part 4: Communicating Through Letters and Memorandums. The four letter-writing chapters, 9–12, complete the course.

The second course in a two-course program is devoted primarily to report writing but also includes the job-search chapters. Factors affecting communication effectiveness, Chapters 4–6, could be covered in greater detail than in the first course.

SOUND PEDAGOGY THAT LEADS TO WRITING PROFICIENCY AND UNDERSTANDING

This text is carefully designed to facilitate students' understanding of crucial communication principles and to develop effective writing skills.

Specific features that promote learning include the following:

1. Students are allowed to build a strong theoretical foundation for writing (Chapters 1–8) before encountering the writing applications (Chapters 9–18)—an organizational pattern reviewers and users have recommended consistently. If you prefer to have your students write earlier, you can easily adapt the sequence and content of this flexible text to meet your students' specific needs. Changes in the organization to the eleventh edition include

   a. Beginning the eleventh edition with the chapter on "Interpersonal Communication and Listening," (formerly Chapter 2), an engaging, highly relevant beginning for a study of business communications.

   b. Refocusing Part 3, "The Writing Process," on the process of writing—from determining the purpose and channel, envisioning the audience, adapting the message to the audience, organizing the message, writing the first draft, and revising and proofreading. Part 3 includes two chapters: Chapter 7, "Organizing and Composing Messages," and Chapter 8, "Revising and Proofreading Messages."

2. Chapter-opening learning objectives guide students through the learning experiences and are reviewed in the chapter summary so students can check their comprehension. End-of-chapter activities are provided for each learning objective.

3. Important terms are printed in bold for easy recognition, and definitions are stated precisely in easy-to-understand language.

4. Marginal questions and notes serve as handy self-checks that help students identify important concepts on each page. Some marginal notes require students to analyze and apply information just read and present real-world communication situations.

5. Before-and-after examples of writing with sentence-by-sentence analysis highlight common errors and help students see specific applications of most effective writing principles. Many new examples have been added to the eleventh edition to ensure that models depict effective solutions to timely business problems.

   a. Engaging new letters, memoandums, and e-mail messages include claims related to MIS documentation contracts and front-end charges for mutual funds, notice of company relocation to employees, and a procedural memorandum. Creative persuasive examples focus on promoting ideas rather than products; e.g., an employee's appeal to a supervisor to approve a telecommuting work option, citizens to support a city's youth swim association, and a persuasive claim to a resort hotel to adjust the room rate because exercise facilities were not available to conference attenders as advertised.

   b. A new application letter, a followup letter, and thank-you letters to an interviewer and a reference are based on the company/job profile for the entry-level audit position presented in the text. These letters illustrate how an applicant can identify and emphasize key qualifications that match company and job requirements.

   c. Four excellent new report examples are annotated for optimal learning and address engaging, timely topics that enhance students' understanding; e.g., audit of a company's software policies and inventory, preparation for working in the Kuwaiti market, and issues related to electronic monitoring.

   d. Lively new examples of an effective table, various types of charts, and a flowchart reflect capabilities of advanced presentation graphics software.

6. Full-document format adds realism to letters, memorandums, résumés, and reports and reinforces students' understanding of standard business formats. These visually appealing documents, complete with realistic letterheads, also provide variety in the regular text discussion.

7. "General Writing Guidelines" (Chapter 9) and "Check Your Writing" checklists provide a valuable tool for students to evaluate their documents rapidly. Additional checklists were added for (a) planning and delivering an oral presentation, (b) organizing and composing messages, (c) revising and proofreading messages, (d) interviewing, (e) pre-

paring employment messages, and (f) handling performance appraisals.

8. Completely new, engaging photos and relevant captions that illustrate specific communication concepts or extend the text discussion. At least one photo in each chapter focuses on a real-world communication situation.

9. Appealing graphics that provide students a clear picture of the specific communication theory and concepts being discussed.

10. Grammar and mechanics reviews in Appendix B provide clear examples and self-check quizzes to help students see where grammar review is needed. Plus, basic style in writing is covered in Chapters 7 and 8. Appendix B is also a handy grammar reference for students.

11. Abundant end-of-chapter activities provide students realistic, challenging problems to solve. Activities include review questions, exercises, e-mail application, applications, and cases for analysis. Approximately 25 percent of these activities are new. Activities are carefully written to

    a. Portray business situations relevant in various business disciplines and require students to consider international, ethical, legal, and technological implications. A identification line classifies each writing application (Chapters 9–18) so you can select exercises, applications, and cases relevant to your students interests/needs. The line also indicates the specific implications inherent in the problem.

    b. Encompass a broad range of difficulty to meet various levels of student needs—a repeated request of reviewers and users. The level of each activity is clearly marked in the *Instructor's Resource Manual*. The four levels include

    Level 1: Analyzing the strengths and weaknesses of a poorly written document and revising the document incorporating the critique.

    Level 2: Composing a document based on the information provided in the case problem. Students may provide fictitious details if necessary.

Level 3: Conducting limited library research to locate relevant information needed to solve the problem.

Level 4: Analyzing a complex issue that may require extensive research to reach an informed decision. Students write appropriate document(s) to the intended audience(s) from options provided (e.g., immediate supervisor, client/customer, and any others the students deem appropriate). These analytical cases appear in a separate section, Cases for Analysis.

EXPOSURE TO REAL-WORLD COMMUNICATION CHALLENGES

Advice from a panel of committed executives and exposure to communication dilemmas in real companies help students understand the relevance of effective oral and written communication in their career success. Several pedagogical components are integrated throughout the text to aid students in applying specific communication principles to real companies and situations:

1. A *Student Foreword* ("Effective Communication Skills: Key Ingredient in Career Success") challenges students to approach the course with added incentive. Examples from current literature and personal anecdotes of executives help students see the role of communication in the real world and the strong link to career success.

2. Communication Mentors give your students a priceless opportunity to "look over the shoulders" of a panel of communication mentors—six of the thirteen mentors are new to the eleventh edition. These corporate leaders represent numerous disciplines and various levels of management. As students study a particular principle, one or more of the communication mentors discuss how the principle actually works in today's dynamic business environment, share related strategies for communicating effectively, or simply provide concrete advice for developing the needed skill. To acquaint your students with the communication mentor panel, a photo and brief profile appears at the end of the *Student Foreword*. The mentor boxes contain original comments written for this textbook and are not adapted from comments printed elsewhere.

3. *New* **"Communication in Action" cases** integrated in each chapter are built around an executive addressing a communication dilemma in a real company. Cases are original based on personal interviews with these executives are not adapted from comments printed elsewhere. They include **critical thinking questions** and legitimate writing assignments (in chapters where writing has been introduced). Answers to questions and applications appear in the *Instructor's Resource Manual*.

4. *Revised* chapter openers, photographs, marginal notes, and text discussion also highlight communication issues in real companies.

5. Six videotapes with teaching/learning materials take students inside real companies to learn how business executives solve communication problems. Teaching/learning materials in the student textbook and *Instructor's Resource Manual* help instructors use these videos to enliven and supplement learning effectively.

INTEGRATION OF INTERNATIONAL, TECHNOLOGY, ETHICS, LEGAL, AND INTERPERSONAL FACTORS

International, technological, ethical, legal, and interpersonal topics are integrated throughout the text to reinforce the importance of these factors in all phases of communication—oral and written. In addition, to this comprehensive coverage, selected features that focus additional emphasis on these important topics include the following:

1. An **e-mail application** at the end of each chapter develops proficiency in using this important tool in the workplace. Applications include sending the instructor an outline and bibliography of an upcoming oral or written report for approval, minutes of group meetings, and responses to cases where e-mail is an appropriate channel. Students message other students to apply specific communication theory and to facilitate collaborative writing projects. Advanced applications include querying an international agency through Gopher to seek firsthand information about international communication and performing an electronic search of a business research topic using the Internet.

2. A separate chapter on "Ethical and Legal Guidelines" (Chapter 6) builds awareness of ethical issues facing students now and on the job. Using a framework for analyzing ethical issues including legal aspects, students develop skill in finding solutions to ethical dilemmas that do not compromise their own personal values. Specific guidelines help students learn to filter their messages to ensure that they are using effective communication ethically. Numerous examples from students' daily life, the business world, and cases give students ample opportunity to analyze complex issues where right and wrong may not be clear.

3. Separate international and technology chapters (Chapters 4 and 5 respectively) have been updated to reflect current coverage. Expanded coverage includes the Internet, online catalogs and information services, collaborative software, document conferencing and detailed discussion of the ethical and legal implications of technology.

4. End-of-chapter exercises, applications, and cases require students to solve problems with international, technology, ethics, legal, and interpersonal implications. The implications student inherent in the activity appears in bold print above the activity number and name.

CRITICAL THINKING SKILL DEVELOPMENT

The ability to analyze complex issues, organize thoughts logically and communicate these complex ideas concisely is essential for career success. The pedagogy of previous editions of *Business Communications* has involved teaching students to analyze and organize before beginning to write. Other features in the eleventh edition that foster the development of critical thinking skills include the following:

1. Marginal notes marked **Think It Over** pose analytical questions or provide short activities that can be completed individually as as cooperative learning activities. Students analyze and apply the information presented on the page, and discuss personal experiences or locate real-world applications of the principle presented.

2. Use of an ethical framework for finding solutions to ethical dilemmas (Chapter 6). This analysis of ethical issues requires stu-

dents to identify an issue, evaluate critical information, organize and express clear ideas, and persuade others to adopt a different perspective.

3. Practical applications in the *Study Guide* provide critical thinking questions (communication pointers) that help students analyze a situation and then organize their thoughts logically and concisely.

4. Communication in Action cases (see discussion of "Real World Exposure") and selected end-of-chapter activities provide critical thinking questions that help students analyze the situation and organize their thoughts.

5. End-of-chapter activities encompass a broad range of difficulty to meet various levels of student needs. Levels 3 and 4 require extensive critical thinking (Refer to the *Preface* for a detailed explanation and illustration of these levels.) The Cases for Analysis, the most difficult of the four ranges of difficulty, require students to analyze complex issues, conduct extensive research, and communicate the analysis in logical, concise documents. (The level is marked in the *Instructor's Resource Manual*. Many of these cases are designated with the GMAT icon in the textbook.)

6. Selected cases are marked with a GMAT icon indicating that these cases can be used as a sample **Graduate Analytical Writing Assessment (AWA)** for students preparing for the Graduate Management Admission Test (GMAT). The AWA portion of the GMAT includes two writing tasks designed to assess the ability to think critically and communicate complex ideas. The *Instructor's Resource Manual* contains guidelines for scoring the AWA following the holistic scoring method used by GMAT graders to rate analytical writing.

COOPERATIVE/COLLABORATIVE LEARNING ACTIVITIES

Develop meaningful cooperative learning activities that involve having your students work in small groups as an alternative to the traditional lecture method. With this teaching method, you can empower groups of students to achieve communication goals and become more accountable for the product of their work. (See Cohen, 1994 in the Selected References at the end of this section).

Educators' support for cooperative learning is increasing as research continues to document this pedagogical method as a "major ingredient in student learning" (See Johnson, Johnson, & Holubec, 1994; Slavin, 1994; Sharan & Sharan, 1992 in the Selected References at the end of this section.) Furthermore, as working in teams becomes a critical workplace skill in today's total quality management environment, business students must be equipped with the interpersonal skills to work with a wide variety of people and to arrive at common goals. Cooperative learning provides the means for such skills to develop.

Meaningful student interaction is especially valuable in large sections. Consider these suggestions for implementing cooperative learning experiences:

1. *Assign students to heterogenous groups of four or five.* Early in the term, pass a deck of cards to the class, with each student taking one. (For a class larger than 52 students, use a second deck of cards with a dot beside the number; for instance, for a class of 100, distribute 2 decks of cards with all black tens removed.) Have students tape the card into their class notebook. When soliciting student interaction, have "pairs" of students interact with one another (for instance, the five of diamonds and the five of hearts would form a pair. When groups of four are required, for instance, all "four of a kind" card holders could form a team, with spades being the team leaders. The cards can be combined throughout the term in any variety of ways to produce groups of differing sizes as needed.

2. *Develop cooperative learning activities that continue for short periods: informal (continues for one class period) or formal (continues for one to three class periods).* These short-term activities help students (a) focus attention on important concepts, (b) process material already taught through critically thinking, and (c) apply the group's collective information to the solving of problems.

Examples of short-term cooperative learning activities include

a. Asking student groups (or variations discussed in Step 1) to discuss concepts you have introduced in class (e.g., compare and contrast the deductive and inductive outline, identify various techniques for de-emphasizing bad news, define or explain concepts in your own words, etc.).

b. Completing the Think It Over marginal notes—a rich source of cooperative learning activities that will develop students' critical thinking skills.

c. Completing a short quiz. You might have individuals take the quiz first with closed books, and then have the group take the quiz with open books. The individual grade will make each member accountable for assigned readings. Discussing the questions allows students to examine the text more thoroughly and to share information and learn from one another.

d. Critiquing poorly written documents and revising to incorporate suggestions generated by the group and composing solutions to problems. Select problems from the to the end-of-chapter activities. An acetate or master of poor and good solutions to problems are provided for numerous problems. Chapter 5 contains several technology problems that lend themselves to effective cooperative learning activities.

3. *Develop long-term collaborative assignments for various written and oral communication tasks.* These assignments may continue over the entire term or a majority of it. Traditional research projects with an oral and written report are typical assignments.

4. *Devise a method for assessing group performance on short-term and long-term cooperative learning activities.*

Short-term cooperative learning activities: Informal cooperative learning assignments designed primarily to enhance learning may *not* be graded (e.g., discussion of concepts and Think It Over marginal notes). You can give the group credit (minor number of points) for completing the activity. Assigning credit will cause groups members to place pressure on other members to be prepared and present for each class period.

An individual and group grade can be given for quizzes and involved activities such as critiquing, revising, and composing documents. To simply recordkeeping, you might average the individual and group grades and record only one grade for the assignment.

The individual and group grade could be weighted equally, or the weighs could vary.

Long-term cooperative learning activities: Various methods can be used; however, we recommend assigning the same grade to the each group member for the quality of the product submitted. A second grade should be given to the each individual based on the quality and the quantity of the individual work contributed and should account for 10 to 20 percent of the student's grade on the assignment. The individual grade is based on (a) evaluations of team members and (b) your observations of team dynamics.

The following suggestions will aid you in facilitating the group's evaluation of individual's performance:

a. Ask students to assign a percent grade to each team member including him/herself midway into the project. This grade should reflect the quality and quantity of the team member's contribution. You may require that this assessment be submitted via e-mail. If an individual receives low marks from team members, you can contact the student to correct the problem. Knowing that they are accountable to the team tends to motivate students.

b. Have students complete a formal evaluation of each team member, including themselves, at the time the project is completed. The evaluation form should use a likert scale rating method that assesses effort, quality, and quantity of contribution. A sample evaluation sheet is included at the end of the Introduction of the *Instructor's Resource Manual.*

Another method for assigning an individual grade is to allow each group member a designated number of participation points to divide among members as they deem appropriate. The division may be equal or with more points given to one member and fewer to another. however, the point assignment must be a group decision.

c. Have students submit a post-project status report in memorandum form. The memorandum should include (1) a summary of their group performance, (2) a description of what they learned from the group experience, and (3) an analysis of what they would do differently the next time they are part of a team project. Such as assignment requires students to assess the group dynamics and the success of various strategies to bring about a successful group experience.

Selected References

Boyette, J. H., & Conn, H. P. (1992). *Workplace 2000: The revolution reshaping American business.* New York: Penguin.

Cohen, E.G. (1994). *Designing group work* (2nd ed.). New York: Teachers College Press.

Johnson, D., Johnson, R., & Holubec, E. (1994). *Circles of learning: Cooperation in the classroom.* Edina, MN: Interaction Book Co.

Sharan V., & Sharan S. (1992). *Expanding cooperative learning through group investigation.* New York: Teachers College Press.

Slavin R. (1994). *Cooperative learning: Theory, research, and practice.* Boston: Allyn & Bacon.

GENERAL TEACHING SUGGESTIONS

1. *Encourage class discussion using the inductive teaching approach.* This approach guides students as they derive conclusions (instead of *telling*, as would be done in the deductive approach). Let students know (in the first class session or two) that the *purpose* of discussion is to *learn* by sharing experiences related to the discussion.

   Frequency of participation should not be used as a factor in calculating semester grades. (Without clarification of this point, students may choose to speak often but contribute little.) Control students who overparticipate; encourage students who underparticipate. Students who are reluctant to contribute may be learning the most. By facial expression, students frequently reveal whether they have an idea to share or a question to ask. If an instructor's invitation to respond is well timed, the student may contribute with enthusiasm. Avoid embarrassing a student or making the student regret having tried to participate in a discussion that has been invited. If students sit in class "sweating it out" for fear that their names will be called, an instructor's purpose is defeated.

2. *Integrate the communication mentor comments into class lectures to reinforce the concepts in the chapter.* Comments may focus on communication strategies proven in the workplace or concrete advice on developing specific communication skills. So that you can test students' understanding of this valuable content, the *Test Bank* and the *Study Guide* contain questions from the communication mentor comments.

3. *Integrate the Communication in Action (CIA) cases into class lectures to add a real-life dimension to text coverage.* Questions following each case may be used to stimulate class discussion on topics related to the chapter coverage. CIA cases may also be assigned as outside reading, with students turning in the answers to the questions or answering the questions in class as a quiz.

4. *Use the acetates provided as well as make transparencies directly from the Instructor's Resource Manual.* A list of transparency acetates (designated as **TA**) and transparency masters (designated as **TM**) for each chapter is included in the *Instructor's Resource Manual*. Additionally, make transparencies from assignments submitted by students (blot out names). Critique them in class.

5. *Use the marginal statements, questions, and hints as learning reinforcement tools and to develop critical thinking skills.* Think It Over marginal notes require students to analyze and apply the information just read. These serve as an excellent means of encouraging critical thinking and soliciting class dialogue. Think It Over notes may also be used as discussion questions on exams.

6. *Enrich class lectures by integrating information from the Additional Readings included in the teaching suggestions for each chapter.* You may assign these readings and have students contribute major points when the relevant topic is discussed in class. Taken from current business magazines and practitioner journals, these readings will help capture students' attention as they read about real-world communication strategies.

7. *Assign activities from the Study Guide for each chapter.* Assure students that completing the review questions for each chapter will be an excellent review for an objective test on the material and for completing future writ-

ing assignments successfully. Each chapter includes 15 true/false and 15 multiple choice questions. Solutions clearly explain why each incorrect response is wrong and direct the student to a page in the textbook for further study.

Writing Applications are available in the *Study Guide* for Chapters 9–18. These applications walk students through three writing problems related to each chapter. Students answer critical thinking questions that help them organize their thoughts and outline correctly, write solutions using their outlines, and then compare their solutions with a sample solution.

Even if you do not require students to use the *Study Guide,* you may use the objective questions, practical applications, and grammar exercises to supplement quiz and test materials.

8. *Integrate the videotape prepared for each part of the text.* Require students to read the "Video Connection" in their text (follows the chapter to which the video relates), which previews the videotape and provides several questions reviewing major points presented. After showing the videotape, initiate a class discussion using the review questions. You may prefer assigning review questions and cases (that require students to write a letter or memorandum) to be completed for homework.

A video is available for each of the following chapters:

3	Public Speaking and Oral Reporting
4	Intercultural Communication
8	Revising and Proofreading Messages
11	Writing to Persuade
14	Job Interviews, Employment Messages, and Performance Appraisals
15	The Report Process and Research Methods

Suggested answers to the video activities and five multiple choice questions (to add to an objective test for this unit or to use as pop quiz items) are included in the videotape teaching suggestions immediately following each chapter.

9. *Expose students to Appendix B if you identify weaknesses in grammar or mechanics.* Refer

to teaching suggestions in Chapters 7 and 8. Prepare handouts and pretests directly from the *Instructor's Resource Manual* to inventory students' needs and to provide additional drill. Many of these items can be used for pretests, tests, quizzes, and class discussion. Answers are provided in the *Instructor's Resource Manual.* CIPS, the computerized grammar-review program, is still available with the eleventh edition. Designed for use on IBM compatibles, the program reviews 36 principles of grammar and punctuation. It is self-explanatory; students can proceed at their own pace without any instructor assistance. Unique as a computerized grammar review program, it presents each principle inductively. Students are encouraged to think; they are able to derive a principle before the computer presents and confirms it.

HOMEWORK AND GRADING

1. *Place primary emphasis on homework on letters, memorandums, and reports submitted for checking or evaluation.* Grammar and mechanics homework exercises should not be graded but should be considered reviews to sharpen tools for letter and report writing.

2. *Assign writing assignments to be written during class time.* The purpose is, of course, to assure that the student is doing his/her own work and to determine if the quality of the impromptu work is consistent with the student's homework. Additionally, the class period imposes a time constraint consistent with workplace requirements. Some unannounced assignments may be given during the course, using the last half hour of the class period for students to complete and turn in the assigned problem. Use a problem from the text or one prepared on a transparency to be displayed during the writing time. Tell the students in your course introduction that the unannounced assignments will count the same as a homework letter assignment. If you administer three, tell students you will count the highest two marks. In other words, if they take all three, the low mark will be discarded. In this way, the impromptu nature of the unannounced assignment will be compensated for when a student misses one.

3. *Assign about ten homework assignments (one or two pages) and at least one short and one*

long report. If you choose not to assign the long report, assign two problems from the short report and proposal chapter (Chapter 17). The weight given reports may vary, but instructors often make a short report equal to three to five letter assignments and a long report equal to five to ten letter assignments.

4. *Devise a fair grading system and communicate it clearly to students.* If students understand the grading system and see it as something objective, they will likely accept it. Papers graded on an A–B–C–D–F basis generally tend to group around B with today's grade inflation, and the result is a hazy distinction between any two letter grades. A method that tends to provide more marks and avoid the + and – after letters is a 10-point system. A perfect paper would be worth 10 points, earned on either of the following scales:

Scale 1		*Scale 2*	
	Points		*Points*
Content	2	Letter planning	4
Organization	3	Writing style	3
Style	3	Tone	2
Mechanics	2	Appearance	1
Possible points	10	Possible points	10

Scale 1 uses the same criteria used in the *"Check Your Writing"* checklist provided for students at the end of each chapter. The 2 points for Content allow credit for understanding the assignment and selecting the right ideas for inclusion in the letter. Because organization and style are major problems for students, the text devotes primary attention to these criteria. Therefore, they are weighted more heavily on the scale—3 points each. With 2 points allowed for good mechanics (spelling, formatting, and punctuating), students are rewarded for meeting high standards; but substandard mechanics will not result in a failing score for a paper that is otherwise good.

Like Scale 1, Scale 2 places major emphasis on organization (planning) and style. Allowing 2 points for tone encourages concern for human relations. By allowing 1 point for appearance, the scale provides a small reward for good mechanics. Yet, students need a negative reward for sloppy proofreading, misspelling, and faulty punctuation.

Such errors would result in deductions from total points earned on a paper. For example, a paper that earned 6 points but contained an error in spelling and another in punctuation would have a net mark of 4.

As a general guide, A=9 and 10 points, B=7 and 8, C=5 and 6, D=4, F=3 and below. For work over an academic term, total the points and divide by the number of assignments to obtain an average. An average of 6.4, for example, would be a high C but not a B. Let students know that your grading becomes stricter as the term progresses. What might be 9 or 10 work early in the course could be only a 6 or 7 if it were submitted later.

For reports that carry five times the weight of a letter assignment, you may use a 50-point basis and then divide the total into five marks. A report earning 38 points would receive five marks such as 8–8–8–7–7 and appear in the record book in that way to match the single-letter assignment marks.

Both suggested grading scales can be adjusted to reflect a higher number of points, for instance 50 or 100 points instead of 10. The relative weights of components would remain the same, but more latitude for grading is provided. *"Check Your Writing"* checklists appear at the end of Chapters 9–13, and 18 and can be used as gradesheets for letter, memorandum, and report assignments. The following gradesheets appear at the end of the Introduction to this *Instructor's Resource Manual:* (a) speech/oral report, (b) pleasant and routine messages, (c) unpleasant messages, (d) persuasive messages, (e) analytical reports, and (f) group evaluation. These gradesheets are based on the *"Check Your Writing"* checklists at the end of the chapters. You can easily change the total weight of the assignment, weights for the various components (organization, style, content, and mechanics), and the checklist items being graded for a specific assignment.

When points are awarded for each assignment, students can keep their own records and know where they stand at any given time.

5. *Save some paper-evaluation time by using the correction symbols in Appendix C.* If you have correction symbols of your own, students may add them to the textbook page. You may

simply write an abbreviation to identify the major area needing improvement. Or to provide additional feedback, you may write the number and letter designating the *specific* principle violated and the textbook page where the concept is covered.

6. *Coordinate grading so that the primary instructor grades all students' work on a rotating basis.* If a grading assistant is utilized, some "norming" sessions would be helpful to assure that the instructor and assistant use the same criteria and evaluation level in grading student work.

7. *Allow students to do some peer grading, especially of homework assignments.* This strategy not only saves valuable time for the instructor, but allows the student the opportunity to critique another student's work, comparing it to a gradesheet checklist or a sample solution provided by the instructor.

8. *Administer objective tests and quizzes to keep students "in step" during the course.* Objective test results should account for *no more than 25 percent* of a final course grade.

The *Test Bank* contains at least 50 true/false and multiple choice questions and five short answer questions for each chapter and Appendix A. To accommodate the needs of your class, you can readily select an appropriate balance of factually oriented and application questions. A marginal notation shows the correct answer, the page number on which the answer appears, and **F** (fact) or **A** (application) to identify the question type. These questions are also available on the *MicroExam,* which allows you to edit, add, or delete questions to produce a customized test. *MicroExam* is available for IBM compatible and Mac systems.

Collaborative Writing Projects

Refer to Cooperative/Collaborative Learning Activities section for suggestions for grading cooperative/collaborative learning activities.

E-mail Application

Assign the e-mail activities at the end of each chapter to develop students' proficiency in communicating electronically. The first e-mail assignments should not be graded for content and style but recorded for credit. For some students, these assignments will be their first attempt at using electronic mail. Furthermore, the editing limitations of the e-mail system should be considered in grading elements such as message structure and format.

E-mail assignments can be considered as part of the homework component of the course and may be recorded simply for credit rather than attempting to grade each of them. The instructor should, however, respond to each message received from students so that they will know that the message has been successfully delivered. The response may be a simple acknowledgment or may reflect on some aspect of the content of the student message.

Analytical Writing Assessment for the Graduate Management Admission Test

Introduce students to the scoring technique used for the written portion of the Graduate Management Admission Test (GMAT). The recent addition of a writing assessment to the GMAT exam, used as a determinant of entry into most graduate programs in business, has focused attention on holistic grading of student writing. In holistic scoring, a single score is assigned to a writing sample, based on the overall quality of thinking and writing. Holistic scoring emerges from the idea that writing is a complex process and that the effectiveness of a response depends upon the integration of many different elements. The GMAT method uses a six-point scale for evaluation, with scoring criteria based on organization, development, and grammatical structure. A disadvantage of holistic grading for classroom assignments is that students typically perceive them to be vague and arbitrary.

For students who plan to take the GMAT, however, some exposure to the writing assessment technique used will be helpful. Selected end-of-chapter activities which are marked with the GMAT icon can be used to illustrate this evaluation technique. In the GMAT writing assessment, a score from 0–6 is assigned based on the following criteria:

6 Outstanding

A cogent, articulate analysis of the complexities of the issue or argument, demonstrating mastery of the elements of effective writing. It is marked by the following: insightfully explores the issue; is clearly organized; demonstrates superior control of language, including diction and syntactic variety; and demonstrates superior facility with the conventions of standard English but may have minor flaws.

5 Strong

A well-developed analysis of the complexities of the issue or argument, demonstrating strong control of the elements of effective writing. It is marked by the following: clearly develops the issue using well-chosen reasons or evidence; is generally well organized; demonstrates clear control of language, including diction and syntactic variety; demonstrates facility with the conventions of standard written English but may have minor flaws.

4 Adequate

A competent analysis of the issue or argument, demonstrating adequate control of the elements of writing. It is marked by the following: develops a position using relevant reasons, examples, or features; is adequately organized; demonstrates adequate control of language, including diction and syntax but may lack syntactic variety; displays control of the conventions of standard English but may have some flaws.

3 Limited

A competent but clearly flawed analysis of the issue or argument, demonstrating some control of the elements of writing. It is marked by the following: demonstrates a vague or limited position or argument; is poorly organized; is weak in the use of relevant reasons or examples; uses language imprecisely and/or lacks sentence variety; contains occasional major errors or frequent minor errors in grammar, usage, and mechanics.

2 Seriously Flawed

A paper demonstrating serious weaknesses in analytical writing skills, demonstrating little control of the elements of writing. It is marked by the following: Is unclear or seriously limited in its main points; is disorganized; provides few, if any, relevant reasons or examples; has serious, frequent problems in the use of language and sentence structure; and contains numerous errors in grammar, usage, or mechanics that interfere with meaning.

1 Fundamentally Deficient

A paper demonstrating fundamental deficiency in analytical writing skills, with a pervasive pattern of errors in the elements of writing. It is marked by the following: provides little evidence of organization or coherence; has severe and persistent errors in language and sentence structure; and contains a pervasive pattern of errors in grammar, usage, and mechanics that severely interferes with meaning.

0 Unscorable

A paper that is totally illegible or obviously not written on the assigned topic.

Tell students that the Analytical Writing Assessment (AWA) score is reported, along with the numeric GMAT score, to the institution. Universities and professional schools may use this information as they choose, with an increasing number of institutions requiring a minimum AWA score for admission into graduate programs.

THE FIRST CLASS SESSION

The importance of a good start by the instructor and students cannot be overemphasized. During the first week, student opinions and attitudes are formed. A good beginning is achieved when the instructor introduces students to business communication in a manner that will create interest in the subject and causes students to feel that the instructor is personally interested and concerned about their success in the course. The beginning should be well planned. Because of the many interruptions during the first few days, the schedule should be flexible.

1. *Facilitate a mixer exercise.* A room without fixed seating is desirable for the "mixer," an activity used in many interpersonal communication courses.

   a. Move chairs to the sides of the room and have the entire class stand in a "crowd" in the center of the room.

   b. Ask the students to walk about randomly. But they should not purposely look at or touch others. They must not talk. (Most will look at the floor while walking.)

   c. After about two minutes of milling about, students should be told to make eye contact with other students—to look them in the eye but not to touch or talk—and to continue to walk about.

   d. After about 30 or 45 seconds, ask students to touch the hands or arms of others they look at as they walk.

   e. After another 30 or 45 seconds, ask students to take the nearest person they did not know previously as a partner and move to two seats or to a convenient location.

f.   The "new" pairs will have about five minutes to learn all they can about each other. After five minutes, ask each pair to join with another pair, so the four of them can become acquainted.

This exercise may be done with some triads (threesomes) particularly when someone might otherwise be left out because of an odd number of students. In about 15 minutes, your class will have broken the ice. Immediate friendships are often formed.

Why do the mixer? In addition to the get-acquainted aspects, students will react about being lost in a crowd, about the power of making eye contact, and about the increased impact introduced by touching. Additionally, you might ask if noise in the room prevented their listening to their partners. Invariably, the answer is no. People are selective listeners, able to turn off some distractions and listen to what they want to know. In addition to these aspects, your class will have formed the basis for group work and participating.

Recall some aspects of the mixer during your discussion of interpersonal communication and the Johari Window in Chapter 1.

2.   *Allow time for student introductions.* A variation of the mixer is an activity designed to assist students in learning about one another. On the first class day, have students write down and turn in to you a list of three interesting or unusual facts about themselves. Devise a list of about 15 characteristics taken from the student lists, with a space by each for a signature. On the second class day, distribute a copy of the list to each student, with the instructions to find someone in the class with each of the characteristics and obtain a signature beside them. Students should take their seats when all spaces are filled. Bonus points can be given to the student who completes the assignment first.

A more traditional introduction activity involves two people seated near each other learning what they can about each other. After a short time to prepare, one person will introduce the other to the class, and then the process is reversed.

Although these activities may seem to be time consuming, they are important to establishing an open environment for learning.

3.   *Administer a "Word-Usage Checkup."* Use the checkup in the *Instructor's Resource Manual* as a "pretest." Make enough copies for the entire class, give them a few minutes to complete the items, and then give them the correct answers. Let students retain the pretest so that they will know how well they did. Explanations for questions missed are found in Chapters 7 and 8 or the Words Frequently Misused section of Appendix B.

4.   *Administer a grammar-punctuation pretest.* On the first day of class, lecturing for a full hour is not normally the best approach. Ten minutes or so could be profitably devoted to a pretest of grammar and punctuation. Choose one of the exercises from the *Instructor's Resource Manual.* When the page is returned at a subsequent class period, encourage students to retain it for future reference. Later in the semester, after the principles have been reviewed, let students take the test again and compare the results with results of their first day's effort. For most, evidence of progress will be encouraging.

5.   *Allow students to prepare a written exercise.* Because writing and communicating are closely related, let students write the first day. Select one of the writing assignments at the end of Chapter 9 or 10. Reproduce it at the top of a page. Allow students ten or fifteen minutes to write the letter, placing the solution in the space beneath the problem definition (and on the back side if extra space is needed). Tell them to write the paragraphs they think the letter should include (omit date, address, salutation, and so on).

Keep the letters until after Chapters 9 and 10 have been covered. Then, return letters and invite students to critique their own papers. Some students will laugh aloud at mistakes they made the first day. Most will be able to see that they can write much better now than they could the first day.

6.   *Initiate a brief discussion about the importance of communication in career success.* Use the information from the *Student Foreword,* "Effective Communication Skills: Key Ingredient to Career Success," including the mentors' real-world statements about the relevancy of communication skills. Remind students that a major problem in *written* communication is the *unwritten* message

that is also transmitted. Project on the screen some sentences such as these:

I don't care what he does. (Mrs. Armstrong's response to a reporter who asked—while Neil was on the moon—if she would be in favor of his making subsequent trips.)

I'm waiting for a gentleman. (A woman's response to a man's invitation to join him for lunch. She was waiting at the door of the dining room.)

I have to miss class tomorrow. Will we be doing anything important? (Student's question, addressed to a professor.)

For each statement, invite students to answer such questions as "What do the words actually mean?" "What *un*written message might the statement convey?" "How might the unwritten messages strain the relationship of the sender and receiver?" Students will have ready answers to such questions.

7. *Learn students' names on the first day.* Try this method:

   a. After students are in their seats and the class is underway, hand a sign-up sheet to the first student in each row. Printed instructions at the top will read: *"Print your name, first name first."* (Make sure the row number appears on the sheet for each row.) Say, "Print your name and pass to the next student."

   b. Later, while students are completing the pretest or writing exercise, collect the sign-up sheets at the end of each row. Look at the students in each row, associating the first student with the first name on the sheet, the second student with the second name, etc. Drill yourself. Within a minute or two, you can put the sheet aside and mentally call the names of students in the first row. Work fast, the faster the better. Very quickly, you will have associated a face and a seat location with each name on the sheet in Row 1. Do other rows in the same manner. Then, challenge yourself to recall the name of every student; drill yourself again on the names of students in each row. By the time students have completed the exercise they have been doing, you may be able to call every student's name.

   c. Use the seating chart to check attendance each day.

8. *Build student-instructor relationships.* A major reward of teaching is the opportunity to associate with people who have careers ahead of them. Being genuinely interested in students and getting along well with them cannot compensate for lack of knowledge or poor teaching methods; but without a positive student-instructor relationship, effectiveness suffers.

   a. *Get acquainted with each student.* For the same reasons that businesspeople benefit from getting acquainted (see the text's discussion of the Johari Window), instructors and students benefit from getting acquainted. Invite students to think about this question: "Can you communicate more effectively with a stranger than with an acquaintance?" Readily, they will agree that knowledge of another person's background is an aid in communicating with that person. For that reason, you will share some of your background in exchange for some information about theirs. Reveal whatever you think your students should know about you (alma mater, number of years in business, consulting work, number of years on the present job, special interests, etc.). In exchange, you invite them to give you information about themselves.

      Distribute a sheet that invites students to share their major field of study, number of college credits earned thus far, and professional aspirations. On the last line, invite students to use the remainder of the page (and the back side if more room is needed) to give additional information about themselves (such as personal interests, accomplishments, concerns, disappointments—anything that they would reveal to a new friend). Let students know of your plans to *use* the information provided—to assist in getting acquainted with your students, to assist in any subsequent counseling about the course, and to assist in writing subsequent letters of recommendation. (Of course, they are free to tell little or nothing if they so choose; but almost every student will appreciate an opportunity to share pertinent information with an instructor who seems to care.)

b. *Be available to students.* Keep your posted office hours. By letting students know that certain office hours are set aside for them, you demonstrate concern for students (which positively influences classroom effectiveness). Sometimes, a student's visit to the office provides an opportunity to remove barriers that interfere with learning. In a student's mind, an instructor's credibility depreciates when posted hours are not kept. Provide alternate ways for students to contact you. Besides visits to your office, the telephone and e-mail are other avenues that students may prefer for communicating with you.

c. *Practice punctuality.* Instructors enhance their credibility by being in the classroom and ready to begin when the last notes of the bell fade and by not extending the session beyond the scheduled dismissal time. Preferably, return papers (other than the major report) at the class session following the one in which they were collected. By considering students' desire for prompt feedback and by doing their own work on schedule, instructors are in a position to encourage promptness on the part of students.

Except for the report or other extended assignments, collect assigned papers at the class session following the session in which they were assigned. Beforehand, let students know that late papers are not accepted. (If they are, time will be wasted in discussing the reason for lateness, the fairness of the penalty may become a problem, and students may get unneeded practice in making excuses.) Before collecting any papers, explain the plan. For example, you may explain that a portion of the class session that precedes the final exam will be set aside for students to complete makeup exercises. Students who were not able to meet a schedule but had good reasons can avoid penalty. Students who are not serious about meeting deadlines usually choose to meet them rather than risk taking makeup tests at the end of the semester. An alternative plan is to allow each student to submit one late assignment on the next class day after it is due. This generally takes care of the genuine illness or emergency.

d. *Require students to keep a notebook or folder.* Students will find that keeping a notebook specifically for their communication course will be helpful in preparations for tests and in office discussions with the instructor. The notebook should contain the course syllabus; class notes; class handouts; and tests, quizzes, and letter-writing assignments that have been returned. With such records in hand, students can expect more productive discussions with instructors (and sometimes avoid unpleasant discussions).

e. *Include the grading policy in the course syllabus and explain it before the first papers are graded and returned.* Usually, students will accept a system for determining the semester grade if the system is explained in advance. However, if the grading system is discussed on the first day of class, grading may get more attention than it deserves.

From prior experiences with composition classes, students are well aware that evaluation of letter-writing assignments is subjective. Unless instructors have some safeguards, too many students will challenge the grade on every paper that is returned. Those unproductive and stressful discussions can be avoided: (1) Let students know you are aware of the subjective nature of grading but will try to be objective; (2) Project or distribute copies of the grade sheet to be used for each assignment prior to the completion of the assignment; (3) Tell students what to do if they disagree with a grade. They are to keep all papers returned to them in their notebook. About a week before the end of the semester, you will let them know what their grade averages are up to that point. If they disagree, they are to bring their notebook to your office for review. If a consistent bias is detected, or if errors in checking or recording are discovered, make whatever adjustments are justified. Thank the student for giving you a chance to make amends.

By the end of the semester (after students have had many graded papers returned), students will almost certainly see that you have been generous more frequently than you have been stingy. Besides, if an extra point had been awarded here and there, the grade probably would not change.

f. *Explain the policy on absences in the course syllabus*. Some instructors include a small component in their grading system for attendance, with a deduction made for each absence over two. Bonuses may also be given for perfect attendance. If a point deduction or other grading penalty is not made for absences, you may consider the following plan: To a student who asks, "How many absences am I allowed?" the answer is "As many as you want. While you are absent, I will be spending every possible minute trying to help your classmates learn some principles that they can apply in their personal lives, in school, and in their careers. I will be preparing them for their assignments and their tests. Those with a good attendance record have a chance of making good scores. For students who must be absent on a day in which assignments are submitted or tests given, a makeup session is planned for the last class-meeting time before the final exam. If you must be absent, your reason is considered valid. You need not report it to me (unless for some reason you just want me to know)."

Such a policy is a reminder to students that education is their responsibility. It minimizes the amount of time spent in discussing upcoming or past absences. It also removes an instructor from the process of assessing the validity of an excuse and determining the severity of a penalty for absence. Normally, students who have more than three or four absences have already penalized themselves to the extent that making enough points to pass the course is difficult.

As an attendance motivator: Ask students to do some calculation. From the amount of money spent for tuition and the number of class sessions they will attend in the present semester, they can determine the tuition cost per class session. (Students are sometimes shocked at the figure.) Would they buy a ticket for a concert or a professional sporting event and just toss it? Do they see education as one thing people should pay for but not receive?

√CHECK YOUR WRITING—SPEECH/ORAL REPORT		
Component	Possible Score	Your Score
Organization ☐ Effective opening is used that presents purpose and initiates rapport with audience. ☐ Ideas are sequenced logically and smoothly. ☐ Time limit is observed. ☐ Effective ending is utilized that summarizes and/or makes a call for action.	20	
Delivery ☐ Appropriate eye contact is used. ☐ Irritating "nonwords" and other annoying speech habits are avoided. ☐ Lectern is used appropriately; leaning, tapping, etc. is avoided. ☐ Jargon and technical terms that the audience may not understand are avoided. ☐ Careful and tasteful dress is exhibited. ☐ Gestures and body language are used appropriately. ☐ A confident appearance is exhibited.	20	
Content ☐ Information is accurate and current. ☐ A few major points are included, with adequate support for each. ☐ Statistics, anecdotes, quotes, and/or humor are used appropriately. ☐ Visual aids are discussed appropriately.	40	
Visual Aid Usage ☐ Visual aids are appropriate to audience and setting. ☐ Only one major idea is related on each visual. ☐ Design is simple, clean, and appealing. ☐ Visuals are error-free. ☐ Distortion of facts and relationships is avoided. ☐ Readability is assured through adequate size and clarity. ☐ Information is accurate and current. ☐ Audience viewing is not obstructed by the speaker. ☐ Speaker paraphrases rather than reads visual line by line.	20	
Comments:	100	

√CHECK YOUR WRITING—PLEASANT AND ROUTINE MESSAGES		
Component	**Possible Score**	**Your Score**
Content ☐ Major idea is clearly identified. ☐ Supporting details are sufficient. ☐ Facts, figures, and names are accurate. ☐ Message is ethical and abides by legal requirements.	30	
Organization ☐ Major idea appears in the first sentence ☐ Supporting details are in a logical sequence ☐ Final sentence seems appropriate for an ending.	20	
Style ☐ Active voice predominates. ☐ Reader-oriented (first person is used sparingly or not at all). ☐ Words are readily understood, are informal, but not slang or clichés. ☐ Significant or positive thoughts appear in simple sentences in independent clauses; significant words are in emphatic positions. ☐ Sentences are relatively short and vary in length and structure. ☐ Paragraphs are relatively short—especially first and last paragraphs. ☐ Ideas cohere (changes in thought are not abrupt). ☐ Expression is original (sentences are not copied directly from problem, sample letters in text, or other students' papers).	30	
Format ☐ Appropriate letter or memorandum format specified in the instructions. ☐ Contains all standard parts positioned at left margin (dateline and closing line appear at horizontal center in modified block letter format). ☐ Contains appropriate special parts (writer's address, mailing notation, subject line, enclosure notation, copy notation, etc.) ☐ Uses mixed or open punctuation as specified in the instructions. ☐ Letter is balanced on page; memorandums begin 1½ from top of page. ☐ Spacing as shown in Appendix A. ☐ Jagged right margins for letter and memo. ☐ Has single-spaced paragraphs with blank space between paragraphs; no paragraph indentation; 1-inch side margins ☐ Signs letter or initials memo in black ink.	5	
Mechanics ☐ Keyboarding ☐ Spelling ☐ Grammar ☐ Punctuation	15	
Comments:	100	

√CHECK YOUR WRITING—UNPLEASANT MESSAGES		
Component	**Possible Score**	**Your Score**
Content ☐ Major idea is clearly identified. ☐ Supporting details are sufficient. ☐ Facts, figures, and names are accurate. ☐ Message is ethical and abides by legal requirements.	30	
Organization ☐ Begins with buffer that does not state the bad news, mislead reader, or state the obvious. Sets stage for reasons. ☐ Reasons precede the bad news. ☐ Presents logical details from which main idea (unpleasant idea) emerges. ☐ Ends with a positive idea (an alternative, resale, or sales promotion,etc.).	20	
Style ☐ Principal idea (unpleasant idea) is sufficiently clear. ☐ Subordinates bad news (complex sentence, positive language, positive idea, indirect refusal, counterproposal, subjunctive mood, etc.). ☐ Reader-oriented (first person is used sparingly or not at all). ☐ Words are readily understood, are informal, but not slang or clichés. ☐ Sentences are relatively short and vary in length and structure. ☐ Paragraphs are relatively short—especially first and last paragraphs. ☐ Ideas cohere (changes in thought are not abrupt). ☐ Expression is original (sentences are not copied directly from problem, sample letters in text, or other students' papers).	30	
Format ☐ Appropriate letter or memorandum format specified in the instructions. ☐ Contains all standard parts positioned at left margin (dateline and closing line appear at horizontal center in modified block letter format). ☐ Contains appropriate special parts (writer's address, mailing notation, subject line, enclosure notation, copy notation, etc.) ☐ Uses mixed or open punctuation as specified in the instructions. ☐ Letter is balanced on page; memorandums begin 1½ from top of page. ☐ Spacing as shown in Appendix A. ☐ Jagged right margins for letter and memo. ☐ Has single-spaced paragraphs with blank space between paragraphs; no paragraph indentation; 1-inch side margins ☐ Signs letter or initials memo in black ink.	5	
Mechanics ☐ Keyboarding ☐ Spelling ☐ Grammar ☐ Punctuation	15	
Comments:	100	

√CHECK YOUR WRITING—PERSUASIVE MESSAGES		
Component	**Possible Score**	**Your Score**
Content ☐ Writer is convinced that the idea is valid. ☐ Receiver benefits are stressed throughout. ☐ A primary appeal (central selling point) is incorporated. ☐ Evidence is convincing—factual, objective, and nonexaggerated. ☐ Message is ethical and abides by any legal requirements.	20	
Organization ☐ Sequence of ideas is inductive. ☐ First sentence gets attention and reveals the subject of the message. ☐ The primary appeal is introduced in the first two or three sentences and reinforced throughout the message. ☐ Receiver benefits are pointed out throughout the message. ☐ Cost to the receiver is not introduced until after the receiver benefits have been presented and is connected closely with what the receiver receives in return. ☐ Desired action is associated with the receiver's reward for taking action. ☐ Final paragraph includes a reference to the specific action desired and the primary appeal. The paragraph emphasizes the ease of action and includes a stimulus for quick action (if appropriate).	30	
Style ☐ Language is objective and positive. ☐ Active verbs and concrete nouns predominate. ☐ Sentences are relatively short but vary in length and structure. ☐ Significant words are in emphatic positions. ☐ Paragraphs are relatively short—especially first and last paragraphs. ☐ Ideas cohere (changes in thought are not abrupt). ☐ Primary appeal is frequently called to the receiver's attention through synonyms or direction repetition of the word. ☐ Unity is achieved by including in the final paragraph a key word or idea (the primary appeal) that was used in the first paragraph. ☐ Expression is original (sentences are not copied directly from problem, sample letters in text, or other students' papers).	30	
Format ☐ Appropriate letter or memorandum format specified in the instructions. ☐ Contains all standard parts positioned at left margin (dateline and closing line appear at horizontal center in modified block letter format). ☐ Contains appropriate special parts (writer's address, mailing notation, subject line, enclosure notation, copy notation, etc.) ☐ Uses mixed or open punctuation as specified in the instructions. ☐ Letter is balanced on page; memorandums begin 1½ from top of page. ☐ Spacing as shown in Appendix A. ☐ Jagged right margins for letter and memo. ☐ Has single-spaced paragraphs with blank space between paragraphs; no paragraph indentation; 1-inch side margins ☐ Signs letter or initials memo in black ink.	5	
Mechanics ☐ Keyboarding ☐ Spelling ☐ Grammar ☐ Punctuation	15	
Comments:	100	

√CHECK YOUR WRITING—ANALYTICAL REPORTS

Component	Possible Score	Your Score
Transmittal Letter or Memorandum ☐ Opening sets "Here is the report" tone. ☐ Subject is established in first sentence. ☐ Those who assisted with study are acknowledged. ☐ Brief summary of study is included. ☐ Close reflects thank you and forward look.	10	
Title Page ☐ Title is concise and descriptive. ☐ Full identification of authority for report is provided. ☐ Full identification of preparer is provided. ☐ Completion date is given. ☐ Attractive layout is used.	5	
Contents and Figures Page(s) ☐ Appropriate title(s) for page(s) is (are) used. ☐ Tabular arrangement is used to indicate heading degrees. ☐ Appropriate arrangement is used.	5	
Executive Summary ☐ A concise title (*executive summary, abstract, synopsis*) is used. ☐ A condensation of major sections of report is provided. ☐ Effective, generalized statements are used to avoid detail.	5	
Writing Style ☐ Use of *I* and *we* pronouns is avoided. ☐ Active/passive voice is used effectively. ☐ Proper verb tense is used. ☐ Ambiguous pronoun references (*this*) are avoided. ☐ Expletive beginnings (*There is, It is*) are avoided. ☐ Lists of three or more items are enumerated. ☐ Transition sentences are incorporated for coherence. ☐ Proper grammar and sentence structure are applied.	15	
Format/Layout ☐ Headings are descriptive of the contents of the sections. ☐ Consistency of contents is maintained; talking headings are used. ☐ Parallel construction is used in headings at the same level. ☐ Picture-frame layout is used for all pages; proper margins are used. ☐ All pages are numbered appropriately.	15	

√CHECK YOUR WRITING—ANALYTICAL REPORTS (continued)		
Component	Possible Score	Your Score
Graphic/Tabular Support ☐ All figures are numbered consecutively. ☐ Each graphic is given a descriptive title. ☐ Each graphic is introduced within the text that precedes it. ☐ Each graphic is placed as close to the textual reference as possible; analysis is more than repetition of ideas that can be seen in the graphic. ☐ Adequate graphic support is used to clarify information.	25	
Introduction ☐ A clear statement of the problem/purpose is provided. ☐ Scope or limits of the study are described. ☐ Method of research, with justification, is given. ☐ A definition of terms section is included, if necessary.	20	
Report of Findings ☐ Each statement is meaningful in its contribution to the solution of the problem. ☐ Ideas are logically sequenced. ☐ Large, unwieldy numbers are reduced to understandable ones through units, percentages, or ratios. ☐ Objective reporting style is used rather than persuasive or emotional language; opinions and assumptions are identified. ☐ Items are tabulated or enumerated for simplification. ☐ Careful use of primary and/or secondary data are evidenced. ☐ Adequate facts and figures are provided to support statements.	60	
Summary, Conclusions, and Recommendations ☐ Major information of findings section are briefly restated. ☐ Conclusions are stated carefully and clearly and are a logical outgrowth of findings. ☐ Recommendations grow naturally from conclusions.	20	
Citations/Referencing ☐ A citation is provided for each quoted and paraphrased source. ☐ An acceptable, authoritative referencing style is followed. ☐ Adequate information is provided to locate each source. ☐ Reference list includes a complete, accurate entry for each source cited.	15	
Appendix ☐ Items are included that are useful but not important enough to be in the body of the report. ☐ Each item is labeled and identified with an appropriate title.	5	
Comments:	200	

√EVALUATION OF GROUP MEMBERS

1. List the name of each member of your group (including yourself) in the space below.
2. Consider the quality of the contribution you believe each member of your group made (including yourself). Assign a percentage of the group's overall grade you believe each person in your group should earn. The total of the assigned percentages must equal 100%. (For instance, assigning 25% to each of four members should signify an equal contribution by each member.)
3. Write a brief, but **specific** justification for each rating. General judgments without evidence are not acceptable.

Name: _____ | **Percentage**

Justification:

Name: _____ | **Percentage**

Justification:

Name: _____ | **Percentage**

Justification:

Name: _____ | **Percentage**

Justification:

PART I

COMMUNICATION FOUNDATIONS AND ORAL COMMUNICATION

Chapters 1 and 2 are designed to provide knowledge about interpersonal and group communication, environmental aspects of business communication, and communication in organizations. Listening is included in Chapter 1 to provide an introductory course module composed of communication theory, speaking, and listening as preparation for the written and oral content and activities. Chapter 3, "Public Speaking and Oral Reporting," is included in Part 1 because so many reviewers recommended its introduction early in the course.

While text coverage of this three-chapter content is generous, you can supplement your own course coverage by referring to any of the excellent texts in these areas and the Additional Readings listed for each chapter in the text and *Instructor's Resource Manual.*

Build time in your schedule for integrating the videotape for Chapter 3, "Public Speaking and Oral Reporting." Require students to read the "Video Connection" after Chapter 3 in their texts, which previews the videotape and provides several questions covering major points presented. After showing the videotape, initiate a class discussion using the review questions. Alternatively, review questions and applications can be assigned as homework. Suggested answers and five multiple choice questions (to add to an objective test for this unit or to use as a pop quiz) are included in the videotape teaching suggestions immediately following Chapter 3.

CHAPTER 1

INTERPERSONAL COMMUNICATION AND LISTENING

CHAPTER OVERVIEW

Understanding what communication is and how it occurs is central to successful transactions in the workplace. Whether verbal or nonverbal messages are involved, the successful communicator will benefit from an understanding of appropriate behavioral and management theories related to the role of communication. Listening is emphasized as a vital communication skill for successful interpersonal and group communication.

LEARNING OBJECTIVES

1 Define communication and describe the main purposes for communication in business.

2 Discuss the importance of nonverbal messages and explain the difficulties involved in interpretation.

3 Explain the communication process model and the ultimate objective of the communication process.

4 Explain how behavioral sciences and management theories (Maslow, McGregor's Theory X and Y, total quality management, stroking, and Johari Window) help management understand the role of communication in the workplace.

5 Discuss the benefits of good listening and identify causes of poor listening.

6 Identify the four styles of listening and specify strategies for improving listening for each style.

CHAPTER OUTLINE AND TEACHING SUGGESTIONS

1   LEARNING OBJECTIVE

I.   Purposes of Communication
   A. An invigorating start is vital for this first chapter, because everything in the chapter contributes background for the remainder of the text coverage.
   B. Conduct a mixer activity to help students relax and get to know each other better:
      1. If you have not used one of the "mixer" exercises described previously in "The First Class Session" section of the Introduction, now is a good time to do so. The experience students gain provides an excellent departure point for discussions about interpersonal communication and listening.
      2. Another mixer activity would involve having students find all other class members who have the same major, assemble into a group, and meet one another. Each person would then introduce one of the persons in the group. A variation would be to have students find all other class members who share the same birth month.
   C. Students need to be impressed with the importance of communication to business success. Managers spend up to 80 percent of their time communicating—working in small groups, writing reports, and speaking with employees and clients. The following teaching suggestions may help reinforce this point:
      1. Show **TA 1–1** (Student Foreword Opener) to show the importance of communication skills.
      2. Show **TA 1–2** (Chapter Opener) to enforce the idea that international business activity increases the

need for strong communication skills.

2   LEARNING OBJECTIVE

II. Nonverbal Communication
   A. Metacommunication
   B. Kinesic Communication
   C. Teaching Suggestions:
      1. Make a transparency of **TM 1–2** (Kinesic Communication) and display it as you discuss this section.
      2. Show **TM 1–1** (Metacommunications) to illustrate implied and inferred meaning.
   D. Overcoming Barriers Created by Nonverbal Messages
      1. Make a transparency of **TM 1–3** (How Might Other Cultures React to Nonverbal Messages?) and display it as you discuss this section. Encourage students to share examples. **TM 1–4** (Cultures' Reactions to Nonverbal Messages) gives some correct responses.
      2. Demonstrate several nonverbal signals and have students write down what they perceive to be their meanings. You might include some of the following: folded arms, raised eyebrows, scratching the head, hands on hips, shrug of shoulders, etc. Have students share their perceptions. Were there differences in what students perceived? Explain. How might those signals be interpreted differently when accompanied with various word messages?

3   LEARNING OBJECTIVE

III. The Communication Process
   A. Show **TA 1–4** (Communication Process Model) as you discuss this section.
   B. The Sender Encodes the Message
   C. The Sender Selects an Appropriate Channel and Transmits the Message
      1. Show **TA 1–3** (Communication

Channels). Lead a discussion of the advantages and disadvantages of each channel. Under what circumstances would each channel be preferred?

2. Show **TM 1–5** (Selecting an Appropriate Communication Channel). Lead a discussion of why a certain channel would be preferred in certain circumstances. Include such issues as privacy, confidentiality, speed, impact, access, etc.).

D. The Receiver Decodes the Message

E. The Receiver Encodes a Message to Clarify Any Misunderstandings

F. Interferences Hinder the Process

   1. In small groups, ask students to complete Exercises 4–5 at the end of the chapter. Compare lists for commonalities.

   2. Using the lists generated above, have each student record the habits that he or she personally needs to overcome.

G. Summarize the section by emphasizing the following points:

   1. Communication is complete only when the message has been decoded at its destination.

   2. Although it is not always readily available (as in written communication), feedback normally provides senders with information about the effectiveness of their messages.

   3. Decoding and encoding are mental activities drawing on an individual's reservoir of experience.

H. To illustrate the complexity of the communication process, complete the following activity:

   1. Ask one student to study the diagram in **TM 1–7** (Origami Drawing) that illustrates the steps for folding paper to make a drinking cup.

   2. Tell the class that the student will give them instructions for making something from a piece of paper.

   3. Ask the student to give the instructions, giving only verbal instructions (no nonverbal cues) and answering no questions from the class.

4. Initiate a class discussion to identify breakdowns in the communication process. You may repeat the activity, this time allowing the speaker to use nonverbal signals and to answer questions from the class. Consider any improvements in the communication process and lead students into a discussion of the communication process model.

4	LEARNING OBJECTIVE

IV. Behavioral Factors Affecting Communication

A. Human Needs

   1. Discuss Maslow's needs hierarchy and relate it to McGregor's management styles. Managers who practice Theory Y help satisfy workers' social and ego needs. By satisfying these needs, people gain in personal maturity, which helps lead to trust in management. On the other hand, managers who practice Theory X tend to assume that workers are concerned only with satisfying lower-level physiological and security-safety needs, and so these managers fail to assist in people's efforts to satisfy higher-level needs.

   2. Integrate the communication mentor comments into class lectures to reinforce the concepts in the chapter. Mention, for instance, Hugh Jacks' comment concerning the importance of being a good listener and giving people "strokes," even when they bring bad news. Solicit discussion from the students.

B. Management Styles

   1. In addition to focusing on McGregor's Theory X, you might briefly discuss William Ouchi's Theory Z. Theory Z, also known as Japanese style management, is marked by a strong bilateral commitment of employer and employee, life-long employment, and slow decision making based on consensus.

Total Quality Management (TQM) is consistent with Theory Y and Theory Z since the contribution of the individual is emphasized.

2. Assign Exercise 8 at the end of the chapter. Results of the article summaries may be shared in discussion or as oral presentation.

C. Stroking and the Johari Window

1. The discussion of Maslow's and McGregor's concepts and the TQM movement eases the transition to the Johari Window concept. Trust in another leads to a person's willingness to disclose personal feelings, beliefs, and problems. Trust in others results from need satisfaction and from mature treatment at work. The Johari Window transparency provides a means to show how trust leading to self-disclosure helps enlarge the free or open area and, in turn, decrease the size of the blind and hidden areas. Self-disclosure leads to further trust and to a higher level of interpersonal "sharing."

2. Show **TM 1-6** (Johari Window: Trust and Self-Disclosure Help Expand the Open Area) as you discuss this concept.

5 | 6   **LEARNING OBJECTIVES**

V. Listening as an Interpersonal Skill

A. Because of its pervasive nature, listening should be a concern of other disciplines in addition to business communication. Training program kits are available from private vendors and from school learning centers, but purchasing such kits for use in one class session probably is not significantly productive. In the business communication course, listening instruction should be related to interpersonal communication and to interviewing practices. Text coverage is adequate for these purposes and for recall throughout other parts of the course.

B. Bad Listening Habits

C. Suggestions for Effective Listening

1. To emphasize that people may not listen as effectively as they think, give the listening test on the following page. (Test reprinted with permission of South Central Bell.)

2. Show **TA 1-5** (Effective Listening Guidelines) as you discuss this section.

D. Communication in Action: Tim Smith, S & S Video

1. Focus on how communication gave Smith a competitive advantage.

2. Lead students in a discussion of the answers to the questions provided in the text.

E. Listening for a Specific Purpose

1. Casual listening

2. Listening for information

3. Intensive listening

4. Listening for feelings with empathy

F. Teaching Suggestions:

1. Make a transparency of **TM 1-8** (Solution, Exercise 6). Lead class in a discussion that focuses on speaker and listener responsibilities.

2. Have students complete Exercise 12, noting their listening weaknesses. Then require them to keep a listening log for 21 days, the time needed to break a habit. They should write down what they did each day to break the bad listening habits which were identified (daydreaming, interrupting the speaker, prejudging the subject, etc.). Have students give a short oral report at the end of the three-week period, summarizing their outcomes.

3. Assign Exercises 14–16 throughout the term to refine student's listening skills.

VI. Summary

A. The following activity may lead to a review of the concepts covered in Chapter 1. Ask one student to stand and tell

Listening Test

Directions: Listen carefully because I will read each question only once. Use a pencil and paper to record the answer after each question has been read.

1. In the series of numbers "5–8–4–1–6," the second number is *8. Yes.*
2. In the list of words "by-of-in-at-on," the word beginning with "a" is *at. Yes.*
3. In the list of names "Adam, Meredith, Timothy, Jack, Suzette," which begins with a "J"? *Jack*
4. In the series of numbers "8–1–9–5–3," the third number is *9. Yes.*
5. Answer true or false to the following: In the list of words "below-go-snow-throw-flow," the third word mentioned is "throw." *False.*
6. Multiply the number 9 by 2, subtract 3, add 10, divide by 5. The answer is *5. Yes.*
7. Listen carefully to this statement: "Send five box tops with your name and address and 25 cents to Box 45, Denver, Colorado 80200, to receive the special gift offer." The number of cents to be enclosed is 25. *Yes.*

the class, in one to two minutes, something about himself or herself. Then select three more students—one at a time and with no forewarning—to do the same. You should jot down the nature of their disclosures. Are they from hidden or open areas? Purely factual? Toward the end of the class period or at the beginning of the following period, ask other students to tell what they "heard" from one student's story. Did listening occur? Ask other students to comment.

B. Assign selected exercises and activities at the end of the chapter.

C. Assign the *Study Guide* activities for Chapter 1. Assure them that completing this assignment will be an excellent review for an objective test on the material and for completing future writing assignments successfully. This chapter includes 15 true/false and 15 multiple choice questions.

D. Have students complete the e-mail assignment at the end of the chapter.

TRANSPARENCIES AND MASTERS

TA 1–1	Student Foreword Opener
TA 1–2	Chapter Opener
TA 1–3	Communication Channels
TA 1–4	Communication Process Model
TA 1–5	Effective Listeners…
TM 1–1	Metacommunications
TM 1–2	Kinesic Communication
TM 1–3	How Might Other Cultures React to Nonverbal Messages
TM 1–4	Cultures' Reactions to Nonverbal Messages
TM 1–5	Selecting an Appropriate Communication Channel
TM 1–6	Johari Window: Trust and Disclosure Help Expand the Open Area
TM 1–7	Origami Drawing
TM 1–8	Solution, Exercise 6

TA indicates a transparency acetate is provided in the transparency packet.

TM indicates a transparency master is provided in the *Instructor's Resource Manual.*

ADDITIONAL READINGS

Baum, N. (1994, April 11). Learn to be a good communicator, and a good listener, *American Medical News,* p. 34.

Berk, L., & Clampitt, P. G. (1991). Finding the right path in the communication maze. *Communication World, 8*(10) 28–32.

Bover, S. F. (1994). CEO serves as chief communicator of TQM program. *Public Relations Journal, 50*(6), 16–18.

Buhler, P. (1991). Are you really saying what you mean? *Supervision, 52*(9), 18–20.

Buhler, P. (1992). Managing in the 90s: Communicating with employees. *Supervision, 53*(5), 19–21.

Finkin, E. F. (1991). Controlling costs through effective communication. *Journal of Business Strategy, 12*(6), 59–61.

Genua, R. L. (1993). How well do you manage your mouth? *Female Executive, 16*(6), 72–73.

Grove, A. S. (1992, February). The fine art of feedback. *Working Woman,* p. 26–27.

Kelly, W. R. (1994, January). Effective words move minds, feelings: Communication tips for salesmen. *Agency Sales Magazine*, pp. 24–25.

Klassen, C. (1993). Improving quality means improving communication. *Canadian Business Review, 20*(2), 15–18.

Murphy, T. (1991, July). Getting your point across to each group. *Working Woman*, p. 47.

Peace, W. H. (1991). The hard work of being a soft manager. *Harvard Business Review, 64*(6), 40–47.

Penley, L. E., Alexander, E. R., Jernigan, I. E., & Jenwood, C. I. (1991). Communication abilities of managers: The relationship to performance, *Journal of Management, 17*(1), 57–76.

Rogers, C. R., & Roethlisberger, F. J. (1991). Barriers and gateways to communication. *Harvard Business Review, 69*(6), 105–111.

Sachs, R. (1991). Overcoming obstacles to communication. *Supervisory Management, 36*(7), 4–5.

Stephens, C., & Loughman, T. (1994). The CIO's chief concern: Communication. *Information and Management, 27*(2), 129–137.

Svehla, T. A. (1994, April). That's not what I meant! Why listening is the key to making yourself heard, *Food Processing*, p. 70.

Weiss, D. H. (1991). How to assure real communication takes place. *Supervisory Management, 36*(12), 4.

ANSWERS TO "COMMUNICATION IN ACTION" CASE: Tim Smith, S & S Video

1. Which of the three typical communication channels does Smith use primarily? Smith primarily uses two-way, face-to-face channels. Telephone calls to customers provide examples of two-way, not face-to-face channels, and letters to customers involve one way, not face-to-face channels.

2. **Identify some effective speaking and listening skills Smith uses when dealing with irate customers.** Smith deals effectively with irate customers by listening carefully to their complaints. He practices good listening by avoiding self-centered conversation and asking questions of the customer. He also takes responsibilities for mistakes. If a customer is given the wrong movie, he quickly assumes responsibility for

the problem by asking, "What would you like me to do?" Smith encountered emotionally charged language. The customer's expectations were not met, and she stereotyped video stores. The customer also was unwilling to communicate by hurrying toward the door.

Smith was involved in psychological stroking by providing accurate feedback to the customer, spending time with her, and listening to her complaints. He also gave her options on movies' categories and discussed other services.

3. **Assume that you are a small business owner. List several approaches you would take to practicing open, honest communication with customers.** Students will list a variety of approaches. Ensure that their comments include specific behaviors relating to their approaches that are listed in the chapter.

4. **What are some payoffs Smith experiences for effective listening on the job?** Effective listening brings repeat customer business, increases video rentals, and increases business growth as well as mailings of announcements and specials.

5. **When Smith states, "Keep communication honest at all times...no exaggeration, no lies," how does this ethical statement encourage that same ethical communication in his customers?** Customers may tend to "mirror" Smith's ethical behavior. In response to Smith's open and honest communication, customers are likely to respond in a similar fashion.

ANSWERS TO REVIEW QUESTIONS

1. The three purposes of communication are to inform, to persuade, and to entertain. Managers spend approximately 60 to 80 percent of their time involved in some form of communication, including attending meetings, writing reports, presenting information to groups, explaining and clarifying procedures and work assignments, evaluating and counseling employees, and promoting company products, services, and image.

2. The primary components of a message are the verbal and the nonverbal. Nonverbal accounts for up to 93 percent of total meaning.

3. Some possible metacommunications are as follows: "You didn't make budget last year; but try to do it this year." "I don't have any confidence in your ability to make budget this year, but try anyway." "The budget that upper management has given us is so ridiculous, I don't expect you to make the budget; so don't worry about it."

4. The five stages of the communication model follow.

    a. The sender encodes a message.

    b. The sender selects an appropriate channel and transmits the message.

    c. The receiver decodes the message.

    d. The receiver encodes a message (feedback) to clarify any part of the message not understood. Sender and receiver give feedback until the message is understood.

    e. The sender and receiver remove or minimize interferences that hinder the communication process.

5. Three typical communication channels are (a) one-way, not face-to-face (e.g., letters, memos and reports, press releases, electronic mail, facsimile, and voice-mail); (b) two-way, face-to-face (e.g., informal conversations, interviews, oral reports, speeches, or teleconferences); and (c) two-way, not face-to-face (e.g., telephone conversations and intercom announcements).

6. Educational, geographic, cultural, religious, social, and a variety of narrower factors lead to barriers. Refer to Figure 1–3 for other communication barriers.

7. Knowledge of Maslow's need hierarchy can assist communicators in identifying and appealing to need levels of various individuals or groups. McGregor's Theory X and Y reinforces to managers the idea that communication with subordinates should be on a mature, adult level.

8. The total quality management movement draws on McGregor's assumptions about Theory Y management and the creation of a more responsible role for the worker. Each employee is expected to solve problems, participate in team-building, and expand the scope of his or her role in the organization. Quality circle programs often did not have the support of top management, and employees were not empowered to carry through with their solutions. Today's management typically understands that empowering employees to initiate continuous improvement is critical for business survival.

9. Stroking is a transactional analysis term for identifying the way others give recognition to a person. It can be in the form of a pat on the back from the supervisor, a congratulatory message, or being listened to. Receiving strokes is essential to a person's mental and emotional well-being. By staying aware of this fact, managers can greatly improve communication and people's attitudes toward their work.

10. Sharing, or disclosing, occurs when people develop trust in each other. Individuals share personal thoughts, ambitions, and inner feelings only with selected persons whom they have learned to trust.

11. Benefits of effective listening on the job are as follows: Good listeners are liked by others; job performance is improved; accurate feedback provides evidence of job performance; greater job security exists for employees and supervisors; good listeners aren't often "taken"; creativity is improved; knowledge and skills necessary for promotion are enhanced; job satisfaction is improved.

12. Bad listening habits are very much attributable to ego involvement—preoccupation with personal problems, and other self-centered, careless attitudes. Refer to the five bad listening habits listed in the "Bad Listening Habits" section.

13. People listen selectively because they can block out barriers and distractions when they want to listen. Poor hearing is seldom a cause of poor listening.

14. Overlistening occurs when a listener attempts to get every detail. As a result, the listener mentally or physically records items, gets behind in this activity, and misses major points. Refer to the six guidelines for intensive listening listed in the "Intensive Listening" section.

15. Good listening for feelings depends on empathy. Refer to six suggestions for empathetic listening listed in the "Listening for Feelings with Empathy" section.

POSSIBLE SOLUTIONS TO EXERCISES

1. Solicit responses that require thought and reflection from students.

2. The lists will probably include items related to interrupting the speaker, ignoring the speaker, not looking at the speaker, fidgeting, exercising poor personal habits of cleanliness and mannerisms, passing the buck, getting too far ahead of the speaker, and failing to provide feedback. Refer to the list of communication barriers in Figure 1–3.

3. This list should reveal for the students some interesting differences between cultures. Some business examples of nonverbal miscommunication might be mentioned by students or introduced for discussion by the instructor.

4. In developing this list, students will synthesize information from various sources: the communication barriers in Figure 1–3, personal experiences, and self-analysis.

5. This exercise should help students appreciate the infinite number of breakdowns in the communication process and make them aware of some of their own communication problems.

6. This exercise offers an alternative way for reinforcing the concept of interferences and barriers to communication.

   Initiate a class discussion based on students' responses to this question. To illustrate the importance of effective listening, encourage students to share experiences where another person did not listen intensively and for feelings with empathy. Refer to the solution on **TM 1–8** (Solution, Exercise 6).

7. Encourage students to think about problems in encoding and decoding, as well as barriers and noise factors. Discuss the importance of feedback in completing the communication cycle. Try to elicit at least one response involving communication with a person of another culture.

8. Have students share information in a group discussion. What companies were discovered? What strategies for total quality management were consistently used in the companies? What novel approaches were reported?

9. Encourage students to share the reactions they received when they gave strokes during the designated time period and their reactions to the experience. Discuss the importance of motive when giving strokes, and emphasize the benefits stroking provides employees, supervisors, and the company.

10. A supervisor understanding Johari's window will realize that trust is essential if employees are to discuss openly and honestly the weaknesses that are affecting their job performance, strengths or special abilities that need to be developed to prepare for advancement or more challenging responsibilities, and other job-related concerns. By creating an open, supportive relationship, the supervisor can foster the trust needed for employees to divulge this information found in the blind, hidden, unknown areas—enlarging the open area.

11. A student's time distribution of communication activities may reinforce studies showing that a manager's time is distributed as follows: listening, 45 percent; speaking, 30 percent; reading, 15 percent; and writing, 10 percent.

12–16. Use these exercises to integrate listening skills throughout the term. These activities will add a welcome variety to the strenuous writing required in Parts 4–6 and will provide opportunities for practicing essential speaking skills while refining listening skills.

   To vary the assignment, select from the following topics: (a) Whatever your career field, communication skills are a key ingredient in your career success (specify a career); (b) Rapidly changing technology has revolutionized the way a business communicates; (c) What would business be like if legality were a company's only ethical benchmark or criterion?

POSSIBLE SOLUTION TO E-MAIL APPLICATION

The primary purpose of this application is to get students online and familiar with e-mail. If students have not received previous instruction in the use of e-mail, the instructor should prepare a simple tutorial for distribution. Students should be able to complete the assignment outside of class and without instructor assistance. The bibliography citation provides application of knowledge that will be developed further in Chapter 18.

```
┌─────────────────────────────────────────────┐
│ ┌───────────────────────────────────────────┐ │
│ │                CHAPTER 2                   │ │
│ └───────────────────────────────────────────┘ │
└─────────────────────────────────────────────┘
```

ORGANIZATIONAL SETTING FOR BUSINESS COMMUNICATION

CHAPTER OVERVIEW

As the setting for most business communication, students should understand the nature of an organization. Intrapersonal, interpersonal, and group communication are components of organizational communication. Communication flows within an organization in several directions, but barriers must be recognized and overcome if communication is to be successful.

LEARNING OBJECTIVES

1 Identify the four levels of communication.

2 Discuss factors affecting group communication.

3 Identify factors leading to the need for formal organizations.

4 Identify three barriers to communicating in formal organizations.

5 Distinguish between external and internal systems of organizational communication.

6 Discuss how information flows within an organization (downward, upward, and horizontal).

CHAPTER OUTLINE AND TEACHING SUGGESTIONS

1 LEARNING OBJECTIVE

I. Levels of Communication
   A. Lecture and discussion for Chapter 2 should not involve much more than one class period because many of the concepts are carried over into other portions of the course.
   B. Show **TA 2-1** (Chapter Opener) as you discuss this section.
   C. Because the course is new to most stu-

dents, vocabulary, theory, and background for later study are introduced here. Major concepts to cover include the following topics:

1. The major purpose of communication is to satisfy needs—personal, social, task, or job.

2. Interpersonal communication grows into group communication, which grows into organizational communication as size and complexity lead to different needs.

3. Formal organizations are marked by characteristics that call for increases in the amount and effectiveness of communication: specialization of individuals and units and interdependence of individuals and units.

4. The concept that all people have task and maintenance goals—get the job done and feel good about themselves—is an important factor in understanding the difference between an externally imposed system and an internally (within the person) generated system.

2 LEARNING OBJECTIVE

II. Communicating in Groups
   A. Show **TA 2-2** (Purposes of Group Communication) as you discuss this section.
   B. Purposes of Groups
   C. Factors in Group Communication
      1. Leadership
      2. Common goals
         a. Make a transparency of **TM 2-1** (Conflict). Lead a discussion of the value of conflict in the group process.
         b. Groupthink is a destructive phenomenon that results

when a group develops one mindset rather than exploring alternative solutions. Groupthink can result because of pressure to conform and to present a unified front. The space shuttle Challenger disaster was a prime example of groupthink at work. After the tragedy, numerous persons involved with the project indicated that they had indeed had reservations about the launch, yet the pressure to not further delay the mission influenced them to say nothing contrary. Conflict is a healthy process that counteracts groupthink.

   3. Role perception

      a. Make a transparency of **TM 2–2** (Roles of Group Members) to display. Which roles are positive? Which are negative? Can an individual group member play more than one role?

      b. Ask students to think of a group of which they are a member (family, club, church, etc.). They should then indicate persons in that group who play each of the roles discussed in 3a above.

   4. Longevity

   5. Size

   6. Status

   7. Group norms

      a. Newly formed groups often find it helpful to set aside time to define their purpose, expectations, and roles.

      b. Refer to Communication Mentor Terence McSweeney's comment comparing a team of employees to a symphony orchestra. Lead students in a discussion of this analogy.

---

3 | 4   LEARNING OBJECTIVES

III. Communicating in Organizations

   A. Specialization of Individuals and Units

   B. Interdependence of Units and Individuals

   C. Communication Barriers Caused by a Functional Organizational Structure

      1. Unclear indication of role vs. status

      2. Excessive competition

      3. Flat organizational structures ·

         a. Flat organizations pose new requirements for communication flow. When mid-level positions are eliminated, communication must be redirected.

         b. Assign Exercise 5 and report in class on the "flat" organizations they researched.

---

5   LEARNING OBJECTIVE

IV. External and Internal Systems

   A. Systems in Action

   B. The Grapevine as an Internal System

      1. To illustrate the workings of the grapevine, try the following serial communication activity:

         a. Ask six members of the class to leave the room and remain far enough away so that they cannot hear what is going on in the room.

         b. Ask the remainder of the class to read the story on **TM 2–3** (Serial Communication), which you have made into a transparency. The six participants should not read the story until the exercise is completed.

         c. When everyone has finished reading, select a volunteer to tell the story, without consulting the overhead, as close to verbatim as possible to the first person who was sent out of the room.

d. Call in the next student and ask the volunteer to reproduce the story as accurately as possible. The student should listen very carefully because he or she will be asked to reproduce the message for the next person. No questions or discussion should occur before, during, or after the reproductions.

2. A slight variation of this exercise is to ask one of the six students (outside the classroom) to read the story silently and then relay the message, in front of the class, to the second student. The second student then relays the message to the third student; the process is repeated until the message has been relayed to all students asked to stand outside the classroom. Because the class is unaware of the "true" message, distortion and confusion caused when oral messages are passed from person to person are emphasized.

| 6 | LEARNING OBJECTIVE |

V. Communication Flow in Organizations
  A. Show **TA 2-3** (Organizational Communication Flow) as you discuss this section.
  B. The directions of communication flow within organizations—upward, downward, and laterally (vertically or horizontally as you view an organizational chart)—describe the efforts of organizational managers to exercise control and effect coordination.
  C. Downward Communication
  D. Upward Communication
  E. Horizontal or Lateral Communication
  F. Communication in Action: Lonnie Uzzell, Southside Bank
    1. Ask students to read the case and answer the questions that follow.
    2. Follow up the case by assigning Exercise 3 at the end of the chapter, which requires students to depict the external system of com-

munication for an organization of choice.

VI. Summary
  A. Integrate the communication mentor comments into class lectures to reinforce the concepts in the chapter. Comments may include a communication strategy proven in the workplace or concrete advice on developing communication skill. So that you can test students' understanding of this valuable content, the *Test Bank* contains questions from the communication mentor comments.
  B. Assign the *Study Guide* activities for Chapter 2. Assure them that completing this assignment will be an excellent review for an objective test on the material and for completing future writing assignments successfully. This chapter includes 15 true/false and 15 multiple choice questions.
  C. Assign selected activities and exercises at the end of the chapter.
  D. Assign the e-mail assignment at the end of the chapter.

TRANSPARENCIES AND MASTERS
TA 2–1   Chapter Opener
TA 2–2   Purposes of Group Communication
TA 2–3   Organizational Communication Flow

TM 2–1   Conflict
TM 2–2   Roles of Group Members
TM 2–3   Serial Communication

ADDITIONAL READINGS
Bush, J. B., & Fronman, A. L. (1991). Communication in a "network" organization. *Organizational Dynamics, 20*(2), 23–36.

Gilberg, K. R. (1993). Open communications provide key to good employee relations. *Supervision, 54*(4), 8–9.

Goddard, W. E. (1994). Don't let internal communication links be bad connections! *Modern Materials Handling, 49*(2), 41.

Kelly, T. (1993). Communication is priority at GM. *Quality Progress, 26*(4), 12–13.

Odom, R. Y., English, D. E., Mills, H. N., & Noe, R. M. (1990). How to conduct meaningful meetings. *Business, 40*(4), 52–54.

Ray, M. (1991, July). The new way to boost morale: Keep your staff informed, *Working Woman*, pp. 16–17.

Sandwith, P. (1992). Better meetings for better communication. *Training & Development, 46*(1), 29–32.

Spaeth, M. (1994). Corporate communications: Do your employees believe you? *Corporate Board, 15*(85), 17–21.

ANSWERS TO "COMMUNICATION IN ACTION" CASE: Lonny Uzzell, Southside Bank

1. **During the working day, how does Uzzell experience listening in the four levels of communication?** Uzzell experiences intrapersonal listening when he prepares for questions about the new computer system. He listens interpersonally when he meets customers in the lobby or talks with customers on the telephone. He listens in groups when talking with and training employees about using the new computer system. Finally, he listens organizationally by his interaction with the president, tellers, and individuals from different departments.

2. **Identify various directions in the flow of listening at the bank. How does good listening and timely, accurate feedback facilitate communication when a new computer system is installed?** Uzzell was involved in upward communication when the president called him. He communicated downward with the staff assisting him with his presentation. He communicates horizontally with the other senior vice president conducting the presentation with him. Good listening through these levels plays a key role in accurate feedback. If Uzzell receives timely, accurate feedback from his staff, the implementation of the computer system will proceed smoothly.

3. **Reflect on your own experiences with a bank. How did your interpersonal communication with bank employees make that experience positive or negative?** Students may comment on their banks' communication about changes in fee structures, computer system changes, or customer service issues. Other students may state that their telephone calls to the bank were answered promptly (or too slowly), a bank officer took time (or didn't take time) to answer their questions and talk to them, or that certain problems were resolved (or not resolved) quickly. Encourage specific comments from students.

4. **Using the organizational chart for Citizen's Bank of Springfield in Figure 1–2 as a sample, distinguish between formal and informal communication at Southside Bank. Provide several examples to illustrate the two distinct systems.** Formal communication generally follows the lines up and down on the organizational chart, from president and vice presidents to various departments. Informal communication does not follow formal lines, but develops its own channels, often crossing lines and jumping between various departments. Communication followed formal lines within the bank when bank employees and officers discussed the change in computer systems. Uzzell also communicated formally with customers about the change through a letter.

ANSWERS TO REVIEW QUESTIONS

1. Intrapersonal is the communication that occurs within a person as the person processes information; interpersonal communication occurs between or among people.

2. The two major goals of both interpersonal and group communication are achieving task and maintenance goals.

3. Synergy is the increased output that results from people's working in groups as opposed to the output of the same people working individually.

4. Long-term groups spend considerable time and effort on maintenance goals, and short-term groups tend to concentrate almost exclusively on tasks.

5. An odd number of group members provides for deciding votes and reducing tie votes.

6. Conformity is easy and comfortable, leads to acceptance, and provides communication opportunities.

7. Factors that characterize organizations are specialization of individuals and units and interdependence of individuals and units.

8. Barriers caused by formal organizational structure include (a) unclear indication of role vs. status and (b) excessive competition.

9. Organizational charts show a hierarchy of authority that is not a hierarchy of importance.

10. Lack of understanding about the nature and roles of other persons or groups is a possible cause of most conflict between or among groups. This shortcoming is a communication problem that leads to conflict.

11. The pyramid shape implies higher status and salaries for those at the upper levels. As a result, competition occurs and often reaches a point at which cooperation is impossible.

12. In a win/win situation, one person's success is not achieved at the expense or exclusion of another. Employees and management must identify a solution everyone can support. Reaching this mutual understanding requires a high degree of trust and effective interpersonal skills, including empathetic and intensive listening skills, and determination to communicate until an acceptable plan is found.

13. In a flat organization, communicating across the organizational chart becomes more important than communicating up and down in a top-heavy hierarchy. Communication is enhanced because the message must travel shorter distances. Much of the communication is face to face.

14. An external system, or bureaucracy, relies on rules, procedures, and formalities.

15. An internal system develops from and is characterized by maintenance activities.

16. Grapevines are difficult to track because they do not follow single patterns.

17. Downward messages grow in size as they proceed through successive organizational levels by people's efforts to prevent distortion.

18. Organizational control is achieved through upward-downward communication. Coordination comes from horizontal communication.

19. Feedback is the term that describes a receiver's reaction.

20. Benefits of accurate upward communication are that it keeps management informed about the feelings of lower-level employees, taps the expertise of employees, helps management identify both difficult and potentially promotable employees, and improves downward communication. Upward communication may be threatening because the subordinate may be held responsible for misinformation or for promising more than can be accomplished. Employees appreciate genuine opportunities to send information to management.

Some risks associated with upward communication are that employees may resent any superficial attempt at open communication with management, and employees often tell superiors what they think the superior wants to hear and not what is true.

POSSIBLE SOLUTIONS TO EXERCISES

1. Focus on activities that cause the student to apply the principles in the chapter, rather than simply recalling facts.

2. A starting place for this activity would be the communication flow for the class. Lead students into discussion of the upward, downward, and lateral patterns of communication that exist. How is the external system structured? the internal?

   Students can also describe communication in groups such as workplace peer groups, student organizations, social groups, athletic teams, academic departments, and religious groups. In addition, analyzing the communication patterns among a group that is not formally organized, such as friends that meet at lunch every day, could illustrate the definite communication patterns present even in informal groups.

3. Encourage students to share with the class or small groups their organizational chart depicting the external communication system of an organization. Good examples may be drawn from workplace peer groups, student organizations, social groups, athletic teams, academic departments, and religious groups. Discuss the formal hierarchies as they compare to informal power structures.

4. Divide students into groups of four to five and instruct them to discuss each student's analysis of the external and internal communication system of an organization. Then as a group, students should attempt to predict management's reactions to the recommendations. A group leader could be asked to give a brief oral report to the class.

5. Discussion of the readings should focus on the common effects on communication that

have been reported. Did some organizations deal more effectively with communication issues than did others? What communication advice would you offer to an organization that is about to undergo "flattening"?

6. Refer to teaching suggestions for Learning Objective 5 for instructions for conducting this activity. Encourage students to discuss how messages enter the grapevine, speed and accuracy of message transmission, types of messages that flow through the grapevine, and the atmosphere that allows the grapevine to thrive. Discuss suggestions managers could follow to use the grapevine effectively. Recall Carroll Perkins' comments about the Salt River Project's use of the grapevine to counteract the rumor that additional employee layoffs were imminent.

POSSIBLE SOLUTION TO E-MAIL APPLICATION

Activity A can be answered from information provided in the chapter. Activity B requires the student to analyze and apply chapter information. Noted advantages of e-mail might include immediacy for the sender (elimination of telephone tag problem), elimination of time-zone differences, and ease of use. Disadvantages are that e-mail does not allow for instant feedback and clarification in most cases (although "chat" mode is available on some systems), and not everyone has access to e-mail. Issues of formality, confidentiality, and verifiability might be raised as issues in selecting e-mail as an appropriate communication channel.

Grading of this assignment should focus on content, rather than format. Completeness of the message and attention to what the assignment requested in the way of information should be the key criterion for evaluation.

CHAPTER 3

PUBLIC SPEAKING AND ORAL REPORTING

CHAPTER OVERVIEW

Speaking before groups poses serious anxiety for most people; to force them into such speaking situations abruptly might be considered cruel and unusual treatment. Group or team projects may be used initially to ease students into speaking roles with the support of their team members. Another way to reduce anxiety is to require the first speaking activity; award bonus points but do not penalize the student.

LEARNING OBJECTIVES

1 Analyze the audience for your oral presentations.

2 Plan and organize public speeches and oral reports.

3 Deliver speeches with increasing confidence.

4 Select, design, and use visual aids effectively.

CHAPTER OUTLINE AND TEACHING SUGGESTIONS

1 LEARNING OBJECTIVE

I. Knowing Your Audience
   A. The speaking chapter is presented at this time because it can be related to the material on listening to form the speaking-listening combination. Additionally, if you plan to have student presentations for portions of several class periods or before video cameras, this material needs to be presented early in the term.

B. Show the videotape "Public Speaking and Oral Reporting." Ask students to complete the related activities in the text. Use **TA 3–5** (Business Tips from Salsbury Communications, Inc. [Video, Part 1]) to summarize the major points.

C. Show **TA 3–1** (Chapter Opener) as you introduce the material.

II. Planning Your Speech or Oral Report

A. Show **TA 3–2** (Guidelines for Planning an Effective Speech) as you discuss this section.

B. Planning Your Strategy

C. Outlining a Public Speech to Persuade

D. Locating Support for Major Points
   1. Effective opening
   2. Well-supported body
   3. Effective ending

E. Outlining an Oral Report to Inform and Explain
   1. Introduction
   2. Body
   3. Summary

F. Assign Exercise 2 at the end of the chapter, which involves planning an oral presentation.

G. Communication in Action: Tom Watson, Watson Communications International, Inc.
   1. Ask students to answer the questions following the case.
   2. Present the following analogy to baseball that Bert Decker cites in *"You've Got to be Believed to be Heard."* Major league baseball players are considered successful if they bat above .300—if they hit the ball 30 percent of the time. Your chances of delivering an effective speech are much better. Why jeopardize your career by not even attempting public speaking?
   3. Use the following teaching suggestions to help alleviate fear:
      a. Show **TA 3–1** (Chapter Opener) to emphasize that fear of

public speaking can be overcome with time and practice.

   b. Ask students to list their fears related to public speaking. Through discussion, compile one master list. Point out to students that the fears they have are common to virtually everyone.

III. Delivering Your Oral Presentation

A. Controlling Speech Qualities
   1. Phonation
   2. Articulation
   3. Pronunciation

B. Using Style in Speeches

C. Keeping Within Time Limits

D. Show **TA 3–3** (Guidelines for Delivering an Effective Speech) to summarize this section.

E. Ask students to observe the oral presentation techniques of television newscasters, commentators, and panel show hosts. Students should prepare a one-page commentary and be ready to report their observations to the class or to members of their smaller group.

F. Assign Exercise 4 at the end of the chapter, which requires students to critique their own speaking skills.

IV. Using Visual Aids

A. Handouts

B. Chalkboards and Whiteboards

C. Flip Charts and Posters

D. Projected Visuals
   1. Transparencies
   2. Slides
   3. Computer presentations
   4. Videos, films, and audiotapes
   5. Models and physical objects

E. Show **TA 3–4** (Guidelines for Using Visuals Effectively) to summarize this section.

F. Show **TM 3–1** (Presentation Design Strategies) to provide further help in preparing appropriate visual aids.

V. Summary

A. Team presentations are usually less threatening than individual ones. Three- and four-person teams can be assigned to prepare and make presentations.

B. A suggested grading sheet for the oral component of a report project completed collaboratively is provided at the end of the Introduction of the *Instructor's Resource Manual.*

1. Officers' reports to a corporate shareholders' annual meeting. Each team may select its own corporation from any available annual report. Students play roles as officers' making financial, marketing, social responsibility, production, or long-range planning reports.

2. Introduction of a new consumer product to the press. Individual team members will represent the manufacturer, the advertising or promotion agency, and the research and development arm of the manufacturer. Teams will "invest" in a product.

3. Roundtable discussion of a current topic. One person serves as moderator, and the other three, as panel participants.

4. Presentation of the advantages and disadvantages of financial investments. Team members should plan the discussion around common stocks, corporate bonds, tax-exempt instruments, bank deposits, and federal obligations such as Treasury bills.

5. Topics in Exercises 3–6 at the end of this chapter.

6. Intercultural communication reports described in the Chapter 4 exercises:

a. Interview an international student, professor, or businessperson (Exercise 5) or a businessperson returning from an overseas assignment (Exercise 6).

b. Prepare a report providing management with specific guidelines for integrating successfully into another culture (Exercise 13).

7. Group presentations of new technologies that are impacting communication (e.g. facsimile, holography, fiber optics, voice synthesis). Team members will discuss the cost, availability, business applications, and guidelines for use of a particular technology.

8. Debate presentations of legal/ethical dilemmas discussed from polar perspectives (e.g., software piracy vs. price gouging by computer software developers, employee right to privacy vs. employer right to monitor electronically). The team will divide into halves which will represent the positions of the opposing interests.

If facilities to videotape presentations are available, schedule team presentations so that other teams constitute the audience. Videotapes should be made available for student review (feedback). Refer students to the checklist at the end of the chapter—"Check Your Public Speaking"—as a guide for planning as well as evaluation of their presentations.

C. Instruct students to complete the *Study Guide* questions for Chapter 3. Assure them that completing this assignment will be an excellent review for an objective test on the material and for completing future writing assignments successfully. This chapter includes 15 true/false and 15 multiple choice questions.

D. Assign selected activities at the end of the chapter. Remind students to study the suggestions in the "Check Your Writing" checklist when planning and delivering a speech or oral report and designing visuals.

E. Assign the e-mail application at the end of the chapter.

TRANSPARENCIES AND MASTERS

TA 3–1   Chapter Opener

TA 3–2   Guidelines for Planning an Effective Speech

TA 3–3   Guidelines for Delivering an Effective Speech

TA 3–4   Guidelines for Using Visuals Effectively

TA 3–5   Business Tips from Salsbury Communications, Inc. (Video, Part 1)

TM 3–1   Presentation Design Strategies

ADDITIONAL READINGS

Critical link between presentation skills, upward mobility. (1991). *Supervision, 52*(10), 24–25.

Fryer, B. (1991, November). Pointers for public speaking. *PCWorld,* pp. 235, 238–239.

How to give a good talk (1992, May). *Agency Sales Magazine,* pp. 32–35.

Hughes, M. (1990). Tricks of the speechwriter's trade. *Management Review, 79*(11), 56–58.

Louw, A. A. (1992). Break your barriers and be a better presenter. *Training & Development, 46*(2) 17, 19–20, 22.

McTague, M. (1991, August). Six rules to get your message across. *Supervisory Management, 36*(8), 9.

Percy, V. R., & Mullen, M. (1993). Getting your message across: Successful business presentations. *Training & Development, 47*(9), 20–23.

ANSWERS TO "COMMUNICATION IN ACTION" CASE: Tom Watson, Watson Communications International, Inc.

1. **Why is preparation so important in handling communication anxiety?** Good organization improves a speaker's impact, influence, and credibility because the audience perceives the speaker as prepared. Good preparation reduces speech anxiety and raises the speaker's self-esteem.

2. **Does good public speaking come naturally for you? Give examples of your personal experiences in public speaking. What technique assisted Watson in overcoming his fear of speaking?** Students' answers about their speaking skills will vary. They should justify their answers with examples of their own successes or failures. Watson was well prepared and concentrated on sharing his topic with the audience rather than being self-conscious. His keen interest in and knowledge of his topic helped him stay focused.

3. **Assume that you are faced with giving a presentation to your class and are experiencing communication anxiety. What are some ways you can reduce speech anxiety?** A speaker can reduce speech anxiety through being well prepared, knowing the subject well, using a good introduction, and using visual aids.

ANSWERS TO REVIEW QUESTIONS

1. Encourage students to discuss their answers in class or in small groups.

2. Refer to the discussion in the "Knowing Your Audience" section. The best source for audience information is the person who invited you.

3. Audiences are usually more alert in the morning, often uncomfortable after lunch, and may be sleepy in the evening. Speakers should take the time into consideration when planning their presentations.

4. A few major points should be developed because of time limitations and the ability of the audience to absorb.

5. The traditional purposes of speeches are to inform, to entertain, and to persuade.

6. Statistical support, anecdotes, quotes from prominent people, appropriate jokes and humor, and visual displays can be used to support the major points of a persuasive speech.

7. Too much persuasion may lead to distrust of the speaker. Would you buy a used car from the speaker?

8. Oral reporting is an efficient way to communicate because several people receive the message at the same time rather than individually at different times and because the audience is able to provide immediate feedback for clarification. As a result, oral reporting can significantly reduce message distortion and misunderstanding. Oral reporting differs from public speaking in several ways: smaller audience, familiar audience, questions from audience during presentation, intimate setting, shorter duration, and a difference in purpose—to inform.

9. The speaker may use the following visuals to assist or reinforce audience understanding: handouts, chalkboards and whiteboards, flip charts and posters, projected visuals (transparencies, slides, on-screen shows), models and physical objects. In terms of methods, the speaker may use anecdotes, jokes, quotes, and statistics.

10. The opening sets the stage and helps to grab audience attention. The closing provides the final "clincher"—a place to drive home the major thrust and to create the final impression.

11. The opening of a public speech and an oral report should identify the subject, grab the audience's attention, and set the stage for the presentation.

12. The ending of an oral report provides a summary and a conclusion or recommendation; the public speech usually ends with an appeal to accept the speaker's idea.

13. Memorization may lead to stiffness, lack of speaker reaction to feedback, and mental blocks (forgetting).

14. Professional speakers primarily use the extemporaneous style.

15. Articulation is the way in which people physically produce and join sounds. Pronunciation is a learned skill, a product of education and experience. To improve speech quality, breathe properly and relax, listen to yourself, and develop flexibility.

16. Encourage students to share their answers with the class or in group discussion. See the list in chapter dealing with using gestures naturally in the "Using Style in Speeches" section.

17. From a personal basis, some speakers should not use jokes under any circumstances because they cannot tell them properly. Jokes should be clean and related to the speech.

18. See the list of 14 suggestions for public speaking in the "Using Style in Speeches" section.

19. See the list of eight guidelines for preparing and using visual aids in the "Using Visual Aids" section.

20. Chalkboards and whiteboards can be used in informal speaking settings, are convenient for small audiences, and are flexible. The user can continue to erase and reuse the surface, and no special equipment is needed.

21. Guidelines for preparing visuals with "at-a-glance comprehension":
    (a) limit ideas to one per visual;
    (b) keep text lines short; and
    (c) do not clutter the page with too many colors, fonts, and graphics.

22. Color can be incorporated to create professional-looking flip charts and posters, and these visuals can be prepared in advance.

23. The advantages of using projected visuals:
    (a) more material can be presented in a shorter amount of time,
    (b) graphic representation of ideas leads to increased retention,
    (c) speaker can move from one visual to another quickly and easily, and
    (d) state-of-the-art visuals indicate a familiarity with technology necessary for success in today's business environment.

24. Computer presentations that run unattended can serve as an attention-getter at a trade show. Computer presentations can be mailed conveniently to potential customers/clients and employees in remote locations. Smaller face-to-face audiences may be overwhelmed or distracted by the special effects used to move from one idea to another. Automation limits the human interaction important in typical meetings or presentations.

25. A model or physical object is useful when
    (a) you want participants to "sample" a product or
    (b) the audience will benefit from seeing an exact replica or a to-scale model of a product or the like.

POSSIBLE SOLUTIONS TO EXERCISES

1. Focus on activities that cause students to apply the principles in the chapter, rather than simply recalling facts.

2. In this activity, you may require that students research the topic selected by locating and reading one or more articles. Evaluate the assignment according to organization and impact. Have students built in essential elements for an interesting and informative presentation?

3. Encourage students to discuss these analyses with the entire class or in a group discussion.

Summarize students' comments by generating a list of strengths and weaknesses in oral communication skills.

4. This exercise will help students assess their own speaking skills and develop strategies for improvement. Attempt to create a non-threatening class environment so that students are willing to evaluate their speaking skills honestly.

5. These exercises provide a way to get the entire class involved in group work, speaking roles, and meaningful content.

6. For this exercise, you might provide students with the Additional Readings listed for appropriate chapters in the *Instructor's Resource Manual*. Evaluation should focus on organization, content, delivery style, and visual aid design and usage.

7. In evaluating this assignment, you may assign a group grade for the overall effectiveness of the presentation, or a portion of the grade may be assessed according to individual performance.

POSSIBLE SOLUTION TO E-MAIL APPLICATION

The student's outline should include an introduction, body with appropriate main points delineated, and a summary, with whatever level of detail you deem necessary. An acceptable referencing method should be used in preparing the resource list. The grade on this assignment may constitute a portion of the overall oral presentation grade.

VIDEO CONNECTION
Salsbury Communications, Inc.

CHAPTER 3:
Public Speaking and Oral Reporting

SUMMARY

I. Widespread Fear of Public Speaking
  A. Number one fear of American adults
  B. Ability to overcome fear of public speaking produces a marketable skill

II. Factors in Effective Public Speaking
  A. Nonverbal dimensions
    1. Pitch
    2. Rate
    3. Tone
    4. Resonance
    5. Nasality
  B. Proper articulation of words
  C. Selection of appropriate topic about which speaker is "expert"
  D. Reduction of nervousness
    1. Planning
    2. Outlining
    3. Structuring
    4. Rehearsal (at least six times)
  E. Proper presentation development
    1. Introduction
      a. It is the most critical part of presentation
      b. Having someone else introduce the speaker is beneficial—so have a written introduction of self ready
      c. Humor is good but tricky
    2. Body
      a. Structure is important for audience acceptance
      b. Gestures are important but can be overdone
    3. Conclusion
      a. Be concise
      b. Plant a seed that will cause the audience to reflect later
  F. Everything in sync
    1. Verbal and nonverbal channels must match
      a. Face
      b. Hands
      c. Words
      d. Posture
    2. Reagan/Mondale comparison
      a. Reagan had everything "in sync"
      b. Mondale was not "in sync"

III. Tips for Effective Public Speaking
  A. Maintain eye contact
    1. Frequent
    2. Direct
    3. Friendly

B. Use visual aids appropriately
1. Bullets—headline information
2. Simplicity—too much information is distracting and results in over-kill
C. Commit to practicing—speaking is a developmental skill

ANSWERS TO DISCUSSION QUESTIONS

1. **What five characteristics does Greg Salsbury mention as nonverbal dimensions of oral communication? Why are they considered nonverbal?** Nonverbal characteristics that were mentioned included pitch, rate, tone, resonance, and nasality. Salsbury classified these as nonverbal because they exist outside the actual words of the message; they do, however, directly bear on the delivery of the verbal message.

2. **What does Salsbury say is the best way to overcome nervousness in public speaking? How much of this technique is desirable?** The best way to overcome nervousness is through practice. Salsbury described a process of planning, outlining, structuring, and *rehearsing* as essential to success. He recommended a minimum of six rehearsals, more if the information is totally new to the speaker.

3. **What is the most critical part of an oral presentation?** The most critical part of the presentation is the introduction because the audience's impression of the speaker and the topic is generally formed in the first 30 seconds.

4. **What role does humor play in public speaking?** Humor is good when used appropriately, but it is tricky. A joke can be the best or worst way to open a presentation, depending on whether the audience receives it positively. Humor can "ingratiate you to your audience or bury you."

5. **Salsbury uses the 1984 presidential race between Reagan and Mondale as an example of the importance of having "everything in sync." Explain the concept, referring to the two candidates for examples.** "Having everything in sync" refers to having a match in the verbal and nonverbal channels. The face, the hands, the posture, and the words must all convey the same message if the speaker is to be perceived as convincing. In the 1984 presidential campaign, Reagan exhibited this "in sync" quality. His face was very expressive, and his gestures matched the verbal message. In contrast, Mondale's face lacked expression much of the time, and his body language did not tend to match the message of his words. Salsbury attributes the outcome of the election, to a large degree, to these vital differences in the communication styles of the candidates.

POSSIBLE SOLUTION TO APPLICATION

(Solutions will vary)

Advertising as a Career

I. Introduction
   A. Would you enjoy having the opportunity to influence the behavior of millions of people?
   B. Would you enjoy the opportunity to contribute to the health of the national economy?
II. Characteristics of the Advertising Career [Body]
   A. Allows creative expression (it's fun)
   B. Investigates the motivations and preferences of consumers (it's enlightening)
   C. Encourages buying and therefore keeps the economy active (it's rewarding)
III. Summary—Advertising is fun, enlightening, and rewarding

MULTIPLE CHOICE QUESTIONS

1. Humor in oral presentations
   a. should be avoided because it can offend or agitate members of the audience.
   b. should be used extensively to reduce boredom.
   ✔ c. is either the best or worst way to open a presentation.
   d. is appropriate for informal conversation but not appropriate for a public presentation.

2. Which of the following does an audience typically *not* enjoy when listening to an oral presentation?
   a. articulation of words
   ✔ b. nasal intonation
   c. pauses
   d. structured information

3. Which of the following statements applies to practicing for public speaking?
   ✔ a. It is a necessary part of preparation and should be done a minimum of six times.
   b. It is needed by the novice speaker but becomes less essential for the polished speaker.
   c. It is helpful in moderation, but once or twice is sufficient.
   d. It tends to make the presentation overly structured and therefore should be avoided.

4. The use of gestures in oral communication
   a. detracts from the message being delivered and should be avoided.
   b. requires careful planning and practice for effectiveness.
   ✔ c. is beneficial when all elements match with the spoken message.
   d. shows genuineness and cannot really be overdone.

5. Which statement is *not* appropriate advice for the use of visual aids in an oral presentation?
   a. Visual aids should focus on "bullet" items and statements.
   b. Visual aids assist even the experienced speaker in keeping audience attention.
   c. The message of visual aids should be short and simple.
   ✔ d. Visual aids should focus on subpoints of the presentation that might otherwise be missed by the audience.

PART 2

ANALYZING CRITICAL FACTORS INFLUENCING COMMUNICATION EFFECTIVENESS

Chapter 4 is concerned with intercultural communication related to the management of people from other cultures and international business. Chapter 5, "Business Communication Technology," concentrates on what electronic tools can do for the manager and management. Chapter 6, "Legal and Ethical Guidelines," focuses on the ethical and legal dimensions of business communication.

Build time in your schedule to integrate the videotape "Cross-cultural Communication at Home," prepared for Chapter 4. Require students to read in their texts the "Video Connection" after Chapter 4, which previews the videotape and provides several questions reviewing major points presented. After showing the videotape, initiate a class discussion using the review questions. Alternatively, review questions and cases (requiring students to write a letter or memo) can be assigned as homework. Suggested answers and five multiple choice questions (to add to an objective test for this unit or to use as a pop quiz) are included in the videotape teaching suggestions immediately following Chapter 4.

CHAPTER 4

INTERCULTURAL COMMUNICATION

CHAPTER OVERVIEW

After reading Chapter 4, students should conclude that they cannot achieve complete proficiency in intercultural communication through classroom instruction, no matter how many courses are devoted to it. Course coverage will hopefully, however, launch students into a life-long pursuit of international understanding. Students should readily conclude that they will face the challenges of interacting with people from other cultures, whether it is part of their work in the United States or part of an assignment in another country.

LEARNING OBJECTIVES

1 Discuss the importance of communicating effectively across cultures, genders, and ages.

2 Identify how culture affects patterns of behavior and communication effectiveness.

3 Identify five potential barriers to intercultural communication.

4 Apply specific guidelines for effective written and oral communication with an intercultural audience.

CHAPTER OUTLINE AND TEACHING SUGGESTIONS

1   LEARNING OBJECTIVE

I. Intercultural Communication Opportunities

    A. Whether you present a lecture on the chapter before students read it or whether you conduct a session of questions and answers, lecture, and discussion after they have read the chapter, you should be able to draw on current examples from magazines, newspapers, and television about problems in intercultural communication:

1. EuroDisney is a good example of what can go wrong when a company tries to create a new venture in a foreign country without taking the context of the national culture into consideration. Executives at EuroDisney presumed U.S. company policies would be equally as successful at EuroDisney. Immediate problems occurred: employees resisted Disney's disregard for national customs—the unpopular dress code prohibiting facial hair and limiting make-up and jewelry and the no-alcohol-in-the-park policy (the French generally include wine with most meals).

2. When Wal-Mart opened a Supercenter in Mexico City, thousands of local residents poured in to see and buy the latest products from the United States. Managers decided to leave the English labels on products when they discovered that Mexican customers actually preferred products in "American" packaging over the ones with Spanish labels. For Mexicans, buying goods from the United States is a mark of status. Make a transparency of **TM 4–1** (Think It Over) and project it to the class.

3. A similar phenomenon occurred in Moscow. When McDonald's opened its first restaurant in the former Soviet Union, Muscovites took home the styrofoam containers as souvenirs and were willing to stand in line just to sample the food Americans take for granted here.

4. Coca-Cola committed an offense similar to McDonald's when they placed the flags of the 24 nations participating in the World Cup on their packaging. Among the flags was Saudi Arabia's, which includes sacred words from the *Koran*. Muslims were incensed, as they believe that holy words should not be used as a sales device, much less on packaging destined for the trash.

B. Show **TA 4–1** (Chapter Opener) to reinforce the need for effective intercultural communication.

C. Working for a Multinational Company Abroad

1. People will have to work in, supervise, and manage businesses in a culturally diverse environment.

2. Integrate the communication mentor comments into class lectures to reinforce the concepts in the chapter. So that you can test students' understanding of this valuable content, the *Test Bank* contains questions from the communication mentor comments.

D. Working for a Foreign-Owned Company

E. Working in a Culturally Diverse Workforce

1. Show **TA 4–2** (The Changing Demographics of the U.S. Workforce).

2. Depending on the cultural mix in your classes, you can do much in the way of relating the chapter to your "community." Virtually everyone is involved with intercultural contacts in some way.

3. The NAFTA treaty has expanded business activity with Mexico, reinforcing the need to better understand and accommodate for cultural differences. The daily flow of people back and forth across the U.S.-Mexican border in Southern California represents the busiest border entry point in the world and provides plenty of evidence of a multicultural society. Asian immigration following the Korean and Vietnam conflicts brought a strong Buddhist influence to the United States. Recent problems in Central America and the Caribbean have also brought a significant number of immigrants to the United States.

4. Show the videotape "Cross-cultural Communication at Home," and have students complete the assignments related to the activity. Use the Video Connection to illustrate Pacific Bell's efforts to work with a diverse workforce in California.

Show **TA 4–5** (Business Tips from Pacific Bell Directory).

| 2 | LEARNING OBJECTIVE |

II. Culture and Communication
   A. Ask students to read and summarize an article dealing with a U. S. cultural subgroup (e.g., Asian Americans, Latinos, Europeans, etc.) What cultural characteristics make the group distinctive?
   B. Divide students into small groups and ask each group to interview a person on the campus or in the community who represents a subculture (Exercise 5). The interview should include questions about the languages, customs, foods, social structure, and behaviors of the particular culture. The interviews can be the basis for preparation of an oral report.
   C. Lead the class in a discussion of the issue of cultural stereotypes. How do movies and television stereotype U.S. citizens? other cultural groups?
   D. Locate a list of common questions for the world traveler and distribute it to students. *(Going International* by Copeland and Griggs is an excellent source.) This activity will help them to assess how much effort may be required to succeed in another country. After students total their scores, discuss the outcomes.

| 3 | LEARNING OBJECTIVE |

III. Barriers to Intercultural Communication
   A. Stereotypes
   B. Timing
   C. Personal Space
   D. Body Language
   E. Translation Limitations
   F. Communication in Action: Jim Bice, APV plc
      1. Lead a discussion of the application questions that follow the case. Ask for suggestions as to what elements

and methods should be included in a company's formal intercultural communication training. Some students may have experiences they can share with the class.
      2. Ask students to role play the international communication situation on **TM 4–2** (Script, Exercise 8). Lead a discussion of the issues in Exercise 6, Part b, using the suggested solution in **TM 4–3** (Solution, Exercise 8).

| 4 | LEARNING OBJECTIVE |

IV. Guide to Good Intercultural Communication
   A. Show **TA 4–3** (Guidelines for Writing to an Intercultural Audience) and **TA 4–4** (Guidelines for Speaking with an Intercultural Audience) as you cover this section.
   B. General Principles
   C. Written Communication
   D. Oral Communication
V. Summary
   A. Role playing, group discussion, and any other techniques that involve students in the coverage of this material will make learning about intercultural communication more meaningful. Specific exercises to achieve this type of class activities are included at the end of Chapter 4. To help students appreciate the importance of cultural differences, have them complete Jameson's international simulation (see 1993 citation in Additional Readings). Rather than reading about cultural differences, your students will assume the characteristics of one of three different cultures, thereby "experiencing" the barriers caused by people with ethnocentric views.
   B. Assign the *Study Guide* questions for Chapter 4.
   C. Assign selected activities at the end of the chapter.
   D. Ask students to complete the e-mail application at the end of the chapter.

TRANSPARENCIES AND MASTERS

TA 4–1   Chapter Opener
TA 4–2   The Changing Demographics of the U.S. Workforce
TA 4–3   Guidelines for Writing to an Intercultural Audience
TA 4–4   Guidelines for Speaking with an Intercultural Audience
TA 4–5   Business Tips for Pacific Bell Directory (Video, Part 2)

TM 4–1   Think It Over
TM 4–2   Script, Exercise 8
TM 4–3   Solution, Exercise 8

ADDITIONAL READINGS

Davidson, E. (1991). Communicating with a diverse workforce. *Supervisory Management, 36*(12), 1–2.

DeVries, M., & Kets, F. R. (1994, May). Toppling the cultural tower of Babel. *Chief Executive,* pp. 68–71.

Dulek, E. R., Fielden, J. S., & Hill, J. S. (1991). International communication: An executive primer. *Business Horizons, 34*(1), 20–25.

Frederico, R. (1992). Boardroom beckons global communicators. *Communication World, 9*(12), 24–25.

Hampden-Turner, C. (1991). The boundaries of business: The cross-cultural quagmire. *Harvard Business Review, 69*(5), 94–96.

Heger, K. (1994). Leadership's changing face: How African-Americans and Latin American leaders communicate in a multicultural age. *Communication World, 11*(8), 24–29.

Jameson, D. A. (1994, September). Strategies for overcoming barriers inherent in cross-cultural research. *Bulletin of the Association for Business Communication, 57*(3), 39–41.

Jameson, D. A. (1993, March). Using simulation to teach intercultural communication in business communication courses. *Bulletin of the Association for Business Communication, 56*(1), 3–11.

Keen, P. (1990). Sorry, wrong number. *Business Month, 135*(1), 62–63, 66.

Knotts, R. (1989, January-February). Cross-cultural management: Transformations and adaptations. *Business Horizons,* 29–33.

Knotts, R., & Hartman, S. J. (1991). Communication skills in cross-cultural situations. *Supervisory Management, 36*(3), 12.

March, R. M. (1989). No-nos in negotiating with the Japanese. *Across the Board, 26*(4), 44–51.

McGarry, M. J. (1994, June 9). Short cuts. *Newsday,* p. A50.

Munter, M. (1993). Cross-cultural communication for managers. *Business Horizons, 36*(3), 69–79.

Neumeier, S. (1989). When somebody wants a payoff. *Fortune, 120*(13), 117–118, 120–121.

Souter, G. (1992). Avoiding a world of problems: Communication is vital for global programs. *Business Insurance, 26*(15), 40–41.

Tixier, M. (1994). Management and communication styles in Europe: Can they be compared and matched? *Employee Relations, 16*(1), 8–26.

Yoshida, S. (1992, June). It's beyond verbal expression (communicating with the Japanese). *Across the Board,* p. 51.

ANSWERS TO "COMMUNICATION IN ACTION" CASE: Jim Bice, APV plc

1. **During an initial greeting with a Chinese businessperson, list several guidelines that help facilitate good communication.** Discuss with students various verbal and nonverbal, intercultural communication skills. Students may list speaking slowly and listening carefully as two of the most important ways to facilitate good communication. When discussing nonverbal skills, talk with students about the importance of eye contact and knowing the right distance to stand from a Chinese businessperson.

2. **Do you feel Bice's training adequately prepared him to communicate interculturally? Explain why.** Point to the fact that Bice's marketing success depends on his intercultural training. Although obtained informally, he appears to be highly successful at marketing internationally. Students may need to understand the advantages of formal training in terms of the breadth and depth formal training provides.

ANSWERS TO REVIEW QUESTIONS

1. Canada and Mexico are major trading partners of the U.S., since the passage of NAFTA. Trade with Western Europe and Japan is also very important to U.S. business activity. U.S. firms have established plants in Europe, Central and South America, and Asia. Asians (primary Japanese) and Europeans have built plants in the United States. Refer to the "Intercultural Communication Opportunities" section or current newspapers and business magazines for additional evidence.

2. The passage of NAFTA, the unification of Germany, the economic reform and restructuring of the former USSR, and the restructuring of the European Economic Community are recent world events that have affected the level of international investment.

3. The real cause of the decline in male dominance in the workforce is a decline in the white male population in relation to the number of jobs available. Recent movements to improve the status of women and minorities in management positions are also a factor.

4. Increasing numbers of companies are offering diversity training seminars to help workers understand and appreciate gender differences and the cultures of co-workers.

5. Culture enables people to acquire a language, to feel social membership, to have standards for behavior.

6. Societies exhibit their culture in various ways including customs, objects, gestures, sounds, images, structures of institutions, and language.

7. Stereotyping may blind a person to the traits of any single individual who is a member of a stereotyped group. Applying generalizations (stereotypes) to individuals is dangerous.

8. Religious beliefs affect how people look at both their time on earth as well as their time in the hereafter. These views of time affect how a person might behave in various circumstances. Remember, however, that time is also affected by other cultural factors, including work, climate, technology, and values related to a variety of daily activities.

9. Messages people receive are translated or interpreted in terms of their own individual life experiences. Individuals' minds serve as emotional filters in the process of decoding messages.

10. Three general guidelines for intercultural communication are: (a) learn about the other culture, (b) have patience, and (c) get help when you need it.

11. Technical jargon and slang expressions are always open to misinterpretation in intercultural communication. Red-flag words shut the recipient's mind to your message and destroy any chance of trust and cooperation.

12. Stereotypes can provide broad generalizations about a people and establish a base from which to depart in intercultural communication. Cultural factors such as religion and family provide accurate information as part of stereotypes. The major caution, of course, is to consider individuals as individuals first, and members of a larger society second.

13. Feedback may be obtained by observing the other person rather carefully when he or she is speaking. The nonverbal cues from body motions, eyes, and vocal tones may be revealing. Additionally, you can be frank about the situation and ask the other person to verify the message in some way. Refer to step 6 in the "Oral Communication" section.

14. Refer to the list of nine suggestions under the "Written Communication" section.

15. Refer to the list of 11 suggestions in the "Oral Communication" section.

POSSIBLE SOLUTIONS TO EXERCISES

1. Emphasis of these activities is to raise awareness and sensitivity to cultural differences.

2. Use students' discussion of their answers to this exercise to supplement the information in the "Intercultural Communication Opportunities" section. Using the students' life experiences as a basis for your discussion will make this topic more relevant and interesting.

3. To vary this exercise, divide the class into groups of four or five members and allow class time to hear their arguments. Hearing each group's persuasive argument for increased international business, the class is more likely to realize the importance of learning to deal effectively with other cultures than from reading the chapter or listening to an instructor-directed lecture. This assignment could be used instead of one of

the assignments in Chapter 3, "Public Speaking and Oral Reporting," allowing you to integrate oral communication and intercultural communication in one assignment.

4. Use an intercultural assessment to guide the students in evaluating their adaptability to other cultures. (An excellent assessment is available with the *Going International* film series by Copeland Griggs Productions.) Divide the class into small groups to discuss their plans for improving their adaptability to other cultures.

5. Provide class time for students to share a one- to two-minute informal report on their interviews with an international student, an instructor, or a businessperson. If possible, invite one of these individuals to give a brief presentation to the class. Initiate a class discussion summarizing suggestions for communicating with a person from another culture. The students' reports and the report from the international speaker will help students see intercultural communication from the perspective of the person from the "other" culture and increase their commitment to improve their ability to communicate across cultures.

6. Provide class time for students to share a one- to two-minute informal report on their interviews with a businessperson returning from an overseas assignment. Initiate a class discussion summarizing suggestions for adapting to work in another culture. If possible, arrange for one of these individuals to give a brief presentation to the class.

7. You might provide students with the Additional Readings list provided for this chapter.

8. The script for this assignment is located on **TM 4–2**. A solution is provided on **TM 4–3**. The nonverbal messages will vary according the role play. In assessing the success of the communication, however, students will likely note several weaknesses: ignorance of each other's form of greeting, her use of an idiom that confused him, his stereotyped idea of the role of women, their difference in perception of time necessary to conduct business, etc. Strengths will likely be less obvious to students; they might include: the civil nature of their conversation in spite of conflicting ideas, the attempt to use appropriate greetings, her moving the conversation to the purpose of the visit, common courtesy shown between them, etc.

9. Students will be able to predict the interaction between the two cultures from reading the chapter or from knowledge of the culture. Some incidents will require research.

a. The event probably caused considerable embarrassment to the individual, for, in Asia, collective effort is valued over individual effort and competition. The dominant North American culture sees public praise as the best reward for a job well done.

b. The Arab-American employees are likely to expect a third-party intermediary, and without one the incident may blow up. Whereas the dominant North American culture is likely to take an individualistic, win-lose approach and emphasize privacy, Arab-Americans tend to value a win-win result that preserves group harmony but often requires mediation.

c. Latino culture teaches that building relationships is often critical to working together, but the dominant American culture encourages "getting down to business." The North American supervisor who hurries the manager through these formalities may be considered rude and ultimately untrustworthy.

d. Although the Indonesian is uncertain about the decision, saying no directly to the person sitting across the desk is culturally inappropriate. He will likely try to remain poised and avoid a direct answer. If the sales representative pushes further, the Indonesian will likely say yes and later send a telegram saying no.

e. The Asian woman keeps her eyes down to show respect to authority. Because this practice violates everything taught to North American managers about interviewing, the manager may think she is not assertive, not strong enough—that maybe she's hiding something, insecure, or not attentive. She sees the manager's eye contact as domineering, invasive, and controlling. Basically they don't trust each other.

f. The team worker with effective interpersonal skills should be hired because his ability to establish cultural rapport with the Asian workforce will far offset any deficiency in technical skills.

g. Crossing the legs is repugnant to Malaysians. Because the soles of shoes (and feet) come in contact with the filth of life, they are properly kept on the ground. The Malaysian would likely consider the U.S. manager very inconsiderate for not learning this very basic cultural preference.

h. In the Mexican culture, time is not considered important. Therefore, deadlines for reports may not be considered important either. The non-Mexican manager in Mexico may have to set an earlier deadline to receive the report by the time it is actually needed. The executive may have to adapt other planning strategies, taking into consideration Mexicans' attitude toward time.

i. Suggesting that the senior-level people meet alone will offend the Japanese, who place great emphasis on consensus. During negotiations, the Japanese deal with the group—not the individual.

j. Unlike U.S. business executives, typically managers in the United Kingdom do not conduct business during dinner or on a golf course. These activities are devoted to social activities only.

k. Because of the low status of females in Middle-Eastern cultures, the U.S. female executive probably would not be accepted as a legitimate company representative.

l. Exchanging business cards is more crucial to the Japanese than to North Americans; therefore, the Japanese executive was likely offended by the U.S. manager's ignorance of business card protocol. The U.S. manager should have made sure the business card was clean and free from smudges and bends, offered the business card immediately with his name and title facing the Japanese manager, held the card with both hands to show respect, taken time to read the card carefully, and placed the card on the table where it could be seen.

10. This exercise will provide an interesting variation from the typical instructor-directed lecture or class discussion.

11. If the majority of your students have limited exposure to international audiences, you may divide students into groups. Alternatively, you may ask students with experience in intercultural communication to share an experience and analyze its effectiveness using the communication process model. Using students' experience as a basis for discussion will bring relevance to intercultural communication.

12. Divide the class into small groups for this exercise. Requiring students to develop this checklist is intended as a preliminary exercise for developing the cultural profile (Exercise 13). To develop this list, students will synthesize information from various sources; information in the chapter, communication barriers discussed in Chapter 1 and those shown in Figure 1-3, and other factors developed by creative brainstorming. You might require students to gather additional ideas by reading several articles related to intercultural communication (see Additional Readings for this chapter).

13. Using the checklist developed in Exercise 12, students working in small groups can begin research immediately to develop a cultural profile for a particular culture or ethnic culture in the United States. Steps (b) and (c) can be varied depending on the time you wish to devote to this topic. Students can use this research to prepare the written report and/or the oral presentation typically required in this course. An added advantage is the incorporation of intercultural communication skills while developing writing and speaking skills.

14. To help students identify possible issues, suggest they focus on one specific area within their disciplines. For example, management students could focus on human resources, production, transportation; accounting majors could focus on financial, auditing, tax, and information systems. In addition to performing library research of printed and electronic sources, students should be encouraged to seek advice from professors in their disciplines. (Knowing that business communication students are researching international business issues in their disciplines should enhance professors' perception of the course.)

POSSIBLE SOLUTION TO E-MAIL APPLICATION

You will need to develop an instruction sheet for accessing Gopher, or one may already be available through your campus's information support services. Basically, the instructions will likely include the following:

1. How to log onto your university's mainframe computer. Your students will likely already know this if e-mail accounts have previously been established.

2. How to select Gopher listings (usually from a menu).

Once the student connects to Gopher, further activity is merely a matter of moving the cursor to the desired source and clicking.

This application is likely to create more interest among students if they print out and bring their responses to class for discussion. List the countries on the board as students indicate the places with which they have communicated. Ask whether any interesting or unusual responses were received which were related to the business communication issues that were addressed. Students may turn in their printouts for homework credit.

> ### VIDEO CONNECTION
> **Pacific Bell Directory**
>
> ### CHAPTER 4:
> **Cross-cultural Communication at Home**

SUMMARY

I. Issues in Maximizing Cross-cultural Communication
    A. Verbal issues
        1. Meanings of words
        2. Grammatical structure
    B. Nonverbal issues
        1. Body language
        2. Meaning of time
    C. Attitudinal issues
        1. Respect
        2. Trust
    D. Stereotype avoidance
        1. Differences of behavior within cultural groups
        2. Broadening of cultural perspective

II. Tips for Better Cross-cultural Communication
    A. Practice courtesy
    B. Use words precisely
    C. Recognize the society "salad bowl" (versus the more traditional "melting pot" idea)

ANSWERS TO DISCUSSION QUESTIONS

1. **Stephanie Dollschnieder refers to an important ingredient in successful intercultural communication as "cutting each other slack." What does she mean? Give examples of how this strategy can be accomplished.** "Cutting each other slack" refers to the willingness of intercultural communicators to excuse errors in customs and social graces when an honest attempt is being made by the other person to respond appropriately. The example used is the Asian custom of bowing to varying degrees upon meeting persons of different status. If we attempt to observe the custom, but inadvertently misjudge the degree of bow that is appropriate, the gracious Asian will likely excuse the error. Similar "cutting of slack" is necessary in other intercultural dealings.

2. **What part do respect and trust play in intercultural communication? How are they related concepts?** Respect must be given to the other person's right to his or her beliefs and customs, no matter how different they may be from one's own. Trust represents the assumption that the other person will also respect your beliefs and customs. The two concepts are inseparable.

3. **To what extent is courtesy a universal concept?** Courtesy is practiced differently from one culture to another, yet all have accepted standards of what is considered courteous or mannerly in various situations. A smile is probably the basic universal act of courtesy. An effective business communicator observes and studies other practices that are appropriate and desirable to a given culture so that proper behavior can be exhibited.

4. **How does the "salad bowl" concept of culture differ from the traditional "melting pot" idea?** The "salad bowl" recognizes the right of each culture to exist as a

separate, definable entity, while existing in harmony with other cultural ingredients. The "melting pot" idea describes a blending of cultures, so that single cultures lose their individual identity and take on a new co-mingled form.

5. **Jan Birkelbach discusses the wide array of behavior within cultural groups and cautions against generalizing that all members of a specific group fit a certain stereotype. Give examples of several such stereotypes.** Cultural stereotypes are broad-sweeping ideas about the people that make up a cultural group. They are, of course, false when applied to every individual within a given group and are often false about the group as a whole. Cultural stereotypes may include the following:

a. North Americans are greedy.

b. Mexicans are always late.

c. Jews are penny pinching.

d. Vietnamese eat dogs.

e. Middle Easterners don't practice good personal hygiene.

f. The French are arrogant.

g. African-Americans are good athletes.

h. The Irish have bad tempers.

SOLUTION TO APPLICATION
(Solutions will vary)

Effective Intercultural Communication: Necessary for (specify community)

I. Effective Intercultural Communication Is Essential
   A. (Community) is culturally mixed
      1. Caucasian: 72.6%
      2. Black: 22.5%
      3. Hispanic: 2.9%
      4. Asian: .6%
      5. American Indian: .1%
      6. Other: 1.3%
   B. Cultural differences exist
      1. Different languages
         a. English
         b. Spanish
         c. Dialects
         d. Other

   2. Different customs
      a. Religious observances
      b. Celebrations
      c. Family life
      d. Nonverbal communication
      e. Other

II. Effective Intercultural Communication Is Possible
   A. Learn as much as possible about cultures
   B. Respect cultural differences
   C. Use words precisely
   D. Use nonverbal communication appropriately
   E. Practice courtesy

III. Effective Intercultural Communication Is Profitable
   A. More satisfied customers
   B. Greater sales
   C. Other

IV. Summary

Part I of the outline would, of course, vary for each community. This solution requires some investigation into the cultural makeup of the student's local community, drawing on local demographic sources. Furthermore, it requires that the student learn firsthand about the characteristics of other cultural groups by utilizing the interview technique. Finally, the student is involved in the preparation of an oral presentation that brings together the information that has been gathered locally, along with the suggestions and tips covered in the videotape. Logic, organization, and synthesis skills are utilized in preparing the requested outline.

MULTIPLE CHOICE QUESTIONS

1. Which of the following is the best advice for communicating interculturally?
   a. Do what is appropriate, verbally and nonverbally, for your culture and hope the other person understands.
   ✔ b. Learn all you can about the other culture and apply it in your communication, realizing that the other person will probably overlook innocent mistakes.
   c. Avoid intercultural communication until you are an expert in the other cultures because mistakes can be offensive.
   d. Forget about cultural differences and concentrate on your message.

2. The cultural "salad bowl" refers to
   ✔ a. The idea that cultures can exist together in a complimentary fashion while still maintaining their separate identities.
   b. Mix-ups that can occur when members of different cultures do not understand one another.
   c. A weaker alternative to the blending of cultures described as the "melting pot."
   d. A traditional view of cultural diversity that emphasizes courtesy and social do's and don'ts.

3. Which of the following statements is *most* accurate concerning people within a specific culture?
   a. Behaviors are not related to cultural norms.
   b. Behaviors are standardized, based on cultural norms.
   ✔ c. A wide array of behaviors occur within the group.
   d. Behaviors will change automatically when interaction with another culture occurs.

4. Which of the following is most universal in its meaning?
   a. Words
   b. Body language
   c. Time
   ✔ d. Smile

5. The best summation of the issue of intercultural communication is
   a. It will become less critical as cultures assimilate into one mega-culture.
   b. It will have greater importance for large international firms than for smaller domestic firms.
   c. It is a business trend that comes and goes in cycles.
   ✔ d. It will remain extremely important as we learn to recognize and respect individual differences among cultures.

CHAPTER 5

BUSINESS COMMUNICATION TECHNOLOGY

CHAPTER OVERVIEW

The goals of this chapter include familiarizing students with the terminology and benefits of business communication technology and helping them learn to cope with problems frequently encountered with various applications of technology. The chapter discusses technology in four major divisions: collection and analysis of data, writing and organizing data, presenting data, and sharing data. The chapter concludes by discussing some legal and ethical considerations for users of communication technology.

Most students are familiar with personal computers, word-processing software programs, and perhaps other programs. Their experiences provide a departure point for the discussion of communication in today's automated environment. However, because student backgrounds in knowledge and skill in the electronic area will vary greatly, you need to adjust your coverage of Chapter 5 accordingly.

LEARNING OBJECTIVES

1 Identify the benefits of using organizational databases and online information services and spreadsheets to collect and analyze data.

2 Identify the benefits of using word-processing, spellchecks, thesauruses, and writing-analysis software to write and organize text.

3 Explain how printers and desktop publishing and presentation graphics are useful to enhance the overall effectiveness of a document.

4 Discuss how e-mail, voice-mail, facsimile machines, cellular telephones, telecommuting, teleconferences, and videoconferences facilitate sharing data effectively.

5 Identify ethical and legal implications associated with technology.

CHAPTER OUTLINE AND TEACHING SUGGESTIONS

1   **LEARNING OBJECTIVE**

I. Collecting and Analyzing Data
   A. Show **TA 5–1** (Chapter Opener) as you begin discussion of the chapter.
   B. Have personal computers and software available for student use or at least for instructor demonstration, if at all possible.
   C. Organizational Databases
   D. Online Library Catalogs and Other Databases
   E. Online Information Services
      1. The Internet
         a. Being able to send messages anywhere in the world instantly is especially helpful for companies such as Panasonic that need to communicate quickly with its many suppliers and customers and its U.S. and Japanese labs. Refer students to the photo of the Internet screen in the text.
         b. Companies are developing other significant uses for the Internet as more people connect and the Internet becomes easier to use. For example, doctors at hospitals with Internet connections consult with faraway specialists by transmitting 3–D brain scans that can be rotated and examined onscreen.
         c. Companies are beginning to use Internet for electronic marketing and for providing customer support. In fact, some vendors have found that placing free and shareware titles online for a specified period without requiring payment is a successful strategy for developing satisfied users. A number of companies that have attempted electronic marketing have met strong resistance from people objecting to "junk" mail being distributed electronically.
         d. IBM engineers at remote locations often use the Internet when developing a new project or when collaborating with engineers in other companies. Knowing that linking its corporation to a public network such as the Internet is risky; IBM has developed an elaborate security program to protect confidential information.
         e. Assign Exercise 2 at the end of the chapter which involves online location of a current article. Require students to write an executive summary of the article and/or give an oral report to the class or to small groups. You could also require students to e-mail you with the highlights of their articles.

2. Commercial Online Information Services

3. Ask students to find out about the subscription fees, services, and usage charges for one of the five major national commercial information services that allow connection to the Internet. Students may consult computer magazines for ads with toll-free numbers or call local providers.

F. Hurdles Involved in Using Online Services

1. Information overload is a real phenomenon when attempting to "surf the net." The user must establish strategies for delineating searches and keying in to the most useful sources for desired information. Otherwise, the Internet user can easily fall victim to the "mouse potato" syndrome, sitting spell-bound in front of the computer screen for hours on end.

2. Ask students to prepare a one-page report on Mosaic, a graphical interface that allows access to sound and motion video, as well as text files. Refer to the e-mail assignment at the end of Chapter 4 for information on gopher access.

G. Spreadsheets

1. Gather samples of computer spreadsheets as further examples of electronic production.

2. Assign Exercise 3 at the end of Chapter 5 in the text to reinforce the guidelines for verifying a spreadsheet data. Project the correct response, using **TA 5–3** (Solution, Exercise 3). This activity illustrates the importance of proofreading types of documents other than letters or memos.

H. Integrate the communication mentor comments into class lectures to reinforce the concepts in the chapter. Comments may include a communication strategy proven in the workplace or concrete advice on developing communication skill. So that you can test students' understanding of this valuable content, the *Test Bank* contains questions from the communication mentor comments.

| 2 | LEARNING OBJECTIVE |

II. Writing and Organizing Data

A. Word-Processing Software

B. Spellcheck, Thesaurus, and Writing-Analysis Software

C. Assign Exercise 5 at the end of the chapter. Project the correct response, using **TA 5–4** (Solution, Exercise 5).

| 3 | LEARNING OBJECTIVE |

III. Presenting Data

A. Printing

1. Dot-Matrix Printers

2. Laser Printers

3. Collect and make transparencies of various typestyles, fonts, and sizes produced on a variety of printers. Project to the class and discuss differences in appearance.

B. Desktop Publishing Software

C. Presentation Graphics Software

D. Graphic Design Principles

E. Gather samples of desktop published documents as further examples of electronic production. The résumés in Chapter 13 and the sample report in Chapter 18 illustrate the desktop publishing capabilities of top-level word-processing software.

F. Ask students to prepare a flier for a product or service of their choice, using presentation graphics software. Encourage the use of varying font choices and sizes and at least one picture graphic.

| 4 | LEARNING OBJECTIVE |

IV. Sharing Data

A. Electronic Mail

1. Make a transparency of **TM 5–1** (E-mail Style Guidelines). Project for

    students to view as you discuss the rules.

    2. Even if you are not requiring the e-mail application at the end of each chapter, you may want to require the one included at the end of Chapter 5 or go back to a simple one in an earlier chapter.

B. Voice Mail

C. Facsimile Machine

D. Telecommuting

E. Cellular Telephones

F. Electronic Meetings

    1. Teleconferences

    2. Videoconferences

G. Guidelines for Communicating Electronically

    1. Project **TA 5–2** (Guidelines for Communicating Electronically) for students to view as you lead a discussion of the topic.

    2. While individuals are afforded a degree of privacy, court cases have affirmed the property rights of computer system owners to monitor the operations of such systems. This fact means that the privacy rights of individual employees are superseded by the property rights of employers. Pending legislation may make it illegal for employers to monitor electronic communications without giving suitable notice that such monitoring will occur.

5	LEARNING OBJECTIVE

V. Legal and Ethical Implications of Technology

A. Make a transparency of **TM 5–2** (Information Ethics Issues) and project it as you lead the class in a discussion of ethics issues.

B. Privacy and Accessibility

C. Communication in Action: Al Walea, USAA

D. Discuss the Communication in Action case involving USAA and customer privacy.

E. Property Rights

    1. Software and intellectual property

    2. Computer crime and abuse

F. Accuracy

VI. Summary

A. Use the content of the chapter, the review questions, and the exercises to develop students' understanding of the terminology and the benefits of the various electronic communication technologies.

B. Assign the *Study Guide* questions for Chapter 5.

C. Assign the e-mail application at the end of the chapter.

D. Throughout the semester, use the exercises and applications at the ends of Chapters 7–18 to develop students' competency in composing and revising documents using word-processing software.

TRANSPARENCIES AND MASTERS

TA 5–1   Chapter Opener

TA 5–2   Guidelines for Communicating Electronically

TA 5–3   Solution, Exercise 3

TA 5–4   Solution, Exercise 5

TM 5–1   E-mail Style Guidelines

TM 5–2   Information Ethics Issues

ADDITIONAL READINGS

Berry, K. H. (1992). Mail call. *Association Management, 47*(2), 48–52.

Brightman, J. (1992, May-June). Meet face-to-face without getting on that plane (video conferencing). *Executive Female*, pp. 14–15.

Coy, P. (1991, June 3). Your new computer: The telephone; voice processing puts a powerful tool at everyone's fingertips. *Business Week*, pp. 126–129.

Dyson, E. (1992, February 3). Who pays for data? *Forbes*, p. 96.

Flanagan, P. (1994). Videoconferencing changes the corporate meeting. *Management Review, 83*(2), 7.

Gull-May, H. (1992, February). Is the world of the communicator shrinking or expanding? *Communication World*, pp. 48–49.

Half, R. (1990, December). Please hold…. *New Accountant*, pp. 21–22.

Quinn, J. C. (1992, November). Using technology to improve communication. *Fund Raising Management*, pp. 21–22.

Strom, B. (1990). Improve your written communications with grammar-checking software. *Computers in Accounting*, 6(9), 70–76.

Sullivan, N. (1991, July). Making a good impression. *Home-Office Computing*, 9(7), 64.

Techno-manners for the millennium. (1990). *Business Month*, 135(1), 66–67.

Warnock, J. (1992, June). The new age of documents (toward full electronic document interchange). *Byte*, pp. 257–59.

ANSWERS TO "COMMUNICATION IN ACTION" CASE: Al Walea, USAA

1. **Why is a current, accurate database so important to USAA's business?** USAA's database contains important information related to its customer's policies, claims, and financial services. An employee can access a customer's records quickly and, in turn, update records quickly. A customer's insurance policy may be generated or a claim processed from the database. If the database is not current and accurate, a customer's claim cannot be processed promptly

2. **Describe USAA's advantage of conducting most business by telephone. What are some disadvantages?** USAA has effectively eliminated the insurance agent by conducting most business by telephone. Conducting business exclusively by telephone can improve the quality of service and improve time and processing of records. The customer doesn't have to make an appointment to talk with an agent. The customer can just pick up the telephone. Loss of "person" contact may be a disadvantage for some customers. The missing component of nonverbal communication, such as eye contact or a smile, may be a barrier in some conversations.

3. **Assume that you are a customer of USAA. What privacy-of-information concerns do you have about personal information existing in a large company's databanks?** Privacy issues concern confidential information being used without the customer's knowledge for purposes for which it wasn't intended. Issues could include the following: someone checks on balances in various accounts (snoops); an agent other than the one who usually works with a customer could snoop into coverages for insurance or investment portfolio. Students may fear sales solicitation calls from unauthorized personnel. Remind students that because USAA is providing insurance services, an employee assigned to a customer could make recommendations for additional services. If an outside company calls, that's a problem. Additionally, students may voice concerns that their personal information will be sold to other companies or be obtained by others illegally.

ANSWERS TO REVIEW QUESTIONS

1. Computers (a) collect and analyze information for messages, (b) shape messages to be clearer and more effective, and (c) communicate quickly and efficiently with others over long distances.

2. Two distinct advantages of electronic communication are (a) the remarkable speed of electronic searches of databases and networks as compared to manual searches of printed sources, and (b) the vast amount of information available to provide for better problem solving.

3. Database information often is vital to the production of necessary reports. Lists represent collections of similar or related information. Businesses have lists that must constantly be created, updated, and maintained. Database software organizes data, permits them to be updated, and allows them to be retrieved in a variety of report formats. Access to accurate information is necessary to produce timely reports for decision making or other purposes. Examples of internal databases might include customers, suppliers, account numbers, dollar and unit sales by salespeople and by product, payrolls, employees, and a vast array of items for special and general needs. External databases may include Dow Jones News/Retrieval, Prodigy, and CompuServe. A personal set of lists might include a different but wide variety of subjects. An example is your personal telephone list.

4. People use online services for two basic purposes: to communicate with others and to obtain information. Using a modem, the appropriate communication software, and an

assigned password, you can obtain information from around the world by subscribing to the Internet or a commercial online service. Users have access, for example, to the NASA-funded computer, transcriptions of the U.S. Supreme Court opinions, software, card catalogs from many libraries, etc. With an Internet connection, you can collaborate with students in your class or other universities.

5. Learning to "tunnel" through the vast amount of information productively can be an overwhelming experience. The experience can also be expensive in terms of time spent and charges incurred for online time.

6. Electronic spreadsheets are useful for preparing reports containing any analysis of numbers. Spreadsheet programs can be used to manipulate and analyze data for more accurate and timely decision making. The spreadsheet's forecasting ability, which allows the user to ask "what if" questions, is one of its main benefits. By arranging data into organized tables, the spreadsheet assists the manager in using the data. Incorporating a spreadsheet or graphic generated from a spreadsheet into a document can be invaluable for communicating complex information efficiently. A graphic can quickly be constructed from the spreadsheet data to reinforce or illustrate a point of discussion. The text describes a manager who inserts a stacked-bar chart in a memo to reinforce her explanation of the change in the composition of billable hours. Using the same spreadsheet, the manager can easily generate a visual aid (transparency, slide, or printed handout) to support an oral report. Answers will vary based on the experience of each student.

7. Two major barriers to be overcome when producing a spreadsheet are (a) using incorrect formulas for manipulating data and (b) falsely assuming confidence in a spreadsheet that may contain "bad" data.

8. The following word-processing features would be appropriate:
   a. Insert
   b. Spellcheck
   c. Delete
   d. Search and replace
   e. Block and move
   f. Automatic contents page, index, and document references
   g. Mail merge
   h. Block and copy
   i. Redlining and document comment
   j. Thesaurus
   k. Writing-analysis software

9. When using collaborative software, each author marks revisions and inserts document comments in much the same way as with word-processing software and then sends the computer file to the co-author. Some collaborative software programs allow multiple authors to work on a document at the same time. Examples of collaborative documents are reports, training materials, manuals, etc.

10. The mail-merge feature of word-processing software allows a writer to send a customer or client an original letter, with his or her name individually keyed instead of a photocopy of the standard text. The sort feature can be used to arrange the addresses in numerical order according to ZIP Code; thus letters and mailing labels are printed in the order required by the U.S. Postal Service for mass mailings. Form letters can be personalized by (a) using original keyboarding, not photocopies; (b) using mail merge to personalize envelopes, inside addresses, salutations, and messages; (c) using better-quality paper and printers; and (d) printing the address directly on the envelope rather than using mailing labels.

11. Spellchecks, thesauruses, and writing-analysis software aid in producing effective messages by detecting misspelling, suggested alternative wording, and identifying grammatical errors. Overreliance on such tools can be hazardous, because they have limitations and still require user judgment.

12. Dot-matrix printers have a printhead with pins that strike the ribbon to create characters on the paper. Laser printers use a process similar to photocopying to produce a page of characters at a time. Dot-matrix printers come with at least two printing modes that produce different print qualities. Printing documents in draft mode is fast, but the quality is not appropriate for external correspondence. The print speed is slow in the near-letter quality mode, and the print quality remains inadequate for external

business correspondence. Laser printing produces characters of the highest quality available for printers commonly used in business. Printing speed is a significant advantage of laser printing. Dot-matrix printers can also be used to print certain graphic images. Laser printers can handle sophisticated graphic images. Laser printers cost approximately three times as much as dot-matrix printers.

13. First, one or more documents are created, edited, and proofread in a word-processing program. Documents are then imported into a page-layout (desktop publishing) program where the user can enhance the text with different typefaces, sizes, styles, and other enhancements such as lines, boxes, and other graphic images. The result is documents that are persuasive and professional looking and produced at a fraction of the cost required by a professional printer.

14. Business graphics help people grasp a point more readily than would a narrative or even a table. As technology allows easier access to more and more information, graphic representation of data becomes even more important and gives decision makers at-a-glance comprehension of key information. The use of graphics in presentations has grown greatly in recent years because of the development of increasingly capable programs for generating this technology on personal computers. Users can produce professional-looking images quickly and efficiently.

15. Sources of graphics include the following: (a) electronic spreadsheet and presentation graphics software; (b) clipart (predrawn graphics stored on disk), which comes with high-end word-processing software; (c) drawing software, which allows desktop publishers to draw their own images; and (d) scanned images including graphics, photos, signatures, letterhead, and text.

16. Inexperienced (untrained) users of desktop publishing and computer graphics often overdo the creative aspects in their enthusiasm and either detract from the intended message or mislead interpreters of the information.

17. See "Graphic Design Principles" in Chapter 5, eight guidelines for preparing and using visual aids in the "Using Visual Aids" section of Chapter 3, and **TM 3–4**.

18. Advantages of the stated technologies are as follows: (a) Electronic mail is much faster than the traditional postage service. It arrives almost instantaneously and promotes immediate feedback. Electronic mail eliminates telephone tag, permits communication with several others simultaneously, and reduces the paper load. (b) Fax is a flexible and inexpensive form of e-mail whose main advantages are speed and ease of use. Additionally, the time zone problem is overcome. (c) Portable computers allow people flexibility by giving access to computing power regardless of location—hotel room, airplane, taxi, or client's office. Managers are able to make every minute of a busy schedule count and are able to generate and communicate current information. Time can be used more efficiently, and information can be accessed more readily. (d) Cellular telephones increase productivity by allowing better use of time. Workers are able to stay in closer contact with co-workers, clients, and customers. Quick, courteous responses build strong interpersonal relationships, which in turn lead to increased employee commitment and a competitive edge. Sales representatives, contractors, lawyers, city officials, and others who work away from the office use cellular telephones frequently. Encourage students to share their experiences with each of the four technologies.

19. Telecommuting is the concept of individuals working at home (or a remote location) and transmitting work to the office electronically via a computer, a modem, and telephone lines. The major advantages of telecommuting include reduced time and expense of commuting and increased flexibility of working hours. Encourage students to share examples of efficient application of telecommunicating.

20. See "Guidelines for Communicating Electronically" in Chapter 5 and **TA 5–2** for suggestions.

21. Four legal and ethical issues include the following: (a) concerns for privacy and accessibility to information; (b) protection of intellectual property such as copyrighted software; (c) computer crime and abuse, including illegal transfer of funds, stealing files, introduction of viruses, disruption of service, and theft of services; and (d) responsibility for the accurate recording of use of data,

including checking the relevance, current-ness, and verifiability of all information.

22. See the Fair Information Practices Principles in Chapter 5. Encourage students to share experiences.

23. To protect individual privacy: (a) collect only that which is needed, (b) develop and use safeguards for the security of information and instill in others the values of privacy and confidentiality, and (c) develop a clear privacy policy that complies with the law and does not unnecessarily compromise the interests of employees and employers.

24. The following guidelines are provided by the Computer Software Copyright Act of 1980: (a) Users are generally prohibited from modifying, transferring, adapting, leasing, or loaning entire programs or parts of programs; and (b) Users generally cannot run software legally on more than one computer simultaneously.

25. Computer crime is the commission of illegal acts through the use of or against a computer. The most damaging computer crimes are introducing viruses, theft of services, disruption of computer services, and theft of tele-communication services. Disgruntled employ-ees may sabotage a computer system to get even with the company, or a hacker may steal information. Employees may use the company computer for personal purposes, thus causing loss of productivity and additional charges to the company for online time. Internet users may transmit hateful, harassing, or obscene messages and violate the rights of others. Encourage students to discuss recent cases of computer crime and the implications of the actions taken by all parties.

POSSIBLE SOLUTIONS TO EXERCISES

1. Focus on activities that expand student understanding of the impact of technology on business communication.

2. This exercise can be assigned in conjunction with other assignments that require library research. Early exposure to the library data-base will facilitate students' completion of the long, formal report and other research projects in this course and the students' other courses.

3. Refer to solution on **TA 5–3**.

4. Assignments will vary.

5. Refer to **TA 5–4** for solution.

Errors Detected by Spellcheck
◆ proceed
◆ necessary
◆ review

Errors Not Detected by Spellcheck	
Par. 2	◆ year's, *not* years
	◆ its, *not* their
	◆ extended, *not* extend
Par. 3	◆ fully, *not* full
	◆ an advantage, *not* a advantage
	◆ seminars, *not* seminar
	◆ effective, *not* affective
Par. 4	◆ capital, *not* capitol
	◆ has, *not* have
	◆ within, *not* with
	◆ your, *not* you

6. You may want to assign a specific passage such as the Gettysburg Address or the Pre-amble to the Constitution. When students run the writing-analysis program, they may be surprised at the volume of "errors" it will report. Discuss how the program's logic works and why the user may not always want to make the corrections which are suggested.

7. When this assignment is made, survey the class to determine whether students can produce samples using the major types of printers—dot-matrix, laser, and color laser. Then you can provide samples from printers that are unavailable to students. Illustrate how document appearance affects message impact.

8. If time is limited, add this topic to your list of approved topics for research report assign-ments. If you require an oral report, the entire class will benefit from informative guidelines for designing effective documents. Principles that may be reflected in students reports include: (a) remember that "more is less" in determining how much to put into a graphic, (b) limit the number of sizes and styles of fonts in a single document, (c) achieve a balanced appearance in layout, (d) work with a theme or focus for each graphic, and (e) keep the design simple.

9. Suggested solutions are as follows:
   a. Electronic mail would be a good choice because the message can be sent simultaneously to many subscribers, thus saving time and money.
   b. E-mail would not be recommended for this situation because it requires tact and sensitivity. A face-to-face meeting would be preferred.
   c. E-mail is not recommended when the content of the communication is confidential. Overnight mail would be a better choice in this case because speed is important.
   d. E-mail could be used in this case because the spreadsheet file could be attached and transmitted.
   e. Voice mail would be preferred because the recipient would not have to log on to the computer to know that the message has been sent. Fax could also be used in this case because it provides the speed needed in this situation.

10. Evaluate student messages for clarity, completeness, and conciseness.

11. Devote class time for students to share their experiences to the class or in small groups. Using student experiences to supplement the communication barriers discussed in the chapter will add relevance to the topic. Students intimidated by computers may receive additional confidence after hearing peers discuss their negative encounters with technology. Experiences will vary, but keep students focused on how such problems can be overcome or minimized by proper procedures and appropriate applications of technology.

12. Suggested solutions are as follows:
   a. Use e-mail for routine internal messages instead of memos.
   b. Use video conferencing instead of traveling to meetings.
   c. Use voice mail or e-mail to eliminate telephone tag.
   d. Require the use of spellcheck on all word-processed documents.
   e. Transfer files to electronic databases.
   f. Use word-processing software for the creation of documents.
   g. Provide a cellular telephone for the vice-president.
   h. Have the writer fax updated scripts rather than mailing them.

POSSIBLE SOLUTION TO E-MAIL APPLICATION

If you are following the sequence of chapters in the text, students will not yet have been exposed to concepts related to message impact, such as adaptation and strategy. Consequently, evaluation of this assignment should not focus heavily on such factors. Depending on the editing capabilities of your e-mail system, you may grade spelling, grammatical content, and basic formatting.

CHAPTER 6

ETHICAL AND LEGAL GUIDELINES

CHAPTER OVERVIEW

Businesses have recently become more aware of the severe implications of the unethical behavior of their employees. In response many businesses have begun training their employees to make ethical decisions and establishing company codes of ethics. Many companies realize that employees must be capable of making ethical decisions to protect the business from legal liability and to maximize long-term profits.

The widespread presence of pressures to compromise personal values requires attention from business professors who aim to prepare students to function effectively in this environment. The ethics topic meshes particularly well with the business communication discipline because the ability to identify and analyze ethical dilemmas relates directly to one's effectiveness in gathering and evaluating critical information, organizing and expressing clear ideas, persuading others to adopt different perspectives, and so on.

As a business communication instructor, you cannot improve your students' personal morals. They come to you with their own sense of right and wrong already instilled. What you can do, however, is give them tools to help them deal with potentially unethical situations in the workplace. By analyzing these dilemmas from multiple perspectives, your students may be able to find solutions that conform to their own personal values. Hopefully, students will be less likely to take the easy way out of ethical quandaries if they are better equipped to deal with them.

LEARNING OBJECTIVES

1 Define ethics and identify the process by which individuals develop a foundation for making ethical decisions.

2 Identify the common causes for unethical behavior in the workplace.

3 Use an ethical decision-making framework to facilitate identifying and effectively communicating solutions that conform to your personal values.

4 Apply the guidelines for taking moral responsibility for all communication (oral and written) transmitted and actions taken.

CHAPTER OUTLINE AND TEACHING SUGGESTIONS

1 | LEARNING OBJECTIVE

I. The Foundation for Ethical Behavior
    A. Project **TA 6–1** (Chapter Opener) as you introduce this material.
    B. Initiate a class discussion to arrive at a definition of ethics, which should lead to the principles of right and wrong that guide individuals in making decisions that affect others. Then, to initiate a discussion of the foundation of ethical behavior, ask how people know what's

right and wrong. Discuss how the actions in the "The Foundation for Ethical Behavior" section might affect a young person's moral development, and ask students to add other actions to the list. Discuss how compromises in personal values can affect a person's value system. This discussion should lead naturally into a discussion of commonplace unethical behavior in a student's academic life and in the workplace. Encourage students to contribute other examples from their own experiences.

C. To create immediate interest in the topic and to emphasize the widespread presence of unethical behavior, ask students to locate in a current newspaper or magazine an example of an illegal act (Exercise 6) and an unethical act (Exercise 7). Ask students to share these incidents with the class to supplement the examples at the beginning of the chapter.

    1. Tonya Harding succumbed to unethical conduct in her bid to become a world-class skater. (Make a transparency of **TM 6–2** (Skating Champion Struggles with Ethical Dilemma) and project it.

    2. Pete Rose, baseball's greatest hitter, gradually acquired a gambling problem that earned him a jail sentence.

    3. Steroid use by Olympic sprinter Ben Johnson caused him to be stripped of his gold medal.

    4. Olympic diving champion, Greg Louganis, failed to disclose the fact that he had tested positive for the HIV virus, even after a diving accident resulted in blood exposure to other athletes and support personnel.

D. Make a transparency of **TM 6–1** (Minor Concessions Weaken an Ethical Foundation) and project it for the class. Using the news items from I–C, lead a discussion of how minor breaches in ethics can lead to the committing of major criminal acts.

| 2 | LEARNING OBJECTIVE |

II. Causes of Unethical Behavior in the Workplace

A. Excessive Emphasis on Profits

1. According to a survey of 4,000 businesspersons conducted in 1993–94, nearly one-third of the respondents sometimes felt pressured to engage in misconduct to achieve business objectives. Also, one-third of employees observed misconduct at work in the last year, but fewer than half reported it to their companies. The majority of those who did report the misconduct were not satisfied with their company's response. One employee in six stated that his/her company overtly encourages misconduct to meet business objectives. Meeting business goals—either schedule pressures or overly aggressive financial or business objectives—was the most common source of pressures to engage in misconduct. (See the Goodell, 1994, article in the Additional Readings section.)

2. Refer to Communication Mentor comment by James F. Hurley that discusses the lack of short-term rewards for ethical behavior in the workplace. Lead students in a discussion of intrinsic rewards for proper behavior.

B. Misplaced Corporate Loyalty

C. Obsession with Personal Advancement

1. In 1993, General Motors filed criminal charges against their former purchasing chief for stealing confidential GM documents.

2. Refer to Communication Mentor comment by James Hurley that discusses the seductive quality of an unethical environment. Lead students in a discussion of risks and remedies.

D. Expectation of Not Getting Caught

1. Many people think they will never get caught making illegal copies of software, one of the most widespread "white collar" crimes in the world. The Software Publishers Association reports, however, that more than 4,000 claims have been settled against such offenders since 1990.

2. Ask students why "fuzz busters" were invented? Is speeding wrong as long as there are no police around?

E. Unethical Tone Set by Top Management

1. Unethical tone set by top managers is a problem which is deep-rooted in the corporate culture of some organizations. Corporate culture is extremely difficult to change and can take years. The time factor should, however, not be a deterrent to efforts to bring about an ethical work environment.

2. Assign Exercise 3 at the end of Chapter 6 in the text. This activity requires students to read an article related to management responsibility for ethics.

F. Uncertainty About Whether an Action is Wrong

G. Unwillingness to Take an Ethical Stand

H. Emphasize that being aware of the major causes of unethical behavior will assist students in recognizing the forces that can cause unethical behavior. Recognizing the causes of unethical behavior is the first step in making business decisions that may require students to compromise their personal values. Discuss the seven causes of unethical behavior in the workplace and each of the examples provided. To increase relevance, encourage students to share incidents they have experienced or those reported in the newspapers and magazines articles collected in Exercises 6 and 7.

| 3 | LEARNING OBJECTIVE |

III. Framework for Analyzing Ethical Dilemmas

A. To introduce the "Framework for Analyzing Ethical Dilemmas," ask students to discuss the ethical principles or systems that they think would be helpful in determining whether an issue is ethical.

This discussion will emphasize the point that various methods are used to resolve ethical dilemmas and can be incorporated into a systematic plan for analyzing ethical dilemmas. Knowing what "tools" to use when faced with an ethical dilemma will help students find solutions that better conform to their own personal values.

B. Show **TA 6–2** (Framework for Analyzing Ethical Issues) as you discuss this section.

C. Legal Considerations

1. Legality is just the first step in determining whether an action is ethical. Many food manufacturers have come under scrutiny by watchdog consumer groups for making products labeled "lite" or "lowfat" when in fact most of the calories in the food are derived from fat or have high calorie content. This misinformation could be potentially deadly for some consumers.

2. Ask students to give examples of actions that are legal but not ethical to some persons (e.g., abortion, gambling). Have students give examples of actions that are illegal but ethical to some persons (e.g., speeding, marijuana use).

D. Company and Professional Codes of Conduct

1. In the recent survey of over 4,000 business persons (Goodell, 1994), 60 percent of respondents reported that their companies had codes of conduct; 33 percent reported that their company had training on business ethics; and 33 percent reported that their company had an ethics officer or ombudsman.

2. Divide students into small groups by major and have them give short oral reports about the code of ethics of their intended professions (Exercise 8). Discuss some of the specific ethical behaviors included and the variations between professions.

E. Ethical Principles and Theories

1. Utilitarian theory

a. The major premise of the utilitarian theory is that in all situations one ought to do that which provides the greatest balance of good over harm for everyone. A related question is whether the ultimate aim is for the good of the group, or whether the company's philosophy is more that what is good for the individual will, de facto, be good for the group. This view boils down to whether people in a particular country have a more individualistic orientation, meaning that people are supposed to take care of themselves, or whether the group occupies center stage. Countries such as the U.S. or Australia tend to be very individual-oriented, whereas countries such Indonesia, Singapore, and Japan are more group-oriented.

b. Assign one or more of the cases at the end of Chapter 6. A central feature of the ethical framework is the identification of stakeholders and the assessment of the effect(s) on them.

2. Doctrine of *prima facie* duties

F. Communication in Action: James F. Hurley, California Federal Bank.

G. After presenting the ethical framework, you could use several of the cases students reported (see II–B). Current ethics cases, especially those occurring in your geographic area, can bring an added level of relevance to your coverage of business ethics.

H. Use **TA 6–2** (Framework for Analyzing Ethical Issues) to discuss the ethical framework. Emphasize the three decision points in the model: (a) Is the alternative legal, and does it comply with relevant contractual agreements and company policy? (b) Is the alternative consistent with the company's and/or the profession's code of ethics? (c) Is the alternative ethical? After discussing the Weyerhaeuser example given in the chapter, ask students to use the ethical framework to analyze one of the ethical issues (personal or workplace) presented in "The Foundation for Ethical Behavior" and "Causes of Unethical Behavior in the Workplace" sections or the incidents students located in newspapers or magazines (Exercises 6 and 7).

| 4 | LEARNING OBJECTIVE |

IV. Communicating Decisions Ethically and Responsibly

  A. The final section, "Communicating Decisions Ethically and Responsibly," emphasizes the importance of taking responsibility for the power of effective communication. Stress to students that they are to communicate for *one and only one purpose*: to uphold their own personal values and their company's standards of ethical conduct.

    1. The six guidelines for communicating responsibly and ethically are an excellent preview of principles that are integrated in the applications chapters that follow: (a) Is the information stated as truthfully, honestly, and fairly as possible? (b) Are the ideas expressed clearly and understandably? (c) Are unpleasant ideas stated tactfully and positively to preserve the reader's self-worth and to build future relationships? (d) Does the message embellish or exaggerate the facts? (e) Is your viewpoint supported with objective, welldocumented facts? (f) Are graphics carefully designed to avoid distorting facts and relationships?

    2. These ethical principles are incorporated in the "General Writing Guidelines," provided in Chapter 9 before the first writing application, and in "Check Your Writing" checklist at the end of Chapters 9–18.

  B. Show **TA 6–3** (Guidelines for Communicating Ethically) as you discuss this section.

  C. Assign Exercise 10 at the end of Chapter 6, which involves identifying distortion of facts in graphics.

V. Summary

  A. Discuss the communication mentor comments, synthesizing the advice these executives have offered for dealing with and avoiding ethical dilemmas. So that you can test students' understanding of this valuable content, the *Test Bank* contains questions from the communication mentor comments.

  B. Assign selected exercises at the end of Chapter 6.

  C. Present the "Cases for Analysis" initially as a class discussion or as an individual or group project. Regardless of the method used, students should be given an opportunity to discuss the case in class or in small groups. This exchange of ideas enables students to observe how other students analyze and support their decisions. Many of the cases provide situations where the line between right and wrong is unclear. As a result, students' final decisions and the documents required to communicate those decisions will differ. Therefore, you should grade solutions to the cases based on the students' analyses of the facts and their objective support of the decision. The decision as to whether a case demonstrates ethical behavior should not be graded. For that reason, an analysis, with no conclusion, is provided with each solution.

  D. Assign the *Study Guide* questions for Chapter 6.

  E. Ask students to complete the e-mail application at the end of the chapter.

  F. Assign one of the applications designated as an AWA (Analytical Writing Assessment) for the GMAT. Refer to pages 12–13 of this *Instructor's Resource Manual* for holistic scoring techniques used by evaluators of this written portion of the GMAT.

TRANSPARENCIES AND MASTERS

TA 6–1 Chapter Opener
TA 6–2 Framework for Analyzing Ethical Issues
TA 6–3 Guidelines for Communicating Ethically

TM 6–1 Minor Concessions Weaken an Ethical Foundation
TM 6–2 Skating Champion Struggles with Ethical Dilemma

TM 6–3 Ethical Messages Disclose Complete and Accurate Information

TM 6–4 Ethical Messages are Expressed Clearly and Understandably

TM 6–5 Solution, E-mail Application

TM 6–6 Solution, Case for Analysis 1, Step 3

ADDITIONAL READINGS

Boyer, E. P., & Webb, T. G. (1992, March). Ethics and diversity: A correlation enhanced through corporate communication. *IEEE Transactions on Professional Communication*, pp. 38–43.

Edwards, G., & Goodell, R. (1994, Fall/Winter). Three years later: A look at the effectiveness of sentencing guidelines. *Ethics Journal*, p. 1, 4, 5.

Goodell, R. (1994, Fall/Winter). National business ethics survey findings. *Ethics Journal*, p. 1, 3, 5.

Half, R. (Ed.). (1991). Managing your career: "How can I determine if a firm is ethical?" *Management Accounting, 72*(7), 13.

Holmes, N. (Ed.). (1991). Ethics: Resolution of ethical conduct. *Management Accounting, 72*(12), 14.

Hunt, T., & Tirpok, A. (1993). Universal ethics code: An idea whose time has come. *Public Relations, 19*(1), 1–10.

Kirrane, D. E. (1990). Managing values: Systematic approach to business ethics. *Training & Development Journal, 44*(11), 53–56, 58.

McElreath, M. P. (1994, April). Was it the devil who made him do it? (violation of standards of professional ethics). *Communication World*, pp. 27–29.

McElreath, M.P. (1993, October). When the press comes knocking: Balancing the public's need to know with the customer's right to privacy. *Communication World*, pp. 33–35.

McElreath, M. P. (1993, April). Who cares if you violate the IABC Code of Ethics? *Communication World*, pp. 10–13.

Neumeier, S. (1989). When somebody wants a payoff. *Fortune, 120*(13), 117–118, 120–121.

Riley, K. (1993). Telling more than the truth: Implicature, speech acts, and ethics in professional communication. *Journal of Business Ethics, 12*(3), 179–197.

Skeddle, R. W. (1990). Business ethics: Dealing in the gray areas. *Financial Executive, 6*(3), 9–13.

Sottosanti, V. (1989). A 12-point ethics plan. *Advertising Age, 60*(9), 20, 24.

Welty, G. (1994, April). Be human…be honest…and scrupulously fair. *Railway Age*, p. 9.

ANSWERS TO "COMMUNICATION IN ACTION" CASE: James F. Hurley, California Federal Bank

1. **Why do you think Hurley considers ending a telephone conversation abruptly when asked to give information that would give the caller an undue advantage?** Hurley avoids even small compromises in his ethical behavior. When a caller asks for "secret knowledge," Hurley understands the legal and ethical consequences of revealing even small bits of unauthorized information. He also realizes that small compromises could lead to more serious consequences.

2. **What might occur if Hurley revealed secret information about a possible merger between California Federal Bank and another large bank?** Legal consequences may follow. In addition, California Federal Bank's stock may be affected negatively and Hurley's position or employment may be affected.

3. **Review the six points of the Pagano Model for ethical decision making. How does Hurley's reaction to requests for information pass point four, the light-of-day test?** The light-of-day test asks, "If your action appeared on television or others learned about it, would you be proud?" Not only were Hurley's actions legal, they were also ethical. By not revealing information that would give the caller undue advantage, he conducted business ethically.

ANSWERS TO REVIEW QUESTIONS

1. Ethics refers to the principles of right and wrong that guide us in making decisions that affect others. Student definitions will vary.

2. Unethical conduct might include distorting or misrepresenting the truth, withholding information, violating confidentiality, theft of goods or information, failure to report wrong

doing, etc. Examples listed in the chapter include Microsoft's infringement of Stac Electronic's patent; General Motors managers accused of stealing documents when they "defected" to Volkswagen; CIA agent Aldrich Ames' selling of top-secret information for the Russians; and Beechnut's selling infant apple juice without a trace of apple juice.

3. Ethical issues do arise frequently in most areas of business, and the pressure to know what is right appears to be felt most strongly by lower-level managers who are least experienced doing their jobs. Many of these managers are recent business school graduates. Only if one has definite beliefs on a variety of issues and the courage to practice them will he or she be able to make sound ethical judgments. Putting ethical business practices first will also benefit one's company by building a reputation for fairness and good judgment in the eyes of existing and potential clients and customers.

4. In order for you to make an ethical decision, you must first know your own values. Second, you must identify a particular situation as an ethical issue. Third, you must safeguard your ability and willingness to act ethically and responsibly by staying keenly aware of common pressures to compromise your personal value system.

5. The common causes of unethical behavior in the workplace are (a) excessive emphasis on profits, (b) misplaced corporate loyalty, (c) obsession with personal advancement, (d) expectation of not getting caught, (e) unethical tone set by top management, (f) uncertainty about whether an action is wrong, and (g) unwillingness to take an ethical stand.

6. No, small ethical compromises desensitize people to unethical practices, possibly causing them to make more serious ethical concessions or take illegal actions.

7. Refer to the list of personal examples of pressure to act unethically and the list of workplace ethical dilemmas in the "The Foundation for Ethical Behavior" section. Encourage students to share, either with the class or in small groups, ethical dilemmas they have faced.

8. The three decision points in the ethical framework include the following: (a) Is the alternative legal, and does it comply with relevant contractual agreements and company policy? (b) Is the alternative consistent with the company's and/or the profession's code of ethics? (c) Is the alternative ethical?

9. Analyzing the legality of an alternative involves determining whether it (a) obeys existing laws, (b) fulfills contracts with resource groups, and (c) adheres to company policy.

10. An organization exchanges information or makes financial transactions with a variety of resource groups. Such groups may include employees, owners, customers, suppliers, creditors, government, and society. When interacting with any of these resource groups, the decision maker must identify the legal implications affecting the appropriate resource group(s).

11. A code of ethics is a written document that summarizes a company's or a profession's standards of ethical conduct.

12. Comprehensive ethics awareness programs help employees understand and adhere to standards; they help management identify breakdowns in the system and then develop solutions to these problems.

13. Utilitarian principles evaluate choices in terms of what provides the greatest good with the least amount of harm for everyone involved. A decision maker must estimate the impact of the alternative on all stakeholders (persons affected by the decision) and then select the one that optimizes the satisfaction of the greatest number of people. The theory of duties involves evaluating an alternative on Ross's five highly desirable moral tenets: (a) not harming innocent people, (b) keeping promises, (c) showing gratitude, (d) acting in a just way, and (e) providing reparations to those who have been harmed by one's actions.

14. Benefits of effective communication include (a) increased likelihood that the message will yield the desired response; (b) courage to deal with ethical issues otherwise ignored because of insecurity in communicating about sensitive and unpleasant issues; (c) positive business relationships built on honest disclosure of information; and (d) justified respect from supervisors as an honest, sensitive, highly effective communicator worthy of challenging and rewarding opportunities.

15. Six guidelines for ensuring that your message is being communicated responsibly and ethically are listed on **TA 6–3** and in IV–A–1.

POSSIBLE SOLUTIONS TO EXERCISES

1. These are best covered as a part of class discussion on the various issues related to ethical behavior.

2. Answers will vary.

3. In addition to the written report, you might utilize the following activities based on the reading of the book. (a) In a class discussion, have students assume they are the sales manager facing the ethical dilemma in the book. Applying the ethical framework, would they succumb to management's pressure to increase profits at any cost or resign the position? (b) In a class discussion, ask students to summarize the ethical principles presented in the book that are not in the text. You may want to suggest other materials for outside reading on ethics. This assignment may also be used as the basis for an oral report.

4. Students are more likely to discuss their own ethical dilemmas in small groups rather than as a class. Each group can summarize the situations and advice and present them to the class.

5. This exercise also works well in small groups. Learning can be enhanced as students share their rationale.

6–7. These exercises require students to read magazines and newspapers and can also be used as the basis for an oral report.

8. Students with the same major may work in pairs or small groups to complete this assignment. Make transparencies of selected codes of ethics located by students, and lead the class in a discussion of the similarities and differences in the codes.

9. Answers may vary as will knowledge of the legal framework for dealing with each resource group. Students may need time outside of class to research the legal implications.

10. Make transparencies of graphics students bring to class to display as you lead in discussion. These examples will be useful again later when you cover "Managing Data and Using Graphics" in Chapter 16.

POSSIBLE SOLUTION TO E-MAIL APPLICATION

See **TM 6–5** for suggested solution. For grading purposes, focus on the appropriateness of content as related to material in Chapter 5 as well as on formatting and grammatical correctness.

POSSIBLE SOLUTIONS AND RECOMMENDED OUTLINES TO CASES FOR ANALYSIS

MANAGEMENT/Ethics	GMAT

1. **Is hiring the homeless to purchase tickets ethical?**

⇨ *Level 4* ⇦

Refer to **TM 6–6** (Solution, Case for Analysis 1, Step 3).

1. Analysis of the problem:

   a. *Relevant facts.* Refer to case.

   b. *Ethical issues.* Is it ethical for a company to hire the homeless to purchase tickets?

   c. *Stakeholders.* Omaha Brokerage Firm, firm's customers, record store, record store customers, homeless, and community/society.

   d. *Legal considerations.* None; the firm can hire anyone to buy tickets.

   Contractual considerations. No union contracts; only contract is the oral contract between the firm and its employees.

   e. *Code of ethics.* No company or professional code of ethics exists.

   f. *Cost/benefit analysis of hiring the homeless to purchase tickets.* See Figure 6–1.

   g. *Obligations to stakeholders.* See Figure 6–2.

   h. Answers should be graded based on students' analyses of the facts and the objective support of their decisions. Therefore, no conclusion is provided with the analysis.

2–3. Refer to suggested solution of completed memorandum in **TM 6–6** (Solution, Case for Analysis 1, Step 3). This solution assumes the student judged hiring the homeless to be ethical (Step 1h).

Stakeholder	Cost	Benefit
Omaha Brokerage Firm	◆ Receiving negative publicity; that is, newspaper articles and record store discontent.	◆ Allows us to maintain profits in competitive market; may allow us to avoid ticket price increases, which in turn could lead to decreased demand.
Firm's customers		◆ Able to purchase tickets at a reasonable rate; do not have to spend time standing in line.
Record store	◆ Homeless people in front of store may damage its image.	◆ Possibly higher profits from increased sales.
Record store customers	◆ Must stand in long lines with what they describe as "shabby" people; they will be dissatisfied when tickets are sold out after they stand in long lines.	
Homeless	◆ Forced to sleep out in cold; may be subjected to ridicule; may do this meaningless task instead of bettering themselves; food is greasy, not nutritious.	◆ Receive money and food for purchasing the tickets; may use cash to better themselves.
Community/ society	◆ Shabby people may attract more public attention—look bad.	◆ May help solve the city's problem with the homeless.

Figure 6–1 ◆ 1. Cost/benefit analysis of hiring the homeless to purchase tickets

Stakeholder	Obligation
Omaha Brokerage Firm	◆ Keeps promise to stockholders to earn profits.
Firm's customers	◆ Keeps promise to customers to charge fair prices.
Record store	◆ May cause harm by hurting store's image (shabby people out front).
Record store customers	◆ May be harmed by losing opportunity to buy tickets. ◆ May not be treated justly if we buy all tickets.
Homeless	◆ Are not harmed because they sleep outside anyway. ◆ Keeps promise—they are paid $50 upon ticket purchase. ◆ Food shows our gratitude for standing in line.
Community/ society	◆ The action is legal; therefore, just. ◆ No harm is caused.

Figure 6–2 ◆ 1. Obligations to stakeholders

FINANCE/Ethics	GMAT

2. Should management compensation be restricted?

⇨ *Level 4* ⇦

1. Analysis of the problem:
    a. *Relevant facts.* Refer to case.
    b. *Ethical issue.* Is it ethical to restrict management compensation?
    c. *Stakeholders.* Golden Value Stores, management, stockholders, and employees.
    d. *Legal restrictions.* None; the stockholders can vote as they desire.
    e. *Code of ethics.* No company or professional code of ethics exists.
    f. *Cost/benefit analysis of restricting management compensation.* See Figure 6–3.
    g. *Obligations to stakeholders.* The company has an obligation to management to reward them for their performance. Compensation incentives should be aggressive but attainable. Incentives should be awarded for partially fulfilling goals. The company owes the stockholders a fair return on their investment. The company should provide its employees with a quality work environment where quality work is rewarded and fairly compensated.
    h. The company goal is to establish policies aimed at increasing stockholders' wealth. Establishing goals that are unrealistic, however, may diminish overall company performance. Management may feel pressured to make risky or unethical decisions that could increase short-term profitability at the expense of long-term profitability. Quality managers and employees may resign if they perceive themselves to be a negative impact on the company environment. Thus, the changes resulting from adopting the proposal could reduce earnings and dividends.

2–3. Answers should be graded based on students' analyses of the facts and the objective support of their decisions. Therefore, no solution is provided.

MANAGEMENT/Ethics	GMAT

3. Is reducing quality to cut costs ethical?

⇨ *Level 4* ⇦

1. Analysis of the problem:
    a. *Relevant facts.* Refer to case.
    b. *Ethical issues.* Is it ethical for a company to reduce the quality of a critical part to reduce production costs? Is it ethical for a vice president to communicate his or her disapproval of a decision when communicating that decision to subordinates?
    c. *Stakeholders.* Haynes-McReynolds Industries, stockholders, airline manufacturers, and passengers.
    d. *Legal restrictions.* None, the new product meets governmental and customer safety standards.
        Contractual considerations. The product meets company standards.
    e. *Code of ethics.* No company or professional code of ethics exists.
    f. *Cost/benefit analysis of adopting the new production method.* See Figure 6–4.
    g. *Obligations to stakeholders.* The company has an obligation to its stockholders to earn a profit but to do so lowers the quality of products delivered to its airplane manufacturer clients. This decline in quality adversely impacts the ultimate stakeholders, the airline, and its passengers.
    h. Although the company is not negligent in producing a lower quality part, it still may be forced to defend itself against litigation. Thus, the company will likely incur higher costs in defending itself against litigation, even if it prevails in court.

2–3. Answers should be graded based on the students' analysis of the facts and the objective support of their decisions. Therefore, no singular solution is provided.

Stakeholder	Cost	Benefit
Golden Value Stores	◆ Proposal (restricting compensation) could encourage managers to take risky or unethical actions to achieve goals. ◆ Quality managers may leave if they perceive new goals to be unachievable.	◆ Will relate compensation costs more directly to company operating results. ◆ Attaining 10 percent growth would improve market position.
Management	◆ Managers may view proposal as a negative evaluation of their past performance.	◆ Successfully achieving new goals would increase compensation and professional growth.
Stockholders	◆ Could reduce long-term return if changes are not managed properly.	◆ Would increase short-term return only slightly with reduced compensation costs. ◆ Could increase long-term return if management achieves new 10 percent goals.
Employees	◆ Work environment will likely change as management reacts to changes. Change will increase stress regardless of whether changes are positive or negative.	◆ Achieving 10 percent growth would increase opportunities for advancement and pay increases.

Figure 6–3 ◆ 2. Cost/benefit analysis of restricting management compensation

Stakeholder	Cost	Benefit
Haynes-McReynolds Industries	◆ Increases the risk of potential litigation.	◆ Reduced production costs can increase profits (increased sales).
Stockholders		◆ Increased return on investment.
Airline manufacturers	◆ Increases the risk of potential litigation.	◆ Any reduction in the price of Haynes-McReynolds' parts results in lower airplane production costs.
Passengers	◆ Increases risk of mental and physical harm in the event of an engine failure.	◆ Any reduction in airplane production costs may result in slightly lower airfares.

Figure 6–4 ◆ 3. Cost/benefit analysis of adopting the new production method

MANAGEMENT/Ethics   GMAT

4.   Is an ethical issue involved in replacing humans with machines?

⇨ *Level 4* ⇦

1.   Analysis of the problem:

    a.   *Relevant facts*. Refer to case.

    b.   *Ethical issues*. Is it ethical for a company to replace workers with automated machines?

    c.   *Stakeholders*. Employees to be terminated, employees to remain employed, Lolley Corporation, stockholders, local community/society.

    d.   *Legal restrictions*. None; the company has justification for replacing the workers (not discriminatory termination).

        Contractual considerations. The action does not violate known company policy. If applicable, management would have to consider any union contracts.

    e.   *Code of ethics*. No company or professional code of ethics exists.

    f.   *Cost/benefit analysis of adopting the new production method*. See Figure 6–5.

    g.   *Obligation to stakeholders*. The company has an obligation to its stockholders to maximize its profits and thus the dividends it pays. Responsibility to employees extends to the community because lost wages impacts the local economy.

    h.   Some students may agree with the action based on their motivation to increase corporate profits. However, many students may contend that the cost to employees (those terminated and remaining) and the community is not worth the small increase in earnings per share (EPS will still be $3.00 per share).

CROSS-DISCIPLINE/Ethics   GMAT

5.   Is the proposed action ethical?

⇨ *Level 4* ⇦

Refer to the solutions in the "Cases for Analysis" in the appropriate chapters.

Stakeholder	Cost	Benefit
Employees to be terminated	◆ Loss of employment.	
Employees to remain employed	◆ May have increased fear of losing their jobs, resulting in lower morale.	
Lolley Corporation	◆ May have a negative impact on employee morale and image within the community.	◆ Increases profits by $15,000.
Stockholders customers		◆ Increases earnings per share by 0.47 cents.
Local community/society	◆ Increases unemployment rate, thus increasing unemployment benefit payments; loss of tax revenues on personal income.	◆ Increases corporate income tax revenues from the additional $15,000 profit.

Figure 6–5 ◆ 4. Cost/benefit analysis of replacing humans with machines

PART 3

THE WRITING PROCESS

Two approaches to teaching letter and report writing are available: (1) Assume students already know the basics of good writing and plunge immediately into business writing exercises. (2) Assume most students would need to sharpen their tools before beginning to work, and conduct some review followed with writing exercises. We have found the second approach to be more effective. For that reason, writing chapters in the text are preceded by Chapters 7 and 8 that focus on the writing process and review basic writing principles.

Chapter 7 focuses on the initial steps in the writing process: determining the purpose and channel for the message, envisioning the audience, adapting the message to the reader, organizing the message, and writing the first draft. Chapter 8 focuses on the final two steps in the writing process: revising and proofreading.

Most students who learn (or relearn) the principles in Chapters 7–8 experience initial success in the writing assignments of Chapters 9–12. Because students make few mistakes, morale is high. For instructors, grading a set of high-quality papers is not overly time consuming. When students master the basics in the first weeks of a term, the remaining weeks provide abundant opportunity for reinforcement. Students can form habits of correctness.

Build time in your schedule to integrate the videotape prepared for Chapter 8, "Revising and Proofreading Messages." Require students to read the "Video Connection" after Chapter 8 in their texts, which previews the videotape and provides several questions covering major points presented. After showing the videotape, initiate a class discussion using the review questions. Review questions and cases (requiring students to write a letter or memo) can be assigned as homework. Suggested answers and five multiple choice questions (to add to an objective test for this unit or to use as a pop quiz) are included in the teaching suggestions immediately following Chapter 8.

The following suggestions are offered to assist in meeting the spectrum of student needs:

1. *Give a pretest*. Use your favorite language test or use one of the three tests included in Section B of the *Instructor's Resource Manual*. Select from the (a) Grammatical Checkup, (b) Word-Usage Checkup, (c) Punctuation Checkup, or (d) combine selected questions to fit your needs. Administer the pretest early in the semester (preferably in the first week). Ten minutes of class time is probably sufficient. Assure students that the pretest score will not be counted in determining the final grade. Before the test, explain its purpose (to find out the extent to which students in this class need a review of grammar, spelling, and punctuation). This information will enable you to tailor instruction to student needs.

2. *Encourage students to learn proper writing techniques*. Instead of *lecturing* students about the value of knowing grammar and punctuation or the consequences of making errors, *lead them* to make statements about the value of knowing. Through focusing on current business events and discussion, guide students in *listing reasons* for knowing and applying principles of grammar.

3. *Provide learning experiences*. The goal is to bring about as much learning and relearning as possible without devoting an unjustified amount of class time to a review of basics. Some possible approaches include:

   a. *Extra class sessions*. Reserve a large room at an hour (possibly in the late afternoon) when most students can attend an announced review session. Do not require attendance, but encourage any students who haven't scored well on the pretest to attend. (Don't be surprised if students who made high scores are present, too.) Based on the pretest results, select a limited number of grammatical and punctuation principles for discussion. Depending on time constraints and progress made in the first session, an additional session or two could be scheduled. If an instructor demonstrates willingness to do extra work in the students' behalf, at least some of them may be inspired to do extra work on their own behalf (like voluntary study of Appendix B).

b. *Two or three entire class sessions.* Announce that two (or three) class sessions will be devoted to a review of grammar and punctuation. Tell students who made high pretest scores that their attendance is optional. (Most of them will choose to attend.) By spending some class sessions in this manner, students can experience reasonable success in their initial writing assignments and instructors can minimize the amount of time devoted to making comments on papers.

c. *Portions of several class sessions.* Devote about ten minutes of each class session to review (for the first weeks only). Such sessions are not long enough to bore students who may already know the basics. In providing learning experiences, *rely mainly on the inductive approach.* That is, instead of telling students a rule and then illustrating or explaining it, help students (through discussion of examples) to *derive* rules. The technique encourages students to *think* (instead of listen) and to phrase principles in their own words (instead of the instructor's). Thus, students are more likely to grasp and remember principles.

d. *Independent practice.* Instruct students to follow these procedures for reviewing the grammatical principles in Appendix B: (1) Complete the Self-Check at the beginning of Appendix B, (2) mark any errors and identify the grammatical principles requiring further study, (3) read the material in Appendix B related to the principles identified in Step 2 and complete the exercises positioned with these principles, (4) complete the Self-Check at the end of Appendix B to assess mastery again. You may wish to administer the Review Quiz at the end of Appendix B after students have reviewed Appendix B. The answers are not provided; therefore, you may give a daily grade as an added incentive to study Appendix B. For additional practice, have students complete the grammar review included in each chapter of the *Study Guide.*

4. *Encourage students to learn the vocabulary used in discussing the writing process.* Initially, some students may have the same attitude that was expressed by one student who had made a low score on a pretest: "I'm a *business* major. As such, I will never be asked to define words like 'gerund' or 'superlative.' Why should I bother to learn them?" Without removal of that barrier, the student would have learned little about the revision process. Labels are essential. As employees or executives, people in business need to have *names* for tools they use or principles they apply. Without knowing what to *call* something, thinking about it is difficult.

An effective way to *test* vocabulary is to ask students for examples. For example, instead of asking for a definition of an appositive, ask them to compose a sentence that contains an appositive.

5. *Reward students for learning.* For motivated students who have put forth effort, instructor recognition of their progress may be sufficient reward. Time spent in commending deserving students is well spent. By learning basics, students will have improved their chances of making an adequate grade in the communication class. Scores on written assignments will be better than they would have been if serious review had not been undertaken. As a reward for knowing grammar and punctuation, include a limited number of grammatical and punctuation items on examinations.

CHAPTER 7

ORGANIZING AND COMPOSING MESSAGES

CHAPTER OVERVIEW

Business communication students will have had prior instruction in composition, but almost all of them will fall into one of these categories: (1) They learned the principles but have forgotten some, (2) they never learned the principles, or (3) they learned the principles but have never thought about ways in which they could be applied in business. The instructor's challenge is to provide a learning experience for students in all three categories.

Administrators in schools of business frequently receive reports about their graduates' weak writing ability. The finger of scorn may be pointed at the whole educational system or at English composition classes; but it is sometimes pointed directly at the business communication instructor. That instructor's task is difficult—teach a class in communication *and* help certain students to master basics that should have been learned previously.

Chapter 7 focuses on effective business writing as process that involves careful analysis, planning, adaptation, and organization before the communication is drafted.

LEARNING OBJECTIVES

1 Identify the purpose of the message and the appropriate channel.

2 Envision the audience so you can adapt the message.

3 Apply techniques for adapting messages to the audience.

4 Recognize the importance of organizing a message before writing the first draft.

5 Select the appropriate outline (deductive or inductive) for developing messages by identifying the central idea and the likely receiver reaction.

6 Apply techniques for developing effective sentences and for developing unified and coherent paragraphs.

CHAPTER OUTLINE AND TEACHING SUGGESTIONS

1	**LEARNING OBJECTIVE**

I.   Determining the Purpose and Channel

   A.   Show **TA 7–1** (Chapter Opener). Develop the analogy of the setting of an athletic goal and the setting of communication goals.

   B.   Make a transparency from **TM 7–1** (Organizing and Composing Messages) to illustrate the components of organizing and composing messages. Discuss the advantages and disadvantages of each communication channel presented in Chapter 1.

   C.   Ask students to recall the various channels for sending messages: person-to-person conversations, telephone, fax, e-mail, meetings, mailed correspondence, etc. Show **TA 1–3** (Communication Channels). Then pose several communication situations and ask students to choose the best and worst channel for each. The situations might include the following: announcement of a layoff, dissemination of new procedures for logging information, response to a colleague's request for routine information, submitting of a bid on a job or project, feedback on an employee's performance appraisal, etc. Discuss the reasons for each choice. Show **TM 1–5** (Selecting an Appropriate Channel) and initiate a discussion of the selection of an appropriate channel for these scenarios or use as a quiz.

   D.   Refer to **TM 1–7** (Origami Drawing) to illustrate the inadequacy of a communication channel in meeting its desired purpose.

2	**LEARNING OBJECTIVE**

II. Envisioning the Audience
  A. Integrate the communication mentor comments into class lectures, emphasizing the advice these executives have offered for mastering effective writing skills.
  B. So that you can test students' understanding of mentor comments, the *Test Bank* contains questions from the communication mentor comments.

3	**LEARNING OBJECTIVE**

III. Adapting the Message to the Audience
  A. Assume an Empathetic Attitude
  B. Focus on the Receiver's Point of View
  C. Use Bias-Free Language
    1. Avoid gender bias
    2. Avoid race and ethnic group, age, religion, and disability bias
  D. Avoid Statements that Destroy Goodwill
    1. Eliminate condescension
    2. Use euphemisms cautiously
    3. Avoid flattering tone
    4. Avoid demeaning expressions
    5. Use connotative tone cautiously
    6. Avoid statements of surprise, doubt, and judgment
    7. Avoid statements of certainty
  E. Project a Positive, Tactful Tone
  F. Ask students to give examples of situations where they have experienced a loss of goodwill toward a business or its employees because of poor communication (self-centered attitude, biased language, condescension, etc.).
  G. Lead students in a discussion of the amount of time necessary to build goodwill and to lose it.
  H. Assign Exercises 1–15 at the end of the chapter to apply principles of adaptation. Show **TA 7–2** (Answers to Exercises 1–15) as you review the answers.

4	5	**LEARNING OBJECTIVES**

IV. Organizing the Message
  A. Outline to Benefit Writer and Receiver
  B. Sequence Ideas to Achieve Desired Goals
  C. Communication in Action: R. D. Saenz, Business Consultant
  D. Ask the students to locate articles in current business periodicals about the value of writing and speaking skills in their field. To help you initiate a class discussion, refer to the list of articles in Additional Readings or others with which you are familiar. Ask students to share specific examples of needed communication skills discussed in their articles. You could also divide the class into groups by academic major for this discussion.
  E. Invite students to relate experiences about the value of communication skills. Compared to students who have gone from high school directly to college, people who currently have responsible jobs seem to have more enthusiasm for an opportunity to improve writing skills. Students will listen attentively to a classmate who begins with something like, "I've been in business for twenty years. I've made progress, but it would have come much faster and easier if I had learned the basics of English and writing."

6	**LEARNING OBJECTIVE**

V. Writing the First Draft
  A. Writing Powerful Sentences
    1. Use correct sentence structure
    2. Rely on active voice
    3. Emphasize important ideas
      a. Sentence structure
      b. Repetition
      c. Words that label
      d. Position
      e. Space
      f. Format
      g. Punctuation

4. Teaching Suggestions:
   a. Make a transparency of **TM 7–4** (Punctuating Compound Sentences) and review the examples with the class.
   b. Ask students to complete Exercises 16–25 at the end of the chapter to reinforce the importance of emphasis.
B. Developing Coherent Paragraphs
   1. Position the topic sentence appropriately
   2. Link ideas to achieve coherence
   3. Keep paragraphs unified
   4. Vary sentence and paragraph length
C. Teaching Suggestions:
   1. Make a transparency from **TM 7–2** (What Would You Think If...) and have students discuss their reactions to each question posed.
   2. Project on the screen some sentences, paragraphs, or short letters that contain errors. Invite students to identify errors and to discuss such questions as these: Does the error (a) keep the message from being understood correctly? (b) cause the reader to waste time? (c) distract your attention, causing you to think more about the error than about the message? (d) raise questions about the author's educational background, self-respect (or respect for the reader? From their own answers, students can increase their appreciation of the necessity for correctness.
   3. Make a transparency of **TM 7–3** (Think It Over) and ask students to give written or oral rebuttals to each statement. Suggested responses are summarized as follows:
   Statement 1: **"As an executive, I will have an administrative assistant who will be responsible for the grammar, spelling, and punctuation in my correspondence; therefore, I need not bother with learning."** Because of downsizing, some executives have little or no administra-

tive support. At best, an executive job may be years away. Until then, is the executive content with making errors? A good assistant may be hard to find. How will the executive who probably has a college education yet lacks grammar skills entrust the task to an assistant who likely is less educated? Assistant or no assistant, the executive is still responsible.

Statement 2: **"If I need to know the answer to a grammatical question, I'll simply use my references."** If basic knowledge is scant, references may be difficult to use. Looking up basics is time consuming, and references may not be available where and when needed. A college graduate who wants to find what percentage one number is of another should be able to make the calculation without referring to a math text. Likewise, a business writer who wants to know whether to use "John and I" or "John and me" should know already, without having to refer to an English text.

Statement 3: **"I can write without making a mistake because I know my limitations. If I don't know whether a certain word is appropriate or how to punctuate a sentence, I can find another way to express myself and thus avoid a problem."** Why work under such limitations? Getting by on a limited amount of knowledge is somewhat like taking only a club or two to the golf course. Why not know the basics and express ideas in the manner you really prefer? Also, knowledge of basics assists in understanding what is read.

VI. Summary
A. Use the "Check Your Writing" checklist at the end of the chapter as a review for students.
B. Assign review questions at the end of the chapter.

C. Assign the *Study Guide* questions for Chapter 7.

D. Assign the *Study Guide* applications for Chapter 7. The applications require students to (a) select the correct word choice and explain the communication principle being applied, (b) select the correct sentence and explain the comunication principle being applied, and (c) rewrite sentences to incorporate effective communication principles. The solutions are provided in the *Study Guide*.

E. Ask students to complete the e-mail application at the end of the chapter.

TRANSPARENCIES AND MASTERS

TA 7–1 Chapter Opener
TA 7–2 Answers to Exercises 1–15

TM 7–1 Organizing and Composing Messages
TM 7–2 What Would You Think If . . .
TM 7–3 Think it Over
TM 7–4 Punctuating Compound Sentences

ADDITIONAL READINGS

Glaseman, J. K. (1990). Where seldom is heard an intelligent word. *Business Month, 135*(6), 14–15.

Lewis, H. G. (1991). The future of "force-communication": Power communication. *Direct Marketing, 54*(2), 48–51.

Lundeen, H. K. (1989). Are your words working for you? *Journal of Property Management, 54*(11), 26–28.

Patterson, P. (1992, March 1). Do you write as clearly as you speak? *Institutional Distribution, 28*(5), 106–107.

Petrini, C., & Shea, G. F. (1992). A case for clear writing. *Training & Development, 46*(1), 63–66.

Stone, P. F. (1990). Would you really want to read your own writing? *The Practical Accountant, 23*(5), 67–70.

ANSWERS TO "COMMUNICATION IN ACTION" CASE: Cynthia Pharr, C. Pharr Marketing Communications

1. **Why was the lighter theme of Pharr's letter to the financial analyst appropriate for a rebuttal?** Pharr reasoned that a lighter theme was appropriate because it was consistent with Showbiz Pizza's fun-loving corporate slogan, "Where A Kid Can Be A Kid!" Discuss with students that Pharr thought the lighter theme may have a persuasive impact on the analyst's thinking and would possibly change his attitude toward Showbiz Pizza.

2. **Assume for a moment you are the financial analyst. What impact do you believe the letter and its enclosures would have on you? Discuss with students the importance of the positive tone of Pharr's letter.** Because the tone is positive, the impact on the analyst will likely be positive or neutral. A negative tone may have reinforced the analyst's skeptical attitude toward Showbiz Pizza. The enclosures were effective visuals; the two free passes may persuade the analyst to visit the restaurant.

ANSWERS TO REVIEW QUESTIONS

1. The purpose of a message is like a sports goal to an athlete. Business messages may have as their purpose to inform or to persuade.

2. Selecting the appropriate channel of communication increases the likelihood that the receiver will understand and accept your message. For example, a written document is appropriate for routine or pleasant information. Complex information may require a written document and follow up with a face-to-face meeting. A face-to-face meeting is appropriate for sending unpleasant or highly emotional messages that may be subject to misinterpretation. E-mail is especially effective when sending the same message to many people and communicating with people in different time zones but should not be used when confidentiality is required.

3. Envisioning the audience helps the writer to tailor the message to the audience's particular needs, values, opinions, preferences, etc. Age, economic level, educational/occupational background, culture, rapport, expectations, and needs of the audience should be considered.

4. Empathy is an attitude that enables a person to identify another's frame of reference (knowledge, feelings, and emotions) and to project or communicate understanding back to the person (or animal).

5. Empathy is an excellent way to establish rapport and credibility and to build long-lasting personal and business relationships. Secondly, seeing a situation or problem from the receiver's perspective not only will permit you to address the receiver's needs and concerns but will also enable you to anticipate the receiver's possible reaction to the message. Encourage students to share hypothetical or personal examples of these.

6. Euphemisms should be avoided that represent excess sugar coating or that appear to be deliberate sarcasm.

7. Connotative words that elicit a favorable reaction are acceptable.

8. The statement could be construed to mean, "Your conduct is such that I recognize your lack of self-control. Because of your condition, you could not be thinking rationally."

9. In each case, the writer seems to be making a declaration of certainty when certainty is hardly possible.

10. Active voice is best for conveying pleasant ideas because the subject of the sentence is the doer, which makes the sentence more emphatic.

11. Subjunctive mood speaks of a wish, necessity, doubt, or contrary conditions and conveys the message in positive language. Because the expression of the negative idea includes a reason, the idea seems less objectionable and the tone is improved.

12. If for any reason a writer suspects the implication is not sufficiently strong, a direct statement in negative terms is preferable.

13. Passive voice is preferred for conveying negative ideas.

14. More emphasis is provided to an idea by using (a) a simple sentence, (b) an independent clause, (c) dashes, and (d) tabulated arrangement.

15. Placing a word first or last in a sentence gives it emphasis.

16. Because each unit in the series is on a line by itself and because the arrangement consumes more space on a page, a tabulated series attracts more attention than a paragraphed arrangement.

17. Outlining before you write encourages brevity and accuracy, permits concentration on one phase at a time, saves time in writing or dictating, provides a psychological lift, and

facilitates emphasis and de-emphasis. Receivers benefit because the message is more concise and accurate, relationships between ideas are easier to distinguish and remember, and reaction to the message is more likely to be positive.

18. Questions to answer in order to select inductive or deductive pattern include the following: (a) What will be the central idea of the message? (b) What will be the most likely receiver reaction to the message? (c) In view of the predicted receiver reaction, should the central idea be listed first in the outline; or should it be listed as one of the last items?

19. When messages begin with the major idea, the sequence of the ideas is called **deductive**. When messages withhold the major idea until accompanying details and explanations have been presented, the sequence is called **inductive**. Consider the receiver to determine whether to use the inductive or deductive paragraph. If the message will please the receiver or be perceived as routine, use deductive approach. If the reader might be antagonized by the main idea or if the writer wants to encourage receiver involvement, used inductive approach.

20. Normally, writing rapidly, with intent to rewrite certain portions if necessary, is better than slow, deliberate writing, with intent to avoid any need for rewriting portions. The latter can be time consuming and frustrating.

21. For coherence within paragraphs, repeat a word that was used in the preceding sentence; use a pronoun that represents a noun used in the preceding sentence; and use connecting words such as *however, therefore, yet, nevertheless, consequently, also, in addition, etc.* For coherence among sections, use good transition sentences and keep paragraphs unified and arranged in a systematic sequence.

22. Paragraphs should not be uniform in length; the length may vary from one line to a dozen or so lines. Average paragraph length should, however, be kept short since short paragraphs enable a writer to emphasize each thought and also appear more inviting to read than longer paragraphs.

23. The effect of the unified message is like a complete circle. It begins with an introduction that identifies the topic and provides necessary background. Systematically sequenced paragraphs follow that provide the facts of the message. A summary or conclusion brings all

major points together. When the "wrap-up" paragraph is missing, the circle is incomplete.

24. A transition sentence bridges the gap between two topics by summing up the preceding topic and leading a receiver to expect the next topic; it confirms the relationship of the two segments.

25. Focus on responses that show understanding and appreciation of the appropriate writing principles.

POSSIBLE SOLUTIONS TO EXERCISES

1–15. See **TA 7–2** (Answers to Exercises 1–15) for identified weaknesses and suggested revisions.

16. More emphasis is given to credit in "a" because it ends the sentence.

17. Sentence "b" gives more emphasis to denial because it is part of a main clause.

18. Sentence "a" is more emphatic since it uses active voice.

19. Sentence "b" is more specific and, therefore, more emphatic.

20. Sentence "a" is less specific and, therefore, less emphatic.

21. Sentence "b" is less negative because it uses subjunctive mood.

22. Sentence "b" places more emphasis on "excuses" because a dash is a more forceful mark of punctuation.

23. Sentence "a" uses the more forceful, active voice.

24. Sentence "a" is more emphatic because it has a concrete subject.

25. Sentence "b" emphasizes the units by enumerating them.

POSSIBLE SOLUTION TO E-MAIL APPLICATION

Students will likely enjoy this activity. Students should print out their encoded message that is received and bring these to class. Ask students to exchange messages and decode them. Recognize some of the more creative emoticon messages.

CHAPTER 8

REVISING AND PROOFREADING MESSAGES

CHAPTER OVERVIEW

Chapter 8 emphasizes revising and proofreading as the essential, final steps in the writing process. Such writing characteristics as vividness, clarity, conciseness, and readability are stressed. Techniques for proofreading are introduced and reinforced. After a review of the writing process in Chapters 7 and 8 and parts of Appendix B, students will write letters, memos, e-mail messages, and reports. Everything that is learned beforehand will make the letter- and report-writing chapters easier. The general teaching suggestions for Chapter 7 apply also to Chapter 8.

LEARNING OBJECTIVES

1 Edit and rewrite messages for vividness, clarity, and conciseness.

2 Identify factors affecting readability and revise messages to improve readability.

3 Revise and proofread a message for organization, content, style, mechanics, format, and layout.

CHAPTER OUTLINE AND TEACHING SUGGESTIONS

1   **LEARNING OBJECTIVE**

I. Editing and Rewriting
   A. Show **TA 8–1** (Chapter Opener) to emphasize the writer's tools for creating excellent documents.

B. A case occurred in Louisiana a few years ago in which a borrower signed a note to the bank, supposedly pledging a boat as collateral. The description of collateral was incorrectly typed as a "boot." The bank was not pleased with their repossession when the borrower defaulted on the loan.

II. Self-check

A. Emphasize to students the value of becoming so familiar with the rules and principles shown in the self-check that correct usage becomes automatic.

B. For reinforcement, ask students to complete the *Study Guide* activities for Chapter 8.

III. Creating Vivid Images

A. Make a transparency from **TM 8–1** (Editing and Rewriting) to project during discussion of this section and the four that follow.

B. Use Precise Words

C. Select Concrete Nouns

D. Eliminate Clichés

E. Choose Descriptive Adjectives and Adverbs

   1. Overly strong adjectives and adverbs

   2. Superlatives

F. Integrate the communication mentor comments, emphasizing the advice these executives have offered for mastering effective writing skills. So that you can test students' understanding of this valuable content, the *Test Bank* contains questions from the communication mentor comments.

IV. Writing Clearly

A. Choose Simple, Informal Words

B. Eliminate Misplaced Elements

C. Eliminate Dangling Modifiers

D. Recast Expletive Beginnings

E. Express Ideas in Parallel Form

F. Assign Exercises 1–15 at the end of the chapter. Show **TA 8–2** (Answers to Exercises) and discuss the correct answers.

V. Writing Concisely

A. Make a transparency of **TM 8–3** (Revising for Conciseness) and project for students to view.

B. Place on transparency a typical business paragraph taken from a letter, textbook, article, etc. Assign students to work in pairs to rewrite the paragraph for better conciseness.

2   **LEARNING OBJECTIVE**

VI. Improving Readability

A. Ask students to calculate readability scores for their own writing, some of their texts, or newspaper or magazine articles.

B. If your department has a writing-analysis software program, demonstrate it in class and/or give students an opportunity to use it and discuss results in class. You might analyze a familiar literary passage such as the Gettysburg Address or the Preamble to the Constitution to show the strengths and limitations of the electronic advice about writing style.

C. Electronic spellcheck features and writing-analysis software are helpful in locating spelling and structural mistakes; however, students need a thorough awareness of their responsibility for correct spelling.

3   **LEARNING OBJECTIVE**

VII. Procedures for Revising and Proofreading

A. Edit for Content, Organization, and Style

B. Edit for Mechanics

C. Edit for Format and Layout

D. Teaching Suggestions:

   1. Make a transparency of **TM 8–2** (Systematic Revision Procedures) and display to reinforce proofreading procedures.

   2. Have students complete the Proofreading Application at the end of the chapter. Show **TA 8–3** (Solution, Proofreading Application) as you discuss the corrections.

E. Communication in Action: Cynthia Pharr, C. Pharr Marketing Communications

1. Lead students in a discussion of the case, including the importance of tone in the overall message impact.

2. Ask students to work in small teams to draft the letter discussed in the case. Show **TA 8–4** ("Communication in Action" Case). If time is short, omit the team writing and concentrate on the actual letter that was written by the company.

3. Ask students to respond to the two questions that follow the case.

4. Lead a class discussion as to why the particular tone used in the letter worked in this case. When would it be inappropriate?

VIII. Summary

A. Show the videotape "Revising and Proofreading." Assign the video case activities. Show **TA 8–5** (Business Tips from Amatulli & Associates, Inc. [Video, Part 3]) to summarize the advice given.

B. Ask students to review the "Check Your Writing" checklist at the end of the chapter to summarize the material covered.

C. Ask students to complete selected activities at the end of the chapter.

D. Assign the *Study Guide* applications for Chapter 8. The applications require students to (a) revise sentences for improved style, (b) edit paragraphs for improved writing style including correct format and punctuation, and (c) key and print the revised paragraphs using an appropriate letter format illustrated in Appendix A of the textbook. Critical thinking questions help students critique the paragraphs; sample solutions for each application are provided in the *Study Guide*.

E. Ask students to complete the e-mail application at the end of the chapter.

TRANSPARENCIES AND MASTERS

TA 8–1 Chapter Opener
TA 8–2 Answers to Exercises
TA 8–3 Solution, Proofreading Application
TA 8–4 "Communication in Action" Case
TA 8–5 Business Tips from Amatulli & Associates, Inc. (Video, Part 3)

TM 8–1 Editing and Rewriting
TM 8–2 Systematic Revision Procedures
TM 8–3 Revising for Conciseness

ADDITIONAL READINGS

Cheney, G. A. (1990, March). Word crunching: A primer for accountants. *Journal of Accountancy*, pp. 50–54.

Dolbear, G. (1990). The expandable page. *Chemical Engineering, 97*(5), 157–158, 160.

Gold, R. (1989). "Reader-friendly" writing. *Supervisory Management, 34*(1), 39–43.

Joseph, A. (1990). Your employees' writing. *Association Management, 42*(7), 46–48, 81.

Matz, L. M. (1991). Writing tips for bankers. *Journal of Commercial Bank Lending, 73*(8) 51–57. [Contains general guidelines applicable to business writing in any discipline.]

O'Brian, J. D. (1994). How you say it does make a difference. *Supervisory Management, 39*(4), 10.

Poor, E. (1992). The memo as project manager: Writing effective memos. *Executive Female, 15*(3), 63–65.

Reigstad, T. (1994, July 11). Give it to 'em in English and watch the profits soar: Plain English usage in business writing. *Business First of Buffalo*, p. 15.

Seitel, F. P. (1991). Getting it write. *United States Banker, 101*(12), 54.

Shea, G. F. (1992). A case for clear writing. *Training & Development Journal, 46*(1), 63–66.

Thomas, D. O. (1992). We've got to stop verbing our nouns. *RN, 55*(8), 84.

Warren, A. (1993). 10 tips for memos that get results. *Women in Business, 45*(3), 8.

ANSWERS TO "COMMUNICATION IN ACTION" CASE: R. D. Saenz, Business Consultant

1. **Why does Saenz consider proficiency in oral and written communication skills basic to the accounting profession today?** Saenz's employees frequently write memos and letters explaining exceptions, discussing procedures, or explaining resolutions. Understanding only the accounting principles behind these issues limits the employee. Good writing skills are needed to communicate these principles clearly to clients.

85

2. Saenz commented that "grammatical errors quickly detract from the credibility of the writer." How might the credibility of a writer be "detracted" by grammatical errors? A credible person is knowledgeable, competent, and an able writer. A reader who encounters grammatical errors may assume the writer is incompetent, unable to use good grammar skills, or lacks knowledge about mechanical rules.

3. Assume that you are an employee for a large accounting firm. Your duties include careful consideration of any employee's written work that leaves your office. Following Saenz's example, discuss some considerations to keep in mind when commenting about another employee's writing. Students' comments should concern maintaining high standards, setting an appropriate tone, using positive word choice, and explaining how the writing can be improved.

ANSWERS TO REVIEW QUESTIONS

1. When an idea needs to be included but does not need emphasis, using an abstract noun as the subject may be desirable.

2. To readers, clichés may seem monotonous and connote the writer's lack of creativity. By using the expressions that have been overused in communicating with others, writers risk implying that readers are receiving standard treatment—that they are nothing special. Additionally, a cliché may not say exactly what the writer really means.

3. When superlatives are totally unsupported or unsupportable, their use is questionable. Knowing that such statements are exaggerations, the receiver may not believe them or even other believable ideas.

4. Professionals in the same field often use technical terms and jargon when communicating with each other. In this case, the jargon is easily understood and saves time. The degree of formality in writing is dictated by the nature of the message and the backgrounds of the receivers. The writing in dissertations, theses, legal documents, and high-level government documents is expected to be formal.

5. Expletives add to sentence length. Expletives also require a little extra mental processing. In English, the normal word sequence of a sentence is subject-verb-complement. Sentences with expletive beginnings present the verb *before* revealing the subject and thus make meaning a little harder to grasp.

6. Select five ways to prepare a concise message from the seven provided: (a) eliminate redundancies; (b) use active voice to reduce the number of words; (c) review the main purpose of your writing and identify the details that the reader needs to understand the message and to take necessary action; (d) eliminate wordy, unnecessary clichés; (e) do not restate ideas that are sufficiently implied; (f) use suffixes and prefixes, and (g) use a compound adjective.

7. Two types of changes should be made to improve readability: use shorter sentences and simpler words.

8. Errors in business letters and reports reflect negatively on the reputation of the company and the writer. Errors distract the reader from the message itself and thereby reduce the effectiveness of the document.

9. Spellchecks are helpful in locating spelling and keyboarding errors. However, they cannot be relied on to detect all errors. Errors undetectable by spellchecks include misused words, numbers that should be spelled out or vice versa, misspelling of proper nouns, incorrect amounts or addresses, and so on. The writer is still responsible for careful proofreading.

10. The person who is familiar with the basics of grammar is more likely to benefit from writing-analysis software. Knowledge of the basics results in an initial draft that meets higher standards. When the program indicates *few* serious criticisms, the writer can devote more attention to each suggestion when revising. Those who know the basics will understand the vocabulary used by the software and have a better chance of seeing the value of its suggestions.

11. Proofread several times, each time for a specific purpose, such as locating errors in (a) content, organization, and style; (b) mechanics; and (c) format and layout. If using word-processing software, run the electronic spell-check and proofread at least once from a printed copy, as errors on the screen are often difficult to locate.

12. Answers will vary; encourage reflective responses that apply information to situations that actually have been encountered.

POSSIBLE SOLUTIONS TO EXERCISES

1–15. See **TA 8–2** (Answers to Exercises) for solutions.

SOLUTION TO PROOFREADING APPLICATION

Refer to the suggested solution on **TA 8–3**. A summary of the errors follows:

Summary of Errors
Format ◆ Insert two-letter state postal abbreviation.
◆ Insert colon after salutation (mixed punctuation).
◆ Add a complimentary close followed by a comma.
◆ Sign letter.
Par. 1 ◆ Spell "congratulations" correctly.
◆ Insert hyphen in "two-day seminar."
◆ Insert comma after Georgia.
◆ Add another day for the two-day seminar.
◆ Refer to six guidelines rather than five.
Par. 2 ◆ Renumber list in consecutive order.
◆ Use "your" rather than "you" in Item 2.
◆ Spell "sincerely" in Item 3 correctly.
◆ Insert a semicolon to join a compound sentence without a conjunction in Item 3.
◆ Use "hear" instead of "here" in Item 4.
◆ Use semicolon before adverbial conjunction ("otherwise") in Item 5.
Par. 3 ◆ Insert "attend" in Sentence 1.
◆ Insert comma after introductory dependent clause in Sentence 2.
◆ Spell "McMahan" correctly.

POSSIBLE SOLUTION TO E-MAIL APPLICATION

Ask students to print out and submit the edited letter. Students may exchange papers and check the assignment in class, using **TA 8–3** (Solution, Proofreading Application) as a guide.

> **VIDEO CONNECTION**
> **Amatulli & Associates, Inc.**
> **CHAPTER 8:**
> **Revising and Proofreading Messages**

SUMMARY

I. The Planning Process
   A. Identify the audience
   B. Identify the purpose of the message
   C. Select the appropriate media
      1. Written
      2. Video
      3. Computer interactive
   D. Identify and <u>understand</u> the message
II. The Drafting Process
   A. Develop the first draft
      1. Choose elements which are appropriate for the audience and the content
      2. Adapt for style, language, and tone
      3. Set collaborative guidelines
   B. Develop the final draft
      1. Revise for accuracy, consistency, format, and mechanics
      2. Use electronic tools carefully
      3. Use two-step proofreading procedure
         a. Two-person read back method
         b. Individual comparing of edited copy with final copy

ANSWERS TO DISCUSSION QUESTIONS

1. **According to Jim Amatulli, what information must a writer identify before writing the first draft of a document?** The writer(s) must identify (a) the audience, (b) the purpose and the outcome expected by the client, and (c) the optimal media combination before writing the first draft.

2. **Describe the process involved in identifying the content of the message and organizing it effectively.** The writer meets with an "internal expert" to gain a clear understanding of the message to be communicated and then decides on an appropriate approach for presenting the information (e.g.,

procedural or situational scenarios). After the writer and the client agree on an outline of the content, a description of the approach, and the media combination involved in reaching the audience, the writer begins writing the first draft.

3. **What process is used to control for consistency, accuracy, and effectiveness of the message when several writers work collaboratively on a project?** The writers meet to establish guidelines for the appropriate style of the document (e.g., first person vs. second person or active vs. passive voice) and then write a first draft of assigned portions of the project independently. Periodically they meet to ensure that they have not varied from the agreed-on patterns.

4. **Describe the (a) editing process and (b) the two proofreading methods used at Amatulli.** Writers are responsible for the mechanical accuracy of documents they write; however, others in the company review documents for mechanical accuracy. The preferred method of proofreading is to have one person read aloud from the edited copy and another person follow along on the final version. A second method involves an individual comparing the edited copy with the final copy.

5. **How have electronic spellchecks affected the writing process according to Jim Amatulli? What <u>two</u> cautions does he offer about the reliability of electronic spellchecks?** Amatulli states that the advance of spellchecks has made the proofreading process more efficient. However, spellchecks cannot detect differences in word meanings (e.g., *your* vs. *you*) or ensure the accurate spelling of technical terms added to the spellcheck by the user.

6. **Study carefully the writing project Jo Huntingdon described. (a) Identify the audience, the purpose and intended outcome, and the media combination selected.** Audience—managers in a particular organization. Purpose/Outcomes—to develop methods and tools needed to improve the planning process. Media—video and study guide. **(b) Describe the content of the message and the specific approach used to present the message.** The content entailed identifying the exact tools and methods the managers needed to develop to

improve planning. The approach involved dramatizing the planning process in a fictional uniform rental business with plans to expand its clothing line. After the video was completed, the writers developed a Study Guide that was consistent with and clarified the video. **(c) Discuss how collaborative writing enhanced this project.** Writers developed characters (age, gender, job duties) and wrote a script for the video collaboratively. By taking a role and reading the script aloud, the writers were able to add personality to the characters and make them seem real and to verify the conciseness, clarity, and accuracy of the document.

7. **What does Jim Amatulli mean when he describes the objective and subjective nature of communication?** The objective nature of communication is critical in the planning stages (identifying the audience, the purpose and the intended outcomes, the content of the message, and the appropriate media combination). The subjective nature brings the message to life by adding style, tone, and personality that enhance the message without distracting from the delivery of the message.

SOLUTION TO APPLICATION

This application will impress upon students the importance of the planning stage of writing and set the stage for the writing application chapters that follow. Allow students to vary the purpose of the project to exploit their interests and experiences. Consider allowing students to complete this application in pairs or small groups to enhance creativity and interest.

Before assigning this application, be sure students can list the steps in the writing process that they read about in Chapters 7 and 8 and that Jim Amatulli explained. Initiate a discussion about the writing project that Jo Huntington described; have students identify each step in the writing process (Discussion Question 6). After completing Chapter 11 ("Writing to Persuade"), require students to write, revise, and proofread the document planned in this application. This follow-up assignment would further emphasize that writing involves a four-step process and is not merely writing a final copy.

MULTIPLE CHOICE QUESTIONS

1. Which of the following is it **not** necessary for the writer to identify before writing the first draft of a document?
   a. the audience
   b. the purpose and expected outcome
   ✔ c. the formatting requirements
   d. the optimal medium/media to use

2. Which of the following tasks presents the greatest challenge to a collaborative project?
   ✔ a. assuring consistency in style
   b. documenting accuracy of information
   c. achieving effectiveness of the message
   d. meeting deadlines

3. Which of the following proofreading methods is preferred?
   ✔ a. One person reads aloud from the edited copy and another person follows along on the final version.
   b. One individual compares the edited copy with the final copy.
   c. Proofreading is handled by electronic tools, such as spellcheck and style check software.
   d. Proofreading is accomplished word by word and line by line as the document is composed, making it unnecessary to proofread once the document is completed.

4. The four-step sequence involved in the preparation of a document is
   a. write, collaborate, proofread, and revise.
   ✔ b. plan, write, revise, and proofread.
   c. write, revise, edit, and proofread.
   d. think, translate, write, and proofread.

5. Which of the following statements accurately describes communication?
   a. Communication is objective in nature because it involves critical planning.
   b. Communication is subjective in nature because it reflects the own writer's style, tone, and personality.
   ✔ c. Communication is both objective and subjective in nature.
   d. Communication is neither objective nor subjective in nature.

PART 4

COMMUNICATING THROUGH LETTERS, MEMORANDUMS, AND E-MAIL MESSAGES

Although the emphasis in Part 4 is on writing business letters, memorandums, and e-mail messages, the principles discussed have broader application. Students will have abundant opportunities to employ these principles while still in school: in oral communication with professors and peers, in their own personal and business correspondence, in their college writing assignments, and so on.

The goal is not to teach students how to write as people in business write (most students can do that already). Rather, it is to teach them how to write clear, tactful messages that are free of distracting errors.

TEACHING SUGGESTIONS

1. *Introduce a chapter before asking students to read it.* Students are more likely to benefit from studying a chapter if a short discussion has already preceded. As discussion stimulators, choose (a) one of the exercises that appear at the end of each chapter and use it as a pretest, (b) a poor solution (with commentary or critical thinking questions) from the transparencies, or (c) a good solution of one of the chapter applications from the transparencies and project on the screen. A guided discussion can raise questions that will be answered when the assigned chapter is studied.

2. *Encourage thoughtful study of examples.* The sentence-by-sentence critique of poor examples followed by the same treatment of good examples is a special feature of the text. Instead of reading an entire document and then reading the commentary, a student will gain more by reading sentence 1 of the document, reading the commentary about sentence 1, then reading sentence 2 and the commentary about sentence 2, and so on.

   The annotated presentation shows specifically how principles are violated or applied. The before-and-after treatment (a poor exam-ple with commentary followed by a good example of the same document with commentary) has these advantages:

   a. Both the poor and the good examples provide reinforcement of principles discussed in the preceding pages.

   b. The poor examples let students see specifically why certain techniques are discouraged.

   c. The good examples let students see specifically how recommended techniques can be applied.

   d. The vivid contrast helps students to see the value of what is being learned. The ⊘ symbol is shown on poor examples so that students can easily recognize these messages as examples of what they should *not* do.

3. *Discuss standard formats and layout.* Several means of assistance are provided to reinforce understanding:

   a. Letter, memorandum, and e-mail examples are included in the text which are positioned correctly on letterhead and formatted with appropriate letter parts. The commentary directs students' attention to specific letter-formatting issues (letter formats, punctuation styles, special parts, right-margin justification, international address formats, and others).

   b. Before students study the examples of the good-news letters in Chapter 9 (or before they complete the first writing assignment), they should study Appendix A, which provides a detailed explanation and realistic illustrations of the standard formats and layout of business letters and memorandums. Transparencies for Appendix A are positioned after Chapter 18. All information related to document format and layout has been conveniently placed in this separate appendix, where it can be easily referenced.

c. For in-class writing exercises done with pen or pencil, you may wish to disregard format. Just have students write the paragraphs that would appear in the message.

4. *Emphasize outlining before writing.* Although the text emphasizes organization, the issue of organization may need even heavier emphasis in the classroom. Many students who "hate to write" or who draw a blank when attempting a writing assignment have the habit of trying to write without having done the necessary preliminary thinking—without an outline. Three suggestions for emphasizing the importance of outlining are as follows:

a. As an ungraded, in-class exercise, give students a writing exercise and insist that they proceed to write without an outline. Then give another exercise, with student help devise a brief outline, and allow time for writing. Discuss the writing experiences. Compare the time required for writing both exercises. Chances are that students will see that outlining has saved time and resulted in a more pleasant writing experience.

b. For the first homework writing assignment, help the students develop an outline in class at the time the assignment is made.

c. When writing is done in class, insist that the outline be jotted down at the top of the page on which the message is composed.

5. *Encourage rapid composition.* If students have done their thinking first (if they have made a good outline), the words should come to mind quickly. Because time is so valuable in business, students need to be put under some pressure to use time wisely. Encouraged to write rapidly with intent to rewrite any portion that may later seem to need rewriting, at least some students will become convinced that rapid writing is preferable to slow writing with long and frustrating time lapses between sentences. In grading in-class writing exercises, do not penalize students for deleting, revising, or inserting sentences.

6. *Discourage copying or paraphrasing examples.* Sample letters in the text are intended to illustrate violation or application of principles. Writing with a model letter in view (with intent to copy or paraphrase) perpetuates dependency. When letters or memorandums are composed in class, let the exercise proceed with books closed. If homework assignments are obvious copies or paraphrases, discourage the practice by reducing the score. Place a plagiarism statement in the course syllabus that explains the offense and its penalties to emphasize your intent to uphold high standards of integrity. Students need to be reminded that plagiarism includes using the ideas, organization, or words of others (including other students), whether it be from a book, article, paper, or file in any assignment without giving proper citation credit.

7. *Review the General Writing Guidelines.* Before completing any letter, memorandum, or e-mail writing assignment, refer students to this checklist at the end of Chapter 9. So that students can locate it easily, the General Writing Guidelines checklist is formatted with a large, boxed heading. The following points are included in the checklist: (a) exercise discretion in selecting information for inclusion in a message, (b) consider the legal and ethical implications of the message, and (c) be certain that the message is conveyed ethically and responsibly (clear, understandable; tactful and positive; complete and accurate; objective, factual support; unembellished or unexaggerated facts, and undistorted graphics).

8. *Encourage students to use the "Check Your Writing" checklist.* A checklist is positioned after the summary in Chapters 9–12.

9. *Project selected solutions to writing activities.* When papers are returned, conduct a short review of the assignment. With names blocked out, some examples can be used profitably for discussion. Some students will glow when they see their letters projected. For the reticent student who writes well, projecting the letter may be a morale builder that encourages the student to participate.

10. *Select appropriate assignments for grading.* For testing purposes, choose from the numerous new applications at the end of each chapter; a recommended outline or solution is provided for each application. Refer to the solution in the *Instructor's Resource Manual* to identify the difficulty of the cases. Level 2

cases, which provided all necessary information, are preferable for in-class testing. If you prefer to use "fresh" writing problems (students have not read them), select from the two writing problems provided for each chapter in the *Test Bank*. These test problems and a recommended outline follow the objective questions for Chapters 9–12.

11. *Devise an effective grading strategy.* Students will expect a preliminary explanation of the factors considered when the papers are graded. Consider the following strategies:

a. Use the "Check Your Writing" checklist that follows the summary of each chapter. The criteria students can use to check their own writing are the same criteria you use as you check their writing:

Organization: Are the ideas presented in the right sequence?

Content: Are the right ideas—and only the essential ideas—included?

Style: Are the ideas well expressed?

Mechanics: Are the ideas well presented on paper?

Format: Is the document formatted according to an accepted document format?

Some students may say, "Business people don't give their correspondence that much thought. Why should I?" Answer: "Their purpose is to get a job done; your purpose is to learn." To the serious student who has been studying and listening, the checklists are appreciated; they enable students to find and correct their mistakes. As the semester progresses, mistakes become less frequent. Possible weights for each of the listed criteria are suggested in the Introduction section of the *Instructor's Resource Manual*.

b. The grading symbols in Appendix C will help you provide feedback to students efficiently. You may write the abbreviation (highlighted to the right of the numbers) to identify the major area needing improvement. To provide additional feedback on all or on only selected errors, just write the number and letter designating the *specific* principle violated. For example, by marking "8e" above the pronoun "his" on a student's paper, you inform the student that he or she should reread the discussion of Gender-Biased Language on pages 179–182. You are encouraged to add grading symbols of your own.

c. Although students expect all papers handed in to be returned with a grade, the grade may be of less significance than the accompanying comments. To a student, an instructor's comment should mean more than "This is my reason for reducing your score." It should also mean "Next time you write, take this suggestion into account; it will help you to be more successful."

d. Some very worthwhile learning experiences can take place without immediate concern for a grade (from a student's point of view) and without paper checking (from an instructor's point of view). For example, an instructor could project a poorly written letter; conduct a discussion of its content, organization, style, and mechanics; turn off the projector; allow students to compose a letter that solves the same problem but avoids the mistakes discussed; and then compare solutions with a well-written example that is projected. Knowing that a grade is not involved, students may be able to relax and write rapidly. By seeing a good solution on the screen immediately after the exercise, students have quick and effective feedback. Students can also critique each other's writing by checking a homework assignment with the aid of a "Check Your Writing" checklist and/or a suggested solution. (Refer to the cooperative learning strategies in the Introduction.)

12. *Build time in your schedule to integrate the videotape prepared for Chapter 11, "Writing to Persuade."* Require students to read the "Video Connection" in their texts, which previews the videotape and provides several questions reviewing major points presented. After showing the videotape, initiate a class discussion using the review questions. Review questions and cases (require students to write a letter or memorandum) can be assigned as homework. Suggested answers and five multiple choice questions (to add to an objective test for this unit or to use as a pop quiz) are included in the videotape teaching suggestions immediately following Chapter 11.

WRITING ABOUT THE PLEASANT AND THE ROUTINE

CHAPTER OVERVIEW

Routine and good-news letters have been included in the same chapter because (1) the outlines for these letters are both deductive and (2) the arrangement enables instructors to assign a routine letter one day and a favorable response the next. Or, instructors may ask one section to write replies to a routine letter written by another section.

LEARNING OBJECTIVES

1 List the steps in the deductive outline and identify the advantages of using it to convey good news or routine information.

2 Write letters presenting claims and making adjustments.

3 Compose letters making and responding favorably to routine requests.

4 Compose letters requesting credit information and credit and letters providing credit information and extending credit.

5 Write letters making orders and responding favorably to order letters.

6 Prepare memorandums and e-mail messages that convey good news or routine information.

CHAPTER OUTLINE AND TEACHING SUGGESTIONS

1 **2**   **LEARNING OBJECTIVES**

I.   Business Letters
  A.   Routine Claims
    1.   Use visuals as you launch the letter-writing portion of the course:

a.   Show **TA 9–1** (Chapter Opener) to emphasize the importance of empathy in the writing process.

b.   Show **TA 9–2** (Can You Predict Each Reader's Reaction?) as you discuss the need to accurately assess the reader's likely reaction.

c.   Show **TA 9–3** (Deductive Outline: When the Reader Will be Pleased or Interested) as you discuss the sequence of the good-news or routine message.

d.   Discuss the advantages of the deductive sequence. Use the "Check Your Writing" checklist as a basis for discussion.

2.   Claim letter

a.   Discuss the difference between routine claims and persuasive claims.

b.   Make transparencies from **TM 9–2** (Poor Example, Routine Claim) and **TM 9–3** (Good Example, Routine Claim) to project as you discuss effective claim letters.

c.   Assign Application 2 from the *Study Guide* that deals with refusing a favor. Ask students to critique the poor solution using the "Check Your Writing" checklist and revise the letter in class individually or in small groups. Discuss the effective writing techniques incorporated in the revision provided in the *Study Guide*.

d.   Ask students to complete Application 2.

(1)   Show **TA 9–6** (Poor Solution, Application 2) as you lead in a discussion of the weaknesses of this solution. Ask students to

assess the effectiveness of their own or another student's letter.

(2) Show **TA 9–7** (Critical Thinking Question, Application 2) as you reinforce the importance of the planning process.

(3) Ask students to edit or rewrite their own letters for maximum effectiveness, using the "Check Your Writing" checklist. Refer students to this checklist in the textbook.

(4) Show **TA 9–8** (Good Solution, Application 2) as an example of a stronger, more effective letter.

e. Assign Application 2 from the *Study Guide*, a positive response to a claim request. Ask students to critique the poor solution using the "Check Your Writing" checklist and revise the letter in class individually or in small groups. Discuss the effective writing techniques incorporated in the revision provided in the *Study Guide*.

f. Project or make copies of **TM 9–4** (Test Problem, Poor Example, Routine Claim) and require students to revise as an assignment to be graded. Project **TM 9–5** (Test Problem, Good Example, Routine Claim) as you discuss appropriate solutions.

3. Favorable response to a claim letter

a. Focus on the three steps involved in the claim letter sequence.

b. Emphasize the value of including resale in adjustment letters.

c. Show **TM 9–6** (Poor Example, Favorable Response to a Routine Claim) as you lead a discussion of the weaknesses in

this solution or allow students to critique the letter in small groups and report to the class. Show **TM 9–7** (Good Example, Favorable Response to a Routine Claim) as you reinforce techniques for writing effective responses to claim letters.

3 ┃ **LEARNING OBJECTIVE**

B. Routine Request Letters

1. Routine requests

a. Emphasize the three steps in the routine request.

b. Refer to Figure 9–6 (good example) as you lead in a discussion of successful routine requests.

c. Assign Application 1 from the *Study Guide*, a request for graduate school information. Ask students to critique the poor solution using the "Check Your Writing" checklist and revise the letter in class individually or in small groups. Discuss the effective writing techniques incorporated in the revision provided in the *Study Guide*.

2. Favorable response to a routine request

a. Ask students to complete Exercise 6 as an in-class or homework writing assignment.

b. Show **TA 9–5** (Good Solution, Exercise 6) as you review the principles of an effective routine response.

3. Favorable response to a favor

a. Ask students in groups of two or three to complete Exercise 5.

b. Show **TA 9–4** (Good Solution, Exercise 5) as you review the principles of an effective response to a favor.

4. Form letters for routine responses

5. Communication in Action: Barbara Barrett, Jackson Zoo
   a. Lead the class in a discussion of Items 1 and 2 of "Applying What You Have Learned" that follow the case.
   b. Ask students to work in groups of two or three to draft the letter requested in Item 3. Make a transparency of **TM 9–1** (Good Solution, "Communication in Action" case) to show as a suggested solution.

| 4 | LEARNING OBJECTIVE |

C. Routine Letters About Credit
1. Emphasize the legal aspects involved in writing letters about credit.
2. Request for information
3. Response to a request for information
4. Request for credit
5. Favorable response to a request for credit

| 5 | LEARNING OBJECTIVE |

D. Routine Letters About Orders
1. Order letter
2. Favorable response to an order letter

| 6 | LEARNING OBJECTIVE |

II. Memorandums and E-mail Messages
A. Memorandums and e-mail are two primary ways that organizations use to keep their employees informed.
1. Studies show that well-informed employees perform better, suffer less stress, and have lower absenteeism that their less-informed counterparts.
2. Disney executive, Rick Neely, reported in an interview in 1994, that in order to keep all employees abreast of company policy and development, Disney executives created employee information booths containing video and telephone hotlines. In addition, LCD displays highlight events in each employee's work area. This service helps Disney employees feel more connected to the company, which is no small accomplishment for such a large corporation.
3. Ask students to locate articles that relate other examples of how organizations are keeping their employees informed.
B. Refer students to Appendix A for information about the format and arrangement of memorandums. The Additional Readings list may be helpful.
C. Emphasize that principles of organizing that apply to letters also apply to memorandums. Empathy is the key to proper organization.
D. Jargon is acceptable when communicating within the organization, as long as everyone understands the terminology. Present analogies that emphasize the value and cautions of using jargon:
1. People who sail for recreation have a language of their own. They communicate using terms like *starboard*, *port*, and *jib*. People who are unfamiliar with these terms cannot communicate without first learning the jargon.
2. Internet users also have a distinctive language. They communicate using terms such as *surf*, *flame*, *GIF*, *gopher*, etc.
3. Ask students to work in groups of three or four to think of other activities, organizations, professional fields, or situations where jargon is used. Ask them to generate a list of jargon words typical to each example.
E. Good-news Memorandums
F. Routine Memorandums
1. Memorandums outlining procedures or giving instructions

a. Review the guidelines in the text concerning the writing of instructions.

b. Make transparencies of **TM 9–8** (Poor Example, Routine Memorandum) and **TM 9–9** (Good Example, Routine Memorandum) to show as you discuss this section and assign as an appropriate cooperative learning activity.

2. Memorandums about personnel changes

3. Memorandum written "to the file"

III. Summary

A. Integrate the communication mentor comments into class lectures to reinforce the concepts in the chapter.

B. Assign the *Study Guide* questions for Chapter 9. This chapter includes 15 true/false and 15 multiple choice questions.

C. Ask students to complete the *Study Guide* applications for Chapter 9. The applications "walk students through" writing (a) a letter requesting graduate school information (routine request) and (b) a "yes" reply to a claim request. Critical thinking questions help students organize and write an appropriate outline. Students compare their solutions with a sample solution and a detailed commentary that highlights the strengths of the outline and the solution. In a third application, students analyze a poorly written letter and identify errors and weaknesses. Critical thinking questions guide students through the analysis.

D. Ask students to complete the e-mail application for Chapter 9.

E. Assign selected questions, exercises, and applications at the end of the chapter. Remind students to study the suggestions in the "Check Your Writing" checklist when planning and revising an assignment.

F. Assign selected cases for analysis at the end of the chapter. **TM 9–21** (Good Solution, Case for Analysis 1, Step 2b), **TM 9–22** (Good Solution, Case for Analysis 1, Step 3), **TM 9–23** (Good Solution, Case for Analysis 2, Step 3) are provided as solutions.

G. Assign one of the applications designated as an AWA (Analytical Writing Assessment) for the GMAT. Refer to pages 12–13 of this *Instructor's Resource Manual* for holistic scoring techniques used by evaluators of this written portion of the GMAT.

TRANSPARENCIES AND MASTERS

TA 9–1	Chapter Opener
TA 9–2	Can You Predict Each Reader's Reaction
TA 9–3	Deductive Outline: When the Reader Will Be Pleased or Interested
TA 9–4	Good Solution, Exercise 5
TA 9–5	Good Solution, Exercise 6
TA 9–6	Poor Solution, Application 2
TA 9–7	Critical Thinking Questions, Application 2
TA 9–8	Good Solution, Application 2
TM 9–1	Good Solution, "Communication in Action" Case
TM 9–2	Poor Example, Routine Claim
TM 9–3	Good Example, Routine Claim
TM 9–4	Test Problem, Poor Example, Routine Claim
TM 9–5	Test Problem, Good Example, Routine Claim
TM 9–6	Poor Example, Favorable Response to a Routine Claim
TM 9–7	Good Example, Favorable Response to a Routine Claim
TM 9–8	Poor Example, Routine Memorandum
TM 9–9	Good Example, Routine Memorandum
TM 9–10	Good Solution, Application 1
TM 9–11	Good Solution, Application 3
TM 9–12	Good Solution, Application 4
TM 9–13	Good Solution, Application 6
TM 9–14	Good Solution, Application 10
TM 9–15	Good Solution, Application 12
TM 9–16	Good Solution, Application 14
TM 9–17	Good Solution, Application 15
TM 9–18	Good Solution, Application 16
TM 9–19	Good Solution, Application 18
TM 9–20	Good Solution, Application 19
TM 9–21	Good Solution, Case for Analysis 1, Step 2b
TM 9–22	Good Solution, Case for Analysis 1, Step 3
TM 9–23	Good Solution, Case for Analysis 2, Step 3

ADDITIONAL READINGS

Basile, F. (1989). Tips for better business letters. *Journal of Property Management, 54*(11), 28–29.

Fahner, H. (1990). The ten commandments of memo writing. *Sales & Marketing Management, 142*(10), 85–87.

Goddard, R. W. (1989). Use language effectively. *Personnel Journal, 68*(4) 32–36.

Gold, R. (1989). "Reader-friendly" writing. *Supervisory Management, 34*(1), 39–43.

Poor, E. (1992). The memo as project manager. *Executive Female, 15*(3), 63–65.

Scott, J. C. (1993). Preparing correspondence the British way. *Bulletin of the Association for Business Communication, 56*(2), 10–17.

Yellen, J., & Mandel, B. J. (1990). Business writing without blood, sweat and tears. *Working Woman, 15*(6), 64, 66–67, 100–101.

ANSWERS TO "COMMUNICATION IN ACTION" CASE: Barbara Barrett, Jackson Zoo.

1. **Discuss how Barrett's letters prepare legislators and other visitors for a fun visit to the zoo.** The personal nature of her letters cultivates goodwill about the zoo. Appropriate humor stimulates positive feelings in the reader, and free family passes add to the goodwill. A simple thank you, related specifically to the reader, helps prepare positive feelings about the zoo.

2. **What questions did Barrett mentally answer before writing her letter to legislators?** Barrett asked herself what the legislator or contributor wanted out of his or her support of the zoo. In doing so, she adapted her letter to her reader and kept a fresh approach to routine correspondence.

3. **Assume that you work as the assistant director for the Jackson Zoo and will correspond with the Honorable Mary L. Jackson, Mississippi State Senate, Capitol Building, P.O. Box 1018, Jackson, MS 39215–1018. Senator Jackson visited the zoo last weekend with her family, having used free family passes you sent her in previous correspondence. Compose a routine letter of support to Senator Jackson, acknowledging her visit to the zoo with her family. Use**
brevity and conciseness, realizing you will have only a few moments to communicate your message. See **TM 9–1** (Good Solution, "Communication in Action" Case) for suggested letter.

ANSWERS TO REVIEW QUESTIONS

1. The steps in the deductive outline are (a) state the main idea, (b) provide details or explanation, and (c) remind receiver of the good news or main idea and/or include a future-oriented closing thought. This sequence is also appropriate for oral messages that convey good or neutral news. The same outlines recommended for *written* messages are recommended for *oral* messages, as they are based on anticipated reaction. Regardless of whether a message is oral or written, good news is pleasant and bad news is unpleasant.

2. A claim letter is a request for an adjustment. Persuasive claims assume that a request will be granted only after explanations and persuasive arguments have been presented. Routine claims assume that a request will be granted quickly and willingly, without persuasion.

3. When the claim is routine, follow these steps: (a) request action in the first sentence, (b) explain the details supporting the request for action, and (c) close with an expression of appreciation for taking the action requested.

4. An adjustment is a response to a claim letter.

5. *Resale* is a favorable remark about a product or service already purchased by the person being addressed. *Sales promotional material* is a low-pressure message about products or services not yet purchased. Students' responses will vary. As an example, a letter reiterating the quality of wallpaper previously purchased would be using the technique of resale. If the letter also mentions complementary paint products, it would be including sales promotional material.

6. The favorable response to a claim letter follows this sequence: (a) reveals the good news in the first sentence, (b) explains the circumstances, (c) closes on a pleasant, forward-looking note.

7. While the word *grant* is acceptable when talking about claims, it is not encouraged in writing such letters as it implies that the writer is in a position of power. Words such

as *respond to*, *honor*, and *comply with* convey a more appropriate attitude.

8. Major weaknesses in Figure 9–4 include: (a) the first sentence contains an empty acknowledgment, rather than the main idea; (b) the explanation section lacks positive emphasis and conveys no specific assurance that the documentation has been sent; and (c) the last sentence casts doubt about value and credibility.

9. Steps in a routine request are as follows: (a) make the major request in the first sentence; (b) follow the major request with details that will make the request clear, using tabulations when possible; and (c) close with a forward look to the receiver's next step.

10. The use of form letters enables businesses to communicate quickly and efficiently with clients and customers. Inputting the customer's name and address and other variables personalizes each letter to meet the needs of its receiver. Inserting appropriate stored paragraphs helps to tailor the letter to the specific needs of the situation. Another type of form letter does not require the keying of individualized information but allows the sender to check options that apply to the specific reader's situation.

11. In reply to a request for credit information, just fill in the blanks and return the letter. If the request does not include a form, follow a deductive plan in writing—the major idea followed by supporting details.

12. In writing credit information letters, the writer should comply with requirements of the Equal Credit Opportunity Act (ECOA). This law requires that the applicant be notified of the credit decision within 30 days of the receipt of the request. In structuring credit information letters, stick to the facts, making sure that all statements can be documented. Omit statements and opinions that could lead to a defamation charge.

13. The simplified block letter style eliminates the need for an impersonal salutation, a plus when the specific recipient of the letter is not known.

14. The recommended outline for favorable replies to requests for credit is as follows: (a) begin by stating that credit terms have been arranged or that the credit shipment has been made; (b) indicate the foundation on which the credit extension is based; (c) pres-

ent and explain the credit terms; (d) include some resale or sales promotional material; and (e) end with a confident look toward future business.

15. The writer should discuss the basis for the decision to extend credit to prevent collection problems that may arise later. Indicating, for instance that credit is being granted on the basis of an applicant's prompt-paying habits with present creditors encourages continuation of those habits. In recognizing a reputation, the applicant is challenged to uphold it. Unless customers know their exact credit terms, they may not make payments on time or may take inappropriate discounts.

16. Order letters are still necessary if the vendor does not provide an order blank, when the customer has not established credit with the vendor, or when the order is too complex to be communicated by telephone. The order letter should include the following: (a) specifically state the order in the first sentence, (b) detail carefully the items ordered, (c) include a payment plan and shipping instructions, and (d) close with a confident expectation of delivery.

17. Sending individualized acknowledgment letters is not cost effective and will not reach the customer in a timely manner. Most orders can be acknowledged by shipping the order; no letter is necessary. Typically, acknowledgment letters are preprinted letters or a copy of the sales order. However, for initial orders and for orders that cannot be filled quickly and precisely, companies send acknowledgment letters. In these cases, customers appreciate the company's response and information as to when the order should arrive.

18. Memorandums and e-mail typically go to people within a business. Principles of writing that apply to business letters also apply to e-mail messages. Outlines for both letters and memorandums and e-mail are based on anticipated reader reaction. In both cases, reader reaction is predictable. Like tact with customers (to whom letters are written), tact with workers within a firm is affected by the proper sequence of ideas. An exception made when writing to those inside the organization is the use of jargon, acronyms, abbreviations, and shortened forms, which is more likely to be useful when communicating with people who do similar work.

19. Sending a single message to multiple receivers simultaneously is a distinct advantage of e-mail. The writer simply inputs one or more addresses or creates a distribution list for a group of people. See "Electronic Mail" and "Overcoming Barriers to Electronic Communication" sections of Chapter 5 for e-mail style guidelines.

20. Yes. Because of similarity in job and background, workers within an organization are likely to understand acronyms and shortened forms used in their workplace. Because customers and clients may not understand technical acronyms and shortened forms used in a business, such terminology should be limited in letters/memorandums to those known by the general population.

21. The subject line tells the receiver what the message is about and sets the stage for understanding the message. The following suggestions apply when writing subject lines: (a) make the subject line as long as necessary; (b) think of the five Ws to provide clues for good subject lines: *Who, What, When, Where,* and *Why*; (c) repeat the subject in the body of the memorandum; and (d) keyboard the subject line in all-capital letters if additional emphasis is desired.

22. When writing instructions: (a) begin each step with an action statement; (b) itemize each step on a separate line to add emphasis and to simplify reading; (c) consider preparing a flowchart depicting the procedures if necessary; (d) complete the procedure by following the instructions step by step, revising as necessary; (e) ask a colleague or employee to walk through the procedures to locate ambiguous statements, omissions, or errors.

23. Enumerations add emphasis and simplify reading. Numbers should be used for each step when steps should be completed in a particular order. Bullets may be used when the sequence is not important.

24. A "to the file" memorandum is used when information needs to be converted into written form and filed for future reference. Writing the memorandum will assist the writer in remembering and using the information. Such memorandums are useful for recording summaries of disciplinary actions taken with employees. They provide documentation in the event of litigation and in responding to specific weaknesses in performance.

25. Lengthy memorandums may be divided into logical sections. Using such divisions will alert the reader to the information that is ahead and make the material easier to comprehend.

POSSIBLE SOLUTIONS TO EXERCISES

1. Focus on exercises that challenge students to apply the principles studied.

2. After removing identifying information, make transparencies of selected letters and memorandums brought in by students. Divide the class into groups of four or five to discuss the letters and to develop a checklist for effective letter writing. Initiate a class discussion, calling on each group (or a spokesperson) to share its analysis with the class.

3. a. Expresses a reluctant, non-enthusiastic attitude. Uses passive voice to present idea; therefore, sentence lacks a reader-centered focus. Finally, it implies that the office, a non-person, deliberated.

   b. Uses passive, rather than active voice, de-emphasizing the person responsible for the outstanding work.

   c. Lacks a reader-centered focus.

   d. Uses passive voice to convey idea; uses gender-biased language ("girls").

   e. Uses a cliché ("Enclosed please find").

4. a. States the obvious; revise to state that credit has been extended or that the order is on its way.

   b. Uses unnecessary statement that conveys an egotistical tone ("prides itself"); continues this tone by using first person ("we have decided") in the clause that extends the adjustment. Revise to eliminate first clause and to extend adjustment using second person.

   c. Uses an expression of certainty; unnecessarily belittles reader for requesting something other than the latest software.

   d. Uses "grant," a word that implies the writer is in a position of power; uses a lecturing tone ("we caution") that likely is demeaning to the reader and also indicates the decision was not made enthusiastically.

   e. Includes obvious statements ("I am writing this informal memo"); the department heads to whom this memorandum is addressed surely know Peter Johnson is the controller); uses passive voice that makes the message less vivid and longer.

5. See **TA 9–4** (Good Solution, Exercise 5) which illustrates the following outline:

   I. Accept the invitation; restate the date and time to ensure accuracy.

   II. Provide the title of your speech and any other details about the speech (equipment needed, etc.)

   III. Verify the exact time the speech will begin, emphasizing that you cannot arrive before 6:30 p.m.

   IV. Allude to the next step in the chain of events—speaking to the group as requested.

6. See **TA 9–5** (Good Solution, Exercise 6) for a suggested solution. A summary of organization, content, and format errors follows:

Summary of Organization, Content, Style, and Format Errors	
Organization	◆ Uses an inductive approach rather than deductive outline required for letters that convey good news.
Content	◆ Does not begin with the good-news—expenses are deductible.
	◆ Describes situations when expenses are *not* deductible, possibly misleading the reader to believe the news is bad.
	◆ Doesn't reveal the good news until the last sentence.
Style	◆ Begins by stating the obvious ("This letter is in reply" and "We have researched").
	◆ Ends with a weak cliché.
Format	◆ Omits the courtesy title before the reader's name in the letter address.
	◆ Omits colon after the salutation (mixed punctuation).
	◆ Appears as a correctly formatted block letter.

POSSIBLE SOLUTION TO E-MAIL APPLICATION

Students may need some additional instructions as to how to create distribution lists on your computer system. In order to assure that each student both sends and receives messages, specify the names to whom each student is to send his/her message. Require students to print a copy of the messages received and submit them. The content of this message is a secondary concern; the grade should, therefore, be based on the successful creation and use of an address macro.

POSSIBLE SOLUTIONS AND RECOMMENDED OUTLINES TO APPLICATIONS

ACCOUNTING

1. **Requesting Adjustment for Billing Error**

⇨ *Level 2* ⇦

See **TM 9–10** (Good Solution, Application 1) for suggested letter.

MANAGEMENT

2. **Customized Drinking Cups Are Wrong Size**

⇨ *Level 2* ⇦

See **TA 9–6** (Poor Solution, Application 2), **TA 9–7** (Critical Thinking Questions, Application 2), and **TA 9–8** (Good Solution, Application 2) in analyzing this case.

Use the transparencies to (a) analyze the poor solution and (b) answer the critical thinking questions designed to help students organize their thoughts. After this thorough analysis of the case problem, have students write an appropriate outline and solution.

Refer to suggested solution in transparencies. Because of the urgency of this message, students may choose to fax this letter; therefore, the solution should include the mailing notation, "FACSIMILE." Refer to Special Letters Parts, Mailing Notation in Appendix A for proper placement.

MARKETING

3. Correct-size Cups Are on the Way

⇨ *Level 2* ⇦

See **TM 9–11** (Good Solution, Application 3) for suggested letter.

MANAGEMENT

4. Order Does Not Meet Minimum Standards: Routine Claim

⇨ *Level 2* ⇦

See **TM 9–12** (Good Solution, Application 4) for suggested letter.

MANAGEMENT

5. Acknowledging an Error in an Order

⇨ *Level 2* ⇦

The letter should

1. State that a new shipment of bolts will be shipped with a probable delivery date of (specify date).

2. Explain the cause of the problem (bolts of a lesser quality were inadvertently shipped). Assure reader that you are taking steps to see that this error does not recur.

3. Conclude with positive comment that expects future business.

ACCOUNTING

6. Routine Request for Accommodations During an Annual Audit

⇨ *Level 2* ⇦

See **TM 9–13** (Good Solution, Application 6) for suggested letter.

CONSUMER

7. Request for Product Information

⇨ *Level 3* ⇦

The letter should

1. State the request for information about a specific product.

2. Present specific information needs. Include a bulleted or numbered list or provide blanks to be completed and returned quickly.

3. Remind reader to send the information; allude to ways the reader can benefit from responding.

FINANCE/Legal

8. Credit Approval for Construction Engineer

⇨ *Level 2* ⇦

The letter should

1. State that a credit line of $100,000 has been extended.

2. Explain why credit was extended; specify reasons.

3. Present and explain the credit terms; refer to the credit-terms pamphlet for details.

4. Allude confidently to future business by assuring her that credit rates will be raised as her business grows (sales promotion).

FINANCE/Legal

9. Credit Information Needed to Approve Line of Credit

⇨ *Level 2* ⇦

The letter should

1. Include a subject line: CREDIT INFORMATION FOR BURNS CONSTRUCTION

2. Ask for credit information for Burns Construction. Assure reader that Burns Construction listed Mobile Brickyard as a credit reference.

3. Emphasize that the information will be kept confidential.

4. Itemize the specific information needed. Use bulleted or numbered list or provide blanks to be completed and returned quickly.

5. Close courteously by stating your willingness to reciprocate.

MANAGEMENT

10. Order for Staff/Alumni Reception

⇨ *Level 2* ⇦

See **TM 9–14** (Good Solution, Application 10) for suggested letter.

COMMUNITY SERVICE

11. Accepting an Invitation to Perform a Civic Duty

⇨ *Level 3* ⇦

The letter should

1. Express your willingness to speak for the occasion.
2. Give any details related to your topic, equipment needs, etc.
3. End with an enthusiastic, forward-looking close.

FINANCE

12. Time to Diversify Stock Portfolio

⇨ *Level 2* ⇦

See **TM 9–15** (Good Solution, Application 12) for suggested letter.

MARKETING/International

13. Successful Sales Campaign: Letter to Parent Company

⇨ *Level 2* ⇦

The letter should

1. State the good news—sales campaign in Finnish market has gone well—citing the increased sales (compare to predictions).
2. Provide specific details about the success of the sales campaign (including those listed in the case or others that you provide). Avoid overly strong adjectives or superlatives, which would make your message sound exaggerated or embellished.
3. Close with positive comments that look to future successes in the Finnish market.

REAL ESTATE/Technology

14. Video Presentations Expedite Real Estate Showings

⇨ *Level 2* ⇦

See **TM 9–16** (Good Solution, Application 14) for suggested letter.

HUMAN RESOURCES MANAGEMENT

15. Request for Intern Approved

⇨ *Level 2* ⇦

See **TM 9–17** (Good Solution, Application 15) for suggested memorandum.

HUMAN RESOURCES MANAGEMENT

16. Controlling Health Care Costs

⇨ *Level 2* ⇦

See **TM 9–18** (Good Solution, Application 16) for suggested memorandum.

HUMAN RESOURCES MANAGEMENT

17. Reaping Benefits of Total Quality Management Program

⇨ *Level 2* ⇦

The memorandum should

1. Announce the extra day of vacation coming as a result of TQM progress.
2. State as bulleted items the benefits the company is enjoying as a result of the TQM program.
3. Tell employees how and when to take advantage of their extra vacation day.
4. Express appreciation to employees for their part in the success.

MANAGEMENT/Technology

18. Memo Announcing Major Change in Operations

⇨ *Level 3* ⇦

See **TM 9–19** (Good Solution, Application 18) for suggested memorandum.

HUMAN RESOURCES MANAGEMENT

19. New Insurance Carrier Announced

⇨ *Level 3* ⇦

See **TM 9–20** (Good Solution, Application 19) for suggested memorandum.

HUMAN RESOURCES MANAGEMENT

20. Memo Announcing Earthquake Preparedness Plan

⇨ *Level 3* ⇦

The memorandum should

1. State that because tremors have become a problem, a systematic plan for responding to an earthquake is needed; lead into the plan that follows.

2. Itemize the exact procedures to be followed, using a bulleted or numbered list to provide needed emphasis. (Research the literature to identify other procedures to be included in your earthquake preparedness plan.) Use first-person, active-voice sentences to help the readers visualize themselves implementing these procedures.

3. End with a positive comment about the benefits gained from a company-wide earthquake preparedness plan. Suggest that employees post the memorandum on their desk where it can be easily seen and followed in the event of an earthquake.

POSSIBLE SOLUTIONS AND RECOMMENDED OUTLINES TO CASES FOR ANALYSIS

FINANCE/Ethics   GMAT

1. Analyzing an Ethical Situation: A Sound Decision or a Clever Way Out?

⇨ *Level 4* ⇦

1. Analysis of the problem:

   a. *Relevant facts.* Your supervisor is insistent that you must secure *The Princess* for this important boating expedition, and the captain's offer is in direct opposition to the owner's policy.

   b. *Ethical issues.* Using boat without authorization of the owner.
   Legal restrictions. None apply.
   Contractual. None apply.
   Code of ethics. No company or professional code of ethics exists.

   c. *Stakeholders.* Harrelson, Inc., owner, captain, and prospective clients.

   d. *Cost/benefit analysis.* See Figure 9–1. Alternative: to accept the captain's offer.

   e. *Obligations to stakeholders.* See Figure 9–2.

   f. Answers should be graded based on the students' analysis of the facts and the objective support of their decisions. Therefore, no conclusion is provided with the analysis.

2. Students' decisions will vary; see possible solutions to the various options.

   a. Some students may be tempted to select this option because they perceive a routine request to be "easier" to write than the persuasive letter to the owner. However, this letter should serve as a formal agreement between the captain and company, confirming dates, fee, services provided (food/beverages); requiring a receipt; and addressing the insurance coverage.

   b. See **TM 9–21** (Good Solution, Case for Analysis 1, Step 2b) for suggested letter.

   c. Encourage students to think creatively about other ethical solutions to this dilemma.

3. See **TM 9–22** (Good Solution, Case for Analysis 1, Step 3) for suggested letter. This solution assumes the student judged the captain's offer to be unethical (Step 2b).

Stakeholder	Cost	Benefit
Harrelson, Inc.	◆ Captain might cancel trip leaving no time to secure another vessel. ◆ Questionable liability coverage in the event of an accident. ◆ Legality of deducting the charter fee as a business expense if captain doesn't provide proper receipt. ◆ Possible damage to company's reputation if public learns of this action.	◆ Improves chances of securing investment accounts with "select" group of clients. ◆ Able to charter vessel at 50 percent lower rate.
Owner	◆ Receives no payment if the captain pockets the money or does not get full price for use of boat.	◆ Could receive revenue typically not earned during a layover.
Captain	◆ Could be fired if owner learns of his offer.	◆ Earns additional money for the charter.
Prospective clients	◆ None	◆ None

Figure 9–1 ◆ 1. Cost/benefit analysis of accepting the captain's offer

Stakeholder	Obligation
Harrelson, Inc.	◆ To secure the investment account while maintaining the company's integrity and protecting its financial resources.
Owner	◆ To provide a fair return for the use of the vessel.
Captain	◆ None.
Prospective clients	◆ To ensure their safety during the expedition.

Figure 9–2 ◆ 1. Obligations to stakeholders

MANAGEMENT/Interpersonal

2. **Communicating Concern for Employees**

⇨ *Level 4* ⇦

Because this case requires students to create a company scenario based on their own interests and experience, students' solutions will vary widely. If you believe your students will require additional direction, you might share with them the following sample scenario and/or the sample memorandum showing how to develop a workable solution from the research and how to handle the documentation. Be sure to instruct students which documentation method you prefer.

1. *Possible Company Scenario:*

Montgomery Metro is a wholesaler for Montgomery, Inc., a regional household appliance manufacturer. Montgomery Metro sells to 60 appliance dealers; each of its five sales representatives work with 12 dealerships.

For the past three quarters, total sales to dealers have fallen below management quotas. The first quarter goals were missed by 5 percent; the second, by 3 percent. Management raised quotas for the third quarter by 3 percent to offset the losses, resulting in sales 10 percent below projections. Until this year, this same sales team had consistently exceeded goals by 2 to 6 percent.

As a result of the lower first quarter sales, the sales manager reorganized work procedures: (a) sales representatives must submit sales reports and projections once a week rather than once a month, and (b) mailouts and advertising campaigns were developed to supplement personal selling.

The downturn in sales, management's decision to increase quotas, and the change in work procedures (without eliciting feedback from the sales reps) have put morale at an all-time low. In fact, two of the most experienced sales reps are considering resignation.

2–3. See **TM 9–23** (Good Solution, Case for Analysis 2, Step 3) for suggested memorandum.

4. Student solutions will vary. This memorandum should differ from the one in Step 3 in terms of showing reader benefit. In this case,

benefit to the individual employee, rather than the company, should be emphasized.

MANAGEMENT/Ethics   GMAT

3. **Is Providing Faulty Swing Sets Unethical?**

⇨ *Level 4* ⇦

1. Analysis of the problem:

   a. *Relevant facts.* Company shipped out products of lesser quality than current products.

   b. *Ethical issues.* (1) Based on your knowledge that quality increases the price, what level of quality is necessary? In other words, what price should consumers pay for absolute security? To what level of responsibility should a company be held for the safety of its products? (2) The manager is faced with the ethical issue of taking what he considers to be a proper action that likely will have negative consequences on his/her career.

   Legal restrictions. Students may assume that the original product met government standards.

   Contractual. None apply. (Company does not have a contract with retailers who sell the product to customers.)

   Company policy. Students may assume that the original model complied with company quality standards.

   Code of ethics. No company or professional code of ethics exists.

   c. *Stakeholders.* Company, stockholders, children/parents, and inspector.

   d. *Cost/benefit analysis.* See Figure 9–3. Alternative: do not recall swing sets.

   e. *Obligations to stakeholders.* See Figure 9–4.

   f. Answers should be graded based on students' analysis of the facts and the objective support of their decisions. Therefore, no conclusion is provided with the analysis.

2. Solutions will vary but should be based on the analysis in Step 1.

Stakeholder	Cost	Benefit
Company	◆ May be subject to potential liability resulting from product failure. ◆ Negatively affects its relationship with this inspector, who may resign or lower his or her standards for quality in response to the tone set by the company.	◆ Maintains its current profitability and avoids negative publicity involved in a product recall.
Stockholders	◆ Are unknowingly involved in the distribution of a product that could cause personal injury.	◆ Maintain current profitability.
Children/parents	◆ May face potential injury and financial loss as a result of a product failure.	◆ Avoid inconvenience caused by product recall.
Inspector	◆ Is knowingly involved in the production of a product that he or she believes could cause personal injury. ◆ May feel disillusioned by management's disregard for his or her judgment, possibly causing lowered morale and quality standards.	◆ Is perceived as a "team player" and will be rewarded for his or her action.

Figure 9–3 ◆ 2. Cost/benefit analysis of not recalling swing sets

Stakeholder	Obligation
Company	◆ Keeps promise to maximize long-term earnings.
Stockholders	◆ Keeps promise to maximize return on investment.
Children/parents	◆ Keeps promise to provide a quality product at an affordable price.
Inspector	◆ Does not show respect for the judgment of an employee placed in a position of responsibility (final inspection of products).

Figure 9–4 ◆ 3. Obligations to stakeholders

CHAPTER 10

WRITING ABOUT THE UNPLEASANT

CHAPTER OVERVIEW

Because Chapter 10 (bad-news messages) presents more delicate human relations problems than were encountered in Chapter 9, plan to devote more discussion time to Chapter 10. Refer also to the teaching suggestions that apply to all letters/memorandums/e-mail messages in Part 4 and to the teaching suggestions for Chapter 9.

LEARNING OBJECTIVES

1 List the steps in the inductive outline and identify the advantages of using it to convey bad news.

2 Write letters denying adjustments.

3 Write letters refusing to complete an order.

4 Write letters refusing a favor.

5 Compose letters denying credit.

6 Prepare memorandums and e-mail messages that convey bad news.

7 List ways to handle special problems about the unpleasant.

CHAPTER OUTLINE AND TEACHING SUGGESTIONS

1   **LEARNING OBJECTIVE**

I. Communicating the Bad News
    A. Show **TA 10–1** (Chapter Opener) as you begin this discussion.
    B. Discuss the sequence of ideas in the inductive process.

1. Show **TA 10–2** (Inductive Outline: When the Reader Will Be Displeased) to illustrate the steps in the inductive pattern.

2. Discuss the advantages of the inductive sequence. Use the "Check Your Writing" checklist as a basis for discussion.

3. Lead the class in a discussion of occasions when the deductive approach for a negative message may better serve the writer's purpose.
    a. The text relates that certain circumstances justify deductive writing of bad news. Yet, those circumstances are rare; students do not generally need that type of practice.
    b. Preferably, writing assignments should require inductive treatment.

4. Integrate the communication mentor comments in class lectures to reinforce the concepts in the chapter.

C. Style
1. Show **TA 10–3** (Techniques for De-emphasizing Unpleasant Ideas) as you discuss ways to minimize the impact of bad news.

2. Refer to Shirley F. Olson's communication mentor comment about choosing words carefully.

D. Ask students to complete Application 9, working in groups of two or three as a cooperative learning activity.
1. Show **TA 10–5** (Poor Solution, Application 9) as you discuss its limitations.

2. Show **TA 10–6** (Critical Thinking Questions, Application 9) as you lead the class in a discussion of the advantages of the inductive pattern.

3. Ask students to rewrite the letter for homework. Show **TA 10-7** (Good Solution, Application 9) as each student critiques another's letter.

4. Present the following scenario as an in-class group assignment:

   a. A second employee of your firm has been arrested on drug-related charges. The company president has directed you to initiate random drug testing immediately. When communicating this message to employees, how can you counteract employees' resistance to testing and assure them that their privacy will not be invaded while minimizing any ill feelings toward management?

   b. Ask students to write the body of the memo. Discuss their solutions.

5. In letters and memorandums that convey bad news, three sentences are critical: the beginning sentence, the statement of bad news, and the final sentence.

   a. In-class and out-of-class writing assignments should include the writing of **entire** messages, but sometimes classes can beneficially concentrate on certain *portions* of messages. For example, after a writing problem is defined, students in certain parts of the classroom could write the first sentence; others, the refusal sentence; and others, the final sentence. Sentences could be collected and some selected for reading aloud or displayed on screen.

   b. As a writing assignment, students could be asked to write certain sentences instead of entire letters. For example, one assignment could be "For (*specify numbers*) of the writing applications at the end of Chapter 10, write only the first sentence that you would use in each letter." Or, "For applications (*specify numbers*) at the end of Chapter 10, write the paragraph in which the bad news is stated."

2	LEARNING OBJECTIVE

II. Saying "No" to an Adjustment Request

   A. Discuss the general sequence of ideas in an adjustment letter that says "no."

   1. Show **TM 10-1** (Poor Example, Claim Refusal) as you discuss its limitations or have students critique as a cooperative learning activity.

   2. Show **TM 10-2** (Good Example, Claim Refusal) as you discuss the preferred sequence of ideas.

   B. Ask students to complete Application 1 in class or for homework. Make a transparency of **TM 10-7** (Good Solution, Application 1) to show as you discuss appropriate treatment of the adjustment situation.

   C. Assign Application 2 from the *Study Guide*, a claim refusal. Discuss the communication pointers in small groups with a spokesperson reporting to the class if time permits. Discuss the effective writing techniques incorporated in the revision.

   D. Display **TM 10-3** (Poor Example, Test Problem, Claim Refusal); have students revise as an in-class writing assignment individually or in groups. Display **TM 10-4** (Good Example, Test Problem, Claim Refusal) as you discuss the results of the test assignment.

3	LEARNING OBJECTIVE

III. Saying "No" to an Order for Merchandise

   A. Lead students in a discussion of possible reasons for not being able to send merchandise that has been ordered.

   B. Emphasize the elements to be included in a "no" response to an order.

| 4 | LEARNING OBJECTIVE |

IV. Saying "No" to a Request for a Favor

   A. Emphasize the importance of a counterproposal.

      1. Offering an alternative instead of a flat "no" keeps communication open and avoids damage to egos.

      2. Discuss possible analogies to help students understand the effect of the counterproposal: The counterproposal is to the "no" response as a highway detour is to the desired route. Although the detour may require more time and be less desirable than the desired route, the driver will reach his or her destination.

   B. Assign Application 1 from the *Study Guide*, a letter refusing a favor. Ask students to critique the poor solution using the "Check Your Writing" checklist and revise the letter in class individually or in small groups. Discuss the effective writing techniques incorporated in the revision provided in the *Study Guide*.

   C. Ask students to complete Exercise 6 for homework. Show **TA 10–4** (Good Solution, Exercise 6) as you discuss the appropriate "no" response for a favor.

| 5 | LEARNING OBJECTIVE |

V. Saying "No" to a Credit Request

   A. Emphasize the legal implications involved in refusing credit and the importance of having legal counsel review credit refusal letters.

   B. Review the requirements of the Equal Credit Opportunity Act.

   C. Discuss the value of resale in a credit refusal letter.

   D. Assign Communication in Action: Shirley F. Olson, F. F. Ferguson, Sand and Gravel/Prestress/Precast.

      1. Ask students to complete the communication in action applications.

      2. Show **TM 10–5** (Good Solution, "Communication in Action" case) as you review an acceptable pattern of response.

| 6 | LEARNING OBJECTIVE |

VI. Writing Bad-news Memorandums and E-mail Messages

   A. Lead students in a discussion of occasions when memorandums and e-mail messages are appropriate and inappropriate means of communicating bad news.

   B. Compare employee morale to customer goodwill in terms of their importance and their fragile nature.

   C. Assign Application 17, 18, or 19. Solutions to these memorandums are provided on **TM 10–19** (Good Solution, Application 17), **TM 10–20** (Good Solution, Application 18), and **TM 10–21** (Good Solution, Application 19).

| 7 | LEARNING OBJECTIVE |

VII. Handling Special Problems About the Unpleasant

   A. First Paragraph

   B. Bad-news Sentence

   C. Last Paragraph

   D. Show **TM 10–1** (Check Your Writing: Unpleasant Messages) as you review the inductive process. Refer students to the copy of the checklist at the end of Chapter 10.

VIII.   Summary

   A. Integrate the communication mentor comments into class lectures to reinforce the concepts in the chapter.

   B. Assign the *Study Guide* questions for Chapter 10. This chapter includes 15 true/false and 15 multiple choice questions.

   C. Require students to complete the applications in the *Study Guide*. The applications "walk students through" writing (a) a letter saying no to a request for students to tour your plant and (b) a letter refusing a claim request. Critical thinking questions help students organize and write an appropriate outline. Students compare their solutions with a sample solution and a detailed commentary that highlights the strengths of the outline and the solution. In a third application, students analyze a poorly written letter and identify errors and weaknesses. Critical thinking questions guide students through the analysis.

D. Ask students to complete the e-mail application at the end of the chapter.

E. Assign selected exercises and applications at the end of the chapter. Remind students to study the suggestions in the "Check Your Writing" checklist when planning and revising an assignment.

F. Assign selected cases for analysis at the end of the chapter. **TM 10–23** (Good Solution, Case for Analysis 1, Step 2) and **TM 10–24** (Case for Analysis 3, Step 3) are provided as solutions.

G. Assign one of the applications designated as an AWA (Analytical Writing Assessment) for the GMAT. Refer to pages 12–13 of this *Instructor's Resource Manual* for holistic scoring techniques used by evaluators of this written portion of the GMAT.

TRANSPARENCIES AND MASTERS

TA 10–1   Chapter Opener
TA 10–2   Inductive Outline: When the Reader Will Be Displeased
TA 10–3   Techniques for De-emphasizing Unpleasant Ideas
TA 10–4   Good Solution, Exercise 6
TA 10–5   Poor Solution, Application 9
TA 10–6   Critical Thinking Questions, Application 9
TA 10–7   Good Solution, Application 9

TM 10–1   Poor Example, Claim Refusal
TM 10–2   Good Example, Claim Refusal
TM 10–3   Poor Example, Test Problem, Claim Refusal
TM 10–4   Good Example, Test Problem, Claim Refusal
TM 10–5   Good Solution, "Communication in Action" Case
TM 10–6   Good Solution, E-mail Application
TM 10–7   Good Solution, Application 1

TM 10–8   Good Solution, Application 2
TM 10–9   Good Solution, Application 3
TM 10–10 Good Solution, Application 4
TM 10–11 Good Solution, Application 5
TM 10–12 Good Solution, Application 6
TM 10–13 Good Solution, Application 7
TM 10–14 Good Solution, Application 8
TM 10–15 Good Solution, Application 10
TM 10–16 Good Solution, Application 11, Step 2
TM 10–17 Good Solution, Application 12
TM 10–18 Good Solution, Application 14
TM 10–19 Good Solution, Application 17
TM 10–20 Good Solution, Application 18
TM 10–21 Good Solution, Application 19
TM 10–22 Good Solution, Application 20
TM 10–23 Good Solution, Case for Analysis 1, Step 2
TM 10–24 Good Solution, Case for Analysis 3, Step 3

ADDITIONAL READINGS

Basile, F. (1989). Tips for better business letters. *Journal of Property Management, 54*(11), 28–29.

Brockman, E. B., and Bellanger, K. (1993). You-attitude and positive emphasis: Testing received wisdom in business communication. *Bulletin of the Association for Business Communication, (56)*2, 1–5.

Fielden, J. (1989). Clear writing is not enough. *Management Review, 78*(4), 49–52.

Harbrough, F. W. (1991). Accentuate the positive: Verbal and written communication expressed in positive, rather than negative, language. *Technical Communication, 38*(1), 73–74.

Jonker, P., & Reeves, T. Z. (1991). The hidden messages in disciplinary memos. *Supervisory Management, 36*(2), 4–5.

Krafft, S. (1991). How to break bad news. *American Demographics, 13*(7), 42–43.

Pollock, T. (1993). How to disagree…without getting punched in the nose. *Supervision, 54*(11), 25.

Vitiello, J. (1993). Breaking the bad news. *Meetings and Conventions, 28*(13), 135.

Wiesendanger, D. (1992). Bad-news meetings. *Sales & Marketing Management, 144*(14), 65–71.

Wiseman, T. L. (1991). How to avoid the transitional ax in indirect bad-news messages. *IEEE Transactions on Professional Communication, 34*(1), 20–23.

ANSWERS TO "COMMUNICATION IN ACTION" CASE: Shirley F. Olson, J. J. Ferguson, Sand and Gravel/Prestress/Precast.

1. **What impact did empathy have on the organization and style of Olson's message when denying credit?** Empathy affected Olson's organization of the message by the arrangement of thoughts. She follows these steps when saying no: (a) expresses appreciation of customer business, (b) acknowledges the customer's loyalty, (c) recognizes previous credit extensions, (d) says "no" in a non-threatening way (the style of the message), (e) offers credit again after cash has been paid, (f) and thanks him again for his request.

2. **Assume that you work for J. J. Ferguson and must correspond with Mr. Jim Read, Read Construction Co., 203 Woolbright Road, Whitehall, OH 43213-2987. A long-standing customer of six years with an excellent credit rating, Mr. Read has requested additional credit of $30,000 for July. Assume further that Mr. Read had extended his credit beyond the company limit of 60 days and was given an additional 30 days' extension. Write a letter saying "no" to his credit request.** See TM 10–5 (Good Solution, "Communication in Action" Case) for suggested letter.

ANSWERS TO REVIEW QUESTIONS

1. The outline for bad-news messages is as follows: (a) begin with the neutral idea that leads to the reason for the refusal; (b) present the facts, analysis, and reasons for the refusal; (c) state the refusal using positive tone and de-emphasis techniques; and (d) close with an idea that shifts emphasis away from the refusal.

2. The first paragraph (a) lets the receiver know what the letter is about (without stating the obvious) and (b) serves as a transition into the discussion of the reasons (without revealing the bad news or leading the receiver to expect good news). The stated sentence does not accomplish either purpose; it is an empty acknowledgment.

3. The disappointment experienced upon reading the bad news might interfere with the receiver's ability to comprehend or accept the supporting explanation. The feeling of disappointment may interfere with understanding and concentration while the explanations are read. From the writer's point of view, the reasons are important. If they are understood, the decision may be accepted readily.

4. Putting bad news in the last sentence would place too much emphasis on the refusal. Also, certain other ideas that need to be included would be out of place if presented *before* the bad news.

5. The final paragraph (a) de-emphasizes the unpleasant part of the message, (b) conveys some useful information that should logically follow bad news, (c) shows that the writer has a positive attitude, and (d) adds a unifying quality to the message.

6. Placing a refusal in the first sentence may be justified when (a) the message is the second response to a repeated request; (b) a very small, insignificant matter is involved; (c) a request is obviously ridiculous, unethical, illegal, or dangerous; (d) a writer's intent is to "shake" the reader; (e) a writer-reader relationship is so close that satisfactory human relations can be taken for granted; or (f) the writer *wants* to demonstrate authority.

7. Writers can reduce the risk that readers will become impatient by (a) keeping explanations concise, (b) including only relevant ideas, and (c) avoiding platitudes.

8. The inductive outline de-emphasizes bad news by placing it in a less important position.

9. Techniques for de-emphasizing a refusal include: (a) using inductive outline, (b) implying bad news if possible, (c) using positive language that accents the good, (d) offering a counterproposal, and (e) using stylistic techniques that minimize the negative. See TA 10–3 (Techniques for De-emphasizing Negative Ideas) for listing.

   a. Although we are unable to approve your request for credit, we are happy to offer you a 2-percent cash discount on all purchases.

   b. An error was made in the column totals.

   c. When warranty provision are not heeded, the warranty protection is forfeited.

d. Persons who receive unsatisfactory performance appraisals are placed on a three-month probation.

e. We are happy to offer you a free inspection and estimate of repairs.

f. When these requirements are met, we are happy to honor the warranty.

10. (a) A direct statement of refusal will stand out more vividly in a receiver's mind than would an implied refusal. Therefore, an implied refusal is normally more tactful.

Direct example: We are unable to repair your computer since you voided the warranty.

Implied example: Had the terms of the warranty been followed, we would have been happy to repair your computer free of charge

11. Adjustment letters that say "no" follow an inductive sequence of ideas: (a) begin with a neutral or factual sentence that leads to the reasons behind the "no" answer; (b) present the reasons and explanations; (c) present the refusal in an unemphatic manner, and (d) close with an off-the-subject thought.

12. A refusal may begin with a resale statement about the product. Sales promotional material would be most appropriate in the *final* paragraph (or even in a postscript). In earlier paragraphs, it would be confusing.

13. The recommended outline to use when refusing to send merchandise that is inappropriate for the customer's needs is as follows: (a) imply receipt of the order and confirm the customer's interest in your products, (b) give explanation or reason for recommending another option, (c) state the relative advantage of the option over the requested merchandise, (d) focus on the customer's satisfaction that will result from the alternative.

14. A counterproposal is an alternative to the action requested. It is an expression of empathy and goodwill for the customer that seeks to strengthen and maintain positive, long-term relationships.

15. The Equal Credit Opportunity Act (ECOA) requires that the credit applicant be notified of the credit decision within 30 calendar days. Applicants who are denied credit must be informed of the reasons for the refusal and be reminded that the Fair Credit Reporting Act provides them the right to know the nature of the information in their credit file. The ECOA also prohibits creditors from discriminating against credit applicants on the basis of race, color, religion, national origin, gender, and marital status.

16. Being able to initiate company messages that convey bad news effectively is as important as responding "no" to messages from customers/clients and others outside the company. A memorandum or e-mail message should be written inductively when it conveys bad news or when the idea being presented involves persuasion.

17. Six recommended ideas for introducing the bad news in the first paragraph are as follows: (a) a compliment, (b) a point of agreement, (c) some good news, (d) resale, (e) a review of pertinent circumstances, and (f) gratitude.

Figure 10–3: Extends a compliment to the reader (keen interest in investment) that leads to the explanation.

Figure 10–4: Presents resale on the quality print produced by the OptiScan.

Figure 10–7: Presents resale on the bulb the customer ordered; incorporates optimal use of the bulb in the resale statement as a transition to the explanation (the bulb is inappropriate for the customers' needs).

Figure 10–8: Extends a compliment for reader's commitment to a worthwhile community project.

Figure 10–9: Uses resale to confirm applicant's good choice of product.

Figure 10–11: Reviews relevant circumstances that preceded the negative decision that will follow (relocation of company headquarters).

18. The closing sentence should not apologize for action taken. Because valid reasons for the refusal have been provided, an apology is inconsistent. Why apologize for doing what is right? The apology weakens confidence in the decision.

19. The last paragraph should bring a unifying quality to the whole message; however, restatement of the refusal would only serve to emphasize it.

20. To close the letter/memorandum positively, the following suggestions are recommended: (a) provide needed information, (b) focus on the counterproposal, (c) use promotional material as a closing sentence, and (d) promote unity by reiterating an idea which appeared in the first sentence.

POSSIBLE SOLUTIONS TO EXERCISES

1. Focus on activities that encourage students to apply their understanding of the inductive process.

2. Divide the class into groups of four or five to discuss their letters and to develop a checklist for effective letter writing. Initiate a class discussion, calling on each group (or a spokesperson) to share its analysis with the class.

3. If time permits following the small-group discussion, ask a spokesperson from each group to summarize the results of the discussion. Discuss how the students' research compares with the material presented in Chapter 10.

4. a. Presents the bad news in the first paragraph (deductive approach); uses company policy rather than reasons as the explanation for the refusal.

   b. Presents the bad news in the first paragraph (deductive approach); includes refusal in a compound sentence, which overemphasizes the unpleasant news.

   c. Presents the bad news in the first paragraph (deductive approach); includes refusal in a compound sentence, which overemphasizes the unpleasant news.

   d. Presents the bad news in the first paragraph (deductive approach); uses negative language ("cannot" and "defective"); uses "grant," which implies the writer is in a position of power.

   e. Includes obvious statement.

5. a. "Applications must be received no later than May 9."

   b. "Smoking is limited to designated smoking areas."

   c. "Because the damages to your car occurred at the dealership and not the factory, please consult with your dealer for an adjustment."

   d. "Because of (*specify reasons*), you will remain in your current position."

   e. "Please revise this report making these changes in organization."

6. Refer to **TA 10–4** (Good Solution, Exercise 6) for a suggested solution. A summary of organization, content, style, and format errors follows:

Summary of Organization, Content, Style, and Format Errors	
Organization	◆ States the bad news before presenting the reasons for the refusal (deductive rather than inductive approach recommended for bad-news messages).
Content	◆ Includes a buffer that may mislead the reader to believe that Clark is accepting the presidency ("pleased and honored to have been asked").
	◆ Includes vague explanation ("obligations kept me from attending") that may not be considered genuine but rather a hurried response to "get the reader off his back."
	◆ Ends by reminding the reader of the disappointing news. Including an apology ("I am sorry") may cause the reader to believe that Clark is not convinced his argument is a good one.
Style	◆ Uses redundancy ("pleased" and "honored").
	◆ "However" positioned as the first word in the second paragraph signals an abrupt change to a negative thought, prior to presenting the reasons for the refusal.
	◆ Uses negative words that accent the bad news ("regret to inform" and "unfortunately").
	◆ Uses overly strong adjective, "tremendous," which could reduce the credibility of the remainder of the letter.
Format	◆ Appears as correctly formatted in block style, mixed punctuation.
	◆ Includes writer's address above the date because the letter is printed on plain paper.

POSSIBLE SOLUTION TO E-MAIL APPLICATION

See **TM 10–6** (Good Solution, E-mail Application) for suggested memo.

POSSIBLE SOLUTIONS AND RECOMMENDED OUTLINES TO APPLICATIONS

MARKETING

1. Wallpaper Cannot Be Returned

⇨ *Level 2* ⇦

See **TM 10–7** (Good Solution, Application 1) for suggested letter.

MARKETING

2. Caterer Must Charge for Additional Guests

⇨ *Level 2* ⇦

See **TA 10–8** (Good Solution, Application 2) for suggested letter.

BANKING

3. Borrowers Cannot Open Up a Locked-in Interest Rate

⇨ *Level 2* ⇦

See **TM 10–9** (Good Solution, Application 3) for suggested letter.

MANAGEMENT

4. Restocking Fee to be Paid on Returned Merchandise

⇨ *Level 2* ⇦

See **TM 10–10** (Good Solution, Application 4) for suggested letter.

MANAGEMENT

5. Policy Covers Material Value Only

⇨ *Level 2* ⇦

See **TM–11** (Good Solution, Application 5) for suggested letter.

MANAGEMENT

6. Dry Sprinkler Is More Appropriate for Cold Climates

⇨ *Level 2* ⇦

See **TM 10–12** (Good Solution, Application 6) for suggested letter.

ACCOUNTING

7. Interim Audit Must Be Scheduled

⇨ *Level 2* ⇦

See **TM–13** (Good Solution, Application 7) for suggested faxed letter. A fax or telephone call is a more appropriate channel than regular mail because the accounting firm must be informed of this scheduling conflict as quickly as possible. The solution of **TM 10–13** is a letter sent by fax (note the facsimile mailing notation) explaining the scheduling conflict, proposing several options, and mentioning a followup telephone call to finalize the solution.

COMMUNITY SERVICE

8. Sorry, But You Did Not Make the Team

⇨ *Level 2* ⇦

See **TM 10–14** (Good Solution, Application 8) for suggested letter.

The solution is formatted as a friendly letter because the receiver is 12 years old. The vocabulary is simple and sentences are short to keep the readability appropriate for young persons.

MANAGEMENT/Public Sector

9. Decision to Relocate Corporate Headquarters Is Final

⇨ *Level 3* ⇦

Refer to **TA 10–5** (Poor Solution, Application 9), **TA 10–6** (Critical Thinking Questions, Application 9), and **TA 10–7** (Good Solution, Application 9) as you evaluate this assignment. Students are required to consult a reference manual to determine that "The Honorable" is the appropriate courtesy title for a city mayor and that "Dear Mayor" is the appropriate salutation.

ADVERTISING

10. Parent Company Refuses to Continue Support of Not-for-Profit Program

⇨ *Level 2* ⇦

See **TM 10–15** (Good Solution, Application 10) for suggested letter.

COMMUNITY SERVICE/Public Sector

11. All Bids Are Over Architect's Estimate
⇨ *Level 2* ⇦

Step 1: The letter should

1. Open with positive remarks about the progress being made on the community center.

2. Explain that all bids exceeded the architect's estimate and suggest that a meeting of the City Council be called to discuss possible options.

3. Enumerate and summarize the costs/benefits of each option.

4. Close with a specific statement about the action that must be taken and specify a deadline. Positive remarks about the benefits the community will gain from the completion of the community center are appropriate.

Step 2: See **TM 10–16** (Good Solution, Application 11, Step 2) for suggested letter.

MIS

12. Price Reductions in Computer Industry Are Inevitable
⇨ *Level 2* ⇦

See **TM 10–17** (Good Solution, Application 12) for suggested letter.

ACCOUNTING

13. Unable to Speak at Seminar
⇨ *Level 2* ⇦

The letter should

1. Imply that the request has been received; for example, include complimentary comment about Beta Alpha Psi's VITA program.

2. Provide a sincere explanation for refusal (e.g., work overload just prior to April 15 tax filing date). Likely can imply the refusal if the reasons clearly convey the refusal.

3. Offer a counterproposal to minimize the disappointment and to increase your genuineness; for example, volunteer to assist Beta Alpha Psi in some other way—professor of the day, guest speaker at chapter meeting, tour of accounting facility, and so on.

FINANCE

14. New Credit Policies Affect Real Estate Loans Adversely
⇨ *Level 2* ⇦

See **TM 10–18** (Good Solution, Application 14) for suggested letter.

FINANCE/Legal

15. Customer Credit Too Risky to Obtain Loan
⇨ *Level 2* ⇦

The letter should

1. Imply receipt of the credit request and lead naturally into the explanation (e.g., providing necessary credit information).

2. Explain the reasons behind the refusal, convincing the reader that the decision was not arbitrary and providing needed guidance for adjusting credit behavior in such a way that credit can be extended later. Diplomatically explain that the law requires that credit be given to *credit-worthy* customers only.

3. Use positive language to state the refusal. May imply the refusal if the reasons clearly convey the refusal. Offer a counterproposal (e.g., purchase on a cash basis).

4. Encourage subsequent application and thus imply expectation of continued business relationship.

FINANCE/Legal

16. Loan Denied for Poor Credit Customer
⇨ *Level 2* ⇦

The letter should

1. Imply receipt of the credit request and lead naturally into the explanation (e.g., providing necessary credit information).

2. Explain the reasons behind the refusal, convincing the reader that the decision was not arbitrary and providing needed guidance for adjusting credit behavior in such a way that credit can be extended later.

3. Use positive language to state the refusal. May imply the refusal if the reasons clearly convey the refusal. Offer a counterproposal (e.g., purchase on a cash basis).

4. Encourage subsequent application and thus imply expectation of continued business relationship.

HUMAN RESOURCES MANAGEMENT

17. Company Downsizing Announced
➪ *Level 3* ⬸

See **TM 10–19** (Good Solution, Application 17) for suggested memo. Directed to supervisors, the memorandum discusses the rationale for and general details of the downsizing plan. It also enlists the supervisors' help in minimizing employee fear and maintaining positive employee relationships. Students will need to search the literature for guidance in handling crisis communication.

HUMAN RESOURCES MANAGEMENT

18. Back to the Road for Sales Reps
➪ *Level 2* ⬸

See **TM 10–20** (Good Solution, Application 18) for suggested memorandum.

MANAGEMENT/Legal   GMAT

19. To Fire or Not to Fire
➪ *Level 3* ⬸

See **TM 10–21** (Good Solution, Application 19) for suggested memorandum.

HUMAN RESOURCES MANAGEMENT

20. Written Disciplinary Action Required
➪ *Level 2* ⬸

See **TM-22** (Good Solution, Application 20) for suggested memorandum.

POSSIBLE SOLUTIONS AND RECOMMENDED OUTLINES TO CASES FOR ANALYSIS

MANAGEMENT/Interpersonal

1. Plant Will Close in Two Weeks
➪ *Level 4* ⬸

Because this case requires students to research ways to communicate negative information to minimize fear and inaccurate rumors, students' solutions will vary widely. If you believe your students will require additional direction, you might share with them the following sample solutions. Be sure to instruct students which documentation method you prefer.

1. Students' research will vary.
2. See **TM 10–23** (Good Solution, Case for Analysis 1, Step 2) for suggested memo.
3. Students' solutions will vary but should reflect a deductive pattern and the inclusion of pertinent research.

MANAGEMENT

2. Minimizing the Negative Publicity Associated with Product Recalls
➪ *Level 4* ⬸

Because this case requires students to research ways to communicate crisis information, students' solutions will vary widely. Public relations majors can be valuable resources; allow them to lead the class in a discussion about this assignment before students write the letter independently or in small groups.

1. Students' research will vary.
2. Student's solutions should effectively apply concepts of the inductive pattern covered in Chapter 10.

ACCOUNTING/Ethics/Legal   GMAT

3. **An Accountant's Knowledge of a Fraudulent Tax Return: What Action Is Legal? Is It Ethical?**
➪ *Level 4* ⬸

1. Diplomatically (and without an accusatory tone) explain the discrepancy in the income statements. Stress the benefits of authorizing you to file an amended return: Paying the tax is ultimately in Mr. Ford's best interest because an IRS examination could result in significant fines and interest payments.
2. Analysis of the problem.

    Ethical issues. (1) Is the accountant obligated to report the fraudulent tax return to the Internal Revenue Service? (2) Should an accountant continue to provide services to a client after learning the client has filed a fraudulent tax return?

    Legal restrictions. None; the IRS does not require tax preparers to report the improper tax filings of their clients.

Contractual. None apply.

Code of ethics. American Institute of Certified Public Accountants' (AICPA) *Statement on Responsibilities in Tax Practices* contains an accountant/client confidentiality statement. This statement precludes the CPA from disclosing information to a government agency without the client's permission. In addition, the CPA must dissociate himself or herself from a client involved in illegal activities.

Cost/benefit analysis. Not necessary; the CPA's action is clearly dictated by the AICPA Code of Professional Ethics. Answers should be graded based on students' analysis of the facts and accurate research to support their decisions.

3. Refer to **TM 10–24** (Good Solution, Case for Analysis 3, Step 3) for suggested memo.

CHAPTER 11

WRITING TO PERSUADE

CHAPTER OVERVIEW

The persuasive principles presented in Chapter 11 have application in face-to-face business relationships, as well as in written activities. The ability to persuade is useful to a variety of life circumstances in which students will need to motivate action, such as selling a product, a service, or their own abilities; gaining acceptance of an idea; or collecting money.

The goals of the collection-writing section are (a) to give students a practical understanding of credit and collections, (b) to give experience in the use of appeals in the process of persuasion, and (c) to emphasize the legal requirements of the collection process.

LEARNING OBJECTIVES

1 Develop effective outlines and appeals for messages that persuade.

2 Write effective sales messages and persuasive requests (claim, favor, information requests, persuasion within organizations) that are persuasive, but ethical.

3 Write collection letters at various stages of the collection process.

CHAPTER OUTLINE AND TEACHING SUGGESTIONS

1   LEARNING OBJECTIVE

I.   Persuasion Strategies
     A. Show **TA 11–1** (Chapter Opener) as you begin the chapter discussion. Discuss how environmentalists "sold" their ideas to manufacturers, who passed along those ideas to the consumers by labeling their products "biodegradable" or "recyclable." Initiate a discussion about other persuasive campaigns that have resulted in pervasive changes; e.g., health consciousness (fitness, low-fat, high-fiber diets, drug and alcohol abuse, violence, adult literacy, conservation, political and advertising messages).
     B. Plan Before you Write.
         1. Know the Product, Service, or Idea
         2. Know the Receiver
         3. Identify the Desired Action
     C. Apply Sound Writing Principles
     D. Impress students with the balance that must be achieved between including sufficient detail and keeping the interest of the receiver.
         1. Keep a file of persuasive letters of differing lengths.

2. Make transparencies of them or pass them around for students to see.

E. In addition to writing complete letters, students gain from extra practice on certain critical parts. For several letter-writing problems, have students write attention-getters only, price-stating paragraphs only, or action endings only.

| 2 | LEARNING OBJECTIVE |

II. Sales Letters

A. Show **TA 11–2** (Persuasive Outline: When the Receiver Must Be Persuaded) as you introduce the persuasive pattern.

B. Compare the use of the AIDA formula in letter writing to its use in television commercials, magazine and newspaper advertisements, and other marketing techniques.

C. First Paragraph: An Attention-Getter
   1. Start with the Product, Service, or Idea
   2. Focus on a Central Selling Feature
   3. Address the Receiver's Needs
   4. Use an Original Approach
   5. Keep Paragraphs Short
   6. Ask students to complete Exercise 4.

D. Introducing the Product, Service, or Idea
   1. Be Cohesive
   2. Be Action Oriented
   3. Stress the Central Selling Point

E. Convince the Receivers with Evidence
   1. Emphasize the Central Selling Point
   2. Use Concrete Language
   3. Be Objective
   4. Interpret the Evidence
   5. Be Careful When You Talk About Price
   6. Know How and When to Use Enclosures, Testimonials, and Guarantees
   7. Ask students to complete Exercise 5.

F. Last Paragraph: Motivating the Receiver to Action.
   1. Mention the Specific Action You Want
   2. Allude to the Reward for Taking Action
   3. Present Action as Being Easy to Take
   4. Provide a Stimulus for Quick Action
   5. Ask Confidently for Action

G. Teaching Suggestions:
   1. Ask students to bring in examples of sales letters.
      a. Project selected letters and invite comments on the way in which the stylistic techniques discussed in Chapters 7 and 8 are applied in the letters.
      b. Ask students to identify the steps in the persuasive pattern. Use the "Check Your Writing" checklist as a basis for discussion.
   2. Define a persuasive problem or a product that is to be sold. Allow students a few minutes in which to write the worst letter they can write. Although the psychology is questionable (who needs practice in doing something the wrong way?), the exercise is fun; and identifying bad practices can help to intensify mastery of good practices.
   3. Show students a product or present an idea and ask them to write a sales letter in class. The exercise is especially valuable because students have no printed words before them (as they do when completing assignments that are defined in writing).
   4. Assign Exercise 6 to be completed in small groups. Show **TA 11–3** (Solution, Exercise 6) as you review the weaknesses in the letter and its revision.

III. Persuasive Requests
A. Introduce this section with current examples of the necessity for persuasion

(inductive approach) to achieve a specific goal.

1. For example, Marvin Runyon, who was appointed Postmaster General in 1992, inherited the management of one of the fattest bureaucracies. A former business executive, Runyon brought to his new post a management style foreign to most employees. While some lauded his efforts at cutting budgets and red tape, others cast doubt on the validity and success of his plans. Refer students to the photo of Archbishop Desmond Tutu and discuss his efforts to "convince" others to adopt his ideas about apartheid in South Africa. In both these cases, receivers were nonreceptive to the proposed ideas; therefore, diplomacy and the inductive approach was an appropriate organizational pattern.

2. Ask students to provide other current examples of the need for persuasion (e.g, political or legislative situations, controversial CEOs, and the ideas discussed in I–A).

B. Making a Claim

C. Asking a Favor

1. Assign Application 1 from the *Study Guide* that deals with a request to speak at a professional meeting. Discuss the communication pointers in small groups with a spokesperson reporting to the class if time permits.

2. Initiate a class discussion related to effective writing techniques incorporated in the revision provided in the *Study Guide*.

D. Requesting Information

E. Persuading Within Organizations

F. Communication in Action: Mike Mills, American Woodmark

1. Ask students to read the case and complete the memorandum described in the case application for homework.

2. Make a transparency of **TM 11–6** (Good Solution, "Communication in

Action" Case) to show as you discuss the memorandum.

G. Present a poorly written sales letter as a classwork/homework activity.

1. Show **TA 11–4** (Poor Example, Sales Letter in **TA 11–4**) as you lead in a discussion of the letter's weaknesses.

2. Show **TA 11–5** (Critical Thinking Questions, Sales Letter in **TA 11–4**) as you discuss the necessary organization, content, style, and format of the letter. Ask students to write the letter for homework.

3. Show **TA 11–6** (Good Example, Sales Letter in **TA 11–4**) as you lead a discussion of the suggested solution of the letter.

3   LEARNING OBJECTIVE

IV. Collection Letters

A. Characteristics of a Collection Series

B. Stages in the Collection Series

1. Reminder

2. Inquiry

3. Appeal

4. Strong Appeal or Urgency

5. Ultimatum

6. Make transparencies of the following: **TM 11–1** (Good Example, Collection, Inquiry Stage), **TM 11–2** (Good Example, Collection, Appeals Stage), **TM 11–3** (Good Example, Collection, Stronger Appeals Stage), **TM 11–4** (Good Example, Collection, Urgency Stage), and **TM 11–5** (Good Example, Collection, Ultimatum Stage). Show these letters to illustrate the progression in emphasis as the collection process is extended.

7. Suggestions for emphasizing effective development of collection letters follow:

a. To emphasize the personal nature of collection letters, encourage students to use the recipient's name in the body of the letter.

b. To encourage originality, caution students against copying examples from the text or transparencies. Certainly, students must use many of the ideas presented. The language of collections almost reverts to specialized jargon, and many people would not feel comfortable without taking a worn expression or two from the literature of collections. Nevertheless, students should be rewarded for writing letters that do not sound like conventional form letters. In-class writing assignments may result in more learning than do homework assignments.

c. For effective collection writing, encourage students to avoid extremes. Assuming that the customer is *always* right or should *never* be written to in straightforward, negative terms is one extreme. On the other hand, issuing an ultimatum or using tough talk in the first letter of a series is the other extreme. If for some reason a student thinks an extreme approach will be successful, let the student key an explanation at the top of the letter and compose the letter accordingly.

8. Assign Application 2 from the *Study Guide* that deals with the inquiry stage of a collection series. Discuss the communication pointers in small groups with a spokesperson reporting to the class if time permits. Discuss the effective writing techniques incorporated in the revision.

V. Summary

A. Show the videotape "Writing to Persuade."

1. Refer to the teaching suggestions for the video listed at the beginning of Part 4.

2. Show **TA 11-7** (Business Tips from Tracy-Locke/Pharr Public Relations [Video, Part 4]) to summarize the video's message.

B. Integrate the communication mentor comments into class lectures to reinforce the concepts in the chapter.

C. Assign the *Study Guide* questions for Chapter 11.

D. Assign the *Study Guide* applications for Chapter 11. The applications "walk students through" writing (a) a letter persuading a person to speak at a business organization meeting (no honorarium) and (b) the inquiry letter in a collection series. Critical thinking questions help students organize their thoughts and outline correctly; students write solutions using their outlines, and compare their solutions with a sample solution and a detailed commentary that highlights the strengths of the outline and the solution. In a third application, students analyze a poorly written letter and identify errors and weaknesses. Critical thinking questions guide students through the analysis.

E. Ask students to complete the e-mail application.

F. Assign selected exercises, applications, and cases at the end of the chapter. Remind students to study the suggestions in the "Check Your Writing" checklist when planning and revising an assignment.

G. Assign selected cases for analysis at the end of the chapter. **TM 11-20** (Good Solution, Case for Analysis 1, Step 3) and **TM 11-21** (Case for Analysis 3, Step 2) are provided as solutions.

H. Assign one of the applications designated as an AWA (Analytical Writing Assessment) for the GMAT. Refer to pages 12-13 of the *Instructor's Resource Manual* for holistic scoring techniques used by evaluators of this written portion of the GMAT.

TRANSPARENCIES AND MASTERS

TA 11–1   Chapter Opener
TA 11–2   Persuasive Outline: When the
           Receiver Must Be Persuaded
TA 11–3   Solution, Exercise 6
TA 11–4   Poor Example, Sales Letter
TA 11–5   Critical Thinking Questions, Sales
           Letter in **TA 11–4**
TA 11–6   Good Solution, Sales Letter in
           TA 11–4
TA 11–7   Business Tips from Tracy-Locke/
           Pharr Public Relations (Video,
           Part 4)

TM 11–1   Good Example, Collection,
           Inquiry Stage
TM 11–2   Good Example, Collection,
           Appeals Stage
TM 11–3   Good Example, Collection,
           Stronger Appeals Stage
TM 11–4   Good Example, Collection,
           Urgency Stage
TM 11–5   Good Example, Collection,
           Ultimatum Stage
TM 11–6   Good Solution, "Communication in
           Action" Case
TM 11–7   Good Solution, Application 2
TM 11–8   Good Solution, Application 4
TM 11–9   Good Solution, Application 5
TM 11–10   Good Solution, Application 6
TM 11–11   Good Solution, Application 7
TM 11–12   Good Solution, Application 8
TM 11–13   Good Solution, Application 9
TM 11–14   Good Solution, Application 10
TM 11–15   Good Solution, Application 13
TM 11–16   Good Solution, Application 17
TM 11–17   Good Solution, Application 18, Step 1
TM 11–18   Good Solution, Application 18, Step 2
TM 11–19   Good Solution, Application 19
TM 11–20   Good Solution, Case for Analysis 1,
           Step 3
TM 11–21   Good Solution, Case for Analysis 3,
           Step 2

ADDITIONAL READINGS

Bacon, M. S. (1988). Persuasive writing: Imitate the prose of pros. *Association Management, 40*(8), 164–168.

Bartolome, F. (1990). When you think the boss is wrong. *Personnel Journal, 69*(8), 66–73.

Berry, S. (1990). Get that payment in full. *Small Business Reports, 15*(10), 55–58.

Boozer, R. W., Wyld, D. C., & Grant J. (1990). Using metaphor to create more effective sales messages. *Journal of Services Marketing, 4*(3), 63–70.

Charney, A. (1991). Five great ways to begin a b-to-b (business-to-business) letter. *Target Marketing, 14*(8), 42–43.

Cone, P. (1991). How to sell in writing. *Sales & Marketing Management, 143*(14), 71–74.

Hornick, L. (1992). Communicating to get results. *Communication World, 9*(12), 17–20.

Lewis, H. G. (1991). The future of "force communication": Power communication. *Direct Marketing, 53*(12), 51–52.

ANSWERS TO "COMMUNICATION IN ACTION" CASE: Mike Mills, American Woodmark

1. **Mills used facts and figures as evidence in the outside carrier proposal. Give an example of a different proposal in which using evidence other than numbers or statistics would be appropriate.** Suggest that students discuss the area of customer service. The proposal may stress improved service rather than "hard" numbers and cost analysis. Students may make this argument: "I don't care if the system makes money. If I have a noticeably better chance of making commitments to my customers, I'm not concerned about the cost. I'm sold on what we're proposing."

2. **Assume that you are a transportation manager at American Woodmark. After preliminary research and analysis, you develop a plan for a Home Delivery Program in which products are delivered directly to residential homes. Normally, American Woodmark uses commercial stores such as The Home Depot to reach its customers. This new program is innovative and will begin on a trial basis in Milwaukee, Wisconsin. Write a memorandum to your supervisor, Cyndi Johnson, convincing her to approve a pilot test of this new distribution system.** Use an inductive outline for this persuasive request: capture the supervisor's attention, present convincing evidence, have a rational response to anticipated resistance, and close with the specific action you want the supervisor to take. See **TM 11–6**

(Good Solution, "Communication in Action" case) for a suggested memorandum.

ANSWERS TO REVIEW QUESTIONS

1. In planning a persuasive message, information must be gathered about (a) the product, service, or idea; (b) the receiver; and (c) the desired action.

2. Effective writing principles include (a) use concrete nouns and active verbs; (b) use specific language, (c) let receivers have the spotlight; (d) be certain the persuasive message presents the facts honestly, truthfully, and objectively; (e) stress a central selling point or appeal; and (f) use an inductive outline.

3. Ethically, the writer should guard against becoming overzealous and painting less-than-accurate perceptions in the minds of receivers. Legal guidelines related to advertising provide clear guidance for avoiding the misrepresentation of products or services. Exaggerating or misleading in a letter sent by the U.S. Postal Service may constitute the federal offense of mail fraud. Penalties can include significant fines and imprisonment.

4. A "central selling feature" is the one idea that is stressed throughout the letter. It is to the letter what a *theme* is to a report. Good possibilities for a central selling point are a major advantage the product has over its competition or a major benefit a buyer would receive from owning it.

5. The four-point outline for the persuasive message: (a) get attention, (b) introduce the product, (c) give convincing evidence, (d) encourage action.

6. A good attention-getter (a) is related to the product/service/idea and its virtues, (b) introduces a central selling feature, (c) addresses the receiver's needs, (d) sounds interesting, and (e) is original. Some ways to get attention include: (a) a personal experience, (b) a solution to a problem, (c) a startling announcement, (d) a what-if opening, (e) a question, (f) a story, (g) a proverb or quote from a famous person, and (h) a split sentence.

7. Sales letters are typically longer than routine letters because specific, convincing language is necessary. This type of writing is space consuming. The first and last para-

graphs are typically shorter than those in the middle of the letter.

8. Superlatives are acceptable in sales letters if they are accompanied with supporting evidence. Unsupported or unsupportable superlatives are likely to do more harm than good.

9. Incomplete comparisons can be unethical, as they lead receivers to over infer.

Incomplete comparison: Model Z outperforms the competition in clinical trials. (Did Model Z outperform all the competition or certain products?)

Complete comparison: Model Z outperformed the XK17 in clinical trials.

10. Several techniques exist for presenting the receiver with evidence of the value of the product, service, or idea: (a) emphasizing the central selling point; (b) using concrete language; (c) being objective; (d) interpreting the evidence; (e) being careful in talking about price; and (f) knowing how and when to use enclosures, testimonials, and guarantees.

11. Effective techniques for presenting the price include the following: (a) introduce price after presenting the product, service, or idea and its virtues; (b) keep price out of the first and last paragraphs, unless price is the distinctive feature; (c) use figures to illustrate how enough money can be saved to pay for the expenditure; (d) state price in terms of small units; (e) invite comparison of like products, services, or ideas; and (f) use facts and figures to illustrate that the price is reasonable.

12. An effective action ending (a) states the specific action wanted, (b) alludes to the reward for taking action, (c) presents the action as being easy to take, (d) encourages quick action, and (e) asks confidently.

13. A routine claim is based on the assumption that the claim will be granted when the facts alone are presented. A persuasive claim is based on the assumption that presenting facts alone will not likely get desired results; incentives must be included.

14. An appeal in a persuasive letter serves the same purpose as a central selling point in a sales letter. Both serve as a central theme that is supported with evidence throughout the letter and reminds the receiver of a benefit that accrues from doing as asked

(e.g., granting a claim, complying with a request, and making a payment.)

15. The persuasive request uses an inductive sequence that (a) arouses a desire to take action, (b) uses a theme appeal, (c) provides a logical argument to overcome any anticipated resistance, and (d) invites action.

16. (b) If sufficient emphasis has been placed on the reward for taking action, action will probably be taken.

17. "If" and "hope" connote doubt. To use them is to risk implying "I recognize that you may not be at all impressed by what you have read," which weakens the message.

18. Yes. Completing the questionnaire may seem objectionable because it is time consuming. Before being asked to *give,* the respondent needs to be reminded of the reward for giving.

19. No. Action represents something the respondent *gives*—a negative. Negatives are preferably subordinated, but simple sentences are emphatic. Subordination of the negative (action) can be achieved by stating it in a compound or complex sentence that also reminds the receiver of the reward for acting.

20. Collection letters are short because debtors already know they owe money and expect to be asked for payment. Therefore, they are not inclined to spend much time in reading. Stated in a short letter, an important reason for paying is likely to be read; and it may make an impression. Stated in a long letter, an important point may be skipped or passed over quickly.

21. Computers are used to generate reminders automatically at specified intervals (30, 40, 45, and 60 days past due). The mail-merge feature of word-processing software is used to merge variables with standard text to produce personalized form letters.

22. No. Asking whether merchandise and service have been satisfactory has two disadvantages: (a) the question may provide the debtor with ideas that can be used against the creditor, and (b) the question connotes an implied confession that merchandise and service are sometimes unsatisfactory.

23. Only one letter should invite an explanation (and it should precede the appeals-stage letters). If an invitation to explain has been ignored, asking again seems pointless. By

referring to a request that was ignored previously, the creditor may imply forgetfulness, lack of organization, or lack of resolve.

24. Each letter should include only *one* appeal. With no competing appeal, the one appeal is emphatic. A long letter may be discarded before it is read. If it is read, one appeal emphatically presented is more likely to generate action than multiple appeals that compete for attention.

25. (b) An ultimatum letter would have greater justification for use of negative terms. On the assumption that the debtor had experienced a special problem, positive language in the inquiry letter was useful in conveying an attitude of understanding. In the later stages, prior techniques have not worked. Negative words (like losing a credit rating) can make the debt seem more serious.

POSSIBLE SOLUTIONS TO EXERCISES

1. Use one or more of the activities as lecture openers or pop quiz items.

2. Divide the class into groups of four or five to discuss their letters and to develop a checklist for effective persuasive letter writing. Initiate a class discussion, calling on each group (or a spokesperson) to share its analysis and letter with the class.

3. To vary this exercise, you might divide the class into small groups with instructions to (a) select a product/service/idea, preferably one that someone in the group has used or is familiar with; (b) analyze the product/service/idea using the questions in the "Knowing the Product" section as a guide; (c) identify the central selling point; and (d) outline an unsolicited sales letter.

4. Analyses of sentences:

   a. Invites a negative answer which may make reading the rest of the letter needless. Asks for response before presenting adequate benefit for doing so.

   b. Uses a quote that is inappropriate to the message that follows.

   c. Starts with an exaggerated statement that may damage the credibility of the rest of the letter.

   d. Presents price too early before adequate presentation of the product; uses unsupported superlative ("best high-pressured washer").

e. Mentions enclosure before presenting benefits of ownership; thus the receiver may not read the entire letter.

f. Gives an overly exaggerated description of the product that does not provide an incentive to continue reading.

g. States the obvious ("I am writing") using first person; does not present an incentive to continue reading.

h. Includes dissatisfaction before presenting a logical appeal with supporting evidence that leads logically to the request for an adjustment.

5. Analyses of sentences:

   a. Uses deductive approach when the receiver must be persuaded to make the change.

   b. Uses first person; does not provide an incentive to continue reading.

   c. Lacks a receiver-centered idea to capture attention.

   d. Uses a deductive approach when the receiver must be persuaded to make the decision.

6. Refer to **TA 11–3** (Solution, Exercise 6) for solution. A summary of organization, content, style, grammatical, and format errors follows:

Summary of Organization, Content, Style, Grammatical, and Format Errors	
Organization	◆ Uses inductive approach appropriately.
Content	◆ Includes weak attention-getter—states the obvious.
	◆ Is not developed around a central selling point; presents numerous features of the schooner, but does not describe the satisfaction receiver will gain from chartering the schooner.
	◆ Includes weak action ending that does not motivate the receiver to act.
Style	◆ Begins receiver-oriented attention-getter that provides no incentive to continue reading. Changes from first- to second-person and overuses "we" throughout the letter.
	◆ Uses clichés ("please find the enclosed" and "do not hesitate to call me") and the doubtful expression ("I hope").

Style *(con't)*	◆ Omits comma after Georgia.
	◆ Uses expletive beginning ("there will be") in paragraph 3.
Grammatical Errors	◆ Includes "th" and "st" after day of the month.
	◆ Does not hyphenate "103-year-old" (compound adjective).
	◆ Spells "accommodate" incorrectly.
	◆ Omits comma after introductory clause in final sentence.
Format	◆ Needs a courtesy title in letter address.
	◆ Uses a weak salutation; change to "Dear Mr. Singer."
	◆ Needs a colon, not a comma, after the salutation (mixed punctuation).

POSSIBLE SOLUTION TO E-MAIL APPLICATION

Encourage students to choose situations that involve creativity in applying the inductive persuasive pattern. Assist students in identifying persuasive messages they can actually mail to the receiver and evaluate the effectiveness of the message when a response is received. Some students might choose to write a message they had wanted to write previously but did not have the expertise or confidence to do so. Additionally, consider allowing students to work in small groups to enhance creative thinking and to provide a diversity of personal and work experiences to be drawn upon for a realistic persuasive problem.

Send each student (or group) an e-mail message approving or disapproving the persuasive topic and providing necessary guidance for continuing the project. Instruct students to send the completed assignment to you via e-mail or a printed copy. Evaluate the persuasive message for organization, content, style, and format.

POSSIBLE SOLUTIONS AND RECOMMENDED OUTLINES TO APPLICATIONS

MARKETING

1. Promoting a Home Security System

⇨ *Level 2* ⇦

The letter should

1. Seek to gain attention using one of the techniques presented in the "First Paragraph: An Attention-Getter" section. The opening should appeal to the target audience, i.e., families with small children.

2. Introduce the product in the context of the receiver's benefits. Focus on a central selling point.

3. Present objective evidence needed to convince the receiver to act. Subordinate price using de-emphasis techniques.

4. Provide an incentive for quick action (the free, six-month service contract); restate the central selling point to remind receiver of the benefits being received in exchange for the cost.

FINANCE/HUMAN RESOURCES MGT

2. Persuading Employees to Enhance Financial Planning

⇨ *Level 2* ⇦

See **TM 11–7** (Good Solution, Application 2) for suggested letter.

MARKETING

3. Promoting a Product of Your Choice

⇨ *Level 3* ⇦

Content of letters will vary but should

1. Seek to gain attention using one of the techniques presented in the "First Paragraph: An Attention-Getter" section. Present central selling point.

2. Introduce the product in the context of the receiver's benefits.

3. Present objective evidence needed to convince the receiver to act. Subordinate price using de-emphasis techniques.

4. Provide an incentive for quick action, restating the central selling point to remind receiver of benefits being received in exchange for the cost.

MARKETING/International

4. Earning a Finder's Fee for Exceptional British Stamps

⇨ *Level 3* ⇦

See **TM 11–8** (Good Solution, Application 4) for suggested letter. Students must locate the currency exchange rate for British pounds so that they can give the prospective buyer the price in U.S. dollars. If students require assistance, direct them to the "Money" section of *The Wall Street Journal*, *BusinessWeek Index* (follows contents page of *BusinessWeek*), or other sources for the currency exchange rate. The formula to compute the selling price in U.S. dollars plus the 10-percent finder's fee is $200 \div$ currency rate $\times 1.10$.

MARKETING

5. Securing a Radio Advertisement to Promote a Grand Opening

⇨ *Level 2* ⇦

See **TM 11–9** (Good Solution, Application 5) for suggested letter.

REAL ESTATE

6. Exposing Potential Members to Resort Property and Privileges

⇨ *Level 2* ⇦

See **TM 11–10** (Good Solution, Application 6) for suggested letter.

GENERAL

7. Party Time: Special Request

⇨ *Level 2* ⇦

See **TM 11–11** (Good Solution, Application 7) for suggested letter. Possible arguments students could use: mention other clubs where your sorority/fraternity has held functions with no damage; could provide club managers' names and telephone numbers for references; publicity gained from allowing group to use the facility (particularly convincing if the event is being sponsored to raise money for a worthwhile cause).

MANAGEMENT

8. **Beauty Lies in the Eyes of the Beholder**

⇨ *Level 2* ⇦

See **TM 11–12** (Good Solution, Application 8) for suggested letter.

COMMUNITY SERVICE/Ethics

9. **Volunteer Must Complete Commitment**

⇨ *Level 2* ⇦

See **TM 11–13** (Good Solution, Application 9) for suggested letter.

PUBLIC RELATIONS

10. **Advertising Inconsistent with Company Philosophy**

⇨ *Level 2* ⇦

See **TM 11–14** (Good Solution, Application 10) for suggested letter.

FINANCE

11. **Using Effective Persuasion Techniques to Prevent a Hostile Takeover**

⇨ *Level 2* ⇦

The letter should

1. Open with a positive statement about the stock's performance and its prospects for the future.

2. Continue to develop reasons the future looks optimistic; for example, advantage over competitors who must renegotiate union contracts, which will lead naturally into the benefits of retaining current management and ownership—long-term investment opportunities.

3. Encourage stockholders to reject offers for short-term gains such as the one forthcoming from Winton-Pearson, Inc. Instead, stockholders should retain their Carroll stock, to ensure receiving the long-term benefits they have come to expect from Carroll Industry.

MANAGEMENT/Public Sector

12. **Proposed Tax Hike: Persuasive Campaign**

⇨ *Level 2* ⇦

The letter should

1. Seek to gain attention by mentioning something related to the 2-percent tax on prepared food and beverages and of interest to the receivers. Introduce a central appeal.

2. Introduce the benefits gained from supporting the tax hike. State in the context of the receivers' (community) benefits, focusing on the central appeal.

3. Present objective evidence (vivid examples) needed to convince the receivers to act; continue to focus on the central appeal.

4. Request that the receivers support the tax, restating the central appeal so that they remember the benefits being received in exchange for the costs (increased taxes).

MANAGEMENT

13. **Music Video Missing Creative Symbolism**

⇨ *Level 2* ⇦

See **TM 11–15** (Good Solution, Application 13) for suggested letter.

CONSUMER

14. **Equipment Malfunction Justifies an Exchange**

⇨ *Level 2* ⇦

The letter should

1. Seek to gain attention, for example, resale on the VCR or complimentary remarks about the company. Introduce the VCR and a central appeal, for example, company's commitment to stand behind what it sells, fulfilling stipulations of a warranty on a top-of-the line product.

2. Present the details of the problem with the VCR, stating them in terms of the central appeal and leading logically to the request. Avoid strong adjectives and adverbs and superlatives that decrease your credibility.

3. Request a new VCR, linking your request to the central appeal.

HOTEL MANAGEMENT

15. Disappointing Services: Request for Adjustment

⇨ *Level 2* ⇦

The letter should

1. Seek to gain attention and introduce a central appeal, for example, complimentary remarks about the exemplary reputation of the hotel, the reason you chose it for your fifth wedding anniversary.

2. Present the specific reasons you were disappointed with your stay, stating them in terms of the central appeal and leading logically to the request. Use objective, verifiable statements presented as tactfully as possible. Avoid strong adjectives and adverbs and superlatives that decrease your credibility.

3. Request the amount of refund you believe you deserve—for example, difference between luxury hotel and mid-level hotel (your second choice)—linking your request to the central appeal—exemplary reputation (or central selling point you develop).

COMMUNITY SERVICE

16. Securing Volunteer Services for Service Organization

⇨ *Level 2* ⇦

1. Seek to gain attention by using one of the techniques presented in the "First Paragraph: An Attention-Getter" section; e.g., compliment on receiver's past involvement with community activities. Present a central appeal.

2. Describe the organization's needs (services the receiver can contribute) in context of the receiver's benefits. Continue to focus on the central appeal.

3. Present objective evidence to convince the receiver to provide the services; continue to focus on the central appeal.

4. Request that the receiver provide his/her services, restating the benefits to be gained from volunteering.

MANAGEMENT/Technology

17. Investigating Online Connections Important for Company Productivity

⇨ *Level 3* ⇦

See **TM 11–16** (Good Solution, Application 17) for suggested memorandum. Ask students to refer to the "Online Information Services" section of Chapter 5 for background information. Consulting additional resources will allow students to learn more about the benefits businesses are gaining from online connections and thus equip them to develop convincing evidence to include in the memorandum.

MANAGEMENT/Technology

18. Persuading a Manager to Start a FaxFood Line

⇨ *Level 3* ⇦

1. See **TM 11–17** (Good Solution, Application 18, Step 1) for suggested memorandum.

2. See **TM 11–18** (Good Solution, Application 18, Step 2) for suggested letter.

3. Solutions will vary; however, the form should have the following sections: (a) heading with deli name and title (FaxFood Order Form), (b) delivery address and telephone and fax number, (c) numbered menu items with prices, and (d) a table with columns for customer's name, and items ordered. Include several rows in the table for multiple individual orders from one office. Ask students to refer to the "Graphic Design Principles" section in Chapter 5 for assistance in designing the form.

MIS/Technology/Ethics/Legal

19. Convincing Employees to Follow Computer Security Policy

⇨ *Level 3* ⇦

See **TM 11–19** (Good Solution, Application 19) for suggested memorandum. Ask students to refer to the "Sharing Data" and "Legal and Ethical Implications of Technology" sections in Chapter 5 for background information. Consulting additional resources will allow students to identify computer security safeguards. The suggested solution focuses on lack of confidentiality in e-mail and the importance of logging out when leaving a terminal. Students' solutions might include requiring the use of a password and enforcing routine changes of passwords, writing passwords that are difficult to break, assigning user identification passwords that limit information a person can observe and change, and others.

COLLECTION/Legal

20. Collecting an Overdue Payment

⇨ *Level 2* ⇦

Inquiry:

1. State that the payment is past due.

2. Use empathy to seek an explanation for the nonpayment; however, do not provide an excuse or mention that payment was overlooked.

3. Request that Stan explain any special problem that prevents his paying or send a check for $100. Refer to the enclosed pre-addressed envelope (included to encourage quick action).

Appeal:

1. Open with an appeal to Stan's sense of fairness—you prepared the signs, and he agreed to pay by specified dates.

2. Review the situation, leading to the necessary action he must take to meet his side of the agreement—the fair thing to do.

3. Request payment. Refer to the enclosed pre-addressed envelope (included to encourage quick action).

Second Appeal:

1. State exactly how long overdue the payment is.

2. Introduce an appeal to Stan's prestige as an upstanding member of the community, a candidate for public office.

3. Continue to build the appeal by stressing he can maintain his prestige by paying his bill and commencing with a regular payment schedule.

4. Request the payment, emphasizing his pride in his community stature.

Stronger Appeal:

1. Restate the status of his overdue account.

2. Emphasize firmly but tactfully the reasons the amount must be paid—for example, continually accumulating interest, fairness of paying for work performed, possible negative effects nonpayment has on his credit standing, possibility of turning his account over to a collection agency, and possible litigation.

3. Request payment within specified time. If company policy permits, offer to accept an interest-bearing note for payment.

4. Remind Stan that he must pay or accept the consequences of nonpayment. Letter should be signed by top company executive.

Ultimatum:

1. Review briefly the sequence of events leading to the present—a time when payment *must* be received or Stan must face the consequences of his actions.

2. Use forceful but tactful language to demand payment by a specified date. State your action (turn the account over to a collection agency, courts, or an attorney) and the consequences of a poor credit rating.

3. Restate the deadline, emphasizing the positive results of paying by that date. Letter should be signed by top company executive.

POSSIBLE SOLUTIONS TO CASES FOR ANALYSIS

MARKETING/Legal

1. Determining the Legal Implications of Using a Person's Photograph in an Advertisement

⇨ *Level 4* ⇦

1. Students will research answers to the questions provided. Encourage them to talk to public relations professors or practitioners as well as to consult the literature.

2. Sources will vary; however, research should reveal the following legal guidelines: Car dealership must get the person's consent and clarify how the picture will be used (e.g., assure the family their photograph will not be used in an objectionable manner; if the picture is to be altered, describe the alteration). No specific legal guideline requires you to pay a fee. However, because this advertising should increase your sales, you probably should offer the family a small fee. (Students could seek advice from advertising professors or practitioners to determine a fair fee.)

3. See **TM 11–20** (Good Solution, Case for Analysis 1, Step 3) for suggested letter.

MARKETING/Ethics   GMAT

2. Charitable Contributions or Shrewd Public Relations?

⇨ *Level 4* ⇦

1. The letter should follow the inductive, persuasive pattern.

2. Analysis of the problem:

   a. *Relevant facts*. Refer to the case.

   b. *Ethical issues*. Is donating bottled water to the troops ethical?

      Legal restrictions. None apply.

      Contractual. None apply.

      Code of ethics. No company or professional code of ethics exists.

   c. *Stakeholders*. Bottled water company, stockholders, troops, competitors, society.

   d. *Cost/benefit analysis*. See Figure 11–1. Alternative: Donating the bottled water.

   e. *Obligations to stakeholders*. See Figure 11–2.

   f. Answers should be graded based on students' analysis of the facts and the objective support of their decisions. Therefore, no conclusion is provided with the analysis.

3. Solutions will vary.

MARKETING/Technology

3. Developing Support for a Worthy Community Effort

⇨ *Level 4* ⇦

1. Basic revisions to the letter include the following:

   a. The first paragraph seeks to gain attention by providing a more enticing title and introducing a familiar phrase that introduces the central selling point.

   b. The deductive sequence-of-idea pattern is changed to persuasive because the message is not routine. The receiver must be *persuaded* to participate in the community project.

   c. The idea of sharing with others is introduced as the central selling point in the first paragraph, developed throughout the message, and mentioned at the end

   to reinforce the benefit of participation in the project.

   d. The reference to "we" is eliminated, and the receiver is used as the subject in active-voice sentences.

   e. The presumptuous ending is replaced with a reference to the central selling point. To assure easy action, a date and place are added for delivery of the toys.

   f. The unnecessary abbreviations and ciphers after even amounts are eliminated.

   g. The form is moved to the bottom of the page so that it can be detached, leaving the receiver access to pertinent information about the project. Also, checking the date the receiver is available to work reduces effort and the chance of error.

2. See **TM 11–21** (Good Solution, Case for Analysis 3, Step 2) for suggested layout.

Stakeholder	Cost	Benefit
Bottled water company	◆ Cost of the water donated; possible criticism for "exploiting" a military conflict to enhance company image and for exposing troops to product.	◆ Enhanced company image as result of the donation (patriotic support); exposure of product to troops may develop future product loyalty.
Stockholders	◆ Short-term reduction in profits; risk that short-term costs will not be offset by increased sales resulting from product's exposure.	◆ Exposure of product to troops could lead to increased long-term profitability.
Troops	◆ None.	◆ Have access to fresh, sterile water necessary for survival.
Competitors	◆ May lose an opportunity to develop product loyalty and enhance company image.	◆ None.
Society	◆ None.	◆ Reduces the cost of military operation.

Figure 11–1 ◆ 2. Cost/benefit analysis of donating the bottled water

Stakeholder	Obligation
Bottled water company	◆ Keeps promise to maximize long-term earnings.
Stockholders	◆ Keeps promise to maximize return on investment.
Troops	◆ Shows gratitude for service to country.
Competitors	◆ Acts justly by using fair and ethical marketing strategies.
Society	◆ Shows gratitude by accepting civic responsibility.

Figure 11–2 ◆ 2. Obligations to stakeholders

```
VIDEO CONNECTION
    Tracy-Locke/Pharr Public Relations
CHAPTER 11:
    Writing to Persuade
```

SUMMARY

I. Characteristics of a Sales Letter
   A. Call to action
   B. Persuasive
   C. Parallel to a personal sales call
   D. Receiver oriented

II. Responsibilities of the Writer of Persuasive Letters
   A. View self as a medium to connect the receiver to the product/idea
   B. Have a good opening
      1. Must grab the receiver
      2. Must compel the receiver to continue reading
   C. Know the needs of the audience
   D. Prioritize features of your product/service in order of the needs of the audience
      1. Stress top needs
      2. Build your case
      3. Give the receiver reasons to take action

III. Tips for Persuasive Writing
   A. Be concise—value the time of others
   B. Use facts and figures to convince
   C. Avoid pitfalls—misspellings, wrong titles (assuming gender incorrectly), and the like.

ANSWERS TO DISCUSSION QUESTIONS

1. **Cynthia Pharr likens the sales letter to a personal sales call. Explain how the two activities are similar.** In both the persuasive letter and the sales call, the purpose is to convince the receiver to take action or accept an idea. In both cases, the opening is crucial: The salesperson has 10 to 15 seconds to capture the attention of the client; the writer must have an effective opening sentence that compels the receiver to continue reading. The writer and the salesperson must know the needs of the audience as well as being expertly versed in the product/idea.

2. **Michael Fleming puts forth the idea that practicing conciseness shows concern for your receiver/audience. Explain this concept.** Conciseness means that every word is necessary for a clear understanding of the message; no words are wasted. Because businesspeople view time as money, the considerate writer will get to the point and not mince words.

3. **What constitutes an effective opening for a sales letter? Give examples of techniques that may attract the receiver's attention. What should the writer guard against in structuring the opening?** An effective opening catches the immediate attention of the receiver and compels him or her to continue reading. Pharr mentioned the following techniques as effective openings: a question, an interesting fact, an analogy, a story, and an extreme interest of the receiver. Leonardo described the ideal opening as a fantastic, snappy lead but cautioned against developing an opening that might seem fluffy or cute to the receiver. The writer must guard against uninteresting openings.

4. **Explain the concept of being receiver-oriented. How is this idea applied in a persuasive message?** "Receiver-oriented" implies that every part of the letter is written with the needs of the receiver clearly in mind. Thus, the opening is designed to command the attention of the receiver. The discussion of the selling features is structured according to priorities that appeal to the receiver. Convincing facts and figures that the receiver will need to reach the desired decision are offered. The closing is action-oriented, making responding easy and attractive for the receiver.

5. **How do surface characteristics, such as the envelope and stationery, affect the receivers' responses to a persuasive letter?** The physical appearance of the document is extremely important in making the desired impression on the receiver. Pharr believes that carelessness in this regard kills content. The receiver may make an early negative judgment about the letter based on the envelope or stationery; this negativity may preclude his/her consideration of the written message.

POSSIBLE SOLUTION TO APPLICATION

Solutions will vary.

MULTIPLE CHOICE QUESTIONS

1. An effective sales letter
   a. is writer centered.
   b. lists as many benefits of the product/idea as can be covered in a one-page format.
   ✔ c. uses facts and figures to convince the receiver.
   d. does all the above.

2. Which of the following does *not* apply to the opening of an effective persuasive letter?
   ✔ a. outlines the desired action you want from the receiver.
   b. compels the receiver to continue reading.
   c. is, ideally, a fantastic, snappy lead-in.
   d. may be a question, interesting fact, or an analogy.

3. The strongest reason for practicing conciseness is that
   ✔ a. it shows concern for the value of the receiver's time.
   b. it reveals a thorough knowledge of the writer's product or idea.
   c. it reflects a logical pattern in writing.
   d. it directs the receiver to the desired action.

4. Misspellings, wrong titles, and similar occurrences
   a. may actually have the positive effect of showing the receiver that the writer is human.
   b. are generally overlooked by the receiver because he or she is primarily interested in the message.
   c. are distracting to the receiver but tolerated as a normal part of business letters.
   ✔ d. kill the content of the letter, no matter how creative and well written the message may be.

5. The typical receiver response to an unsolicited sales letter is to
   ✔ a. look for any reason to discard the letter.
   b. read the letter carefully in hopes that it will address a need.
   c. read the letter thoroughly, then put it away for further action.
   d. skip over the less interesting parts of the letter to get to the more pertinent parts.

CHAPTER 12

WRITING SPECIAL LETTERS

CHAPTER OVERVIEW

The special letters covered in Chapter 12 represent a variety of writing tasks that most people face at one time or another. Emphasis should be placed on the human relations aspects of such communications.

Depending on the stress given letters/memorandums in the course, special letters may be covered briefly with the comment that the chapter can be used as a "reference manual" for writing special letters. On the other hand, students may look on this chapter as an opportunity to consolidate previous learning. Like most educators and businesspeople, students are inclined to do each day what *must* be done. Anything that *can* wait *will* wait. Writers often postpone writing letters that express sympathy, congratulations, gratitude, and so on until too long a period of time has lapsed. If students could emerge from the study of Chapter 12 committed to take time to write special letters, the time will have been well spent.

LEARNING OBJECTIVES

1 Write messages that congratulate, acknowledge congratulations, thank you, welcome, wish farewell, and invite.

2 Compose seasonal messages that extend appreciation.

3 Compose a condolence and an apology.

4 Write an effective news release.

5 Write letters that identify situations that deserve commendation and those that need improvement.

CHAPTER OUTLINE AND TEACHING SUGGESTIONS

1	LEARNING OBJECTIVE

I. Congratulations
   A. Show **TA 12–1** (Chapter Opener) as you begin the discussion.
   B. Additional ways to introduce the chapter include the following:
      1. Ask students if they had an outstanding instructor last semester. Ask students if they bothered to express their gratitude. If so, was it an oral expression or a written expression?
      2. Ask students if they have written a thank-you letter or congratulatory letter in the past year? Who thought about it but never got around to it? Responses will almost certainly confirm the point that most people do not take the time.
      3. Because most people do not bother to write special letters, those who *do* write them have a good chance of making an impact. A U.S. congressman says that for every letter he receives expressing a certain point of view, he assumes that at least a hundred others thought about sending the same message but just did not take the time.
      4. A travel agent who has planned tours for thousands says that almost no one has ever bothered to write, call, or stop by her office to thank her after returning from an enjoyable trip. In her mind, anyone who does stop by to express gratitude is a very special person (and will get the utmost in service when a subsequent trip is planned).

5. Emphasize the fact that most special letters may be keyed and printed or written in longhand. Etiquette authorities, of course, much prefer longhand messages to cover very personal circumstances. Have students complete Exercise 2, which requires students to present a documented debate of this issue in small groups.

C. Writing Congratulations

D. Replying to Congratulations

II. Thank-you Messages

A. Ask each student to compose and *send* a letter to someone who has been especially helpful to them in some way.

B. As responses to those letters are received, ask students to share them with the class.

C. Assign Application 1 from the *Study Guide*, a thank you for a scholarship award.

1. Discuss the communication pointers and prepare an outline for the letter in small groups. Ask a spokesperson to report to the class if time permits.

2. Assign the letter to be written individually or in groups. Discuss the effective writing techniques incorporated in the revision in the *Study Guide*.

III. Welcomes and Farewells

A. Assign Application 10, 11, or 12 for classwork/homework.

B. Lead students in a discussion of the benefits that arise for both the writer and the receivers of such letters.

IV. Invitations

A. Ask students to brainstorm in small groups to identify a situation that requires the sending of invitations to prospective guests/attendees. Such situations may be related to college or business activities.

B. Require students to design a printed invitation and to compose a letter invitation for the selected situation. Lead students in a discussion of the advantages of each.

2	LEARNING OBJECTIVE

V. Seasonal Messages

A. Lead students in a discussion as to whether seasonal messages for such observances as Thanksgiving and Christmas are appropriate for businesses to send to clients, customers, or employees in light of international/intercultural concerns.

B. Ask students to compose a secular "Christmas" seasonal message acceptable for Christian, Jewish, and Buddhist receivers.

3	LEARNING OBJECTIVE

VI. Condolences

A. Assign Application 14 for classwork/homework.

B. Lead students in a discussion as to whether sending a printed card would be easier than writing such a letter? Would a card be as effective?

VII. Apologies

A. Assign Application 13 for classwork/homework.

B. Lead students in a discussion as to the preferred channel for communicating such a message: telephone, e-mail, memorandum, etc.

C. Assign Case 1 to reinforce the importance of courtesy to international understanding.

4	LEARNING OBJECTIVE

VIII. News Releases

A. Assign Application 15 for completion in small groups.

B. Ask groups to exchange papers and critique the releases for organization, style, content, and format.

5	LEARNING OBJECTIVE

IX. Commendations and Constructive Criticisms

   A.   Emphasize that writing these letters is a part of civic responsibility and stress the following points:

      1.   The motive of letters that commend should be to encourage and to give deserved recognition; saying something favorable for the purpose of later gaining a reward from the receiver is *not* a legitimate motive.

      2.   The motive of letters that point out negatives should be to help; vindication is *not* a legitimate motive.

   B.   Commendations

      1.   Assign Application 2 from the *Study Guide*, a commendation to a former teacher.

         a.   Discuss the communication pointers and prepare an outline for the letter in small groups. Ask a spokesperson to report to the class if time permits.

         b.   Assign the letter to be written individually or in groups. Discuss the effective writing techniques incorporated in the revision in the *Study Guide*.

      2.   Assign Exercise 5 for classwork/ homework. Show **TA 12–2** (Good Solution, Exercise 5) as you review the commendation.

   C.   Constructive Criticisms

   D.   Assign Application 20 for classwork/ homework.

      1.   Show **TA 12–3** (Poor Solution, Application 20) as you discuss the content of a constructive criticism communication.

      2.   Show **TA 12–4** (Critical Thinking Questions, Application 20) as you continue the discussion of how to structure constructive criticism.

      3.   Show **TA 12–5** (Good Solution, Application 20) as you review the suggested solution.

X.   Communication in Action: Honorable Ronnie Musgrove, Mississippi State Senator

   A.   Ask students to read the case and complete the applications for homework.

   B.   Show **TM 12–1** (Good Solution, "Communication in Action" case) as you review the solution to the letter.

XI.   Summary

   A.   Integrate the communication mentor comments into class lectures to reinforce the concepts in the chapter.

   B.   Assign the *Study Guide* questions for Chapter 12. This chapter includes 15 true/false and 15 multiple choice questions.

   C.   Assign the *Study Guide* applications for Chapter 12. Require students to complete the practical applications that "walk students through" writing (a) a letter expressing thanks for a scholarship and (b) a letter thanking an instructor for an excellent course. Critical thinking questions help students organize their thoughts and outline correctly; students write solutions using their outlines, and compare their solutions with a sample solution and a detailed commentary that highlights the strengths of the outline and the solution. In a third application, students analyze a poorly written letter and identify errors and weaknesses. Critical thinking questions guide students through the analysis.

   D.   Ask students to complete the e-mail application.

   E.   Assign selected exercises, applications, and cases at the end of the chapter. Remind students to study the suggestions in the "Check Your Writing" checklist when planning and revising an assignment.

   F.   Assign selected cases for analysis at the end of the chapter. **TM 12–10** (Good Solution, Case for Analysis 1, Step 2) and **TM 12–11** (Case for Analysis 2, Step 2a) are provided as solutions.

   G.   Assign one of the applications designated as an AWA (Analytical Writing Assessment) for the GMAT. Refer to pages 12–13 of this *Instructor's Resource Manual* for holistic scoring techniques used by evaluators of this written portion of the GMAT.

TRANSPARENCIES AND MASTERS

ADDITIONAL READINGS

Half, R. (Ed.). (1992). Managing your career:
     How do I manage people? *Management
     Accounting, 73*(9), 12.

Harris, T. E. (1988). Mastering the art of talking
     back. *Management World, 17*(3), 9–11.

Honacker, C. (1989). Bad news for news releases.
     Association Management, 41(3), 87–90, 91.

Larson, K. (1991). How to recognize your staffers'
     contribution. *Supervisory Management,
     36*(8), 8.

Longo, D. (1994). Communication, key to being a
     better leader. *Discount Store News, 33*(5), 9.

ANSWERS TO "COMMUNICATION IN ACTION" CASE: Honorable Ronnie Musgrove, Mississippi State Senator

1. **When Senator Musgrove receives a letter from a constituent, what is the importance of a written response expressing genuine concern and interest in the issue the constituent raised?** The issue about which constituents write genuinely affect them. The senator's letter will show his genuine interest in and concern for the constituent. The senator may also empathize with the constituent.

2. **Assume that you work as an aide in Senator Musgrove's office. A constituent, who is an educator working for a public school, had written the senator objecting to the handling of her insurance claim. The educator explained that she lost a portion of her deductible during a change in insurance administrators. The senator asked you to draft a letter for him, expressing his concern for her loss and explaining that the issue will be addressed. Draft a letter to Jolene Forrest, 250 Hampton Circle, Jackson, MS 39288–0250. See TM 12–1** (Good Solution, "Communication in Action" case) for a suggested letter.

ANSWERS TO REVIEW QUESTIONS

1. Sending congratulatory messages provides an excellent way for managers to build goodwill. Elections, promotions, births, weddings, and engagements are all occasions for congratulatory messages.

2. (b) A memorandum or e-mail message is likely to have the stronger impact because (a) few others will bother to write a message, (b) memorandums and e-mail messages (for most people) require more time and thought, and (c) they can be kept or shown to others.

3. Handwritten messages have a personal quality and may seem warmer and more sincere; keyboarded messages permit more to be said, and busy managers can prepare them more efficiently.

4. In most cases, letters of congratulations should be answered. The most common pitfalls are in (a) hinting at unworthiness or (b) sounding egotistical.

5. (a) Deductive presentation is normally preferred for special letters. Appearing in the first sentence, the main idea receives the emphasis it deserves.

6. A thank-you note for a gift should (a) identify the gift, (b) tell something positive about it, and (c) describe how it will be used.

7. An informal invitation resembles a business letter but may be keyboarded on smaller-sized, executive stationery. Wording should be conversational, as though the writer were extending the invitation orally.

8. In a seasonal message, a sales pitch would (a) take emphasis away from the main idea

and (b) risk making the receiver feel "tricked" into reading.

9. Include brief, sincere, personal statements about experiences with the departing person, for example, special interests, skills, accomplishments, or mutual problems.

10. The *closeness of the relationship* determines whether to send a printed card or a personalized letter. For close friends, a personalized letter is better.

11. The outline for a condolence is (a) start with a statement of sympathy, (b) follow with sentences about mutual experiences or relationships, and (3) close with some words of comfort and affection.

12. (a) The deductive sequence is better for news releases. Placed in the first sentence, the major idea gets the emphasis it deserves. Receivers who skim through a newspaper article are more likely to read the first sentence than any other.

13. Major points for news releases are as follows: (a) write deductively with concern for brevity and clarity, (b) give sufficient information, (c) include preferred date for publication of message, (d) include the name of the contact person, and (e) use company letterhead.

14. The rewards for writing a commendation letter are intangible. Writers feel good about saying something that will make another person happy and encouraging continuation of behavior from which many may benefit. Such positive thoughts may have a beneficial effect on the writer's own attitude and performance.

15. If descriptive words are overly strong, the message may seem insincere.

16. The writer risks (a) being categorized as a complainer, (b) being associated with negative thoughts and thus thought of in negative terms, or (c) being willing to challenge supervisors' decisions.

17. Judgmental terms should be avoided. If the facts are well presented, the receiver will form a judgment. To the receiver, a self-derived conclusion is more meaningful than a writer-derived conclusion. Use of judgmental terms invites use of negative language; they may also raise questions about whether the writer is qualified to judge.

18. No. In an apology message, one statement of apology is enough. Stating the apology again (or making a reference to it) makes the message longer than necessary. An apology forces a receiver to recall an unpleasant situation; a second apology unnecessarily amplifies it.

19. (a) "Please accept my apology..." is better. The "would like to" adds unnecessary words and also makes the statement conditional. The words imply "If certain circumstances were different, I *would* apologize." The words "Please accept my apology" do just that. The words "I would like to apologize" merely express a desire to do so.

20. No. The mistake is already large enough in the receiver's mind. Strong descriptive words may magnify it, or the receiver may begin to think of the words as accurate. Such reactions to their use would work against the writer's purpose.

POSSIBLE SOLUTIONS TO EXERCISES

1. Focus on activities that encourage students to reflect on and understand the principles covered in the chapter.

2. Following initial discussion of the topic, organize the class into two groups to debate this topic, using the authoritative sources referred to in the exercise.

3. This student-led discussion will be more effective than having students read the material from the text or listen to a instructor-directed lecture, and the discussion provides an interesting change in the class structure. Ask students to share personal experiences in which sending goodwill messages helped an organization (or an individual) achieve goals. Refer to the discussion of stroking in Chapter 1.

4. a. Uses wordy cliché ("I would like to"); uses first person to present a positive idea, resulting in a writer-centered tone. Revise using second person.

   b. Includes an unnecessary negative comment that overshadows the thank you in the remainder of the sentence.

   c. Uses first person to present a positive idea; therefore, sentence is writer-centered; revise using second person.

   d. Uses superlative ("worst") that the receiver may believe is exaggerated, making the message seem insincere.

e. Uses general, exaggerated comment that makes the receiver question the genuineness of the compliment.

f. Uses overly harsh words ("I am sorry" and "irresponsible") that perhaps the receiver has not considered. "Please accept my apology" is better.

g. Uses a long egotistical description and first person; eliminate the obvious introductory phase and use second person as the subject.

5. Refer to **TA 12–2** (Solution, Exercise 5) for solution. A summary of organization, content, style, and format errors follows:

Summary of Organization, Content, Style, and Format Errors

Organization	◆ Uses an inductive approach rather than deductive outline required for letters that convey good news. Good news does not appear until the third sentence. Timing of memorandum is excellent.
Content	◆ The negative discussion and the term "cut-rate" (possible red flag word to this supervisor) may mislead him to believe this letter is a disciplinary message. The thank you in the last sentence is overshadowed by the lavish praise for the company's products.
	◆ Perhaps the last sentence of the second paragraph is an attempt to empathize with the receiver; however, the graphic description of his job ("boredom and fatigue") could be perceived as demeaning.
Style	◆ "We" orientation defeats the purpose of communicating genuine appreciation for outstanding performance. The receiver is not the subject of a single sentence.
Format	◆ Correctly formatted as a simplified memorandum, an appropriate format for a message sent inside an organization.

POSSIBLE SOLUTION TO E-MAIL APPLICATION

Preferred channels are as follows:

Notice of employee dismissal: mailed memorandum preferred since the situation requires privacy and formality.

Thanks for a job well done on a special project: mailed or faxed memorandum or handwritten note preferred because a tangible communication is more meaningful.

Employee performance appraisal: mailed memorandum necessary for official and confidential communication.

Condolence message: informal mailed letter (or handwritten card) preferred.

Congratulations on marriage: informal mailed letter preferred.

Apology for problem incurred in handling a transaction: mailed letter preferred for adequate apology.

POSSIBLE SOLUTIONS AND RECOMMENDED OUTLINES TO APPLICATIONS

MANAGEMENT/International

1. **Congratulations on Completion of Spanish Course**

⇨ *Level 2* ⇦

See **TM 12–2** (Good Solution, Application 1, Step 2) for suggested memorandum.

MANAGEMENT

2. **Praise to Well-deserving Employees**

⇨ *Level 2* ⇦

See **TM 12–3** (Good Solution, Application 2) for suggested memorandum.

MANAGEMENT

3. **A Job Well Done**

⇨ *Level 2* ⇦

The memorandum should

1. Express congratulations for excellent performance.

2. List some of the specific elements of the service that were effective, enjoyable, or helpful to show that your motive is genuine.

3. Restate the congratulations with expectations of future success.

MANAGEMENT/Ethical

4.   Response to Commendation for High Ethical Standards

⇨ *Level 2* ⇦

The memorandum should

1. Express thanks for president's positive comments in today's e-mail message.

2. Look positively to the future, for example, appreciation for working for company whose managers set high ethical standards.

Because the message was received by e-mail, the receiver may respond in the same manner. If an electronic-mail program is available, pair students and have them send the message to each other. If software is not available, have them prepare the message using word-processing software but format it according to the e-mail format shown in the text.

MARKETING/International

5.   Help from Overseas: Letter of Appreciation

⇨ *Level 2* ⇦

See **TM 12–4** (Poor Solution, Application 5) as a weak solution to the letter. **TM 12–5** (Good Solution, Application 5) illustrates an acceptable thank-you letter.

EDUCATION/Public Sector

6.   A Political Stand for Education: Letter of Appreciation

⇨ *Level 3* ⇦

The letter should

1. Thank the representative for his or her support of the education reform bill.

2. Include thanks for specific actions to increase the genuineness of the letter; for example, discuss the favorable reaction in your hometown to the speech supporting the bill after the speech was aired on national television.

3. Close by restating your support of his or her work as your representative and asking for his or her continued support of education.

Students must (a) locate the name and address of their representative and (b) refer to the "Standard Letter Parts, Salutation" section in Appendix A or a reference manual

to determine that "Honorable" is the appropriate courtesy title and "Dear Mr. or Ms. (Surname)" is the appropriate salutation for a U.S. representative.

CAREER DEVELOPMENT

7.   Writing a letter of Deserved Thanks

⇨ *Level 2* ⇦

See **TM 12–6** (Good Solution, Application 7) for suggested letter.

SMALL BUSINESS

8.   Thank You for Business Referrals

⇨ *Level 2* ⇦

See **TM 12–7** (Good Solution, Application 8) for suggested letter.

CAREER DEVELOPMENT

9.   Letter of Appreciation for Assistance in Job Placement

⇨ *Level 2* ⇦

See **TM 12–8** (Good Solution, Application 9) for suggested letter.

EDUCATION

10. Welcome New Members

⇨ *Level 2* ⇦

The letter should

1. Open with genuine welcome to the business organization *(specify)*.

2. Explain briefly the benefits the member can gain from active involvement; highlight several of the regular activities held by the organization.

3. Invite the member to the next meeting; provide time, place, and program description (or provide a calendar of the semester's activities). Provide the names of several officers (membership director, program chair, adviser) who can answer additional questions.

4. Close with positive thought and expectation that the member will be actively involved in the year's activities.

PUBLIC RELATIONS

11. Welcome to the Club: A Public Relations Tool

⇨ *Level 2* ⇦

The letter should

1. Welcome Ray as a member of the Pueblo Civic Club and a member of the business community; might include complimentary remarks about his delicatessen.

2. Mention the Civic Club is an excellent way to meet the other business owners/managers and to become involved in the Pueblo community immediately. Might mention an annual activity that unites the entire community.

3. Close with expectation of seeing him at the next meeting and the success of his delicatessen.

FINANCE

12. Farewell and Thanks for ...

⇨ *Level 2* ⇦

The letter should

1. Express disappointment to Kent that you will not be working with him any longer now that he is retiring.

2. Express appreciation for his "mentoring" over the years. List specific incidents to increase the genuineness of the message.

3. Wish him happiness and relaxation in his retirement. (Closing statement can be personal and genuine if you allude to specific plans he has for retirement).

HUMAN RELATIONS

13. Apology for Missed Meeting

⇨ *Level 2* ⇦

See **TM 12–9** (Good Solution, Application 13) for suggested memorandum.

MANAGEMENT

14. An Expression of Sympathy

⇨ *Level 2* ⇦

The letter should

1. Extend condolences for recent loss; use general language to soften the negative.

2. Include brief statement about the relationship and memorable experiences you had with the friend.

3. Close with additional words of comfort.

PUBLIC RELATIONS

15. Employee Promotion: News Release

⇨ *Level 2* ⇦

The news release should

1. Open with summary statement that answers the five Ws.

2. Discuss Sonja's history with the company, emphasizing her accomplishments and not the company.

3. Provide biographical information about Sonja for community interest.

EDUCATION

16. To a Professor: A Job Well Done

⇨ *Level 2* ⇦

Solutions will vary, but should

1. Extend thanks for the excellent/enjoyable course you completed under the instructor.

2. Include specifics of what the professor did well to make the message seem sincere.

3. Close by restating appreciation for the professor's excellent performance; may include comment about your plans for the future and best wishes to the professor in his or her work.

Note: Application 2 in the *Study Guide* assists the student in writing a letter of appreciation to an instructor or another person who has influenced the writer. A sample solution and commentary highlighting the strengths of the solution are provided.

MANAGEMENT

17. Excellent Performance Commended

⇨ *Level 2* ⇦

The letter should

1. State enthusiastically, yet sincerely, your satisfaction with Amanda's performance.

2. Include specifics of the commendable job Amanda has done for the firm.

3. Close by restating your satisfaction with Amanda's performance; may include a state-

ment about your looking forward to being assigned other interns of similar caliber.

JOURNALISM

18. Blowing the Whistle: A Positive Evaluation

⇨ *Level 2* ⇦

The memorandum should

1. Congratulate Wayne for his courageous actions.

2. Using specific language, commend Wayne for his ethical standards and let him know that the company values an employee like him.

EDUCATION/Interpersonal

19. An Attempt to Help Others: Constructive Criticism

⇨ *Level 2* ⇦

The letter should

1. Begin with neutral statement indicating your purpose for writing.

2. Present only those negative qualities that can be verified; use de-emphasis techniques and leave judgment to the receiver. Include positive facts to add credibility to the letter.

3. Close with a request for confidentiality and assure the receiver that your motive is to help.

ACCOUNTING/Interpersonal

20. Shortcomings in Professional Behavior Overshadow Strong Technical Skills: Constructive Criticism

⇨ *Level 2* ⇦

See **TA 12–5** (Good Solution, Application 20) for suggested letter. **TA 12–3** (Poor Solution, Application 20) and **TA 12–4** (Critical Thinking Questions, Application 20) may be used to review the assignment with students.

POSSIBLE SOLUTIONS AND RECOMMENDED OUTLINES TO CASES FOR ANALYSIS

MANAGEMENT/International

1. Promoting International Understanding Rather Than Reacting to Problems

⇨ *Level 4* ⇦

1. Students must decide whether the letter should be formatted as a traditional U.S. letter or in an acceptable Mexican format. Refer students to the "Written Communication" section of Chapter 4. Additionally, texts used in collegiate Spanish courses contain a brief section on business communication.

Recommended Outline for Apology:

I. State the apology directly using general terms.

II. State actions you plan to take to ensure that this mistake does not happen again; refer to actions you will take in Step 2 that follows.

III. Close with positive look to the future; do *not* repeat the apology.

2. See **TM 12–10** (Good Solution, Case for Analysis 1, Step 2) for suggested memorandum. Refer students to the "Special Letter Parts: Copy Notation" section in Appendix A to format the copy notation correctly.

3. The cover letter should

   a. Recognize the problem of negative fall-out being felt because U.S. managers are not prepared for overseas assignments.

   b. Encourage Ms. Silva to initiate efforts to alleviate this difficulty for future employees.

MANAGEMENT/Public Sector

2. Gaining Support for a Plastics Recycling Plant

⇨ *Level 4* ⇦

1. The letter should

   a. State your recommendation that the plastics recycling plant be built in Monroeville.

   b. Discuss the pros and cons of the decision.

c.   Support your decision with justifiable reasons.

d.   Restate your wholehearted support of the Monroeville location for the plant.

2.   a.   See **TM 12–11** (Good Solution, Case for Analysis 2, Step 2a) for suggested letter.

b.   Solutions will vary.

c.   Solutions will vary.

ACCOUNTING/Ethics   **GMAT**

3.   **Is Overlooking a Vendor's Error to Your Advantage Ethical?**

⇨ *Level 4* ⇦

1.   Analysis of the problem:

a.   *Relevant facts.* Refer to the case.

b.   *Ethical issues.* (1) Is overlooking a vendor's error to your advantage ethical? (2) Douglas is faced with the ethical issue of taking what he considers to be a proper action that likely will have negative consequences on his career.

Legal restrictions. None apply.

Contractual. None apply.

Code of ethics. No company or professional code of ethics exists.

c.   *Stakeholders.* Company, supplier, Douglas, supervisor.

d.   *Cost/benefit analysis.* See Figure 12–1. Alternative: to take no action (inferring that overlooking a vendor's error is ethical).

e.   *Obligations to stakeholders.* See Figure 12–2.

f.   Answers should be graded based on the students' analysis of the facts and the objective support of their decisions. Therefore, no conclusion is provided with the analysis.

Stakeholder	Cost	Benefit
Company	◆ Will cause ill will if or when the supplier recognizes the error. Negatively affects its relationship with Douglas, who may resign or suffer from low morale in response to the tone set by management.	◆ Saves $5,000.
Supplier	◆ Loses $5,000	◆ None.
Douglas	◆ May feel disillusioned by management's unethical behavior, possibly lowering morale.	◆ Is perceived as a "team player" and thus will be rewarded for his action.
Supervisor	◆ Reinforces his belief that overlooking the vendor's mistake is ethical.	◆ None.

Figure 12–1 ◆ 3. Cost/benefit analysis of taking no action

Stakeholder	Obligation
Company	◆ Keeps promise to maximize short-term earnings but could hinder long-term productivity (e.g., inability to secure suppliers).
Supplier	◆ Provides fair payment for merchandise purchased.
Douglas	◆ Shows respect for the judgment of an employee placed in a position of responsibility.
Supervisor	◆ Shows respect for supervisor's managerial decision.

Figure 12–2 ◆ 3. Obligations to stakeholders

PART 5

COMMUNICATING ABOUT WORK AND JOBS

Chapters 13–14 deal with employment communications. Chapter 13 covers the writing of effective resumes and application letters. Chapter 14 includes job interviews and writing all other employment communication. The interviewing section also includes practical suggestions for ensuring a successful performance appraisal interview from the interviewer's and interviewee's perspective.

Outstanding skills in these areas cannot be expected to overcome the handicap of poor preparation or lack of aptitude for the job sought. Therefore, this section emphasizes the necessity of self-, career, and job analyses before preparing a resume. Through these analyses, students may become aware that they are actually ill prepared for the careers they have in mind. Perhaps they will have time to make adequate adjustments. Just as success in selling begins with having a good product to sell, success in finding a suitable job begins with having good qualifications. Taking appropriate courses; participating in career-related school activities; working at part-time jobs that lead to a possible career; conducting thorough self-, career, and job analyses; practicing positive human relations; learning to accept responsibility—all these endeavors prepare students for job success. They also contribute greatly to successful resumes, application letters, and interviews. Valuable as communication skills are, determination to have good job qualifications could be even more valuable for some students.

Build time in your schedule to integrate the videotape prepared for Chapter 14, "Job Interviews, Employment Messages, and Performance Appraisals." Require students to read the Video Connection in their texts, which previews the videotape and provides several questions reviewing major points presented. After showing the videotape, initiate a class discussion using the review questions. Suggested answers and five multiple choice questions (to add to an objective test for this unit or to use as a pop quiz) are included in the videotape teaching suggestions immediately following Chapter 14.

CHAPTER 13

PREPARING RESUMES AND APPLICATION LETTERS

CHAPTER OVERVIEW

Chapter 13 will aid students in seeing the need for career planning, gathering information for inclusion on a resume, arranging the information on paper. Additionally, students will learn to locate prospective employers to whom the resume might be sent and to write an effective application letter to accompany the resume.

The chapter includes several examples of resumes and application letters for traditional business positions formatted using desktop publishing capabilities. A format and layout checklist aids students in enhancing employment credentials using advanced technology.

LEARNING OBJECTIVES

1 Complete systematic self-, career, and job analyses.

2 Prepare an effective chronological, functional, or combination chronological and functional resume.

3 Locate information about employers' needs for workers.

4 Write an application letter that effectively introduces an accompanying resume.

CHAPTER OUTLINE AND TEACHING SUGGESTIONS

1   **LEARNING OBJECTIVE**

I. Setting Goals and Planning

  A. Because two major topics are covered in this relatively long chapter—writing resumes and application letters—consider breaking the chapter into two parts.

  B. Require students to read to the "Finding Prospective Employers" section for the first reading assignment and the remainder of the chapter after completing discussion of resume writing.

  C. Impress upon the students the importance of preparing highly professional job credentials that sell their qualifications in terms of employers' names.

    1. Discuss the scenario of the qualified applicant who was not invited for an interview at the beginning of the "Planning Your Resume" section.

    2. Show **TA 13–1** (Chapter Opener) as you discuss the analogy presented in the acetate and the photo on page 409: athletes know that only a split second or a fraction of an inch determines who wins. Ask students to give examples of Olympic or other athletic events that were determined by minute amounts; (e.g., Tommy Moe, downhill skiing gold medalist in the

1994 Olympics, depicted in the photo on page 409).

    3. Share recent examples of the intense competition job applicants are facing: When Mercedes-Benz decided to locate its newest North American plant in Vance, Alabama, more than 31,000 people applied for 1,500 openings. Emphasize that with competition this fierce, job applicants must make sure their application package (application letter, resume, and references) is neat, error-free, and attention-getting. See Roundtree, 1994 in the Additional Readings. Have students locate similar examples from the current literature and share with the class.

  D. Invite guest speakers to discuss the job-search process and present guidelines for preparing winning resumes and application letters. Consider former students, local human resources professors and managers, officials in the school's career services division, or local employment agents.

  E. Integrate the communication mentor comments into class lectures to reinforce the concepts in the chapter. Concepts include concrete advice on preparing winning employment credentials.

II. Getting Essential Information

  A. Self-analysis

    1. Most colleges and universities provide free-of-charge counseling and career services for students. Services often include job aptitude screening, personality inventory testing, etc.

    2. Encourage students, especially those who are unsure as to their career choice, to utilize these services.

  B. Career Analysis

  C. Job Analysis

  D. Interview with a Career Person

    1. Recommend that students arrange to "shadow" a career person for a day, rather than merely conducting an interview, if possible.

2. Observing the career person at work will give a more realistic view of what the job entails.

E. Company/Job Profile

F. Ask students to complete Applications 1–2, which require the completion of self-, career, and job analyses, an interview of a career person, and a company/job profile. This research process will enable students to construct a resume and an application letter that relate their qualifications to an employer's needs.

| 2 | LEARNING OBJECTIVE |

III. Planning Your Resume

A. Lead the class in a discussion of ethical reporting of information in resumes.

   1. Share a recent example covered in the media about inflated credentials such as the following one: Dennis Taylor resigned as dean and director of the School of Marine Science and Virginia Institute of Marine Science of the College of William and Mary after college officials were notified that he had listed a bogus degree on his resume. William and Mary President, Timothy Sullivan, called the resignation "regrettable but necessary." Refer to Paust, 1995 in Additional Readings.

   2. Emphasize that executives suspect that one job candidate in three lies or omits relevant information from his or her resume, a practice that seems to be increasing in today's tight job market (Think It Over note on page 164 in Chapter 6). Initiate a discussion about the consequences of providing false information on a resume.

B. Identification

C. Job and/or Career Objective

D. Summary of Achievements

E. Qualifications

   1. Education

     a. Assign Application 1 from the *Study Guide*, the education section of a chronological resume. Discuss the communication pointers and compose the resume section in small groups or individually. Discuss the effective writing techniques incorporated in the revision.

     b. Ask students to begin identifying information to be included in the education section of their resumes.

   2. Work Experience

     a. Assign Application 2 from the *Study Guide*, the work experience section of a chronological resume. Discuss the communication pointers and compose the resume section in small groups or individually. Discuss the effective writing techniques incorporated in the revision.

     b. Ask students to begin identifying information to be included in the work experience section of their resumes.

   3. Honors and Activities

F. Personal Information

G. References

H. Communication in Action: Julie Thompson Stovall, Merck & Company, Inc.

   1. Assign the case and the applications that follow it.

   2. Make a transparency of **TM 13–1** (Sample Resume) to show as you discuss resume components and how to "beat out" fierce competition for available positions.

IV. Constructing A Resume

A. Before discussing guidelines for constructing a resume, ask students to prepare a resume during the class period and submit it. After Chapter 13 has been read and discussed, return each student's resume. If students can find their own errors, the learning experience is genuine. They may be able to use their first draft in refining the next draft.

B. Selecting the Organizational Plan

1. Chronological Resume
2. Functional Resume
3. Combination Chronological and Functional Resume

C. Enhancing the Layout

D. Examples of Resumes

1. To assess students' understanding of the types of information to be included in a resume, ask students to complete Case for Analysis 1 as a cooperative learning assignment. Students are to analyze the information provided by an employee seeking a job and select the information that should be included in the resume. Initiate a class discussion about the case with reports from a spokesperson from each group. If time permits, require each group to prepare a resume for the employee. Otherwise, project **TM 13–3** (Solution, Case for Analysis 2, Step 2) and discuss the organizational plan (chronological resume), content, and format of the suggested resume.

E. Ask students to complete Application 3, which requires the preparation of a resume for a job of the student's choice.

1. Make a transparency of **TM 13–2** (Checklist for Winning Resume) to show as you prepare students for the assignment.

2. If consistent with your teaching philosophy, make the resume-writing assignment optional.

3. Announce that, for students who choose to do the assignment, you will do your best to make helpful suggestions. They will have a resume that they can update and use quickly when they need it. When the purpose is *to learn* (not to *make a grade*), some students will respond favorably.

4. If some students choose not to take advantage of what is probably their final opportunity to get a instructor's help with a resume, you will have more time to make suggestions on papers that *are* submitted.

3 | **LEARNING OBJECTIVE**

V. Finding Prospective Employers

A. Networks

B. Career Services Centers

1. Arrange a class tour of your institution's career services center.

2. Ask the director of career services to share job-search information with the students. This information will likely be more meaningful to students when provided by the director than when presented by the instructor.

C. Employers' Offices

D. Employment Agencies and Contractors

E. Help-Wanted Ads

F. Online Databases and Printed Sources

1. Stress that the Internet and online services contain (a) a wealth of information about interviewing and the job search, (b) job listings, and (c) job research information such as company background information and names and e-mail addresses of people at specific companies.

2. Ask students to read an article related to online job searches and have them report major ideas to the class—identifying and retrieving a job opening from an online source and submitting a resume, following special format requirements for posting resumes online, etc.

3. Group the students by major and have them generate a list of specific directories and user groups that likely post job announcements in their fields.

4. Invite an MIS professor to serve as a resource speaker to supplement your knowledge of this topic. Ask students and alumni who have sought jobs using online sources to share their experience with the class.

G. Professional Organizations

4	LEARNING OBJECTIVE

VI. Application Letters
   A. Before discussing the "Application Letter" section of Chapter 13, give students a few minutes of class time to write an application letter that would be designed to accompany the resume already prepared.
      1. Without grading the letters, look through them for good illustrations to use in subsequent class discussions.
      2. After students have read about and discussed application letters in class, return each student's letter. Students will learn from their mistakes, and their letters may be useful in preparing improved versions.
   B. Organization
   C. Content
      1. Length
      2. Source of Job Information
      3. Knowledge of Employer's Activities
      4. Knowledge of Job Requirements
      5. Discussion of Your Own Problems
      6. Statements of the Obvious
      7. Current Employer's Shortcomings
      8. Self-condemning Statements
      9. Boastful Connotations
      10. Flattery
      11. Biographical Discourse
   D. Style
      1. Use Language Used on the Job
      2. Avoid Overused Words and Expressions
      3. Encourage Action
   E. Mechanics
   F. Examples of Application Letters
      1. Assign Exercise 2 and/or Exercise 3. Ask students to critique the poorly written application letters using the "Check Your Writing checklist" and revise the letter(s) in class individually or in small groups. Discuss the effective writing techniques incorporated in the revision provided in **TA 13–2** (Good Solution, Exercise 2) and **TA 13–3** (Good Solution, Exercise 3).
      2. Assign Application 3 from the *Study Guide*, the middle paragraph of an application letter. Discuss the communication pointers and compose the paragraph in small groups or individually. Discuss the effective writing techniques incorporated in the revision.
      3. Ask students to complete Application 3, which requires the preparation of an application letter for a job of the student's choice or Application 4, an application letter for a scholarship.
      4. After students have written an effective application letter, ask them to evaluate other students' letters. The "Check Your Writing" checklist can serve as criteria for evaluation. Project selected letters for discussion.
   G. Stress that employers are influenced by nonverbal messages transmitted in the application letter when they deciding whether to interview an applicant. To emphasize this point, initiate a class discussion about the statements shown below. Suggested answers appear in italics.

   What nonverbal messages are transmitted by the following?
      1. Being among the first to respond to a newspaper ad? *(Applicant is not inclined to procrastinate, is quick to take advantage of opportunities.)*
      2. Sending an unsolicited letter? *(Has initiative, has strong preference for a certain employer, or may be sending many letters of application.)*
      3. Using paper of an unusual size or color? *(Is different—could be positively or negatively—from other applicants, wants to be thought of as nontraditional, may be willing to take risks.)*
      4. Applying for "any job you have open"? *(Is desperate for a job, not particularly proficient at any certain job, undecided about his or her life's work.)*

5. Writing about upcoming graduation in the first sentence? *(Is attaching great significance to the degree and may think the degree itself is a primary requisite.)*

6. Stating directly the qualities that an employee should possess? *(Is willing to state points already known by the reader, has underestimated reader's awareness of desirable qualities, or is just trying to communicate his or her own possession of those skills.)*

7. Flattering the employer, making obviously exaggerated statements about the employer's products or accomplishments? *(Is hopeful the nice-sounding words will bring a favorable response, even though qualifications may be weak. Possibly expects the employer to arrange an interview rather than feel guilty about refusing.)*

8. Using very general terms in discussing experience? *(Has not seen the precise relationship between experience and the job sought.)*

9. Using "I" repeatedly? *(Is self-centered or just doesn't know how to avoid use of "I.")*

10. Using clichés? *(Is unimaginative, doesn't know how to avoid clichés, or thinks they are appropriate.)*

11. Revealing familiarity with some of the history, plans, or problems of the company to which an application is sent? *(Is informed, is interested in the company, does homework.)*

12. Using judgmental words to describe achievements? *(Overconfident, conceited, or lacks human-relations skills.)*

13. Using a "pushy" ending? *(Too forward, too demanding, may have poor qualifications and think pushiness is essential for getting an interview.)*

14. Making errors in grammar, spelling, punctuation, and keyboarding? *(Careless, ignorant, disrespectful, or disorganized.)*

15. Sending a follow-up letter after waiting a few days for a response to an application letter? *(Reveals continued interest in a job, has additional information to report, or is persistent.)*

VII. Summary

A. Integrate the communication mentor comments into class lectures to reinforce the concepts presented in the chapter.

B. Instruct students to complete the *Study Guide* questions for Chapter 13.

C. Require students to complete the applications in the *Study Guide*. These applications "walk students through" revising (a) the education section of a chronological resume, (b) the work experience section of a chronological resume, and (c) the middle paragraph of an application letter. Critical thinking questions help students organize their thoughts and write effective solutions; a sample solution and a detailed commentary that highlights the strengths of the solution are provided for each application.

D. Ask students to complete the e-mail application.

E. Assign selected exercises, applications, and cases at the end of the chapter. Remind students to study the suggestions in the "Check Your Writing" checklist when planning and revising an assignment.

F. Assign Case for Analysis 1 as an enrichment exercise. Students are required to prepare guidelines for preparing job credentials for outplaced workers. Students must synthesize information presented in the chapter and conduct additional research to supplement the text and to meet the needs of the audience specified in the case. Require students to prepare an appealing layout for this document if time permits.

TRANSPARENCIES AND MASTERS

TA 13–1   Chapter Opener
TA 13–2   Good Solution, Exercise 2
TA 13–3   Good Solution, Exercise 3

TM 13–1   Sample Resume
TM 13–2   Checklist for Winning Resume
TM 13–3   Solution, Case for Analysis 2, Step 2

ADDITIONAL READINGS

Asher, D. (1992, Spring). Show what you know. *National Business Employment Weekly, 22,* 23.

Asher, D. (1992, Spring). Use your resume to show versatility. *National Business Employment Weekly, 20,* 23.

Bohn, S. J. (1994). Writing a winning resume. *Healthcare Financial Management, 48*(9), 108–109.

Cohen, J. (February 27, 1995). To tell the truth...; It's sometimes a fine line between lying and accentuating the positive. *The Wall Street Journal,* p. R14.

Culwell-Block, B., & Seller, J. A. (1994). Resume content and format: Do the authorities agree? *Bulletin of the Association of Business Communication, 57*(4), 27–30.

Dulek, R., & Suchan, J. A. (1988). Application letters: A neglected area in the job search. *Business Horizons, 31*(6), 70–75.

Eigles, L. (1993). Cover letters: How to sell yourself in writing. Women in Business, 45(6), 28.

Kaul, P. A. (1992). Getting the job. *Association Management, 44*(11), 32–37.

Mannix, M. (1994). Your credentials plus a song and dance: Next time you update your resume, try adding sound and graphics. *U.S. News & World Report, 117*(17), p. 102.

Niculescu, D. E. (1993). Legal developments affecting the selection process. *Supervision, 54*(5), 5–7.

Paust, M. (1995, May 16). College dean quits after admitting bogus degree. *Houston Chronicle,* p. 8A.

Roundtree, D. (1994, August 24). 31,000 Alabamians seek jobs with Mercedes–Benz plant. *Montgomery Advertiser,* p. B2.

Shahnasarian, M. (1990). Tools for employee development: Get a job. *Training & Development Journal, 44*(6), 15–18.

Silver, M. (1990, February). Selling the perfect you. *U.S. News & World Report,* pp. 70–72.

Vitello, J. (1995). Recharge your resume. *Computerworld, 29*(4), 106.

ANSWERS TO "COMMUNICATION IN ACTION" CASE: Julie Thompson Stovall, Merck & Company, Inc.

1. **Select from the organizational plans discussed in Chapter 13 the one you think Stovall followed when writing her resume. Explain your choice.** Stovall most likely selected the traditional chronological plan. At the beginning of her resume, she placed her Summary of Qualifications. The education section followed. She included an "Activities and Memberships" section near the end. This arrangement indicates a chronological pattern.

2. **Assume that you were applying for a position in a large medical corporation. What job analysis questions would you ask yourself before you prepared your resume?** Students may ask what background courses relate to the medical field. Stovall's pre-med courses related to the position. A student's courses in science, allied health, or other related areas may apply. If related courses are limited, would the student be willing to continue his or her education?

ANSWERS TO REVIEW QUESTIONS

1. Developing a career notebook assists in selecting a career and job that are compatible with aptitudes, abilities, and interests. Recording the information helps to reinforce it in memory. In a notebook or computer file, the information can be analyzed and reviewed easily. The notebook should include career-related information such as a self-analysis, a job analysis, a resume, clippings of career- and job-related information, addresses and telephone numbers of potential employers, past employer information, references, transcripts, and notes taken during interviews.

2. *The Dictionary of Occupational Titles* is an ideal source for learning about the duties and responsibilities of a certain job.

3. The purpose of the resume is to present a concise, informative, easy-to-read summary of relevant qualifications which will get an interview for the applicant. The standard information included on a resume includes (a) identification, (b) job or work objective, (c)

summary of achievements, (d) qualifications, (e) personal information, and (f) references.

4. Inflating qualifications may (a) lead to discovery of the exaggeration and terminate employment, (b) result in loss of employer trust and opportunity for advancement, and (c) result in the assignment of duties on the job that the applicant is not qualified to perform.

5. A good job objective is specific enough to be meaningful yet general enough to apply to a variety of jobs.

6. The "Summary of Achievements" section summarizes the applicant's major qualifications. Including this optional section is especially beneficial if the applicant has a varied background.

7. Types of information that could be included in the "Education" section are (a) degree(s) held, including major, school, and dates; (b) overall and major grade-point averages above a B; and (c) a list of special skills.

8. Subject-understood sentences enable the writer to (a) eliminate personal pronouns that refer to "you," (b) conserve space, and (c) emphasize verbs. Action verbs emphasize accomplishments and help employers visualize a productive employee. Crisp phrases help the employer to see the applicant's strengths easily. Descriptive but not overly strong adjectives give a vivid, believable picture of the applicant as a productive employee.

9. In deciding what information to include in the resume, answer these questions: (a) How closely related is the information to the job being sought? and (b) Does it provide job-related information that has not been presented elsewhere?

10. Advantages of including a "personal information" section: (a) helps to present the applicant as a well-rounded individual and (b) reveals positive personal qualities that could increase appeal as an employee. Disadvantages of a "personal information" section: (a) could force the use of two pages or devote less space to qualifications, (b) causes personal details to compete for attention with qualifications, and (c) could elicit a negative reaction and cause the resume to be discarded. Including some items of personal information can be a plus, such as "nonsmoker." Including personal information can

be a disadvantage because it may lead to discrimination or, at the least, occupy space that could be devoted to more pertinent information. These criteria should be considered in deciding whether to include personal information: (a) How closely is it related to the job being sought? (b) Does it portray the applicant as a well-rounded, happy individual off the job? and (c) Is it controversial?

11. References could be omitted if (a) you prefer to delay your present employer's awareness of your job-seeking efforts; (b) you are confident they will not be needed until after the interview; or (c) you have registered with the school's career services division, in which case your references will have sent recommendation letters already. Permission should always be obtained before listing persons as references.

12. If references are not listed on the resume, a list of references can be provided after a successful interview.

13. The *chronological* resume is the traditional format for resumes that list education and experience in reverse chronological order; it is effective for applicants who have progressed up a clearly defined career ladder. The *functional* resume presents the points of primary interest to employers—transferable skills—in major headings; it is probably better for applicants who have had little or no experience, since it allows the applicant to emphasize some qualities or attributes in which an employer would be interested. A chronological resume might have the effect of emphasizing the lack of experience. The *combination chronological and functional* resume combines features of the other two types; it is effective for giving quick assurance that educational and experience requirements are met yet still using other headings that emphasize qualifications.

14. Refer to the design enhancements shown in Figure 13–7.

15. Sources of prospective employers' names and addresses include the following: networks, career service centers, employers' offices, employment agencies and contractors, help-wanted ads, online databases and printed sources, and professional organizations.

16. Application letters and resumes should *not* contain the same information. Rather, one should complement the other. The letter

151

should get the reader interested in the facts that appear on the resume, introduce it, and point out some ways in which information presented can satisfy employer needs.

17. The application letter (a) seeks to arouse interest in the resume, (b) introduces the resume, (c) interprets the resume in terms of employer benefit, and (d) requests an interview.

18. The application letter *is* a sales letter; it sells an applicant's service. Like a persuasive letter, the application letter gets attention, introduces the product (qualifications) in context of the reader's needs, presents objective, convincing evidence, and encourages action (an interview). The application has a central selling point as a theme throughout the letter.

19. Including frequently used words in application letters cause the letter to sound like competitors' letters. Frequently overused words include: *applicant, application, I, interview, opening, position, qualifications,* and *vacancy.*

20. The invitation to interview is the objective of the letter; the desired action is for the reader to write a letter or place a telephone call to arrange the interview. The goal is to introduce the idea of action without apologizing for doing so and without being demanding or pushy. Unlike the sales letter, the application letter should leave the choice of action to the employer.

POSSIBLE SOLUTIONS TO EXERCISES

1. Use these activities to initiate class discussion. Students are generally interested in this topic, as they see direct application for the principles presented. Expect more questions and discussion than might otherwise be common.

2. See **TA 13–2** (Solution, Exercise 2) for suggested letter. A summary of revisions in organization, content, style, mechanics, and format follows:

Summary of Organization, Content, Style, Mechanics, and Format Errors

Organization	◆ Uses inductive approach (interview is requested after qualifications are presented).
Content	◆ 1: Does not mention name of newspaper (must get attention in paragraph 1).
	◆ 2: Mentions resume before qualifications are presented; reader may immediately turn to resume without completing the letter.
	◆ 3: Uses statement of certainty "as you know" to precede a fact reader already knows, giving a lecturing tone.
	◆ 4–12: Uses lecturing tone—reader already knows what job requirements are; develops qualifications inadequately; simply repeats information included on the resume.
Style	◆ 1: Uses cliché—a weak attention-getter.
	◆ 4–6: Uses gender-biased "insurance man."
	◆ 7–12: Uses "I" in self-oriented statements that do not interpret qualifications as related to job sought.
	◆ 13: Uses redundancy; omit "which is attached for your convenience." Includes a direct reference to the resume; should use second person, referring reader to resume indirectly.
	◆ 14: Uses overly formal "shall."
Mechanics	◆ 1: Misspells "advertised."
	◆ 9: Includes dangling participial phrase that literally states that the reader is a student in college.
	◆ 14: Misspells "personally."
Format	◆ Should not include writer's name above the date.
	◆ Should use the two-letter state abbreviation (AL).
	◆ Omits salutation.
	◆ Omits enclosure notation.

3. See **TA 13–3** (Solution, Exercise 3) for suggested letter. A summary of revisions in organization, content, style, mechanics, and format follows:

Summary of Organization, Content, Style, Mechanics, and Format Errors	
Organization	◆ Uses inductive approach appropriately (interview is requested after qualifications are presented). Paragraphs are too long for easy reading; first and final paragraph should be short.
Content	◆ 1: Does commendably identify position sought in first sentence but does not capture reader's attention.
	◆ 2–6: Develops qualifications inadequately; does not attempt to interpret experiences as related to job sought; instead, directly states the same information that appears on the resume. Sentences 4–6 state the obvious.
Style	◆ 1: Uses cliché—a weak attention-getter.
	◆ 2–6: Uses "I" in self-oriented statements that do not interpret qualifications as related to job sought.
	◆ 4: Uses statement of certainty ("I am sure") that reader cannot be certain about.
	◆ 7: Is wordy ("resume which you will find enclosed").
	◆ 8: Is a standard cliché used in an application letter.
Mechanics	◆ 1: Misspells "advertised"; does not use possessive form of "night's."
	◆ 8: Misspells "convenience."
	◆ 7: Does not use possessive pronoun before gerund, "your studying," misspells "enclosed."
	◆ 9: Is a sentence fragment.
Format	◆ Omits the writer's address (needed because letter is printed on plain paper).
	◆ Does not address letter to specific individual.
	◆ Does not provide street address.
	◆ Includes inappropriate salutation: "Dear Sirs"; should use "Ladies and Gentlemen" or the simplified block format that omits the salutation if the letter is addressed to a company.
	◆ Omits enclosure notation.

POSSIBLE SOLUTION TO E-MAIL APPLICATION

Encourage students to critique for organization, content, style, mechanics, and format using the "Check Your Writing" checklist as a guide. If a standard resume is distributed, scoring may be based on the number of pre-determined errors the student identifies. If students exchange resumes, ask them to revise their resumes based on the feedback provided.

POSSIBLE SOLUTIONS TO APPLICATIONS

CAREER DEVELOPMENT

1. Getting Essential Information to Make a Wise Career Decision

⇨ *Level 3* ⇦

Solutions will vary. Encourage students to talk to professors in their discipline and employees holding similar jobs to obtain current, accurate information about careers and the requirements for specific jobs. Students majoring in professions with well-defined career paths should be able to find published information related to job requirements. For example, requirements for public accountants are clearly outlined in the *Perspectives on Education: Capabilities for Success in the Accounting Profession.* Commonly referred to as the "White Paper," this document was prepared by the then-Big Eight (now Big Six) public accounting firms to assist accounting educators in equipping accountants for successful accounting careers.

CAREER DEVELOPMENT

2. Preparing a Company/Job Profile

⇨ *Level 4* ⇦

Refer to teaching suggestions for Application 1.

CAREER DEVELOPMENT

3. Preparing a Resume and an Application Letter for a Job of Your Choice

⇨ *Level 3* ⇦

Solutions will vary. Prior to the deadline for the assignment, have students bring a draft of their resume to class (specify the degree of completeness desired), and instruct each student to exchange resumes with another student; allow 15 to 20 minutes for students to discuss possible improvements. As you move around the room listening to the discussion, you may identify several points that need clarification. Students can then revise their resumes, incorporating feedback gained during the class period.

CAREER DEVELOPMENT

4. Preparing an Effective Application Letter for a Scholarship

⇨ *Level 3* ⇦

Solutions will vary. Many students find this assignment meaningful because they already have (or will) need to write an application for a scholarship. With increased confidence in their ability to write the application, students, once unsure of how to "sell" themselves, may apply for needed scholarships.

POSSIBLE SOLUTIONS TO CASES FOR ANALYSIS

HUMAN RESOURCES MANAGEMENT

1. Outplaced Workers Need Employment Advice

⇨ *Level 4* ⇦

This case requires students to conduct library research to develop guidelines for writing job credentials for outplaced workers. Therefore, rather than write a "term paper," they must select the information needed to solve a particular problem. To increase the relevancy of the case, students could develop guidelines for recent college graduates.

Step 1: Rather than assign this case during the study of the employment process, you may add this case as a possible topic for a short report after completing Chapter 17. Students are required to prepare a memorandum report documented with current, accurate references. Tell the students which documentation style you prefer.

Step 2: Be certain that students do more than repeat the information in the chapter;

they should locate practical suggestions from the latest periodicals.

Step 3: Solutions will vary.

Step 4: You might divide the students into small groups and consolidate the guidelines each individual identified into one brochure. A final suggestion is to select a panel of judges (advertising and/or public relations professors or practitioners or other business communications professors) to select the "best" brochure, which would be distributed to seniors or interviewing students as a service to your college and as a public relations tool for the business communication course.

HUMAN RESOURCES MANAGEMENT

2. Preparing a One-page Resume for an Outplaced Employee

⇨ *Level 4* ⇦

Solutions will vary. See **TM 13–3** (Solution, Case for Analysis 2, Step 2) for suggested resume.

Information that should be excluded from the resume includes (a) personal data related to age, marital status, number of children, and health—information covered by civil rights legislation; (b) high school information (irrelevant because it occurred so long ago); (c) references (include "available upon request"). Alternatively, students may list references, excluding the minister and Kevin's relative (Richard Reuter). Information about Kevin's interests (regular exercise and sports) and volunteer activities can be included to depict Kevin as a well-rounded individual; however, some of these items may be excluded to prevent the resume from requiring a second page.

The chronological resume is appropriate because Kevin is progressing up a clearly defined career ladder. Emphasize the importance of stressing accomplishments and benefits gained from work experience, education, and extracurricular activities to provide deeper insight into Kevin's ambition, capability, and personality. Point out examples of these reflective statements in the sample resume in **TM 13–3**.

CHAPTER 14

JOB INTERVIEWS, EMPLOYMENT MESSAGES, AND PERFORMANCE APPRAISALS

CHAPTER OVERVIEW

Because it is probably the type of interview most familiar to students and the one of immediate concern, the employment interview receives primary emphasis in Chapter 14. Additionally, employment interviews are a logical continuation of the resume and application letter topics in Chapter 13. Students also learn to apply interviewing skills to the performance appraisal interview so they can enhance their abilities to perform effectively in this important evaluation process.

No matter what the purpose, all interview types have some common elements. They are structured or unstructured, typically involve face-to-face meetings, and rely for success on effective role performance by interviewer and interviewee. As a result, knowledge gained from the study and practice of employment interviews may be transferred to other interview types. Keep in mind that listening, as discussed in Chapter 1 and hopefully integrated throughout the course, is a major interviewing skill.

Good interviewers should also be good interviewees simply because they know the mechanics and practice skills of an interviewer. If this observation is true, *interviewee* skills may be developed based on a knowledge of what the *interviewer's* role involves.

For college students, we suggest giving special attention to preparation for interviews, interview behavior and feedback techniques (paraphrasing and questioning), and dress and grooming.

LEARNING OBJECTIVES

1 Explain the nature of structured, unstructured, and stress interviews.

2 Recognize the interviewer's role in the interview process.

3 Prepare for and participate effectively in a job interview.

4 Recognize and bypass illegal interview questions.

5 Write effective letters related to employment (follow-up, thank-you, job-acceptance, job-refusal and resignation letters, and recommendation requests) and complete application forms accurately.

6 Write positive and negative recommendations that are legally defensible.

7 Participate effectively in a performance appraisal interview.

CHAPTER OUTLINE AND TEACHING SUGGESTIONS

1   LEARNING OBJECTIVE

I. Types of Employment Interviews
   A. Invite guest speakers to discuss the job-search process, effective interviewing techniques, business protocol, and performance appraisal interviews. Consider former students, local human resources professors or managers, business protocol professors, communication consultants, officials in the school's career services center, or local employment agents.
   B. Show **TA 14–1** (Chapter Opener) as you begin the chapter discussion.
   C. Structured and Computer-Assisted Interviews
   D. Unstructured Interviews
   E. Stress Interviews
   F. Integrate the communication mentor comments into class lectures to reinforce the concepts in the chapter. These comments include practical advice for developing effective interviewing skills.

<table>
<tr><td>2</td><td>LEARNING OBJECTIVE</td></tr>
</table>

II. Job Interviewer's Role
   A. Make a transparency of **TM 14–1** (Effective Interviewing Techniques for Interviewers) to show as you progress through the discussion of this section.
   B. Preparing for the Interview
   C. Meeting Face to Face—The Interchange
   D. Evaluating the Interview
   E. Some Interviewer Guidelines
   F. Interviewer Prohibitions

<table>
<tr><td>3</td><td>LEARNING OBJECTIVE</td></tr>
</table>

III. Job Interviewee's Role
   A. Show **TA 14–2** (Effective Interviewing Techniques for Interviewees) as you progress through the discussion of this section.
   B. Preparing for the Interview
      1. Study the Company
      2. Study Yourself
      3. Plan Your Appearance
      4. Plan Your Time
   C. Meeting Face-to-Face—The Interchange
      1. Opening Formalities
      2. Interviewing Guidelines

<table>
<tr><td>4</td><td>LEARNING OBJECTIVE</td></tr>
</table>

      3. Handling Illegal Interview Questions
         a. Initiate a discussion about recognizing and handling discriminatory questions referring to the "Interviewer Prohibitions" and the "Handling Illegal Interview Questions" sections.
         b. Assign Case for Analysis 1 that requires students to conduct further research on discriminatory hiring practices. This case could be assigned as a short report to be completed after you have discussed Chapter 17.
      4. Asking Questions of the Interviewer
      5. Handling Salary and Benefits Discussion
      6. Closing the Interview
   D. Practicing for Interviews
   E. Communication in Action: William Montes, RE\MAX of Florida, Inc.
   F. Arrange for two volunteers to demonstrate an effective (and ineffective) job interview before the entire class to provide a model for mock interviews in teams. This demonstration is an excellent opportunity to use the expertise of resource persons, for example, human resources management professors or practitioners, career services personnel, or students with special communication abilities (students who have completed a full semester course in interviewing).
   G. Have students participate in mock interviews as outlined in Application 3. As a suggestion, have four students work as a team. One plays a role as interviewer, another as interviewee, and two serve as observers to provide critiques of the effectiveness of the interview.
      1. Teams should continue mock interviews until all members have an opportunity to be both interviewer and interviewee.
      2. Require students to distribute copies of their resumes to other team members.
      3. To increase the effectiveness of the mock interviews, complete these activities prior to the interviews:
         a. Assign Application 1 that requires researching a company and writing ten original questions that could be asked during a job interview.
         b. Assign Application 1 from the *Study Guide* to be completed in small groups or individually. Students are required to analyze six interview questions and provide the information the interviewer is seeking in the question and an appro-

priate response. Ask students to compare their answers with the solution provided.

c. Complete the e-mail application and discuss students' responses in class. Refer to the teaching suggestions in the "Possible Solution to E-mail Application" that follows.

d. Assign Application 2 that requires students to write answers to the interview questions in Figure 14–3, insert them in their career notebook, and practice answering them.

e. Have students select three or four of the questions in Figure 14–3 (or other questions they locate from other sources) and use them to develop an outline for the mock interview.

f. Discuss some of the nonverbal signals that create good/bad impressions—especially during the first four minutes.

g. Discuss possible illegal interview questions and strategies for answering them.

H. Following the interviews, have students discuss the interviewer's and the interviewee's strengths and weaknesses and offer suggestions for improvement. Have the interviewing student insert a page in his or her career notebook containing these points:

1. Summary of the strengths and detailed description of the areas needing improvement before the next interview.

2. Significant points discussed during the interview that can be used in a thank-you letter.

<table>
<tr><td>5</td><td>LEARNING OBJECTIVE</td></tr>
</table>

IV. Preparing Other Employment Messages

A. Follow-Up Letters

B. Thank-You Letters

1. Assign Application 2 from the *Study Guide*, a thank-you letter following an interview. Discuss the

communication pointers and compose the letter in small groups or individually. Discuss the effective writing techniques incorporated in the revision.

2. Ask students to complete Application 5, which requires the preparation of a thank-you letter for an interview.

C. Application Forms

D. Job-Acceptance Letters

E. Job-Refusal Letters

F. Resignation Letters

G. Assign one or more of the following applications: Application 4 (follow-up), Application 5 (thank-you), Application 6 (job acceptance), Application 7 (job refusal), Application 8 (job resignation), Application 9 (request for recommendation), and Application 10 (extended job search report to reference). Remind students to study the suggestions in the "Check Your Writing" checklist when planning and revising these letters.

<table>
<tr><td>6</td><td>LEARNING OBJECTIVE</td></tr>
</table>

H. Recommendation Letters

1. Applicant's Request and Thanks for Recommendation

2. Employer's Request for Recommendation

3. Negative Recommendations

a. Initiate a discussion about the three options for responding to a request to write a recommendation that will be negative.

b. Discuss the six guidelines for writing a legally defensible recommendation.

c. Assign Case for Analysis 2 that requires students to consider the consequences of the three options for replying to a specific request to write a recommendation that will be unfavorable and then respond to the request in the manner they deem ethical. Students who choose to ignore the request must write a memo to the file justifying their action; students who choose to telephone must write the dialogue of the call.

4. Positive Recommendations

---

7   LEARNING OBJECTIVE

V. Performance Appraisals

A. Make a transparency of **TM 14–2** (Guidelines for Effective Performance Appraisals) to show as you progress through discussion of this section.

B. Guidelines for Employees

C. Guidelines for Supervisors

D. Repeat the procedures for employment interviews described above to aid in conducting mock performance appraisal interviews. Solicit the help of a human resources management professor or manager to conduct and evaluate the interviews.

E. Record some of the job and performance appraisal interviews on videotape if facilities are available.

F. If career services officers or job counselors are available, ask them to make a short presentation before the class, or visit the career services office on your campus.

VI. Summary

A. Show the videotape, "Job Interviews."

1. Refer to the teaching suggestions for the video, listed at the beginning of Part 5.

2. Show **TA 14–3** (Business Tips from Venture Stores, Inc. [Video, Part 5]).

B. Integrate the communication mentor comments into class lectures to reinforce the concepts presented in the chapter.

C. Assign the *Study Guide* questions for Chapter 14.

D. Require students to complete the practical applications in the *Study Guide*. These applications "walk students through" (a) analyzing a list of indirect interview questions to identify the information sought and to compose responses to the questions and (b) writing a thank-you letter following an interview. Critical thinking questions help students organize their thoughts and write effective solutions; a sample solution and a detailed commentary that highlights the strengths of the outline and the solution are provided. In a third application, students analyze a poorly written letter and identify errors and weaknesses. Critical thinking questions guide students through the analysis.

E. Ask students to complete the e-mail application.

F. Assign selected exercises, applications, and cases at the end of the chapter. Remind students to study the suggestions in the "Check Your Writing" checklist when planning and revising an assignment.

G. Assign selected cases for analysis at the end of the chapter.

TRANSPARENCIES AND MASTERS

TA 14–1   Chapter Opener

TA 14–2   Effective Interviewing Techniques for Interviewees

TA 14–3   Business Tips from Venture Stores, Inc. (Video, Part 5)

TM 14–1   Effective Interviewing Techniques for Interviewers

TM 14–2   Guidelines for Effective Performance Appraisals

ADDITIONAL READINGS

Alderman, L. (1995). What you need to ace today's rough-and-tough job interviews. *Money, 24*(4), 35–37.

Cunningham, W. P. (1993). Careful selection: Interviewing for ethics. *Managers Magazine, 68*(7), 15–17.

Fletcher, C. (1992). Ethical issues in the selection interview. *Journal of Business Ethics, 11*(5–6), 361–367.

Jenks, C. M. (1991, March/April). The prying eye: How to sidestep job-interview questions that invade your privacy. *Executive Female*, pp. 30–31.

Lee, C. (1989). Poor performance appraisals do more harm than good. *Personnel Journal, 68*(9), 91, 93, 95–97, 99.

Lucht, J. (1994). Ace the job interview. *Female Executive, 17*(2), 42–46.

Reticker, P. (1993). The five toughest interview questions. *Healthcare Financial Management, 47*(9), 82–83.

Saunders, P. R. (1993). Job interviewing: How to make it work for you. *Journal of Systems Management, 44*(7), 17–21.

Sligo, F. (1994). Role-playing the employment interview. *Bulletin of the Association for Business Communication, 57*(1), 36–39.

Walley, E. N. (1993). Successful interviewing techniques. *The CPA Journal, 63*(9), 70–71.

Yoo-Lim, L. (1994). More Companies rely on employee interviews. *Business Korea, 12*(5), 22–23.

ANSWERS TO "COMMUNICATION IN ACTION" CASE: William Montes, RE\MAX of Florida, Inc.

1. **According to Montes, what is the most important part of the interview process?** The most important part comes before the actual interview. Montes believes applicants must first analyze what behaviors a position requires. Montes also assesses an applicant's previous work experience. This analysis is an important part of the interviewing process.

2. **What steps does Montes suggest recent graduates take when preparing for an employment interview?** Montes recommends students study a company and learn as much as possible about it. He also believes students can gain a competitive edge in an interview by understanding their personal goals and strengths. If students are required to keep career notebooks, refer them to the company information and job information sections in the text. Montes also recommends personal contact with the company, sending resumes directly to a decision maker.

ANSWERS TO REVIEW QUESTIONS

1. Structured interviews follow set plans, and unstructured interviews are free-wheeling exchanges; good interviewers are capable of having one seem like the other. Using computer-assisted interviewing to screen applicants during preliminary interviews, recruiters obtain standard, reliable information about each applicant. Using computer-assisted interviewing for preliminary job interviews enables the human interviewer to decide reliably and quickly whether to invite the applicant for a second interview and to identify the specific information that must be obtained from the applicant in the second interview.

2. Direct questions usually call for a "yes" or "no" response. Indirect questions require an answer of the what-how-why nature.

3. Answers to this item will take varying forms but should meet some of the criteria mentioned for discrimination discussed in the "Interviewer Prohibitions" section.

4. Employees, business periodicals and newspapers, the Internet and other online sources, chambers of commerce, placement offices, and friends are good sources of information about companies. Facts that should be located include the name, status, latest stock quote, recent news and developments, scope, corporate officers, and products and services.

5. An interviewee can show good intentions by leaning slightly forward in the chair, maintaining eye contact, and providing eye and motion feedback.

6. Answers to this item will vary but should reflect understanding of guidelines mentioned for interviewing. You might ask students to pair with another student to practice verbalizing their strengths in an interview.

7. Tendency not to listen, lack of credibility, lack of interest in the subject, a hostile attitude, profanity, and poor organization of ideas are six leading barriers to interview communication shown in Figure 14–2.

8. Three ways to handle illegal interview questions: (a) refuse to answer the illegal question, (b) answer the question knowing it is illegal and your answer is not related to job requirements, or (c) answer the legitimate concern that probably lies behind the illegal question. Option A risks offending or embarrassing the interviewer; Option B is more likely to keep one in the running for the job but may compromise important principles. Option C is the more effective alternative

because it answers the legitimate concern underlying the illegal question.

9. A good strategy is to admit to some weakness that will not have a negative effect on your job worthiness. In all cases, do not say you have no weaknesses.

    Example: Tendency to expect too much from yourself and others.

10. Follow-up letters include (a) a reminder that an application for a certain job is on file, (b) a report of additional education or experience and its relationship to the job, and (c) a reference to desired action.

11. Referring to a point discussed in the interview can imply that the interview was meaningful or interesting (the interviewer should react favorably). Also, because the reference is specific, the letter is original; it is something more than a standard passage that could be said to someone else.

12. When completing employment forms, (a) follow instructions, (b) complete forms neatly, (c) respond to all questions, and (d) answer questions accurately.

13. (a) An acceptance letter should be written deductively. It accepts the job in the first sentence. To an employer who, with good reason and after much deliberation, had offered you a job, a refusal in the first sentence would seem harsh. The acceptance letter should include the acceptance, details (salary, benefits, starting date, and anything else negotiated), and a closing (that confirms the report-for-work date). The rejection letter should include a beginning that reveals the nature of the subject, explanations that lead to the refusal, and a pleasant ending.

14. The resignation letter is written inductively. It calls attention to the specific job, gives reasons for leaving it, conveys the resignation, and closes on a positive note.

15. Yes, a letter to Professor Ulmer would alert her to the possibility of a request for a recommendation. Your letter would also give you a chance to bring her up to date on your progress. By including a resume, you could give her specific, up-to-date information that would enable her to write specifically about you.

16. Yes. Including both positives and negatives gives the letter a tone of objectivity. Let the reader judge whether the positives are sufficient to counterbalance the negatives.

17. See the six guidelines for writing defensible recommendations included in the "Negative Recommendations" section.

18. The primary purpose of the performance appraisal interview is to evaluate an employee's performance. Refer to the list of five guidelines in the "Guidelines for Employees" section.

19. Refer to the list of seven in the "Guidelines for Supervisors" section.

20. Start the class session by asking the class one or more of these questions.

POSSIBLE SOLUTION TO E-MAIL APPLICATION

Make transparencies and show some of the more interesting questions posed, along with their answers. Lead a discussion of other possible appropriate answers to the questions. Lead students in a discussion of some unusual questions they have been asked in interview situations and how they responded.

POSSIBLE SOLUTIONS AND RECOMMENDED OUTLINES TO APPLICATIONS

CAREER DEVELOPMENT

1.   **Researching a Company and Asking Questions of an Interviewer**

⇨ *Level 3* ⇦

Require students to conduct thorough research of a company in preparation for a mock interview. Divide students into groups by major to reduce the amount of time required to complete this application. Refer to the suggestions in III–G for planning an effective mock interview experience.

CAREER DEVELOPMENT

2.   **Preparing to Answer Interview Questions Effectively**

⇨ *Level 3* ⇦

To shorten this assignment without sacrificing content, divide the questions equally among class members. Discuss each question, giving students ample time to write notes about questions they were not required to answer. Alternatively, require students to complete Application 1 in the *Study Guide*. Students analyze several indirect interview questions to identify the information being sought and then compose answers. Suggested answers are provided.

CAREER DEVELOPMENT

3. Practicing a Job Interview
⇨ *Level 2* ⇦

Refer to Chapter Outline III–G for ideas.

CAREER DEVELOPMENT

4–9. Writing Employment Messages
⇨ *Level 2* ⇦

Stress the importance of writing fresh, original employment letters. Each of these letters should reflect the writer's personality, should not sound like a form letter, and *must not* be a copy of a sample in a job-search manual. Letters should follow the outlines shown in the following figures:

Application	Letter Type	Figure
4	Following Up on a Job	14–5
5	Saying Thank You for an Interview	14–6
6	Accepting A Job Offer	14–8
7	Refusing a Job Offer	14–9
8	Resigning a Job	14–10
9	Requesting a Letter of Recommendation	14–11

CAREER DEVELOPMENT

10. Informing a Reference of an Extended Job Search
⇨ *Level 2* ⇦

The letter should (a) thank the reference for his/her assistance thus far; (b) relate some details about how the search process is progressing; (c) refer to the updated resume which is enclosed (if applicable); (d) express thanks for his/her continued support.

POSSIBLE SOLUTIONS TO CASES FOR ANALYSIS

HUMAN RESOURCES MGMT/Legal

1. Discrimination Hiring Needs Must Be Watched
⇨ *Level 4* ⇦

This application requires students to conduct library research to develop guidelines for nondiscriminatory interviewing. Emphasize that they are not to write a "term paper." Instead they must analyze pertinent information and then develop practical suggestions to be used during interviews. Encourage students to read the "Interviewer Prohibitions" section to become familiar with the topic and then to continue their research in the literature.

Rather than assign this case during the study of the employment process, you may add this case as a possible topic for a short report (Chapter 17). Students are required to prepare a memorandum report documented with current, accurate references. Instruct the students which documentation style you prefer.

If technology is available, require students to design an attractive brochure containing these guidelines. You might divide students into small groups and consolidate the guidelines each individual identified into one brochure.

MANAGEMENT/Ethics/Legal

2. A Negative Job Recommendation: What Is the Appropriate Course of Action?
⇨ *Level 4* ⇦

This application requires the student to consider carefully the consequences of (a) ignoring a request for a recommendation for an employee he or she was pleased to see leave; (b) writing a neutral recommendation; or (c) writing a positive recommendation, omitting the negatives. Divide the class into groups or initiate a class discussion about the legal and ethical implications of each of these options.

> **VIDEO CONNECTION**
> **Venture Stores**
>
> **CHAPTER 14:**
> **Job Interviews, Employment Messages, and Performance Appraisals**

SUMMARY

I. The Resume
   A. Main sections
      1. Name
      2. Address
      3. Telephone number
      4. Job sought
      5. Educational level
      6. Experience
   B. Purpose—introduction of self
   C. Questions to answer before drafting
      1. What do I like to do?
      2. What jobs are out there for me?
   D. Characteristics
      1. Organized
      2. Neat
      3. Easy to read
   E. Mistakes to avoid
      1. Spelling errors
      2. Keyboarding errors

II. The Cover Letter
   A. Purpose
      1. Supplements the resume with information unique to that employer
      2. Tells things you can't say in the resume
      3. Gets the reader to want to know more about you
   B. Characteristics
      1. Follows the sales letter strategy
      2. Is short
      3. Is concise
      4. Is businesslike
      5. Has a call to action in the last paragraph
   C. Areas to avoid
      1. Salary demands
      2. "Dear Sir" opening

III. The Interview
   A. Goals of the interviewer
      1. Understand the person being interviewed
      2. Decide if the candidate will fit into the company
      3. Decide if the candidate has what it takes for the job
   B. Alternative interview formats
      1. Structured vs. unstructured
      2. High stress vs. low stress
   C. Responsibilities of interviewee
      1. Do research on the company ahead of time
      2. Remember that you must decide on the company as well as the company's deciding on you
      3. Be prepared to discuss weaknesses
         a. be above board
         b. tell what you have done to overcome them
      4. Dress appropriately
         a. conservative
         b. in keeping with type of business
      5. Conduct oneself appropriately
         a. stay focused
         b. realize that behavior is being observed from the time you enter the building

IV. Tips for Communicating for Employment
   A. Have self-awareness
      1. Assess your assets and liabilities
      2. View your weaknesses as opportunities
   B. Design two resumes
      1. One specific to a particular job
      2. The other broader in scope
   C. Be relaxed

ANSWERS TO DISCUSSION QUESTIONS

1. **Hyman Albritton suggests that a job seeker should prepare two resumes. Explain the two and tell the purpose of each.** The two resumes suggested by Albritton were (1) one that is specific to a particular position and (2) one that is

broader in scope. The specific resume responds to the job requirements of a particular position; i.e., qualifications listed in an advertisement. The broad resume relates a wider array of qualifications and may "open more doors" because it does not lock the candidate into a tight mold.

2. **List three "dos" and three "don'ts" for resume preparation.** Do include pertinent information such as name, address, telephone number, etc. Do plan and organize the resume carefully. Do prepare two types of resume—specific and broad. Don't allow misspellings in the resume. Don't include unnecessary information. Don't crowd too much into the resume.

3. **What is the "call for action" John Cripe mentions as essential in the application letter?** The "call to action" is a confident, polite request that the employer contact you to schedule an interview. It is the culmination of a well-written application letter.

4. **What advice does Marie Mulvoy have concerning dress for the interview?** Mulvoy advises that conservatism be practiced. She added, however, the type of business should be considered in determining appropriate dress. For example, retail is more fashion forward, while banking is more conservative.

5. **Conducting a self-awareness activity is suggested as a helpful prelude to the employment search process. What is involved? How does it benefit the job seeker?** A self-awareness activity allows the job seeker to assess his or her own assets and liabilities and determine what it is that he or she would enjoy doing. A second phase of this activity is to determine what jobs are available that will match the job seeker's characteristics. Such an activity benefits the job seeker by helping him or her focus attention on appropriate jobs. It also helps him or her honestly face weaknesses so that comfortable answers can be given concerning them, should the subject arise in the interview.

POSSIBLE SOLUTION TO APPLICATION

Responses will vary depending on the individual interviewed.

MULTIPLE CHOICE QUESTIONS

1. An effective application letter that accompanies a resume
   a. describes as many of an applicant's characteristics as a one-page format will allow.
   ✔ b. supplements the resume with information unique to the particular employer.
   c. traces the applicant's accomplishments in chronological order.
   d. begins with "Dear Sir" when an individual's name is not known.

2. Salary expectations are best mentioned
   a. in the resume.
   b. in the cover letter.
   ✔ c. during the interview.
   d. after accepting the position.

3. Which of the following is *not* recommended for inclusion in a resume?
   ✔ a. salary.
   b. job sought.
   c. educational level.
   d. experience.

4. The "call to action" in the cover letter is best placed
   a. in the first paragraph.
   b. in the middle paragraph.
   ✔ c. in the last paragraph.
   d. no where in the letter—it is inappropriate.

5. When asked about his or her weaknesses, the applicant should
   a. tactfully turn the interviewer's attention away from the subject.
   ✔ b. be honest and view weaknesses as opportunities.
   c. view the question as a high-stress tactic and decline to respond.
   d. tell the interviewer that he or she would prefer to discuss strengths.

PART 6

COMMUNICATING THROUGH REPORTS

Part 6 is composed of four chapters beginning with the report process and research methods and proceeding through report preparation methods to the final product. The chapter content is flexible enough to permit intensive coverage of reports or to conclude treatment with short reports and proposals if time is limited.

If students are to complete their reports in teams, consider the method for organizing the groups. If students are permitted to form their own groups, you will want this decision to be made at the beginning of the discussion of this section. Many believe that instructor-appointed groups are more typical of real-world work assignments and also eliminate the pressure and isolation that can occur when students choose their own groups.

When appointing work groups, consider the following factors:

1. *The schedule and preferred work times of each student.* You may ask students to indicate at least 10 hours a week that they would have available for working with their groups (days of the week with specific times). Although working all ten hours each week is unlikely, this information will form a basis for you to match students who have compatible schedules.

2. *Specific areas of strength of each student.* You may want, for instance, to assure that each group has at least one member with some computer skills, someone with demonstrated success in English and/or writing classes, and someone who has participated in a group

process previously. You may devise an information sheet for students to complete that will include such information.

3. *Cultural, gender, and age diversity.* Attempt to form heterogeneous groups so that students have the experience of working with various people.

Completing a business report through the team process produces a great deal of incidental learning about group dynamics, negotiation, collaboration, and consensus. Some pre-planning and organization on your part can help to assure a successful endeavor. Refer to the "Cooperative/Collaborative Learning Activities" section on pages 7–9 of this *Instructor's Resource Manual* for suggestions in assigning students to groups, identifying collaborative projects, and assessing group performance. An evaluation form for group members is provided on page 24.

Build time in your schedule to integrate the videotape prepared for Chapter 15, "The Report Process and Research Methods." Require students to read the "Video Connection" in their texts, which previews the videotape and provides several questions reviewing major points presented. After showing the videotape, initiate a class discussion using the review questions. Review questions and cases (require students to write a document) can be assigned as homework. Suggested answers and five multiple choice questions (to add to an objective test for this unit or to use as a pop quiz) are included in the videotape teaching suggestions immediately following Chapter 15.

THE REPORT PROCESS AND RESEARCH METHODS

CHAPTER OVERVIEW

After having written letters and memorandums and prepared job credentials, students seem to understand the objective nature of reports simply because of the contrast. Chapter 15 follows a sequence that begins with report characteristics and then covers the four steps in problem solving. Considerable attention is given to sampling and designing survey instruments used in normative surveys.

LEARNING OBJECTIVES

1 Identify the characteristics of a report and the various classifications of business reports.

2 Identify the four steps in the problem-solving process.

3 Select an appropriate secondary and/or primary method for solving a problem.

4 Explain the purpose of sampling and two sampling techniques.

5 Apply techniques for developing effective questionnaires.

6 Discuss the common problems encountered in collecting and interpreting data.

CHAPTER OUTLINE AND TEACHING SUGGESTIONS

1 LEARNING OBJECTIVE

I. Knowing the Characteristics of Reports
   A. Show **TA 15–1** (Chapter Opener) as you introduce the material.
   B. Integrate the communication mentor comments into class lectures to reinforce the concepts in the chapter.

C. Show **TA 15–2** (The Formal-Informal Continuum) as you contrast the purpose and style of informal communication, with which students are already familiar, with formal communication, which reports approach.

D. As you introduce report characteristics and the various terms used in report classifications, you may want to prepare transparencies of a complete report such as the one shown in Chapter 18. You will be able to give students a better idea of what the characteristics mean and the role of research in gathering data. Students can then refer to this report in handling the remainder of the report chapters.

E. What is a Report?
   1. Formal or Informal Reports
   2. Short or Long Reports
   3. Informational or Analytical Reports
   4. Vertical or Lateral Reports
   5. Internal or External Reports
      a. Periodic Reports
      b. Functional Reports
   6. Proposals
   7. Instruct students to discuss Exercise 2 in small groups. Initiate a class discussion as students share their classifications of several business reports with the class.

F. Basis for a Report: A Problem

2 LEARNING OBJECTIVE

II. Recognizing and Defining the Problem
   A. Show **TA 15–3** (The Problem-Solving Process) as you discuss this section.
   B. The logic of problem solving may be confirmed by using any everyday problem as an example.

1. Your automobile is low on gasoline.
   a. You have a problem that you define as how to replenish the gas supply as quickly, conveniently, and perhaps as economically as possible.
   b. Having defined the problem, you select a method of solution—probably observation (you do not have to do any library research).
   c. Using this method, you observe how much gas probably remains and how far it will take you. You watch (observe) the surroundings for a service station(s).
   d. You analyze the data your observations provide (third step in problem solving) and finally reach a conclusion about where to obtain gasoline.
2. Other problems you could use to describe the four steps include:
   a. How to study effectively for an exam.
   b. Which side of the bed to get out of when you awaken the first time in a hotel or motel room.
   c. What product brand and quantity to purchase off a grocer's shelf.
   d. What to select for lunch in a college cafeteria.

C. Using Hypotheses and Statements of Purpose
1. Because of elementary school science, virtually every student will know the basic definition of a hypothesis (an educated guess).
2. Ask students to recall hypotheses they tested in their fifth or sixth grade science class and lead into a discussion of hypotheses that might be tested in business settings.
3. Many students will be familiar with the term *thesis statement* as the basis for a literary paper. Use this as a springboard into discussing the similarity to a problem statement or purpose in a business report.
4. Assign Exercise 3 that requires students to write a positive and null hypotheses for business problems. Discuss the answers in class or in small groups.

D. Limiting the Scope of the Problem
1. Place a great deal of emphasis on limiting the problem. Many new researchers, even those working for doctorates, fail to limit problems and give the impression they are going to reshape the world.
2. Limiting problems adds to the credibility of research and permits sound structuring of research procedures.
3. Compare the scope of the report to a scope on a rifle. What purpose does the rifle scope serve? (Makes target larger, more defined, seem closer, etc.) The scope of the report serves in a similar way.
4. Emphasize the 5 Ws of the scope—*what, why, when, where,* and *who.*
   a. The discussion of *when* is an excellent occasion to talk about developing a timeline for completing the report project.
   b. If, for instance, students have six weeks to complete their reports, discuss what should be done during each of the weeks that make up the project.
   c. You may want to require students to submit various parts of their reports at intervals throughout the project. This strategy helps keep students on a timetable and also allows the instructor to provide feedback for improvement.
5. Instruct students to discuss Exercise 4 in small groups. Initiate a class discussion about limiting the scope of a problem.

E. Defining Terms Clearly

F. Require students to design a research study from (a) one of the five problems listed in Application 1, (b) the problem discussed in the Think It Over note on page 504, or (c) a problem students have observed in their academic or work experience. Require students to work in teams of three or four members to design the research study and to make a short oral presentation of their solutions to the class.

3   **LEARNING OBJECTIVE**

III. Selecting a Method of Solution

A. Make a transparency of **TM 15–1** (Primary and Secondary Sources of Data) to show how the two categories of data complement one another.

B. Secondary Research

1. Locating Secondary Data

a. Libraries are absolutely essential to research. Arrange a tour and orientation by your campus's business librarian; ask him/her to emphasize the location and use of various types of business resources, both printed and electronic. Sources of business information such as governmental statistical data on national and international business, employment, and other economic data are of interest to students.

b. Develop a library assignment that requires students to locate various types of resources (books, magazines, journals, newspapers, and government documents) and record the call number, title, and author information for each. Have students photocopy or retrieve relevant articles from online sources. This type of activity forces students to begin the necessary process of researching a topic, eliminating procrastination that often occurs.

c. Assign the e-mail application that requires students to research a topic using the Veronica index. Vary this application by requiring students to use other online sources available to them.

d. Figure 15–3 shows how library research defines boundaries of knowledge so researchers do not make the mistake of reinventing the wheel.

e. Emphasize the use of computer-assisted data searches to simplify time-consuming research. Use the printout of a data search shown in Figure 15–5 to help students see the value of this technology, namely, *a research process that may have taken several hours can be completed in a matter of minutes.*

f. Suggestive or Cue Note

g. Card System

(1) Emphasize the consequences of plagiarism and be certain students understand that a citation must be included for a direct quotation and paraphrased text. Students will learn citation methods (in-text parenthetical and footnote/endnotes) for APA and MLA in Chapter 18.

(2) The traditional note card is illustrated in Figure 15–6; however, the text discusses the effective use of the photocopier.

(3) Portable computer use is introduced as an efficient method of research to be used by increasing numbers of researchers as the price of portables decreases. Researchers input notes using the keyboard in the library and then return the references to the shelf.

2. Organizing and Summarizing Secondary Research
C. Primary Research
    1. Normative Survey Research
        a. Validity and Reliability

| 4 | LEARNING OBJECTIVE |

b. Sampling
    (1) Make a transparency of **TM 15–2** (Sampling Methods) to show as you discuss some of the methods for sampling. Give examples of each.
    (2) Discuss the role of *convenience sampling* in business research. While it is non-scientific, why is it widely used?
    (3) Instruct students to discuss Exercise 6 that requires students to construct a sampling procedure for a business problem. Discuss students' answers in class.
    (4) An outstanding example of the fallacy of making inferences and projecting survey results into the future occurred in the Truman-Dewey presidential race in 1948 (seems like ancient times). Eastern newspapers predicted Dewey as the winner and proceeded to release editions with "Dewey Wins" headlines. Some researchers neglected to include western states in their samples and also forgot that surveys are good only for the time they are made. People tend to change their minds. By morning, the East Coast learned that Truman had won the election. Some of the survey "experts" were not heard from again. Encourage students to discuss other examples.

        c. Show **TA 15–4** (Common Research Errors in Data Collection) as you discuss other problems encountered in survey research.
    2. Observational Research
    3. Experimental Research
D. Communication in Action: David Martin, INTELECO
E. Instruct students to discuss Exercise 5 in small groups and report to the class. This exercise requires students to select a research method for several business problems. Initiate a class discussion as students share their answers with the class.

| 5 | LEARNING OBJECTIVE |

IV. Collecting Data Through Surveys
    A. Selecting a Data-Collection Method
    B. Developing an Effective Survey Instrument
        1. Make a transparency of **TM 15–3** (Guidelines for Designing Effective Questionnaires) to show as you lead the class in discussion.
        2. In discussing questionnaire design, emphasize that, no matter what types of questions are asked, the responses will have to be counted or tallied either by hand or by machine.
            a. Design questions and questionnaire format so that tabulating will be relatively easy and contribute to report organization.
            b. Make a transparency of **TM 15–4** (Common Item Types for Questionnaires) to show as you discuss this section.
        3. Assign Application 1 from the *Study Guide* that deals with composing questions for a questionnaire to be completed individually

or in groups. Ask a spokesperson from each group to share questions with the class; ask students to compare their questions with the questions provided in the *Study Guide*.

4. Require students to develop a survey instrument for a research study. Assign Application 2 if students were required to design a research study for one of the problems in Application 1. The Video Connection at the end of the chapter provides a research problem requiring a survey instrument. Project **TM 15–7** (Solution, Video Connection) as you compare this solution with students' solutions.

5. Chapter 16 begins with construction of tables and data analysis from questionnaire surveys.

6	LEARNING OBJECTIVE

V. Arriving at an Answer
   A. Organizing the Data
   B. Collecting the Appropriate Data
   C. Interpreting Data
      1. Show **TA 15–5** (Common Research Errors in Data Interpretation)
      2. Discuss the common errors made in interpreting data, using the Disney example in the text and other examples from businesses with which students are familiar. Coca Cola's fiasco with its 1985 introduction of New Coke is an excellent example of researchers' failing to consider important factors. Coca Cola did not realize that many Americans consider Coke to be more than a soft drink; its flavor is an American tradition—something not to be changed on a whim.
      3. Ask students (especially marketing majors) to provide other examples they have discussed in their business classes. Attempt to identify an example for each of the seven errors listed on page 520.
      4. Assign *Study Guide* Application 2 that requires students to distin-

guish among findings, conclusions, and recommendations and Application 3—compose a conclusion and a recommendation. Instruct students to compare their work with the solutions provided in the *Study Guide* and discuss these problems in class.

VI. Summary
   A. Show the videotape, "The Report Process and Research Methods."
      1. Refer to the teaching suggestions for the video, listed at the beginning of Part VI.
      2. Show **TA 15–6** (Business Tips from Sygnis, Inc. [Video, Part 6]) as you lead the class in a discussion of the video's content.
   B. Integrate the communication mentor comments into class lectures to reinforce the concepts presented in the chapter.
   C. Instruct students to complete the *Study Guide* questions for Chapter 15.
   D. Assign the applications in the *Study Guide*. These applications involve (a) composing questions for a questionnaire and (b) distinguishing among findings, conclusions, and recommendations. Critical thinking questions help students organize their thoughts and write effective questionnaire questions; solutions are provided.
   E. Ask students to complete the e-mail application.
   F. Assign selected exercises and applications at the end of the chapter.

TRANSPARENCIES AND MASTERS

TA 15–1	Chapter Opener
TA 15–2	The Formal-Informal Report Continuum
TA 15–3	The Problem-Solving Process
TA 15–4	Common Research Errors in Data Collection
TA 15–5	Common Research Errors in Data Interpretation
TA 15–6	Business Tips from Sygnis, Inc. (Video, Part 6)

ADDITIONAL READINGS

Abelson, H. I. (1989). Focus groups in focus. *Marketing Communications, 14*(2), 58–61. [Discusses another effective data-collection method.]

Cragg, J. G. (1994). Making good inferences from bad data. *Canadian Journal of Economics, 27*(4), 776–800.

DiGregoria, D. (1991). Pick up the pace of your writing. *Chemical Engineering, 98*(12) 117–122.

Futrell, D. (1994). Ten reasons why surveys fail. *Quality Progress, 27*(4), 65–69.

Howard K., & Peters, J. (1990). How should questionnaires and interviews be planned? *Managing Management Research, 52*(9), 28–31.

Jameson, D. (1994). Strategies for overcoming barriers inherent in cross-cultural research. *Bulletin of the Association for Business Communication, 57*(3), 39–40.

Maidment, R. (1988, September). Seven steps to better reports. *Management Solutions, 33*(4), 31–34.

Mohn, N. C., & Land, T. H. (1989). A guide to quality marketing research proposals and reports. *Business, 39*(1), 38–40.

Schabacker, K., & Burden, D. (1992). How to get the real scoop on a company. *Executive Female, 15*(2), 65–66.

Semon, T. T. (1994). How to plan a survey. *Marketing News, 28*(18) 14.

Vischer, J. C. (1991). Communicating through surveys. *Journal of Property Management, 56*(6), 9–11.

ANSWERS TO "COMMUNICATION IN ACTION" CASE: David Martin, INTELECO

1. **Why is research so important to many of the clients with whom Martin works?** Martin's research saves his clients time and money. When Martin uses a database for finding information about an electorate's demographics, he is using a method which is more cost efficient than a telephone survey. Martin's marketing research provides cost efficient information for his telecommunication companies.

2. **Why does Martin believe no one research method gives a complete perspective on information gathering?** A single research method reveals information on only one part of a research problem. Using more than one method gives the researcher a broader, more accurate perspective of the total research problem.

3. **Assume that Martin asked you to conduct research, describing political party affiliations in your community. What research methods would you consider using in gathering this information?** The student should utilize more than one research method or source. A telephone survey of those who voted in the last election may be conducted. In addition, databases which include past voting results from previous political races may be used. Library sources may be consulted to locate census demographics.

ANSWERS TO REVIEW QUESTIONS

1. The purpose of informational reports is to provide information; analytical reports attempt to solve problems.

2. Reports generally travel upward because they are requested by higher authority in the organization.

3. Internal audit reports might be formal or informal, short or long, informational or analytical, vertical or lateral, periodic, and functional. Within the description of the purpose and distribution, all of these categories are implied.

4. When a tire is going flat, the driver (a) recognizes the problem and mentally decides on a method of solution; (b) judges the distances to the curb, to the nearest service station, or

to a telephone and combines this knowledge with the estimated distance the car can travel, the condition of the spare tire, and the ability of the driver to change tires; (c) analyzes the options; and (d) arrives at a conclusion. These steps normally take place rapidly.

5. No difference exists in the influence of newspaper and television advertising on cereal sales.

6. Library research reveals how much has already been done in the area of the research. It may save researchers much time and wasted effort.

7. Computer-assisted data searches, cue notes, and a card system aid in learning and protect against accumulating too much information.

8. Reliability is the quality of measuring accurately, and validity is the quality of measuring what is intended to be measured.

9. Random sampling means that each member of the population has an equal opportunity to be included in the sample.

10. Experimental research measures the effect of a variable added to one of two samples.

11. What will you do with the results? Will you use computer methods to tabulate and test the data? Can you get what you want with simple checklist answers?

12. An even number of responses avoids the problem created when responses tend to converge in the middle. An even number of possible responses does not have a middle figure.

13. Poorly constructed questionnaires, failure to get enough information, and gathering too much information are instrument-related errors.

14. Assuming that people behave consistently may lead researchers to make inaccurate generalizations about a different time or a different cause.

POSSIBLE SOLUTIONS TO EXERCISES

1. Use these activities as points of discussion as you discuss the chapter material.

2. (a) external, analytical, formal report
   (b) vertical report, analytical
   (c) periodic, lateral report
   (d) functional, vertical report

   (e) informal, informational report
   (f) informal, informational report

3. (a) *Positive Hypothesis:* Chief executives advanced primarily through the legal area.

   Null Hypothesis: No relationship exists between chief executives' advancement and functional field backgrounds.

   Note: In a hypothesis, the word *significant* usually is added when tests of significance are to be used. Of course, variations are easily possible. Avoid "There will be no difference..." because of the expletive beginning.

   (b) *Positive Hypothesis:* By their fiftieth birthday, people will have a net worth that is directly related to their educations.

   Null Hypothesis: No relationship will exist between people's net worth at age 50 and their educational levels.

   (c) *Positive Hypothesis:* The Fog Index readability rating of business textbooks is directly related to student interest in the courses using the textbooks.

   Null Hypothesis: No relationship exists between the Fog Index readability rating of business textbooks and student interest in the courses using the textbooks.

4. Studies may be limited by sampling selection and size and by methods used to gather data. In experimental studies, limitations might include time of day, different teaching abilities, student differences, and a variety of other factors. Students should recognize that limitations do exist and that to generalize findings beyond the sample requires meticulous research methodology.

5. Research methods used in addition to library research:
   (a) Normative survey
   (b) Normative survey
   (c) Normative survey and observation

6. A sample could come from a telephone list, tax assessor's files, or other numeric sources at random. Perhaps 10 percent might have to be included.

POSSIBLE SOLUTION TO E-MAIL APPLICATION

Helping students develop proficiency in electronic search techniques is the major purpose of this assignment. If students have their report topics at this point, have them search on those topics. The assignment should be evaluated according to appropriateness of the source list generated.

POSSIBLE SOLUTIONS TO APPLICATIONS

1. **Designing a Research Study**

⇨ *Level 4* ⇦

(a) **Campus, Job, or Organization Problem**

See TM 15–5 (Solution, Application 1a) for the suggested solution.

(b) **Internet Ordering for Pacific Electronics**

Statement of the Problem: Should Pacific Electronics allow customers to order computer accessories and software packages via the Internet?

Research Method and Sources of Information: A normative survey by questionnaire to a random sample of customers will be conducted.

Nature of Data to Be Gathered and Analyzed: Data will be gathered on customer attitudes of Internet ordering, including likelihood of using Internet ordering, frequency of using Internet ordering, and preference for Internet ordering as compared to traditional ordering methods.

Hypothesis or Hypotheses to Be Proved or Disproved: Internet ordering is an attractive alternative for customers who are placing orders to the company.

(c) **Adding Breakfast Pizza to Karen's Frozen Foods, Inc., Line**

Statement of the Problem: Should Karen's Frozen Foods add breakfast pizza to its product line?

Research Method and Sources of Information: A normative survey by questionnaire to a random sample of teenagers and working couples will be conducted.

Nature of Data to Be Gathered and Analyzed: Data will be gathered on customer attitudes about breakfast pizza, specifically, preference for breakfast pizza over other breakfast alternatives, likelihood of purchasing breakfast pizza, and frequency of choosing breakfast pizza.

Hypothesis or Hypotheses to Be Proved or Disproved: Breakfast pizza will be an attractive breakfast choice for teenagers and working couples.

(d) **Aggressive Investment Plans with George-Parsons & Associates**

Statement of the Problem: What actions can be implemented by George-Parsons & Associates to attract investment clients to initiate more aggressive tax-saving investment plans recommended by the company?

Research Method and Sources of Information: A normative survey by telephone to investment clients will be conducted.

Nature of Data to Be Gathered and Analyzed: Data will be gathered on customer attitudes about promotion of aggressive tax-saving strategies; specifically, whether they are interested in such opportunities and, if so, what would attract them to such investments.

Hypothesis or Hypotheses to Be Proved or Disproved: Given appropriate promotional information, investment clients will initiate more aggressive investment plans.

(e) **An Annual National Sales Conference for Allied Pharmaceutical Company**

Statement of the Problem: Should Allied Pharmaceutical Company schedule a second national sales conference?

Research Method and Sources of Information: Observation research will be done to determine whether any performance indicators other than sales (absenteeism, turnover, etc.) have shown a positive change following the sales conference. A normative survey will also be conducted of members of the sales force.

Nature of Data to Be Gathered and Analyzed: Performance indicators will be examined to determine whether the previous sales conference had positive effects; members of the sales force will be surveyed to determine their attitudes toward the value of the sales conference.

Hypothesis or Hypotheses to Be Proved or Disproved: Sufficient benefit was derived from holding the national sales conference to justify offering it again.

2. **Developing a Survey Instrument**
⇨ *Level 4* ⇦

See **TM 15–6** (Solution, Application 2a) for suggested solution.

VIDEO CONNECTION
Sygnis, Inc.

CHAPTER 15:
Communicating Through Reports

SUMMARY

I. Steps in the Research Process
  A. Accurately define issues to be researched
  B. Select research methodology
    1. Secondary—referring to information that already exists
    2. Primary—pursuing information that does not exist anywhere else.
      a. direct mail surveys—reach largest number of people but may produce low response rate
      b. mall intercepts
      c. focus groups—bring people together with common interests; researcher obtains thorough information through observing
      d. personal interviews—give indepth understanding of how a person feels
      e. telephone surveys—reach many people quickly
  C. Select sample
    1. Subset of total population or larger group
    2. Random sample accurately represents the larger group
    3. Must be representative for data to be valid
  D. Develop questionnaire
    1. Recognize it as the core document for primary research
    2. Start with simple items and progress to the more complex
    3. Test it on a small group
  E. Compute results

  F. Prepare reports
    1. Visual data representation
      a. helps present complex data or interrelationships
      b. helps in presenting data to large numbers of people
    2. Written-word presentation
      a. organized
      b. concise
      c. does not editorialize
      d. meets reader's needs
II. Tips for Research Report Preparation
  A. Define the problem clearly
  B. Build logical survey questionnaires
    1. Move from simple to complicated
    2. Apply a logical discussion format
  C. Start skill development early
    1. Learn how to be a good interviewer while still in school
    2. Find part-time work with a marketing research firm

ANSWERS TO DISCUSSION QUESTIONS

1. **David Martin and Bruce Brown mention several primary research methodologies. List five and for each give a major consideration in choosing it for data collection.** Primary research methodologies include:

   (a) **Telephone surveys**—useful for reaching many people quickly.

   (b) **Direct mail surveys**—reach a large number of people but generally has a low response rate.

   (c) **Focus groups**—bring people with common interests together, thus the researcher can obtain more thorough information than through other means.

   (d) **Personal interviews**—provide indepth understanding of how a person feels.

   (e) **Mall intercepts**—effective for reaching large numbers of people.

2. **How are the concepts of sampling and validity related?** Validity of data can only be assured when accurate random-sampling techniques are applied. Otherwise, the researcher has no assurance that the results of

the sample are typical of the total population in question.

3. **What role do computers play in research report preparation?** Computers are extremely useful in the tabulation, management, and analysis of data. They are also useful in preparing the text of the report and in generating appropriate graphics.

4. **List four characteristics of a well-designed questionnaire.** A well-designed questionnaire (a) is logical, (b) progresses from simple to complex, (c) is tested on a small group before general use, and (d) serves as the core document by adequately covering issues to be researched.

5. **Explain the role of visual and written presentation in producing an effective research report.** Visual representation is just as important as the written portion of the report. Visual support helps present complex data and interrelationships. Visual representation does not, however, substitute for the written word. The report is judged by the written word. It should be organized, concise, and non-editorializing; and it must meet the reader's needs.

POSSIBLE SOLUTION TO APPLICATION

See TM 15–7 (Solution, Video Application) for suggested questionnaire.

MULTIPLE CHOICE QUESTIONS

1. Considering the probable response rate for the following research methodologies, which combination represents the sequencing from lowest response to highest response?
   a. focus group, telephone survey, direct mail survey
   ✔ b. direct mail survey, telephone survey, focus group
   c. personal interviews, mall intercept, telephone survey
   d. mall intercept, focus group, direct mail survey

2. Which of the following statements does *not* reflect the proper development of effective questionnaires?
   a. Start with easier items and end with complex ones.
   b. Test the questionnaire on a small group before finalizing it for distribution.
   ✔ c. Reserve the use of questionnaires for mailed surveys, and use an unstructured approach for telephone surveys, and intercepts.
   d. Develop the questionnaire after defining the issues to be researched.

3. Which statement best describes the proper use of visual representation in a research report?
   a. Proper use of visuals eliminates the need for written commentary.
   b. Visuals should be used sparingly, as they trivialize serious data reporting.
   c. Visual representation is not generally necessary in the written document although it is helpful in presenting data to a large audience.
   ✔ d. Visual representation is vital in the written text for presenting complex data or interrelationships.

4. Valid data
   a. are tabulated and analyzed by the computer.
   ✔ b. are based on good sampling methodology.
   c. refer to all information collected through primary research techniques.
   d. do not require visual representation.

5. The major value of valid primary research is that it
   a. reinforces secondary data that already exist.
   b. allows the researcher to editorialize on findings.
   ✔ c. reveals information that does not exist elsewhere.
   d. focuses on views of individuals rather than groups.

```
CHAPTER 16
```

MANAGING DATA AND USING GRAPHICS

CHAPTER OVERVIEW

Following data collection as described in Chapter 15, the content of Chapter 16 focuses on handling and presenting quantitative data. Emphasis should be given to reducing large amounts of data to manageable size through tabular and graphic means.

The statistical methods described in the chapter are basic; thus, many students may be familiar with them. Although students have recently completed a course in quantitative analysis and statistics, many appreciate the review.

The text supports the practice of labeling all tables, graphs, and other illustrations as Figure 1, Figure 2, and so on, and numbering them consecutively. This practice makes following the narrative easy and does not confuse the reader with "Graph 1, Table 1, etc.," which might lead to sentences such as "...as shown in Table 8 and Graph 3." Using consecutive numbering, the sentence would read "...as shown in Figures 8 and 9." Businesspeople seem to prefer this approach, and it is generally followed in publishing. On the other hand, some instructors prefer to label graphs and charts as Graph 1, 2, 3, and so on, and tables as Table 1, 2, 3, and so on. They encounter problems, however, when other types of figures, such as maps, photos, and diagrams, must be included.

If at all possible, incorporate computer graphics, either as a means for students to complete assignments requiring the construction of graphics or through demonstration as part of the lecture process.

LEARNING OBJECTIVES

1 Learn ways to manage quantities of data efficiently.

2 Analyze quantitative data using measures of central tendency.

3 Design and integrate graphics within reports.

CHAPTER OUTLINE AND TEACHING SUGGESTIONS

1   **LEARNING OBJECTIVE**

I.   Managing Quantitative Data
  A.   Show **TA 16–1** (Chapter Opener) as you introduce the chapter.
  B.   To gain students' attention, use the statistics instructors' technique of saying that at least two people in a class of 35 will have the same birth month and day. Try it by starting with those born in January and moving through the months. For each month ask those raising hands to give the date. More often than not, two will have the same date of birth. This activity raises student interest in quantitative management techniques.
  C.   Integrate the communication mentor comments into class lectures to reinforce the concepts in the chapter.
  D.   Common Language

2   **LEARNING OBJECTIVE**

  E.   Measures of Central Tendency
  1.   A good way to approach the statistical problems is to put an array of 35 to 50 numbers on the chalkboard or on a transparency. Be sure the numbers are related closely enough to make sense as a statistical distribution when they are tabulated in data classes. For example, call the numbers *student scores on a test*. Have them range between 40 and 99, with a median around 75.
  2.   As students review the array, ask them to pick out the high and low scores (values). Subtracting the low

from the high value and adding 1 to the result gives the range size; that is, high 99 - 40 = 59 + 1 = 60. The range is from 99–40, and the size of the range is 60, which includes both 40 and 99.

3. Ask students to suggest how many data classes to use in tabulating the values. They will probably arrive at ranges of 40–49, 50–59, 60–69, and so on, which would provide 6 classes.

4. Once tabulation into data classes is completed, ask students to prepare a table showing the number and percent of values in each class. From there, you can talk about central tendency.

5. The Mean

6. The Median

7. The Mode

8. The Range

9. Assign the following exercises to reinforce the concept of central tendency:

    Exercises 2–3. Requires students to compute the measures of central tendency of a distribution of ungrouped and grouped data. Refer to the "Possible Solutions to Exercises" and **TM 16–3** (Solution, Exercise 2) and **TM 16–4** (Solution, Exercise 3) for the solutions.

    Applications 1–3 in the Study Guide. Require students to (a) compute the mean, mean, median, and mode, (b) select appropriate measures of central tendency from a distribution, and (c) identify the range and interquartile range.

---

3 | **LEARNING OBJECTIVE**

II. Using Graphics

A. Emphasize not only *how* to prepare each of the graphics described, but *when* to use each of them.

B. Illustrate the various types of graphics as you discuss this section.

1. Make transparencies of actual graphics taken from company documents, newspapers, magazines, journals, etc., to use for illustrations of the various types of graphics.

2. As an alternative or supplement, prepare a variety of types of graphics using a presentation graphics computer package. These visuals can be used throughout your coverage of this section.

3. Discuss the ethical use of graphics. Incorporate examples of graphics that distort or misrepresent data such as the pictogram on page 540, the bar chart on page 166 of Chapter 6, and others you locate in annual reports, *USA Today*, and other printed sources.

C. Tables

D. Bar Charts

1. Multiple-Range Bar Chart

2. Stacked-Bar Chart

    a. Discuss the Think It Over note on page 535. Based on the data in Figure 16–4, the company should concentrate its efforts to reduce defects in the automotive supplies division.

    b. Discuss the Think It Over note on page 535. Based on the data in Figure 16–5, products in the introduction and growth stages are becoming an increasingly larger proportion of the company's total sales. Therefore, management must continue to allocate resources to the research and development of new products.

E. Line Charts

F. Pie Charts

1. Discuss other graphics that can be used to show how the parts of a whole are distributed: stacked-bar and area charts.

2. Discuss the Think It Over note on page 539. A user documentation manager's interpretation of Figure 16–9 follows: Approximately 25 percent of the company's total sales

is database software; however, nearly half the hotline inquiries concerning software operations during January related to database software. Therefore, additional effort should be directed toward improving user documentation for the database software to increase customer satisfaction.

G. Pictograms

H. Maps

I. Flowcharts

J. Other Graphics

K. Provide graphics applications that require students to develop increasing levels of competency:

Drawing a specific graphic. Assign Applications 1–4 that direct students to draw a specific graphic. As you discuss the solutions in **TM 16–5, 16–6, 16–7, 16–8** (Solutions, Applications 1–4 respectively), discuss why each graphic type is effective for portraying the data in the application.

Selecting an appropriate graphic for specific data and preparing an effective graphic. Choose from the following applications:

1. Applications 4 and 5 in the *Study Guide.* Application 5 also requires students to write an effective introduction; therefore, be sure you have discussed Section III of this outline.

2. Assign Application 5 that requires students to select and draw a specific graphic. Project **TM 16–9** (Solution, Application 5) and discuss the solution.

3. Assign the following activity to be completed for reinforcement or for a daily grade:

Prepare a graphic or table to illustrate the following information:

Total consumer credit at the end of March was $184.3 billion, of which $32.8 billion was noninstallment credit. The $151.5 billion of installment credit was composed of $51.6 billion for personal loans, $50.5 billion for automobiles, and $49.4 billion for other consumer goods.

See **TM 16–10** (Solution, Reinforcement Assignment) for suggested table. A pie chart could also be used to represent the data.

Evaluating and revising an ineffective graphic. Assign Application 6; instruct students to evaluate the effectiveness of the three graphics in small groups or individually during class and revise the graphics incorporating the suggestions for homework. Project the solutions on **TA 16–2, 16–3, 16–4** (Solutions, Application 6a, 6b, 6c respectively) during the next class period.

Applying knowledge of graphics to a real-world situation. Assign Application 7 and/or the e-mail application. Students are required to critique and revise graphics included in a company's annual report. The one-page memorandum report required in Application 7 would be an excellent topic for a short report after you have covered Chapter 17.

III. Introducing Tables and Graphs in Text

A. The best way to relate information in this section is to make transparencies of an actual report to display to the class.

B. Reinforce the pattern for including graphics in text:

1. introduce it

2. show it

3. tell about it

C. Discuss the Think It Over note on page 544. The graphic should be positioned at the top of page 9; page 8 should be filled with text that would have ideally followed the graphic.

D. Lead the class in a discussion of the appropriateness of placing graphics in an appendix rather than in the text.

E. Communication in Action: Paul Lehman, Macom Corporation

1. Assign the applications that follow the case.

2. Make a transparency of **TM 16–1** (Solution, "Communication in Action" Case, Question 1) and **TM 16–2** (Solution, "Communication in Action" Case, Question 3) to show as you review the solutions.

F.   Assign Application 5 in the *Study Guide* that requires students to select an appropriate graphic and compose an effective introduction.

IV. Summary

A.   Integrate the communication mentor comments into class lectures to reinforce the concepts presented in the chapter.

B.   Ask students to complete the *Study Guide* questions for Chapter 16.

C.   Require students to complete the applications in the *Study Guide*. These applications "walk students through" (a) computing measures of central tendency, (b) selecting appropriate measures of central tendency, (c) determining effective graphics for selected data, and (d) composing introductions to graphics. Students compare their answers with sample solutions.

D.   Assign selected exercises and applications at the end of the chapter. Although business students tend to be quantitatively capable, those who may not be can often learn from others. Therefore, develop three- or four-person groups to work on some end-of-the-chapter exercises. If you assign exercises as homework, ask volunteers to put their solutions on the chalkboard or on a transparency for class presentation by them.

E.   Ask students to complete the e-mail application and share solutions with the class.

TRANSPARENCIES AND MASTERS

ADDITIONAL READINGS

Antonoff, M. (1990). Presentations that persuade. *Personal Computing, 14*(7), 60, 62–68.

Gruin, L. (1994). Captivated audience: Desktop presentations. *PC Magazine, 13*(16), 257–263.

Holmes, N. (1989, March). Get smart about charts. *Publish,* pp. 42–44.

Horton, W. (1993). The almost universal language: Graphics for international business. *Technical Communication, 40*(4), 682–693.

Horton, W. (1993). Visual literacy: Going beyond words in technical communications. *Technical Communication, 40*(4), 447–451.

Kosslyn, S. M., & Chabris, C. F. (1992). Minding information graphics. *Folio: The Magazine for Magazine Management, 21*(2), 69–71.

Search, P. (1993). Computer graphics: Changing the language of visual communication. *Technical Communication, 40*(4), 629–637.

Williams, T. R. (1993). What's so different about visuals? *Technical Communication, 40*(4), 669–676.

ANSWERS TO "COMMUNICATION IN ACTION" CASE: Paul Lehman, Macom Corporation

1.   **Prepare a stacked-bar chart Lehman could use to explain price variations for lots along the golf course. Factors such as proximity to lakes, a green, a tee, the clubhouse, and a fairway affect the perceived value of a lot. Assume that lot prices range from $100,000 to $150,000.** See **TM 16–1** (Solution, "Communication in Action" Case, Question 1) for suggested graphic.

2.   **Why is a stacked-bar chart appropriate for assessing the progress of Lehman's builders?** Stacked-bar charts enable Lehman to compare sets of data from several builders' activities over time. He tracks the number of completed homes, homes under construction, and vacant lots. Stacked-bar charts allow Lehman to see a contractor's progress toward converting vacant lots to completed lots. The stacked-bar graph shows him how the number of lots in each of the

three categories has changed over a period of time. Pie charts would not show close, side-by-side comparisons of the builders' activities. Tables would not allow adequate comparisons of different activities and builders.

3. **Prepare a stacked-bar chart using first-quarter data. In January Lehman's top builder (provide name) had 80 completed homes, 20 homes under construction, and 50 vacant lots. In February, the builder had 95 completed homes, 15 under construction, and 40 vacant lots. In March, the builder had 105 completed homes, 20 under construction, and 25 vacant lots. Provide a descriptive title. What topics does the graph suggest Lehman should discuss with the builder at tomorrow's meeting? See TM 16–2** (Solution, "Communication in Action" Case, Question 3) for suggested chart. Lehman should encourage the builder to purchase additional lots. The builder should be reminded that having an adequate number and variety of lots available for potential customers' selection are important factors in making a sale.

ANSWERS TO REVIEW QUESTIONS

1. Managing data consists of reducing large amounts of data to tables and graphs and of using measures of central tendency to describe populations. These steps protect researchers from distortion of their material.

2. Common language consists of easy-to-understand terms for most people: percentage, ratios, and fractions.

3. The mean is the measure most people call the "average." It is calculated by dividing the sum of the individual amounts by the total number of amounts.

4. The median represented by the middle amount of 73 would probably be best. The mean of 68 is smaller than six of the remaining eight figures and is too low. The mode is 85, which is too high. The median reduces the impact of the bottom figure of 12.

5. Refer to the list of six guidelines in the "Using Graphics" section.

6. Refer to the list of four guidelines in the "Tables" section.

7. Variations in vertical increments can drastically change the slope of lines and the con-

trast of bar heights. Horizontal variations may contribute to the same problems.

8. A broken chart is one that has portions deleted and clearly indicated because the amounts involved would otherwise be too large for the graphic to fit because of space restrictions.

9. Although both a stacked-bar (component) chart and an area (cumulative line) chart reveal parts of a whole, the stacked-bars show parts for a given time; and the line components depict how those parts relate over some designated period.

10. Pie charts show the division of 100 percent. Line charts show changes over time.

11. Software may limit your ability to follow rules explicitly. The nature of the data or the presentation may require slight deviations to increase the clarity of the graphic. (Refer to the example of changing the top placement of a title when exploding slices in a pie chart.) Rules may be varied for dramatic effect.

12. In pictures, doubling the height and width enlarges the area four times, thus exaggerating differences.

13. A graphic should be placed as near as possible *after* the introduction of the graphic in the narrative.

14. Yes, under *no* conditions should a graphic be included without an introduction. Yes, if readers are told about the graphic and its implications, the graphic will supplement what is said.

15. Refer to the examples in the "Introducing Tables and Graphics in the Text" section. The graphic should immediately follow the introduction.

POSSIBLE SOLUTIONS TO EXERCISES

1. Use these questions to initiate discussion.

2. (a) In computing salaries, omit the thousands (000) and add 000 to answers; that is, multiply answers by 1,000.

    Mean: 1,652 (sum of all salaries) ÷ 25 = 66.1 ($66,100).

    Median: $70,000 (middle salary)

    Mode: $74,000 (most frequent salary).

    (b) Refer to the solution in **TM 16–3** (Solution, Exercise 2).

Mean: This computation used midpoints of 94.5, 84.5, 74.5, and so on; assuming values ranging between 89.5 and 99.5, for example, fall in the 90–99 group or class. If 95, 85, 75, and so on, are used as midpoints, the total of all values would be 1,665; and the mean would be 66.6. Interestingly, the grouped data and the ungrouped data means are the same, indicating that the values were fairly well distributed within each class.

Median: The median is determined by the middle or thirteenth value. In the grouped data, that value is the lowest, or first one in the 70–79 class. Thus the median is found by determining 1/6 of the range of the 70–79 class and adding it to the bottom value of the class, 69.5 or 70. A sixth of 10 is 1.6, which when added to 69.5 or 70 results in a median of either 71.1 or 71.6.

Mode: The modal group is 70–79 because it contains the greatest number of values of any group. Although it is not necessary, the mode could be defined as the midpoint of the modal group.

Any differences existing in the measurements are, of course, attributed to the assumption that in grouped data the assumption is that data are distributed evenly throughout each group. When raw data are used, this assumption is unnecessary.

3. An appropriate table for the data in Exercise 4 may look similar to the one shown in **TM 16–4** (Solution, Exercise 3).

   Introduction: Over half the executives had salaries of $70,000 and above, as shown in Figure 1.

4. (a) organizational chart; provides a picture of the authority structure and relationships of an organization.

   (b) line; provides changes in quantitative data over time and illustrates trends. (A stacked-bar chart would be appropriate to show a breakdown of the various minority groups represented in the total. A table would be appropriate if the writer is required to present actual figures.)

   (c) line chart; depicts changes in quantitative data over time and illustrates trends.

   (d) simple bar chart to compare quantities; pie chart to show the relationships among the counties.

   (e) stacked-bar chart; shows how components over time periods contributed to a total figure.

   (f) flowchart; step-by-step diagram of a procedure.

   (g) map; shows geographical relationships.

5. (a) Move the reference to Table 5 to the end of the sentence. If readers study the table before they are told about it, they will draw their own conclusions.

   (b) Integrate the reference to Figure 6 in the text rather than put it in parentheses. Position the reference at the end of the sentence so that readers read the interpretation before studying the figure.

   (c) Move the reference to Figure 3 to the end of the sentence so that readers read the interpretation before studying the figure. Rewrite using third person if statement is included in a formal report.

   (d) Integrate the reference to Figure 4 in the text rather than put it in parentheses. Position the reference at the end of the sentence so that readers read the interpretation before studying the figure.

POSSIBLE SOLUTION TO E-MAIL APPLICATION

Review the e-mail messages and identify the five graphics that represent most of the major weaknesses. Use one or more of the following class activities:

1. Ask the students who evaluated the weakest graphics to give a short oral report to the class; instruct them via e-mail about how to prepare a suitable transparency.

2. As a variation, have a student show the poor graph and have the class as a group critique it; the student could then display a bullet chart outlining the weaknesses and a good rendition of the chart.

3. Allow all students who critiqued a particular graphic to discuss in a small group how it could be improved. Allow each group to give a brief report of their suggestions to the class.

POSSIBLE SOLUTIONS TO APPLICATIONS

1. Drawing a Bar Chart
⇨ *Level 2* ⇦

See **TM 16–5** (Solution, Application 1) for suggested bar chart.

Introductory sentence: The number of injuries in each plant location over the last year is reflected in Figure 1. The number of injuries in the Memphis plant has increased; the Joliet plant has decreased; and the Knoxville plant has remained steady.

2. Drawing a Stacked-Bar Chart
⇨ *Level 2* ⇦

See **TM 16–6** (Solution, Application 2) for suggested stacked-bar chart.

Introductory sentence: Despite growth in total sales from 1993–1995, the company has not experienced an increase in pretax income, as shown in Figure 1.

3. Drawing a Line Chart
⇨ *Level 2* ⇦

See **TM 16–7** (Solution, Application 3) for suggested line chart.

Introductory sentence: Injuries for the company have been declining over the past four years, as depicted in Figure 1.

4. Drawing a Pie Chart
⇨ *Level 2* ⇦

See **TM 16–8** (Solution, Application 4) for suggested pie chart.

Introductory sentence: The majority of city tax dollars are spent on education, as shown in Figure 1.

5. Selecting and Drawing an Appropriate Graphic
⇨ *Level 3* ⇦

See **TM 16–9** (Solution, Application 5) for suggested table.

6. Evaluating and Revising Graphics
⇨ *Level 3* ⇦

(a) *Suggestions:* The exact sales figures need not be reported in a bar chart; if exact figures are desired, a table would be more appropriate. Begin with the earliest year; otherwise a reader reviewing the figure quickly might interpret sales to be declining.

Introductory sentence: The company has experienced a 300 percent growth in sales over the last six years, as shown in Figure 1.

Title and revision: See **TA 16–2** (Solution, Application 6a) for suggested revision.

(b) *Suggestions:* A bar chart should be used rather than a line chart, because no time period is being charted. The y-axis should start at 0.

Introductory sentence: Unit production for the third quarter varied considerably among plants, as shown in Figure 1. The Memphis plant had the highest unit production and Dallas, the lowest.

Title and revision: See **TA 16–3** (Solution, Application 6b) for suggested revision.

(c) *Suggestions:* A pie chart would be a more effective graphic for showing the contribution each sales representative has made. Convert the number of customers to a percentage.

Introductory sentence: Jan Peterson led the sales force, obtaining 33 percent of the total number of new customers for October, as shown in Figure 1.

Title and revision: See **TA 16–4** (Solution, Application 6c) for suggested revision.

7. Evaluating Graphics in Annual Reports
⇨ *Level 3* ⇦

Papers will vary. Annual reports reflect both good and bad application of the use of graphics. Because of time and accessibility restrictions, you may want to collect and distribute copies of annual reports for evaluation by the class. In evaluating the memos, the following factors might be considered: (a) evidence of the application of principles and guidelines for effective graphic presentation, as covered in Chapter 16; (b) ability to write an effective deductive-pattern memo; and (c) application of analytical processes to practical problem solving.

CHAPTER 17

ORGANIZING AND WRITING SHORT REPORTS AND PROPOSALS

CHAPTER OVERVIEW

Short reports and proposals may be prepared as letters, as memorandums, or as formal reports. Emphasize the problem-solving, research-based orientation of short reports to distinguish them from simple, everyday memorandums.

For many students, the content of this chapter supplements that of Chapters 15 and 16 to provide all the report-writing skill and knowledge they may be required to use. However, documentation methods for formal reports that are presented in Chapter 18 should be included in a discussion of short reports if report coverage should formally end with Chapter 17.

LEARNING OBJECTIVES

1 Identify the parts of a formal report and the contribution each part makes to the overall effectiveness of a report.

2 Prepare short reports in letter and memorandum formats.

3 Prepare proposals for a variety of purposes.

CHAPTER OUTLINE AND TEACHING SUGGESTIONS

1   LEARNING OBJECTIVE

I. Parts of a Report
   A. Show **TA 17–1** (Chapter Opener) that draws an analogy to help students understand that reports are composed of several distinct components (preliminary parts, report text, and addenda) in the same way as an atom has a distinct structure. Tie this discussion with the chapter opening scenario about careful planning in a home improvement project. A third analogy you might develop is discussing the craft that went into every component of a Stradivari violin—

the finest violins the world has ever known. The artisans who constructed them put care into craving each piece of wood and preparing each string before all the pieces were put together into one unique and perfect whole. Likewise, each part of a report must be carefully "crafted" and then reviewed to make sure it is as perfect as possible.

   B. Integrate the communication mentor comments into class lectures to reinforce the concepts in the chapter. These comments include communication strategies proven in the workplace and concrete advice for developing report-writing skills.

   C. Show **TA 17–2** (Parts of a Formal Report) to help students understand that reports are made up of (a) preliminary parts, (b) the report text, and (c) addenda. Emphasize that a report might include most or all of the parts shown in each of the three categories.

   D. Refer to Figure 17–2 to show how a report develops from a simple memorandum to a long, formal report.

      1. Indicate that short reports are presented as memo, letter, and expanded letter reports (the text contains illustrations of these report formats).

      2. Describe how writers tend to add parts as their work grows in volume.

         a. A title page is often added when the text exceeds two or so pages. It also serves as a transmittal in a short report. As the report grows, a letter of transmittal might be added.

         b. A writer might add a contents page if headings appear in the report.

         c. The writer also may prepare a bibliography to demonstrate scholarship and to impress the receiver.

E. Preliminary Parts
  1. Half-title Page
  2. Title Page
  3. Authorization
  4. Transmittal
  5. Contents
  6. Figures
  7. Executive Summary
     a. Refer to other names for this part: *abstract, overview, synopsis*, etc. Emphasize that the executive summary gives the reader a "bird's eye view" of the report and also serves the distant reader who may want only an overview of the project. Stress Pharr's discussion of the importance of "boiling down" a report to its barest essentials yet providing enough information that a decision can be made (mentor note, page 553).
     b. Many new MBA hirees receive assignments to prepare for their supervisors abstracts of business literature and condensations of professional meetings and seminars.
     c. Require students to identify practitioner journals in their fields that include an executive summary with each article and evaluate the quality of the summary (Think It Over note, page 552).

F. Report Text
  1. The "report text" can be compared to the events of a courtroom trial.
     a. The "introduction" can be thought of as the opening statements.
     b. The "body" can be thought of as the testimony and evidence phase.
     c. The "summary and conclusions" can be likened to the closing arguments.
     d. The "recommendation" can be compared to the verdict, which should not come as a surprise if careful evidence has been presented.
  2. Introduction
  3. Body
  4. Summary, Conclusions, and Recommendations
     a. Assign Application 2 in the *Study Guide* that requires students to compose recommendations from data provided.
     b. As students compare their recommendations with the solution provided in the *Study Guide*, reinforce the definitions of *fact, conclusions*, and *recommendations*. Refer students to the definitions and examples on pages 520–521 of Chapter 15.

G. Addenda
  1. References
     a. Re-emphasize the importance of referencing to avoid plagiarism.
     b. Emphasize that although numerous ways to reference exist, the important requirement is consistent use of the method selected. Guidelines for preparing citations and references are covered in Chapter 18.
  2. Appendixes
     a. Emphasize the criterion for deciding whether to place material in the text or in an appendix: How closely related is the material to the text discussion?
     b. Emphasize that appendix items should be sequenced in the order mentioned in the text.
  3. Index

H. Refer students to the chapter summary that includes a list of each report part with a concise explanation of its purpose. To ensure that students understand this concept before attempting to write a report, you might prepare a matching exercise that requires students to match the report part with its purpose. Use the chapter summary to generate this pop quiz.

2	LEARNING OBJECTIVE

II. Organizing Report Findings

   A. Implement the following activity to emphasize the importance of organization:

   > 1. Give a deck of cards arranged in suit order to one student and a deck of cards arranged randomly to another student.
   >
   > 2. Ask class members to call out four cards at random; for instance, four of clubs, jack of diamonds, ten of spades, and ace of hearts.
   >
   > 3. Write these on the board and ask the two students with the cards to indicate as they find each of the cards listed.
   >
   > 4. One student will have a much easier time finding the cards and will finish well ahead of the other.
   >
   > 5. When the first student has found the four cards, ask the two students to show the arrangement of their decks.
   >
   > 6. Ask the class what made finding the selected cards easier for the first student: **Organization.**

   B. Begin with the concept that report preparation takes place after the research has been completed. Data have been gathered, tabulated, and converted into figures for a report. Library research (printed and online sources) provided the report writer with information about research methods and literature related to the subject.

   C. Discuss the organizational pattern of an analytical report.

   1. Make sure students can distinguish an informational report that presents objective information and an analytical report that presents suggested solutions to problems. Review the definitions of an informational and analytical report presented in the "What Is a Report" section of Chapter 15. Introduce the term *justification report* to designate reports that present conclusions and recommendations for managerial decisions.

   2. Ask students what two questions the reader of an analytical report wishes to have answered as he/she reads an analytical report: (1) What is the solution and (2) why. Next, emphasize that the writer should present the information in the report in this same logical order: the conclusion presented first in a deductive pattern (the solution) and the body divided into sections that clearly inform the reader of the criteria used (why).

   3. Lead students through the poor and good outlines for an analytical report to select a personal computer on page 556. Discuss the advantages of dividing the report into sections that reflect the criteria used to make the decision and *not* the alternatives compared: (a) emphasizes the criteria used for the decision, (b) makes comparison of each alternative easy and eliminates overlap of information, and (c) uses original headings that relate to the specific problem being solved (problem, method, findings, conclusions would fit any research topic but would not reveal the nature of a specific problem).

   4. Reinforce the idea of using **talking headings** in parallel form throughout a report.

   D. Show **TA 17–3** (Basic Outline Grows into a Contents Page) to illustrate that the basic outline of the report expands into the contents page. Point out that the divisions reflect the criteria used to make the decision and talking headings reveal the conclusion drawn in each major section.

E. Assign Application 1 in the *Study Guide* that requires students to identify format, composition, and spelling errors in an outline. Instruct students to compare their work with the revised outline provided in the *Study Guide* and discuss principles for developing an effective outline.

III. Form Reports
A. Introduce form reports as tools for managerial and organizational control.
   1. Forms increase the likelihood that repetitive information will be reported uniformly. Every piece of data has the same place to be recorded on identical forms.
   2. Accuracy is also increased. Lenders, for example, may not accept real estate appraisals reported on the Uniform Residential Appraisal Report form if certain information is missing or incorrectly reported.
   3. Bank tellers frequently spend considerable time attempting to balance their cash reports. The reports reflect on teller performance and also receive supervisory review.
   4. Ask the class if they know of other form reports. Suggestions: inventory reports from a variety of businesses, automobile sales and purchases reports (to state governments), marriage license requests, and income tax returns. All are forms used for repetitive occurrences.
B. Refer to Figure 17–4 to illustrate the use of the computer to generate form reports.
   1. Using the example of a hospital's automation of repetitive patient reports, discuss how computer-generated form reports increase efficiency and minimize errors.
   2. The discussion should lead naturally to the human relations benefits gained from producing error-free reports; e.g., minimizing clerical errors that may lead a patient to question the hospital's ability to deliver quality health care.

IV. Characteristics of Short Reports

A. Show **TM 17–1** (Characteristics of Short Reports) as you discuss this section.
B. Refer to **TA 15–2** (The Formal-Informal Report Continuum) to illustrate that short reports tend to appear closer to the informal side of the model than do formal reports.
C. Review the report-writing principles applied in the short periodic report in Figure 17–5 (memorandum format) and the audit report in Figure 17–6 (letter format).
D. As an in-class writing assignment, assign a short report that may be written in about 200 words. The goal of this exercise is to demonstrate how a rapid writing style can produce a rough draft in a short time. The report should contain two pieces of quantitative data that must be converted to tables or graphs. Impose a one-hour or one-class-session time restraint. The idea is for students to assemble the data and write the report as rapidly as possible without bothering to make minor editorial changes. If at all possible, have students compose the assignment using computers to simplify composing and revising.
   1. Have students prepare rough tables from the quantitative data. Using these rough tables, they may prepare computer-generated graphics outside of class to incorporate into their reports later.
   2. The following suggestions will assist students:
      a. Develop an understanding of the problem.
      b. Assume you have conducted whatever research is necessary to gather the data provided.
      c. Prepare the rough tables.
      d. Arrive at a conclusion to the problem.
      e. Make a rough outline—even a mental one—to get an idea of the sequence of your report. Keep in mind the four-step, problem-solving process.
      f. Begin writing with the familiar: the analysis of tabular

data, the conclusion, the purpose, the method of research. Then proceed to another easy portion.

g. Take a fast look at your work. Add transitions where necessary.

3. At the end of the allotted time, have students save their work to a computer disk; if students are handwriting the assignment, collect the papers to be kept until the next class meeting.

4. Return the disk files or written reports to students for editing and refinement at the next meeting. Students will also incorporate their graphics.

5. Have students submit the final product at the end of the class meeting or a time you designate.

3	LEARNING OBJECTIVE

V. Proposals

A. Treat proposals as a form of a short or a long report.

B. Review the definition of a proposal, making sure students understand the proposal is a competitive instrument that attempts to convince the reader that the bidding firm can do the work or make a product better than the competition can. You might ask students to reread the discussion of proposals in the discussion of the types of business reports in Chapter 15.

C. Discuss the purpose of internal and external proposals. *Internal proposals* justify or recommend purchases or changes in the company. *External proposals* are critical documents written to generate business.

D. Distinguish between a solicited and an unsolicited proposal. *Solicited proposals* are generated when a potential buyer submits exact specifications or needs in a request for a proposal (RFP). *Unsolicited proposals* are prepared when a person submits a solution to a problem to be solved.

E. Parts of a Proposal

1. Emphasize that proposals may be prepared in a variety of ways, and the content will also vary. The outline of what is to be included in a proposal is provided when a firm and governmental agency issues a "Request for Proposals."

2. Often, written proposals are followed by oral presentations to provide opportunity for feedback.

3. Problem and/or Purpose

4. Scope

5. Method and Procedures

6. Materials and Equipment

7. Qualifications and Recommendations

8. Follow-up and/or Evaluation

9. Budget, Cost, and Summary

10. Addenda Items

F. Sample Short Proposal: Make a transparency of **TM 17–2** (Good Example, Brief Letter Proposal) to show as you discuss this section.

G. Review the report-writing principles applied in the proposal in Figure 17–8 (letter format)

H. Communication in Action: Jim Ratchford, Cherry, Bekaert & Holland

1. Discuss the use of an unsolicited proposal to generate business. Initiate a class discussion about the computerized perpetual inventory example in the text and Ratchford's promoting the firm's expertise in current accounting changes and issues (hot buttons).

2. Instruct students to complete the applications that follow the case. Students are required to generate an idea and/or outline for an unsolicited proposal. They are encouraged to select a key issue or "hot button" that could be promoted as a specialized service in their chosen field. Refer to the teaching suggestions that follow in the "Communication in Action Case" section.

I. Proposals are excellent projects for team contributions. Organize the class so about five teams will compete to develop the best proposal. Application 12, developing a proposal for a franchise to open a miniature golf course, is an excellent application for this purpose. Entrepreneurial-spirited students get enthusiastic about making assumptions and can picture themselves as aspiring business owners.

VI. Summary

A. Integrate the communication mentor comments into class lectures to reinforce the concepts presented in the chapter.

B. Assign the *Study Guide* questions for Chapter 17.

C. Require students to complete the applications in the *Study Guide*. These applications involve (a) applying parallel structure to report headings and (b) composing recommendations. Critical thinking questions help students revise the outline; students compare their outline and recommendations with sample solutions.

D. Ask students to complete the e-mail application.

E. Assign selected exercises, applications, and cases at the end of the chapter. Remind students to study the suggestions in the "Check Your Writing" checklist at the end of Chapter 18 when planning and revising a short-report assignment.

F. Assign one of the applications designated as an AWA (Analytical Writing Assessment) for the GMAT. Refer to pages 12–13 of this *Instructor's Resource Manual* for holistic scoring techniques used by evaluators of this written portion of the GMAT.

TRANSPARENCIES AND MASTERS

TA 17–1   Chapter Opener
TA 17–2   Parts of a Formal Report
TA 17–3   Basic Outline Expands into a
          Contents Page

TM 17–1   Characteristics of Short Reports
TM 17–2   Good Example, Brief Letter Proposal
TM 17–3   Solution, Application 5
TM 17–4   Solution, Case for Analysis 1, Step 3

ADDITIONAL READINGS

Budish, B. E., & Sandhusen, R. L. (1989). The short proposal: Versatile tool for communicating corporate culture in competitive climates. *IEEE Transaction on Professional Communication, 32*(2), 81–85.

How to make sure your reports are read and acted on. (1989). *Agency Sales Magazine, 19*(3), 40–43.

Mohn, N. C., & Land, T. H. (1989). A guide to quality marketing research proposals and reports. *Business, 39*(1), 38–40.

Sweeney, K. (1991). Bridging communication gaps in management (preparing annual appraisals, asset management plans, and budget proposals. *Journal of Property Management, 56*(2), 54-56.

ANSWERS TO "COMMUNICATION IN ACTION" CASE: Jim Ratchford, Cherry, Bekaert & Holland

1. **Why are proposals so important to Cherry, Bekaert & Holland?** Proposals give prospective clients a "first look" at the accounting firm? The proposals often determine whether the firm secures the account or makes a short list. Although most proposals follow the highly, standardized format of an RFP, the firm demonstrates through the proposal a current knowledge of recent accounting pronouncements.

2. **Generate an idea for an unsolicited proposal you might write for providing a service in your chosen field (e.g., an architect major might develop a proposal for renovating an old building) or recommending a change in your work environment or your university (e.g., change in procedures or work schedule). Consider "hot buttons" or key issues in your field requiring specialized services that you could promote to a prospective client through an unsolicited proposal. Develop an outline for the proposal and describe briefly the information you would develop within each major section.** This assignment is designed to help students recognize the importance of writing *unsolicited* proposals to generate new business. Students are required to identify a "hot button" or key issue in their fields (work environment or university) that could be

developed into a proposal that meets the needs of clients/customers and generates revenue for the company. This proposal may even create a new specialized area of service for the company. The assignment could be expanded into a term project by requiring the student to conduct necessary research and write the proposal. Allow students to work in groups composed of students in the same major to enhance the generation of a number of creative solutions. If time is limited, have groups give a brief oral report discussing the key issue they believe could be developed into an effective unsolicited proposal.

ANSWERS TO REVIEW QUESTIONS

1. Problem, Method, Findings, and Conclusion are the four headings that could be used in many reports.

2. As they grow in length, reports require more support from beginning and ending items to communicate ideas clearly.

3. **Preliminary parts:**

   Half-title page. A single page containing the title that adds formality to the report.

   Title page. Serves as a transmittal; includes title, author, date, and name of person/organization requesting the report.

   Authorization. Provides written authorization for completing the report; becomes a formal part of the report.

   Transmittal. Presents the report to the reader; may summarize the major conclusions (analytical report) or major points (informational report).

   Contents. Lists the name and page number on which every report part appears—except for half-title page, title page, and contents. This list provides the reader an overview of the report.

   List of Figures. Indicates the page number on which graphics appear in a report.

   Executive Summary. Summarizes the essential elements in the report to simplify understanding.

   Report Text:

   Introduction. Orients the reader to the problem (topic) and previews the major divisions.

   Body. Presents the information collected and relates it to the problem; the heart of the report.

   Summary. Adds unity to the report by reviewing main points presented in the body.

   Conclusions. Interprets data collected.

   Recommendations. Presents the writer's opinions on a possible course of action based on the conclusions.

   Addenda:

   References. Lists alphabetically the sources used in preparing the report.

   Appendixes. Contain supplementary information that supports the report but is not appropriate for inclusion in the report.

   Index. Lists alphabetically the subject matter in the report with the page numbers on which each subject appears.

4. If the title is longer than one line, arrange it in the inverted pyramid format; that is, make each succeeding line shorter than the line preceding it. Arrange the title consistently wherever it appears.

5. Write a title that is descriptive and comprehensive. Use concise wording to identify the content of the report adequately.

6. Report writers add report parts to achieve four purposes: (a) add formality to the report, (b) repeat report content, (c) aid reader in locating information, and (d) aid the reader in understanding the report more easily.

7. Preliminary parts are numbered with small roman numerals (i, ii, iii); the remaining pages (beginning with the introduction and ending with the index) are numbered with arabic numerals (1, 2, 3).

8. Using the deductive approach, develop the following outline: (a) present the report and remind the reader that he or she requested it; (b) summarize the research methods and the major points in an informational report or the conclusions and any recommendations in an analytical report; and (c) close cordially, expressing appreciation for the help of others.

9. Word-processing software automatically generates preliminary parts (contents, list of figures) and addenda items (references, index). If last-minute changes are made, these parts are instantaneously updated to reflect any pagination changes.

10. The executive summary presents a miniature version of the report by (a) briefly introduc-

ing the report and previewing the major divisions, (b) summarizing each major report section, and (c) summarizing the report summary (and conclusions and recommendations if included in the report). The executive summary is also referred to as an *abstract*. (Students will note that the *APA Manual* uses the term *abstract* when they study the formal report in Chapter 18.)

11. An effective introduction includes (a) what the topic is, (b) why it is being reported on, (c) the scope and limitations of the research, (d) where the information came from, and (e) a preview of the major sections of the report to provide coherence and transition into the report. The preview tells how the topic is divided into parts and the order in which the parts will be presented.

12. No. Introducing a new idea in the summary may make the reader wonder why the point was not developed earlier. It may suggest that the study was not adequately completed or that the writer did not plan adequately before writing.

13. Findings are the facts (evidence) uncovered by the research. Conclusions are interpretations of the findings. Recommendations present the writer's opinion on a possible course of action based on the conclusions. The summary, conclusions, and recommendations can be placed in three separate sections for a long report. For shorter reports, the conclusions and recommendations can be combined into one section, or all three sections can be combined.

14. The references page (works cited) is an alphabetical list identifying the sources used in preparing the report. The bibliography (works consulted) includes sources not cited in the text to acknowledge that a writer is influenced by any information consulted.

15. If a report contains more than one appendix, label each one with a capital letter and a title (Appendix A, Appendix B...). Yes, each item included in the appendix must be mentioned in the report.

16. Because criteria, not things, are the basis for making judgments and decisions, they are ideal elements for organizational sections of the findings in a report.

17. An inductively organized report becomes deductive when the conclusion is placed at the beginning through such parts as a trans-

mittal message, an executive summary, and the conclusions reported in the introduction.

18. Form reports increase accuracy by requiring that the same information be placed in the same location on each form.

19. Writers use carefully designed input screens to complete a form report. If designed correctly, the writer's inputting selected information will prompt the computer to access a database to retrieve related information (e.g., retrieve address after inputting name, calculate age from birth date), not only saving time but eliminating the chance of making an error. Information is stored on disk and used to generate numerous reports. By increasing efficiency and minimizing the likelihood of clerical errors, the company fosters credibility in its ability to perform quality services.

20. Refer to the list of four in the "Characteristics of Short Reports" section.

21. Memorandum format is for internal reports; letter format, for external reports.

22. The primary purpose of a proposal is to win business. RFP means "Request for Proposal."

23. Because reports and proposals consist of rather discrete parts, writers may begin wherever they like—usually with the easiest or most familiar part.

24. Original writing of sections of a long proposal is divided among the members of a collaborative-writing team. One person compiles all the sections, creates the preliminary and addenda parts, and produces and distributes the final copy.

25. Focus on student responses that indicate understanding of the three major categories of report parts, the purpose of each report part, organizing reports effectively, and preparation of a convincing proposal.

POSSIBLE SOLUTION TO E-MAIL APPLICATION

This activity gives students experience in recording of minutes and also serves to make them accountability to you for progress during the project. Information received from this process will be helpful to you in assessing group as well as individual performance. Intervention may be made when a group seems to be experiencing problems. For instance, if you note that a particular member of the group has been absent from team meetings, you may message him/her about the situation. Other situations that you might want to take note of are the holding of an adequate number of meetings, equitable allocation of work, the setting and meeting of interim deadlines, and adequate planning by the groups. Students will benefit from receiving a return message from you each week to provide feedback as to your informal evaluation of their individual and group progress.

POSSIBLE SOLUTIONS TO APPLICATIONS

PROFESSIONAL DEVELOPMENT

1. Summarizing a Professional Meeting
⇨ *Level 3* ⇦

Suggest that students consult a reference guide for the proper format for recording minutes.

TECHNOLOGY

2. Researching the Information Highway
⇨ *Level 3* ⇦

This information-level report could later be expanded into an analytical report in which a recommendation about the use of the electronic superhighway is made to a particular organization.

CAREER DEVELOPMENT

3. Evaluating a Career Field
⇨ *Level 3* ⇦

Evaluate the currentness of the information presented.

MANAGEMENT/Technology

4. Auditing a Computer Lab
⇨ *Level 3* ⇦

You might require students to include graphics such as tables, pie charts, and/or bar charts in their reports.

FINANCE

5. Evaluating the Performance of a Stock Portfolio
⇨ *Level 3* ⇦

See **TM 17–3** (Solution, Application 5) for suggested memo.

MANAGEMENT/Technology   GMAT

6. Protecting Against Computer Viruses
⇨ *Level 3* ⇦

You might want to require that several different types of reference sources be cited; for instance, a book, a magazine article, and a newspaper article on the subject. An interview could also be required with a business person involved with computer operations or information management.

FINANCE   GMAT

7. Comparing the Merits of Franchising vs. Starting an Independent Business
⇨ *Level 3* ⇦

Secondary sources could be consulted to strengthen the proposal. Some industry figures related to survival of franchise owned versus independently owned businesses would be useful. Interviews with businesspersons in each category might also be specified.

MANAGEMENT   GMAT

8. Assessing the Feasibility of Constructing a Recreational Complex
⇨ *Level 3* ⇦

Emphasize the importance of using graphic representation in the report. You might require that at least two different types of visuals be included.

CROSS DISCIPLINE   GMAT

9. Preparing an Analytical Report
⇨ *Level 4* ⇦

In evaluating these analytical reports, consider the following factors: (a) the thoroughness of secondary data support; (b) the use of an appropriate method of primary research (i.e.,questionnaire survey, interviews, observation, etc.); (c) the use of appropriate graphic support; and (d) inclusion of logical conclusions and a supported recommendation.

(a) Recommend one of three laptops.
     ♦ MANAGEMENT/Technology
(b) Recommend investment of $2 billion of excess cash. ♦ FINANCE
(c) Recommend a computer printer.
     ♦ MANAGEMENT/Technology

(d) Recommend whether uniforms should be required. ♦ HUMAN RESOURCES MANAGEMENT

(e) Recommend network configuration. ♦ MANAGEMENT/Technology

(f) Recommend the form of organization for a business. ♦ ACCOUNTING/Legal

(g) Recommend whether to purchase or lease automobiles. ♦ MANAGEMENT

(h) Recommend whether to invest in cellular telephones. ♦ MANAGEMENT/Technology

(i) Recommend whether to obtain WATS-line service. ♦ MANAGEMENT

(j) Recommend whether to install exercise equipment or subsidize membership in a health club. ♦ MANAGEMENT

(k) Recommend whether to introduce background music to improve productivity. ♦ MANAGEMENT

(l) Recommend whether to implement decentralized photocopiers or a central copy center. ♦ MANAGEMENT/Technology

CROSS DISCIPLINE   GMAT

10. Analyzing Legal and Ethical Issues
⇨ *Level 3* ⇦

In evaluating these reports dealing with legal and ethical issues, consider the following factors: (a) the thoroughness of secondary data support, (b) the proper application of the framework for analyzing an ethical dilemma (see Chapter 6), (c) the use of appropriate graphic support, and (d) inclusion of logical conclusions and a supported recommendation. For additional information, refer to the solution in the chapter in which the case appears.

(a) *Chapter 10, Case 3:* Determine appropriate action when a client has filed a fraudulent tax return. ♦ ACCOUNTING/Legal

(b) *Chapter 11, Case 1:* Identify the legal implications of using a person's photograph in a television advertisement.
♦ MARKETING/Legal

(c) *Chapter 6, Case 1:* Decide whether hiring the homeless to purchase concert tickets is ethical. ♦ MANAGEMENT/Ethics

(d) *Chapter 6, Case 2:* Decide whether management compensation should be restricted.
♦ MANAGEMENT/Ethics

(e) *Chapter 6, Case 3:* Decide whether reducing the quality of engine parts to cut costs is ethical. ♦ MANAGEMENT/Ethics

(f) *Chapter 6, Case 4:* Decide whether to replace humans with robotics to cut costs. ♦ MANAGEMENT/Ethics

(g) *Chapter 9, Case 1:* Decide whether to accept an offer to make an "unapproved" charter. ♦ FINANCE/Ethics

(h) *Chapter 9, Case 3:* Decide whether inferior products should be recalled. ♦ MANAGEMENT/Ethics

(i) *Chapter 10, Case 3:* Determine appropriate action when a client has filed a fraudulent tax return. ♦ ACCOUNTING/Ethics

(j) *Chapter 11, Case 2:* Decide whether a company's donating bottled water to military troops as a public relations maneuver is ethical. ♦ MARKETING/Ethics

(k) *Chapter 12, Case 3:* Decide whether overlooking a vendor's error to your advantage is ethical. ♦ ACCOUNTING/Ethics

MARKETING/Public Sector

11. Bidding for a Convention Site
⇨ *Level 4* ⇦

In evaluating this proposal, consider the following factors: (a) the accuracy and currentness of information related to the city; (b) the thoroughness of information related to the city's appeal; and (c) the creativity shown in making the proposal attractive, readable, and effective.

MANAGEMENT

12. Applying for a Franchise to Open a Miniature Golf Course
⇨ *Level 4* ⇦

Allow students to choose a city for the proposed location and gather appropriate data about that locale. In evaluating this letter report, the following factors may be considered: (a) the accuracy and currentness of information related to the city, (b) the thoroughness of information related to the city's appeal, and (c) the convincing quality of the report.

MANAGEMENT/Technology

13. Proposing to Install an Office System
⇨ *Level 4* ⇦

In evaluating this proposal, the following factors may be considered: (a) the reasonableness of recommendations, (b) the convincing quality of the arguments presented, and (c) the overall appeal of the proposal.

POSSIBLE SOLUTIONS TO CASE FOR ANALYSIS

MANAGEMENT/Technology   GMAT

1. Are Cellular Telephones Affecting Gross Profit at Cannon Engineering

⇨ *Level 4* ⇦

Steps 1–3: Students are provided instructions for computing the change in gross profit, including and excluding cellular telephone costs. These computations are used to prepare the comparative bar-line chart necessary for making an informed decision about the effectiveness of cellular telephone use. If you believe your students will have difficulty with this case, allow them to work in groups with a quantitative major assigned to each group.

Students are to generate the spreadsheet (shown in the case) and add two columns containing the change in gross profit. The increase in gross profit, including cellular telephone costs for the first sales representative, is calculated using the formula *H10 - G10*. The increase in gross profit, excluding cellular telephone costs for the first sales representative, is calculated by the formula *(D10 - C10) × .20*.

Step 4: To reduce the time required to complete this assignment, you may wish to have students complete the analysis portion of this case in small groups during class and then write the memorandum independently. Explain briefly the need to see the change in gross profit including and excluding cellular telephones to make an informed decision. Then, display the comparative bar-line chart on

TM 17–4 (Solution, Case for Analysis 1, Step 3); allow student groups to analyze the data and develop a recommendation. Graphing the values given by the formulas with the quantity of cellular telephone minutes reveals three distinct groups of sales representatives.

a. Five sales representatives (10, 18, 21, 16, 12) made minimal use of cellular telephones and experienced small changes in gross profit. Thus, cellular telephones were not effective for these sales representatives.

b. Three sales representatives (8, 11, 14) made moderate use of cellular telephones and experienced significant positive increases in gross profit. For these sales representatives, the increase in gross profit exceeded the additional expense of cellular telephones.

c. Three sales representatives (9, 5, 6) made extensive use of cellular telephones, but their increase in gross profit failed to offset the increase in telephone costs.

The students' recommendation should focus on learning how the sales representatives in group b utilize cellular telephones. This information should be used to train the sales reps in groups a and c, thus increasing the effectiveness of cellular telephones.

Step 5: Students using spreadsheet or graphics software will import the comparative bar-line chart into the memorandum created with word-processing software. Students creating the graphic using the graphing feature of an advanced word-processing software will simply input the memorandum in the same computer file. If software is unavailable, provide students a reduced copy of the graphic, **TM 17–4** (Solution, Case for Analysis 1, Step 3) to arrange in the appropriate location in their memorandums.

CHAPTER 18

WRITING A FORMAL REPORT

CHAPTER OVERVIEW

Chapter 18 completes Part 6, "Communicating Through Reports." By the time students study Chapter 18, they should have acquired an understanding of research methodology, management of data, use of graphics, and short-report preparation.

If long, formal report projects are not formally taught, you probably will refer students to some of the content of Chapter 18. When studying short reports, for example, students would be concerned with documentation and organizational strategy.

LEARNING OBJECTIVES

1 Specify writing techniques that enhance the credibility and formal writing style of a report.

2 Identify formal report-writing procedures that are effective for you.

3 Use appropriate levels of headings.

4 Use appropriate documentation methods.

5 Write effective formal reports in an acceptable format and writing style.

CHAPTER OUTLINE AND TEACHING SUGGESTIONS

1   LEARNING OBJECTIVE

I. Writing A Convincing and Effective Formal Report
   A. Show **TA 18–1** (Chapter Opener) that presents an analogy that professional builders must depend on the expertise and support of others and stable supporting devices such as scaffolding as report writers rely on outside sources to

support or bolster their ideas. Tie this thought with the chapter opening scenario that contrasts undocumented tabloid headlines with objective, well-documented, and credible reports.
   B. Integrate the communication mentor comments into class lectures to reinforce the concepts in the chapter.
   C. Guidelines for Enhancing Credibility
   D. Writing Style for Formal Report
   E. Communication in Action: James F. Hoobler, U.S. Small Business Administration

2   LEARNING OBJECTIVE

II. Creating an Environment Conducive for Writing
   A. Make a transparency of **TM 18–1** (Suggestions for Creating an Environment Conducive for Writing) to show as you discuss this section.
   B. Lead the class in a discussion as to how each of the ten suggestions is important to the final product and encourage them to identify the suggestions they should incorporate into their own writing procedures.

3   LEARNING OBJECTIVE

III. Using Headings Effectively
   A. Remind students that the two rules related to outlines also relate to headings:
      1. You must have at least two subdivisions to justify an additional heading level.
      2. Headings at the same level must be treated consistently (capitalization, typestyle, grammatical construction, etc.)

B. Assign Application 1 from the *Study Guide* that requires students to compose the appropriate headings for the third section of a formal report. Instruct students to compare their solutions with the one provided in the *Study Guide*.

C. Remind students of the importance of using "talking headings" especially in analytical reports.

| **4** | **LEARNING OBJECTIVE** |

IV. Documenting Reports

A. Show **TA 18–2** (Reasons for Accurate, Complete Documentation) as you stress the relationship between documentation and scholarly or professional integrity and discuss the other reasons for accurate documentation.

B. Initiate a discussion of the plagiarism suit against Michael Bolton (photo, page 592) to help students understand that plagiarism is illegal, and offenders must face the consequences. Ask the students to share other examples of plagiarism in the workplace. You might require them to research this topic using an online database and report to the class. Information systems students might mention copyright infringements such as the suit between Microsoft and Stac Electronics (photo, page 157).

C. Discuss the three guidelines for documenting a report: (a) choosing an authoritative manual to follow, (b) being consistent, and (c) providing enough information for the reader to locate the source. These guidelines lead to the point that any number of documentation methods are appropriate. APA and MLA methods are illustrated in the text because students may be required to use either of these styles on the job or in other courses.

D. Citations

   1. Source Notes

   2. Explanatory Notes

E. Citation Methods

   1. Show **TA 18–3** (Citation Methods) as you discuss the three citation methods: in-text parenthetical,

bottom-of-the-page, and end-of-report.

2. Use examples in the text to cover this concept. The text contains the following examples:

   APA (4th Edition)
   In-text parenthetical citations
   References

   MLA (4th Edition)
   In-text parenthetical citations
   Works cited

   MLA (3rd Edition)
   Traditional footnotes and endnotes

   Note: The 4th Edition of *The MLA Handbook* requires the use of in-text parenthetical citations. Students must follow the *MLA* (3rd Edition) if they are required to use traditional endnotes/footnotes.

3. In-text Parenthetical Citations

   a. Explain that in-text citations eliminate much of the repetition required when preparing traditional footnotes/endnotes. Abbreviated information in parentheses (in-text citation) refer the reader to a list of sources at the end of the report (references).

   b. Instruct students to complete the Think It Over notes on pages 595–596 in groups and discuss their solutions in class. The solutions follow:

      Page 595: APA and MLA in-text citation for business communications text

      APA: (Lehman, Himstreet, and Baty, 1996)

      MLA: (Lehman, Himstreet, and Baty 15)

      Page 596: In-text citation for Robock text; authors' names not included in text

      APA: (Robock & Simmons, 1983)

      MLA: (Robock & Simmons 15)

Page 596: In-text citation for Robock text; authors' name included in text

APA: Robock & Simmons (1993)...

MLA: Robock & Simmons concluded...

    4.   Bottom-of-the-page Citation Method

    5.   End-of-report Citation Method

F.   References (or Works Cited)

    1.   Require students to write a bibliographic entry for their business communication text:

APA: Lehman, C. M., Himstreet, W. C., & Baty, W. M. (1996). *Business communications* (11th ed.). Cincinnati, OH: South-Western.

MLA: Lehman, Carol M., Himstreet, William C., and Baty, William Murlin. *Business Communications.* 11th ed. Cincinnati: South-Western, 1996.

    2.   Point out that examples for writing references for online sources (articles from online source and abstracts on CD-ROM) are provided in MLA and APA formats. Explain that providing a printed source for an electronic document is preferred if the printed source is the same as the electronic source. As technology progress, this guideline will change.

    3.   Assign Application 2 from the *Study Guide* that requires students to prepare the references/bibliography using the APA and MLA methods. Project the solution provided in the *Study Guide* and emphasize major rules in preparing the various entries. When discussing the APA references, discuss the major differences between APA and MLA and other traditional formats shown on page 601. You may require students to complete the application using only the method they will follow in completing the report assignments for your course.

V.   Analyzing A Formal Report

A.   Stress that students should study the sample report that follows Chapter 18 carefully as it serves as a comprehensive report guide.

    1.   The commentary explains the sound report practices applied in the report, including organization, content, style, formatting, page numbering, and documentation.

    2.   The format uses the default (preset) formats set by business-level word-processing software to simplify the formatting process and to follow business practices. In addition, the report is formatted using desktop publishing to help students identify methods to enhance the overall effectiveness of a report, making it "look as good as it sounds."

        a.   The report is singled spaced to save space. The commentary explains that this particular company overrides the APA rule to double space reports; however, drafts are double spaced with five-space paragraph indention.

        b.   Emphasize that businesses often single space lengthy reports to be distributed to multiple readers. If you prefer reports to be double spaced so that reports follow APA style precisely or simply to allow additional space for comments, instruct students to do so. The references page is double spaced as required in the APA style.

        c.   The sample report also uses the term *Executive Summary,* the term used frequently in business; however, APA refers to this document as an *Abstract.*

B.   Obtain copies of formal reports prepared in various businesses to illustrate to students the organization of such documents. Point out the differences and consistencies in style and format.

VI. Summary

A. Integrate the communication mentor comments into class lectures to reinforce the concepts presented in the chapter.

B. Refer students to the "Check Your Writing" checklist at the end of the chapter as you review. This checklist includes guidelines for preparing each part of a formal report. Using the checklist and the sample report, students should find answers to most problems they will encounter in preparing a formal report.

C. Assign the *Study Guide* questions for Chapter 18.

D. Require students to complete the applications in the *Study Guide*. These applications "walk students through" (1) composing appropriate report headings and (2) preparing a bibliography in APA and MLA style. Students compare their solutions with a sample solution.

E. Ask students to complete the e-mail application at the end of the chapter.

F. Assign selected exercises, applications, and cases at the end of the chapter. Remind students to study the suggestions in the "Check Your Writing" checklist when planning and revising an assignment.

G. Assign one of the applications designated as an AWA (Analytical Writing Assessment) for the GMAT. Refer to pages 12–13 of this *Instructor's Resource Manual* for holistic scoring techniques used by evaluators of this written portion of the GMAT.

TRANSPARENCIES AND MASTERS

TA 18–1   Chapter Opener
TA 18–2   Reasons for Accurate, Complete Documentation
TA 18–3   Citation Methods

TM 18–1   Suggestions for Creating an Environment Conducive for Writing
TM 18–2   Possible Solution, Case for Analysis 1, Step 3
TM 18–3   Possible Solution, Case for Analysis 1, Step 4

ADDITIONAL READINGS

DiGregoria, D. (1991). Pick up the pace of your writing. *Chemical Engineering, 98*(12) 117–122.

Norwood, J. L. (1993). Perception or reality: Can we trust federal statistics? *Business Economics, 28*(3), 25-29.

Smeltzer, L. R., & Gilsdorf, J. W. (1990). How to use your time efficiently when writing. *Business Horizons, 33*(6), 61–64.

Smeltzer, L. R., & Gilsdorf, J. W. (1990). Revise reports rapidly. *Personnel Journal, 69*(10), 38–42.

Straub, J. T. (1991). Memos and reports: Write them right the first time. *Supervisory Management, 36*(7), 6.

ANSWERS TO "COMMUNICATION IN ACTION" CASE: James F. Hoobler, U.S. Small Business Administration

1. **How will a reader be affected by a sloppily written Small Business Administration report?** When a report is sloppily written, the writer's credibility may be questioned by the reader. The attractiveness of a well-written report may actually increase the writer's credibility. A well-written report may also attract prompt readership. The sloppily report may also be placed at the bottom of the reader's "to-do" list.

2. **Explain how Hoobler adapted formal reports to various audiences.** To adapt to various audiences, Hoobler made distinctions by determining which parts were included in a certain report. Investigative reports contain findings not included in audit and evaluative reports. Audit reports are anchored in hard data and empirical support. Media personnel receive only summary reports and not complete reports.

ANSWERS TO REVIEW QUESTIONS

1. *Fantastic, superb, brilliant, sensational, stupendous, dismal,* and *miserable* are examples of emotional terms. Note that most emotional terms are adjectives.

2. Because of the objective nature of research, the use of personal pronouns should be limited. The first person (*I*, for example) may detract from the credibility of objective information.

3. Transition sentences bind portions of a report together. Coherence ties sentences together to create better paragraphs and compositions.

4. Because—cause and effect;
   for example—similarity; then—time;
   although—contrast.

5. Not true. Things often look acceptable immediately after they have been written, but later review may change the impression. Writers should plan to review and to rewrite if necessary.

6. Reading aloud slows reading speed to speaking speed, and this slow rate helps reveal awkwardness and grammatical errors that might otherwise go undetected.

7. The symbol outline (I, A, 1) includes report headings of various degrees, which are physically placed in the report to reflect the outline organization. For example, the following format is common: first level (roman numerals) shown as centered heads, second level (A, B, C...) shown as side headings, and third level (1, 2, 3...) shown as paragraph headings.

8. Reasons for documenting reports: (a) citations give credit where credit is due, (b) documentation protects writers from plagiarism, (c) documentation supports your statements, and (d) documentation can aid future researchers pursuing similar material.

9. (a) Select a documentation method and follow it precisely, (b) be consistent, and (c) include more than enough information when in doubt about whether to include certain information.

10. A source note acknowledges the contributions of others and provides enough information so that the reader can locate the original source if desired. An explanatory note (a) comments on a source or provides information that does not fit easily in the text, (b) supports a statistical table, or (c) refers the reader to another section of the report.

11. In-text citations (APA or MLA provided in text) refer to a list of sources at the end of the report; a separate footnotes or endnotes section is not included. To cite material in an in-text citation, place the author's name (date of publication and/or page number are required depending on the method being used) in parentheses.

12. Refer to the list under the "References (or Works Cited)" section.

13. The organization of formal reports is a writer's prerogative but should be done within the framework of the problem-solving steps. Variations available are in the handling of the introductory material (purpose and methods), heading designs, documentation practices, and judgmental variations in what appendix items to include.

14. Using separate pages for the content outline (contents page) and a list of figures is a good idea, particularly when both are rather long. When both can be accommodated on one page, the reader has access to these related topics in one location.

15. No. The introduction portion of the report body need not include headings because most readers expect the beginning part of something to be an introduction. Writers decide which style to use, of course; but some report writers simply do not feel comfortable omitting headings in the introduction.

16. The sample report has a title and two levels of headings. Centered headings denote major sections of the report (roman numerals); side headings denote subdivisions of the major sections (A, B, C).

17. Each of the four graphics is numbered consecutively and positioned as close as possible after its textual introduction. Introductions include (a) an interpretation of the data that appears before the figure so that the reader will not draw his or her own conclusions and (b) a reference to the figure number.

18. The sample report (a) uses centered headings to denote major divisions and side headings to move the reader from one minor divisions to another; (b) includes section introductions that preview the material to be covered in the major section (includes the conclusion to be drawn in that section); and (c) summarizes each major section before moving to the next.

19. Enhancements may include (a) using a laser printer and a proportional font to achieve a professional typesetter quality; (b) including graphic design on the title page; (c) using larger font sizes to emphasize the title and headings; (d) using italics, boldface, and underline to emphasize limited amounts of text; (e) integrating computer-generated

graphics; and (f) generating the contents page and list of figures automatically.

20. Use these questions to generate discussion or as pop quiz items.

POSSIBLE SOLUTION TO E-MAIL APPLICATION

Refer to the group evaluation form provided on page 24 of this *Instructor's Resource Manual* for a suggested evaluation format. Be sure that students rate themselves as well as their team members. Consider the justifications given by students in assessing their scores. Compare group member assessments for possible inconsistencies. You might also ask each student to send an e-mail message that describes the group process that occurred during the project (whether successful or unsuccessful, and why); what he/she learned from the group experience; and what he/she would do differently with the next group assignment.

POSSIBLE SOLUTIONS TO APPLICATIONS

MIS/Technology

1. **Shareware vs. Commercial Software**

⇨ *Level 4* ⇦

Some ideas for this assignment are as follows:

(a) Specify the use of several different types of data sources; for instance, books, magazines, newspapers, and journals, and government documents (if applicable).

(b) If the same report topic has been assigned to the entire class or to several groups of students, consider requiring students to submit photocopies of their source articles prior to writing their reports. Choose the best articles from each of the designated categories and place copies of them on reserve in the library as a notebook of readings. In this way, all students will have access to a sufficient number of sources, which can otherwise be a problem when many students are attempting to research the same topic.

(c) Require that some visual aid be incorporated from a secondary data source.

(d) Require at least two different types of graphic aids from the primary data; for example, pie charts, bar charts, and tables.

(e) Evaluate the format of the report as well as the content.

(f) Evaluate the recommendations according to the strength of the data presented.

(g) Use the evaluation sheet for analytical reports on pages 22–23 of this *Instructor's Resource Manual* or develop your own instrument for purposes of evaluation and grading.

MANAGEMENT

2. **Merits of Mentoring**

⇨ *Level 4* ⇦

See the teaching suggestions for Application 1.

INFORMATION SYSTEMS/ Technology/Ethics/Legal

3. **Attitudes Toward Software Piracy**

⇨ *Level 4* ⇦

See the teaching suggestions for Application 1.

MANAGEMENT

4. **Spiraling Health Costs: Do Employee Assistance Programs Help?**

⇨ *Level 4* ⇦

See the teaching suggestions for Application 1. Optionally, you may require that students conduct an interview with an appropriate businessperson regarding the issue to be addressed in the report.

MANAGEMENT/International

5. **Intercultural Misunderstandings**

⇨ *Level 4* ⇦

See teaching suggestions for Application 1. Optionally, you may require that students conduct an interview with an appropriate businessperson regarding the issue to be addressed in the report.

CROSS DISCIPLINE

6. **A Business Problem To Be Solved**

⇨ *Level 4* ⇦

See teaching suggestions for Application 1. Additionally, you may require students to

(a) Conduct a questionnaire survey to gather research data. If so, consider developing the instrument in class and distributing copies to each student to use in their data gathering. Data collected by all students can be tabulated to produce a single data set that students can then use in writing their findings. Students may also develop appropriate graphic aids from the tabulated data.

(b) Interview an appropriate businessperson regarding the issue to be addressed in the report. The information gained should be incorporated into the report and accurately referenced.

CROSS DISCIPLINE

7. A Business Problem with International, Ethical, Legal, or Interpersonal Implications

⇨ *Level 4* ⇦

See teaching suggestions for Application 6 and the solution in the chapter in which the case appears.

POSSIBLE SOLUTIONS TO CASE FOR ANALYSIS

MANAGEMENT

1. The Riverside Cafe

⇨ *Level 4* ⇦

This case is designed to develop written and oral communication skills and develop creative thinking skills. Allow students to work in small groups. Form teams that represent a cross section of students from various disciplines to exploit the diverse knowledge and experience of the individual members.

Initiate a short discussion about the importance of creative thinking in the competitive business world. Share several anecdotes of companies whose success has been attributed to the creative thinking of its executives. Refer to Lehman, C. M., & Spencer, B. A. (1991). Creative thinking: An integral part of effective business communication, *Bulletin of the Association for Business Communication, 54*(1), 21–27 for additional information.

Steps 1 & 2: Certainly the answer to this case is not as clear as the answer to case problems students are usually assigned; therefore, be prepared for students to be frustrated. To assuage their frustration: (1) remind them that in realistic business situations, the answer is not always immediately evident and (2) allow class time immediately for the teams to discuss the case and to begin to feel more comfortable with this new learning experience.

Your role in this learning experience is facilitator. Assure each team that no one solution is correct, and be sure that they understand the instructions. All necessary information has been provided, and the client, Mr. Becker, (you) cannot be reached. Stress that creativity is the ability to look at the same thing as everyone else, but see something different. Therefore, they should not share ideas with other teams. Each team's work can and *should* be different if the teams work independently.

Step 3: See **TM 18–2** (Possible Solution, Case for Analysis 1, Step 3) for suggested report. (If time is limited, you can require students to present the findings and recommendations in a letter report, as shown in the solution and to omit Step 4 (preparation of a letter of transmittal and a title page).

Step 4: See **TM 18–3** (Possible Solution, Case for Analysis 1, Step 4) for suggested title page and transmittal letter.

Step 5: Solutions will vary widely based on the recommendations presented in Step 3. Creativity in presentation should be considered in grading this assignment. This application could also be used as a bonus assignment for extra credit.

Step 6: Refer to the oral presentation guidelines presented in Chapter 3 and the evaluation form for a speech/oral report on page 18 of this *Instructor's Resource Manual.*

DOCUMENT FORMAT AND LAYOUT GUIDE

In Chapter 9, students are instructed to study Appendix A carefully before reading the good and poor examples of the letters, memorandums, and e-mail messages. The letters and memorandums are positioned correctly on letterhead or plain paper and are formatted with the appropriate parts. The commentary on the examples also reinforces students' understanding of the formats and layout principles presented in Appendix A.

Document format and layout principles likely will be integrated with Chapter 9. Therefore, the teaching suggestions for Appendix A are included in Chapter 9.

To be sure students understand this material *before* doing the first written assignment, you can give a short objective exam covering this material.

Fifty true/false and multiple choice questions are provided in the *Instructor's Resource Manual*. Or, you may use selected questions from Appendix A on the objective test covering Part 4.

TRANSPARENCIES AND MASTERS

TA A–1	Block Style Format, Open Punctuation
TA A–2	Modified Block Format, Mixed Punctuation
TA A–3	Simplified Block Format
TA A–4	Business Letter Printed on Plain Paper
TA A–5	Formal Memorandum
TA A–6	Simplified Memorandum
TM A–1	Special Letter Parts

GRAMMAR REVIEW AND EXERCISES

Some instructors may want students to use Appendix B as a reference only. Others may want to devote class time to present the material—especially the grammar and punctuation principles. Some of the principles in Chapters 7 and 8 are also in Appendix B—for reference, reinforcement, and drill. Refer to the teaching suggestions for Part 3 and Chapters 7 and 8 of the *Instructor's Resource Manual*.

SOLUTIONS TO EXERCISES

Exercise 1
1. (a) More specific.
2. (a) More specific.
3. (a) Subordinates the negative through use of general language.
4. (b) Active voice is more vivid; sentence is shorter.
5. (b) A concrete noun is more vivid than an abstract noun.

Exercise 2
1. their
2. his or her
3. his
4. their
5. her
6. its
7. its
8. me
9. her
10. she
11. my
12. Who
13. whom
14. who
15. this oversight

Exercise 3
1. were
2. was
3. were
4. were
5. were
6. is
7. has
8. rotates
9. doesn't
10. started

1. Susan Woodward edited the booklet.
2. Our accountant checked the figures.
3. The supervisor recommended Ms. Jackson for promotion.
4. A committee is screening the applications.
5. The manager has approved your request for a leave.

Exercise 4
1. frequently
2. angry
3. quickly
4. better
5. any other

Exercise 5
1. The sentence begins with an expletive.
   You must sign and return the enclosed form.
   Your signing and returning the enclosed form are essential.
2. The introductory phrase dangles.
   When I was a small girl, my brother taught me to play basketball.
3. Other words are placed between a pronoun and its antecedent.
   I am submitting an article, which I wrote last summer, to *Time*.
4. The units of a series are not stated in parallel form.
   Almost all of my time is spent in planning, organizing, and controlling.
5. The infinitive "to bring" is split.
   We want to bring the project to a conclusion quickly.
   We want to bring the project to a quick conclusion.

Exercise 6
1. When I was interviewed during Interviewing 101, the first question was "Why do you want to work for us?"
2. The summer season is much slower than the rest of the year, according to the sales manager.
3. We paid for *The Power of Ethical Management* with Check No. 527 on December 10.
4. The NCAA meeting, moderated by President Stanton, will be held in New York.
5. A retirement ceremony is being planned for President Schwada.

Exercise 7
1. The question was answered by 61 percent of the respondents.
2. The meeting will be at 9 a.m. on February 21.
3. Three figures appeared on the expense account: $21.95, $30.00, and $35.14.
4. Go to the service station at Fifth Street and Hardy Drive.
5. We ordered five 16-ounce hammers.
6. This MIS manager ordered ten 40-mb hard drives.
7. Twenty-one members voted in favor of the motion.
8. The cost will be approximately $1 million.
   The cost will be approximately $1,000,000.
9. Mix 2 quarts of white with 13 quarts of brown.
10. Examine the diagram on page 7.

Exercise 8
1. company's
2. weeks'
3. West's and Johnson's
4. Pablo's
5. Morris'

1. Correct
2. Our meeting is scheduled for Monday, Tuesday, and Friday.
3. We liked this car because of its price, durability, and appearance.
4. Correct
5. We are enthusiastic about the plan because (1) it is least expensive, (2) its legality is unquestioned, and (3) it can be implemented quickly.

Exercise 9
1. The man who came in late has not been interviewed, but all other applicants have been interviewed.
2. Margie Harrison, a new member of the board, remained silent.
3. Ammonium sulfate, which is available at almost all home-supply stores, is ideal fertilizer for citrus.
4. This carpet is available in three colors: brown, tan, and blue.
5. We had a long, bitter discussion.
6. Costs have doubled in the last two years as the following graph illustrates.
7. By the time I arrived at the meeting, the issue had been discussed thoroughly and put aside.
8. If you approve of the changes on page 3, please place your initials in the margin.
9. We surveyed the entire population, but three of the responses were unusable.
10. Because only 21 percent of the members were present, the motion could not be considered.

11. John was awarded $25; Bill, $40.
12. We have lost our place in the production line, haven't we?
13. We should be spending less money, not more.
14. On November 20, 1995, all related documents were submitted.
15. Yes, I agree that the meeting in Oxford, Tennessee, should be scheduled in April.

Exercise 10
1. (a) italicizes a book title; (b) encloses the title of an article for a report within quotation marks.
2. (b) uses quotations marks to introduce doubt about whether "accomplishments" is the right label. His undertakings may have been of little significance.
3. (a) does not necessarily state Tim's exact words; (b) does.
4. (a) is about an indefinite number of people who have each won ten games; (b) is about ten people, each of whom has won at least one game.
5. (a) omits some words from quotation; (b) does not.

Exercise 11
1. Expense tickets were not included; otherwise, the request would have been honored.
2. The following agents received a bonus this month: Barnes, $400; Shelley, $450; and Jackson, $600.
3. The bid was not considered; it arrived two days late.
4. This paint does have some disadvantages; for example, its drying time is too long.
5. Soon after the figures have been received, they will be processed; but a formal report cannot be prepared before June 15.

Exercise 12
1. except	11. fewer
2. affect	12. infer
3. advice	13. Regardless
4. among	14. its
5. number	15. lend
6. sight	16. personnel
7. compliment	17. principal
8. credible	18. They're, their
9. one another	19. to, too
10. further	20. Although

Review Quiz
1. Will you please find out whether first- and second-year students are eligible to receive that scholarship?
2. George was once in charge of security at the capitol building; he is not impressed with our firm's security system.
3. The questionnaires, which were mailed on June 1, have been returned; but only a few of those mailed later in the month have been returned.
4. Our stockbroker has written an article on fiscal policy; the article will appear in the March 21 issue of *Newsweek*.
5. Although the committee agreed with Ms. Sims' conclusions, several members raised serious questions about the questionnaire that was used as an information-gathering instrument.
6. John has submitted more suggestions than anyone else in his department, but he has yet to receive an award.
7. Although the procedure has been highly successful, it is not popular in our department.
8. The man who came late to the meeting is the new sales manager for the Southwest Region.
9. The three applicants were waiting to interview for the same job; therefore, they had little to say to one another.
10. Only one of my recommendations was considered; this fact was very disappointing to the superintendent and me.
11. The majority of the discussion was devoted to personnel benefits, but that topic was not listed on the agenda.
12. After you have completed your term, please write to me; we have some highly important matters to discuss.
13. When you rewrite the final draft, please change the word *charge* to *debit*.
14. Each of our assistants is required to take a short, intensive training course.
15. Thirteen respondents thought the company was losing sight of its objectives.
16. On June 3, 1995, the Jackson, Tennessee, location was officially approved.
17. John insisted on our listening to his play-by-play recap of the game.
18. No, the comforter comes in these colors only: burgundy, hunter green, and khaki.
19. The site for the new plant is five blocks southwest of East Lampkin Street.
20. While presenting the proposed change in distribution, the manager was required to leave abruptly when he received an emergency call.

SECTION B
GRAMMAR TESTS

```
GRAMMATICAL USAGE TEST
```

Circle the correct word in each sentence.

1. The manager, not the administrative assistants, (is, are) responsible for this fiasco.
2. Only one of the employees (is, are) going to visit corporate headquarters.
3. My colleague and I (was, were) invited to speak at the seminar.
4. Neither the project manager nor the technical editors (was, were) notified.
5. Neither the technical editors nor the project manager (was, were) notified.
6. Swafford & Associates (was, were) the only firm to send representatives.
7. "Procedures and Policies" (was, were) written by Pat, our administrative assistant.
8. The office manager (don't, doesn't) need to attend the seminar.
9. Jack reminded me that Vancouver (was, is) north of Victoria.
10. Jane finished her project and (leaves, left) before 5 p.m.
11. I wish she (was, were) the office manager.
12. He acted as though he (was, were) in agreement, but he really was not.
13. In this unit, everyone is responsible for (their, his or her) own obligations.
14. The public relations firm has developed (its, their) mission statement.
15. The marketing manager and the finance manager will present (his and her, their) proposals.
16. The recommendation is endorsed by Richard and (I, me).
17. It was (she, her) who provided the justification report to the manager.
18. For (who, whom) was the reprimand intended?
19. I am trying to discover (who, whom) leaked the confidential information.
20. Gaining experience in developing multimedia presentations prepared (me, I) for advancing into my present position.
21. I shall appreciate (you, your) responding before May 1.
22. I was alarmed about (him, his) arriving late for the interview.
23. My score was lower than (yours, your's), but both were acceptable.
24. We have discouraged overtime for the last three (years, years', year's).
25. Mr. Wagner's article appeared in this (weeks, week's, weeks') newspaper.
26. Two (months, month's, months') have passed since the due date.
27. She felt (bad, badly) about the incident and offered to make amends.
28. Of the three managers, Robert has been the (more, most) effective.
29. Pat has traveled more than (anyone, anyone else) in her division.
30. We will appreciate your writing a summary of your findings, taking a copy to the inspector, and (preparation of charts, preparing charts) for an oral presentation.

WORD-USAGE CHECKUP

Circle the correct word in each sentence.

1. The (amount, number) of accidents are decreasing.
2. The questionnaires are to be mailed in No. 10 (envelops, envelopes).
3. If I (was, were) related to the president, I'd be promoted.
4. The company must evaluate (its, it's, its') financial condition.
5. Your answers are different (from, than) mine.
6. Of all our problems, taxation had the greatest (affect, effect).
7. The speaker (implied, inferred) that he favored the candidate.
8. The two lawyers constantly annoyed (each other, one another).
9. Because of her dedication to the job, Margaret considered her promotion a (complement, compliment).
10. The (principal, principle) reason for the change was the proximity of the supplies.
11. Cost was the main (criteria, criterion) in our decision.
12. (Irregardless, Regardless) of weather conditions, we must proceed.
13. We've had (less, fewer) responses this week than last week.
14. We must not (lose, loose) sight of our objective.
15. The sale will be announced (formally, formerly) at tomorrow's meeting.
16. Location A is three miles (further, farther) from the airport than any of the other locations being considered.
17. The office manager's recommendation has been (accepted, excepted).
18. (Although, While) I understand your point, I must follow instructions.
19. Of all the proposals, we chose the one (which, that) was presented first.
20. The reason is (because, that) expenses have been exceeding income.
21. Few prices are expected to (raise, rise) this year.
22. The manager is making plans to computerize (personal, personnel) records.
23. Please (lend, loan) me a couple of dollars for lunch.
24. The profits will be divided (between, among) the two partners.
25. She is an outstanding researcher; she is also a (real, very) good speaker.
26. The researcher developed an appealing design to (complement, compliment) the simple questionnaire format.
27. First, we should seek legal (council, counsel).
28. The leader's role is to (advice, advise) the participants.
29. Writers must (cite, sight, site) quoted and paraphrased ideas.
30. (Their, There, They're) having difficulty with the elements to include in the design.
31. Only one of John's answers was correct; therefore, he decided (to, too, two) withdraw.
32. Only two accidents have been reported in the (passed, past) month.
33. Mr. Lowell was (continually, continuously) asking for time off.
34. The proposal was approved (accept, except) for the timeline.
35. One part is movable; the other is (stationery, stationary).

PUNCTUATION TEST

Insert needed punctuation; delete unnecessary punctuation.

1. All the information has been downloaded, but your's will not be added until Friday.
2. When I am offered a promotion I will accept this responsibility.
3. To ensure a convincing presentation the manager prepared an on-screen slide show.
4. The new president is an excellent, team player.
5. Fifty people have applied for the position but their references have not been verified.
6. Because Laura asked for a three week extension she was transferred to another department.
7. When I left the office four project managers were meeting in the conference room, but I don't know how long they stayed.
8. The documents were sent electronically, and via first class mail.
9. Will you please return the expense report to my desk by noon.
10. Bids have been reviewed, however an opening date has not been set.
11. Only three components were missing; the VCR, the overhead projector and the flip chart.
12. The following employees have worked more than ten hours of overtime this month: Jackson, 20, Ponce, 22, McNeally, 15, and Haley 10.
13. A new company car has been issued, the old one was wrecked.
14. We appreciated his quick accurate response.
15. I plan to work on Saturday, and take a vacation day on Monday.
16. Without a moments hesitation the president said "We can do better".
17. The presidents first question was "How much will it cost"?
18. The contracts which were received on May 21 have been approved.
19. On May 14, 1996 I submitted a hastily-written report.
20. Plan to read "Theory Z" its a book about the management of Japanese business firms.
21. Warrenville, Illinois is the proposed site for the plant expansion.
22. Mr. Lincoln director or the finance committee presented his forecast of interest rate fluctuations.
23. Only two thirds of the membership participated in the project which was of vital importance to the organization.
24. All three, four, and five year contracts were rewritten.
25. In the final draft, principle should have been changed to principal.

SOLUTIONS

Grammatical Usage Test

1. is
2. is
3. were
4. were
5. was
6. was
7. was
8. doesn't
9. is
10. left
11. were
12. were
13. his or her
14. its
15. their
16. me
17. she
18. whom
19. who
20. me
21. your
22. his
23. yours
24. years
25. week's
26. months
27. bad
28. most
29. anyone else
30. preparing charts

Word-Usage Checkup

1. number
2. envelopes
3. were
4. its
5. from
6. effect
7. implied
8. each other
9. compliment
10. principal
11. criterion
12. Regardless
13. fewer
14. lose
15. formally
16. farther
17. accepted
18. Although
19. that
20. that
21. rise
22. personnel
23. lend
24. between
25. very
26. complement
27. counsel
28. advise
29. cite
30. They're
31. to
32. past
33. continually
34. except
35. stationary

SOLUTION, PUNCTUATION TEST

1. All the information has been downloaded, but <u>yours</u> will not be added until Friday.

2. When I am offered a promotion, I will accept this responsibility.

3. To ensure a convincing presentation, the manager prepared an on-screen slide show.

4. The new president is an excellent team player.

5. Fifty people have applied for the position, but their references have not been verified.

6. Because Laura asked for a <u>three-week</u> extension, she was transferred to another department.

7. When I left the office, four project managers were meeting in the conference room; but I don't know how long they stayed.

8. The documents were sent electronically and via first class mail.

9. Will you please return the expense report to my desk by noon?

10. Bids have been reviewed; however, an opening date has not been set.

11. Only three components were missing: the VCR, the overhead projector, and the flip chart.

12. The following employees have worked more than ten hours of overtime this month: Jackson, 20; Ponce, 22; McNeally, 15; and Haley, 10.

13. A new company car has been issued; the old one was wrecked.

14. We appreciated his quick, accurate response.

15. I plan to work on Saturday and take a vacation day on Monday.

16. Without a <u>moment's</u> hesitation, the president said "We can do better."

17. The <u>president's</u> first question was "How much will it cost?"

18. The contracts that were received on May 21 have been approved. *[restrictive clause]*

19. On May 14, 1996, I submitted a hastily written report.

20. Plan to read <u>*Theory Z*</u>; <u>it's</u> a book about the management of Japanese business firms.

21. Warrenville, Illinois, is the proposed site for the plant expansion.

22. Mr. Lincoln, director or the finance committee, presented his forecast of interest rate fluctuations.

23. Only <u>two-thirds</u> of the membership participated in the project <u>that</u> was of vital importance to the organization.

24. All <u>three-</u>, <u>four-</u>, and <u>five-year</u> contracts were rewritten.

25. In the final draft, *principle* should have been changed to *principal*.

SECTION C
TRANSPARENCY MASTERS

Kinesic Communication

■ Visual
- Gestures
- Eye contact
- Facial expressions (smile, frown, wink)
- Attire
- Grooming

■ Vocal
- Intonation
- Projection
- Resonance

How Might Other Cultures React to Nonverbal Messages?

- Nodding head up and down.

- Maintaining consistent eye contact.

- Forming a circle with forefinger and thumb.

- Observing personal space (distance between people in conversation).

- Respecting attitude toward time (e.g., prompt or late for appointments).

- Allowing sole of shoe to be visible.

Cultures' Reactions to Nonverbal Messages

Nodding head up and down
U.S.: Agreement
Eastern Europe: Disagreement; side-to-side movement indicates agreement.

Eye contact
U.S.: Interested, involved
Asian and others: Disrespectful

Forefinger and thumb forming circle
U.S.: Okay
Japan: Money
France: Zero
Brazil: Vulgarity

Personal space
U.S.: 2–3 feet (casual); 4–12 feet (business)
Other countries: Much closer

Time
U.S.: Time is money; punctuality is expected.
Mexico: Time is not perceived to have value; frequently late for appointments.

Sole of shoe visible
U.S.: Unimportant
Arab countries: Insulting because the foot has touched unclean ground.

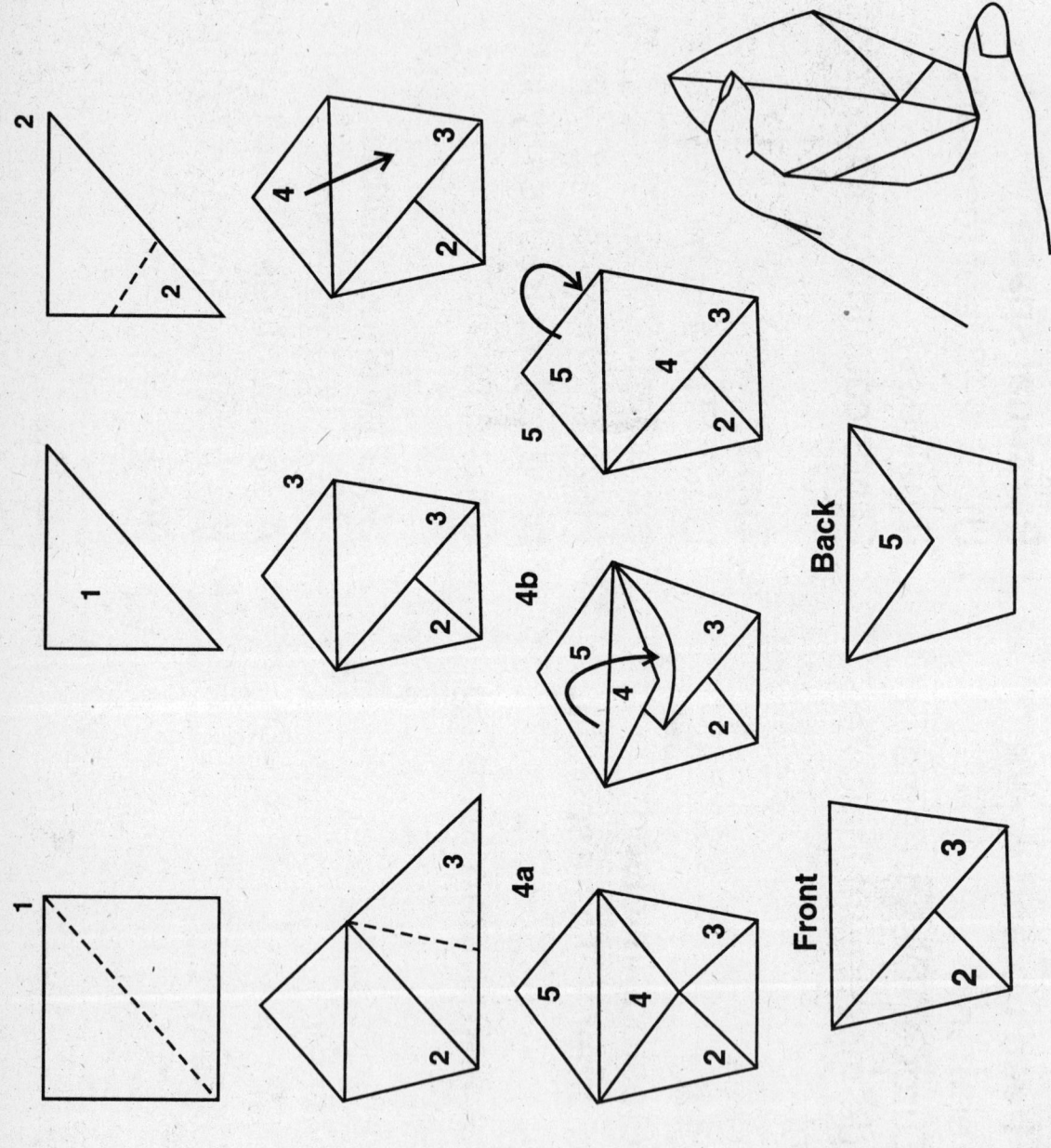

Source: Illustration from *The Art of Chinese Paper Folding for Young and Old* by Maying Soong. Adapted and reprinted by permission of Harcourt Brace & Company.

SENDER

ORIGINAL MESSAGE

ENCODES MESSAGE

"Just look at this report..."
Verbal:
- Vague, nonspecific message.
- Highly emotional.
Nonverbal:
- Highly emotional.

SELECTS CHANNEL AND TRANSMITS MESSAGE

Two-way, face-to-face: Channel is appropriate for this unpleasant issue. However, allowing others to overhear is insensitive and could be distracting to Allison.

DECODES MESSAGE

Verbal:
- Ambiguous and highly emotional; therefore, Allison is unsure of the exact nature of the problem.
Nonverbal:
- Reinforces Rick's emotional state.

DECODES MESSAGE

Rick's specific feedback about the nature of the problem (market risk disclosure) allows Allison to understand this specific concern.

ENCODES MESSAGE

"Obviously you are very concerned..."
Verbal:
- Shows empathy for Rick by acknowledging his concern.
- Encodes specific, open-ended questions to clarify the problem.
Nonverbal:
- Reinforces verbal message.

SELECTS CHANNEL AND TRANSMITS MESSAGE

Changing the channel is impossible because Rick is in control. Therefore, Allison must focus on the message and attempt to disregard that others can overhear.

SELECTS CHANNEL AND TRANSMITS MESSAGE

Unchanged

ENCODES MESSAGE

"The industry specialists in our New York..."
Clear, complete explanation assures Rick that the report is correct; reference to written documentation of research provides additional assurance.

DECODES MESSAGE

Allison understands message; no further feedback is necessary. Finally sender and receiver are mutually satisfied.

SELECTS CHANNEL AND TRANSMITS MESSAGE

Unchanged

ENCODES MESSAGE

"Fine, that disclosure..."
Rick offers a compliment to close conversation and attempt to restore goodwill possibly lost by his outburst.

DECODES MESSAGE

Rick understands the explanation but needs to make final statement to bring closure to the conversation.

SELECTS CHANNEL AND TRANSMITS MESSAGE

Unchanged

ENCODES MESSAGE

"I've read through this report..."
Verbal and nonverbal message are more specific and less emotional.

DECODES MESSAGE

Rick responds to Allison's empathy (becomes calmer) and is prompted to encode a more specific, less emotional message.

I N T E R F E R E N C E S

RECEIVER

— Original message
— Receiver functioning as sender
— Sender functioning as sender

Communication Process Model

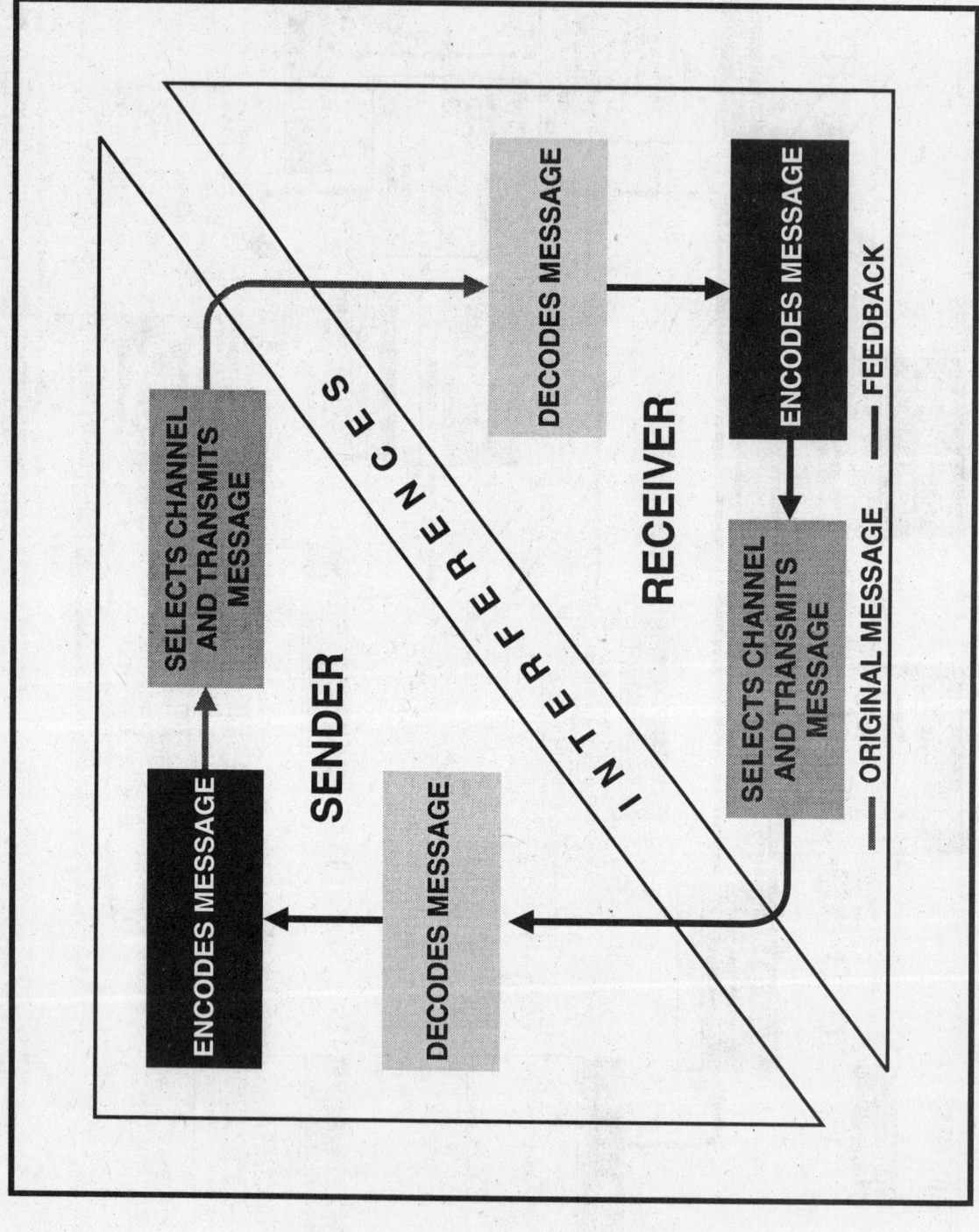

Alternate Topics: Exercise 15

Write a 50- to 75-word response to one
of the following statements.

❶ Whatever your career field, communication skills
are a key ingredient in your career success
(specify a career).

❷ Rapidly changing technology has revolutionized
the way a business communicates.

❸ What would be business be like if legality were a
company's only ethical benchmark or criterion?

Conflict

- Is a normal part of group activity.

- Does not signal that a meeting is disorderly or out of control.

- Focuses on issues, not personalities.

- Results from competing goals.

- Can help to optimize outcomes.

Roles of Group Members

- **Isolate** - one who sits and fails to participate.

- **Facilitator** - one who makes sure that everyone gets to talk.

- **Dominator** - one who speaks too often and too long.

- **Harmonizer** - one who keeps tensions low.

- **Free rider** - one who does not do his/her share of the work.

- **Detractor** - one who constantly criticizes and gripes.

- **Digressor** - one who takes the group on wild goose chases.

- **Airhead** - one who is never prepared for group meetings.

- **Socializer** - one who is a member of the group only for social and personal reasons.

- **Leader** - one who assumes responsibility for organizing and structuring the group's activities.

Serial Communication

Upon entering a taxi (which is a public carrier), Mrs. Stevens found a purse lying in the corner of the seat. She picked it up and looked inside, noticing a roll of bills and some smaller change. She gave it to the driver who told her he didn't know whose it was, but that he would turn it in at the office.

After the company had advertised in the papers for a week and then held the money for one year without anyone claiming the purse, Mrs. Stevens demanded that it be returned to her. There was $1,200 in the purse.

Mrs. Stevens claims that she found the purse in a public carrier and that it belongs to her because the owner failed to claim it. The taxi company claims that because the purse was left in its car, it belongs to them.

Source: From Donald D. White and David A. Bednar, *Organizational Behavior: Understanding and Managing People at Work.* Copyright 1986. Reprinted by permission of Prentice Hall, Englewood Cliffs, New Jersey.

Check Your Public Speaking

PLANNING A SPEECH OR AN ORAL REPORT

☐ Identify characteristics common to the audience and the speech setting (number in audience, seating arrangements, time of day).

• Public speech—attempt to influence the attitudes or actions of the audience.

• Oral report—obtain or exchange information for decision making.

☐ Develop an effective opening that presents the purpose and initiates rapport with the audience.

☐ Select a few major points and locate support for each point: statistics, anecdotes, quotes, and appropriate humor.

☐ Develop an effective ending that calls for the audience to accept your ideas (speech) or provides a conclusion with recommendations (oral report).

DELIVERING A SPEECH OR AN ORAL REPORT

☐ Expect some nervousness.

☐ Insist on a proper, impressive introduction.

☐ Select a few friendly faces in the audience to ensure good eye contact.

☐ Avoid irritating "nonwords."

☐ Avoid other annoying speech habits.

☐ Use a lectern to steady your hands only until you gain confidence.

☐ Use jokes or humor appropriately.

☐ Avoid jargon or technical terms that the listeners may not understand.

☐ Do not overwhelm your audience with excessive statistics.

☐ Watch your audience for important feedback.

☐ Dress carefully and tastefully.

☐ Appear confident and appear to enjoy making the speech.

☐ Keep with the time limits.

Check Your Public Speaking (continued)

DESIGNING AND USING VISUAL AIDS

☐ Limit the number of visual aids used in a single presentation.

☐ Include only one major idea on each visual.

☐ Design the graphic to avoid distorting facts and relationships.

☐ Keep the design simple and clean.

• Design horizontal (landscape) rather than vertical (portrait) visuals.

• Develop a standard design to appear on each visual.

• Be concise and limit words to key points.

• Keep the use of capital letters to a minimum.

• Avoid abbreviations that might confuse the reader.

• Use graphic devices—borders, boxes, shadows, lines, bullets—to separate items and direct attention.

• Use clip-art, scanned art, or cartoons to illustrate important points and break the monotony of a series of visuals containing only text.

☐ Be sure that the visual is large enough to be seen by everyone in the audience.

☐ Proofread the visual carefully to eliminate any errors.

☐ Paraphrase the visual rather than read it line for line.

☐ Step to one side of the visual so the audience can see it.

SELECTING APPROPRIATE VISUAL AIDS

☐ Chalkboard and whiteboard—convenient for small audiences in an informal setting, can erase and reuse the surface, and no special equipment needed.

☐ Flip charts and posters—same advantages as chalkboards, can flip from one visual to another, can use color, and can prepare in advance.

Think It Over

⇨ Why do you think Wal-Mart managers in the Mexico City store decided to leave the English labels on U.S. products?

⇨ Mexican customers prefer "American" packaging over Spanish labels because buying U.S. goods rather than less-expensive Mexican goods is a status symbol.

9 a.m., Monday morning on the shop floor of FTE Enterprises, a major manufacturer of CD players

A Japanese vendor has just arrived at FTE Enterprises for a scheduled appointment to negotiate the delivery date for an order of remote controls. The manager has asked that the vendor be escorted to the shop floor where she was trying to determine why a critical piece of machinery had broken for the third time in two weeks.

The manager notices the vendor's presence but continues her work. The vendor makes his way over to the manager in the middle of the hot, noisy shop floor.

Vendor: Extending his business card, "Good morning, Ms. (provide name)."

Manager: Barely glancing away from a clipboard she had been studying intensely, she takes the card. Without looking at it, she places it in her pocket and continues working.

"Hello."

Vendor: THINKING: "Why can't Americans pay more attention to basic protocol?"
"Is there some place we can sit and talk for a few minutes?"

Manager: "Look, as you can plainly see, I'm very busy. Can't we simply bless this deal and both of us get back to something more pressing?"

Vendor: THINKING: " 'Bless this deal?' "

Trying to initiate a conversation about the order,

"Ms. (provide name), I appreciate the order we received yesterday. . .

THINKING: "She's not listening. So what's new? They all think they already know everything." (Deep breath).

. . . but we need to discuss the delivery date you put on the purchase order. The date you specified is not consistent with the terms we discussed in our meeting two weeks ago."

Vendor: Even more frustrated with the manager's preoccupation and the noise,

"Is there a quiet place we could go to discuss this matter?"

The manager ignores him as she continues to tinker with the machine. Practically screaming over the noise of the machines,

"Again, is there a place we could go to get a cup of coffee?"

Manager: With a sign of resignation and a shrug of her shoulders,

"Oh, ok, the company cafeteria is just around the corner. I need a cup of coffee anyway, but we must make this quick, understand?"

Manager: In the company cafeteria

Motioning for the vendor to take a seat at a nearby table,

"Let's get straight to the point. I have to get back to the line as soon as possible. What's the problem with the order?"

Vendor: "We may have a problem meeting the date you specified."

Manager: THINKING: "Here we go again, as if I don't have enough problems to handle today."

"You said in our meeting last week that you could do a two-week delivery. Isn't that this great 'just-in-time delivery' you people claim is so good?"

Vendor: THINKING: "You people. . . typical reaction. They think we all look alike! Well, see how she likes this:"

"You people just don't quite understand our way of doing things. We can't meet a delivery schedule this tight without a long-term contract. Just-in-time delivery doesn't work that way."

Manager: Manager becomes stiff, leans back from table, and crosses arms.

THINKING: "Well, you're over here now, buddy."

"We have to have the order by noon Friday. You understand what I'm saying? Don't beat around the bush; just get the goods here like you said you would."

Vendor: THINKING: "'Beat around the bush?'" Oh, now I understand. Typical female trying do a man's job. Typical female trying do a man's job. But I'll bet she's a pushover like American women are."

Condescendingly,

Manager: "You see, a just-in-time delivery system puts both of our fine companies on a very strict schedule. We have to protect ourselves because of that. If we enter into a long-term, true just-in-time agreement, then we can meet your schedule. But on a one-time order like yours, three weeks is the BEST we can do."

THINKING: "He's lecturing me! Of all the nerve. Fine, we'll play that way . . ."

Vendor: "I know what just-in-time is, but that isn't acceptable! You saw what's happening on the floor. I have a machine down, my chief mechanic didn't show today, and my supervisor is breathing down my neck about costs. Besides, buddy, it's tough to make a profit these days. Of course, you people wouldn't know anything about that, would you? Here's the bottom line: Deliver the goods by Friday, or you won't see any kind of contract from us!"

THINKING: "Geez, she's not a pushover; she's going for the throat. What'll I do now? I promised my supervisor we'd have this contract. I can't lose face. Besides, I have to get this contract if I am to meet my quota and get my bonus."

Taking a deep breath and speaking carefully,

Vendor: "Ok, ok, let's not be too hasty. We are very interested in pursuing a just-in-time contract with your company. . . I'll talk to my production people. Perhaps we can get the order to you by Friday."

Manager: "Now we're getting somewhere!"

THINKING: "Well, maybe he has a point; I may be asking too much."

"Actually, if you could deliver at least half the order by Friday, we could wait a few days for the rest. Will that help you out?"

Vendor: "That sounds workable, but exactly how many days are you talking about?"

Manager: "By Friday, the 15th. Can we agree on that date?"

Vendor: "That sounds good. I'll call the order in right now."

The manager and the vendor smile and shake hands, pleased with the results of the negotiation.

Sender (Vendor)			Channel	Receiver (Buyer)		
Message	Breakdown	Breakthrough		Message	Breakdown	Breakthrough
"Good morning, Ms. (provide name)."		Offers courteous greeting	Two-way, face-to-face: appropriate. Hot, noisy shop: Inappropriate for negotiating a delivery date.	*"Hello."*	Uses nonverbal behavior to reinforce discourtesy of channel and confirms Japanese stereotype of North Americans—brusque and ill-mannered. Ignores value Japanese place on the proper use of business cards.	
"Is there some place we can sit and talk a few minutes?"		Attempts to alert buyer to her discourtesy politely by suggesting that the channel be altered.		*"Look, as you can plainly see, I'm very busy. Can't we simply bless this deal and both of us get back to something more pressing?"*	Is preoccupied with her work. Uses expression peculiar to the U.S.—"bless this deal."	
"Ms. (provide name), I appreciate the order we received yesterday..."		Attempts to be polite and direct buyer's attention to the order.			Is not listening to vendor's attempt to initiate the negotiation.	
"...but we need to discuss the delivery date you put on the purchase order. The date you specified is not consistent with the terms we discussed in our meeting two weeks ago."		Continues to attempt to get the buyer's attention and initiate the discussion.			Is still not listening to vendor.	
"Is there a quiet place we could go to discuss this matter?"		Tries again to improve communication by changing the channel; does so politely.	Noise and buyer's preoccupation create a barrier; reinforces buyer's discourtesy.		Continues to ignore the vendor's attempt to talk about the order.	

Sender (Vendor)			Channel	Receiver (Buyer)		
Message	Breakdown	Breakthrough		Message	Breakdown	Breakthrough
"Again, is there a place we could go to get a cup of coffee?"		Adapts to U.S. way of doing business in a social setting to divert buyer's attention away from the shop floor; settles for coffee when tea is likely preferred.		"Oh, ok, the company cafeteria is just around the corner. I need a cup of coffee anyway, but we must make this quick, understand?"	Uses verbal and nonverbal messages to reflect continued self-interest and discourtesy for the vendor.	Allows conversation to be moved to less distracting environment.
			Company cafeteria: Removes physical/mental distractions. Is quieter than shop floor. Gets buyer away from the problems on the floor so she can focus on the vendor's agenda.	"Let's get straight to the point. I have to get back to the line as soon as possible. What's the problem with the order?"	Is rude to press vendor to finish quickly so that she can return to more important work. Labels the order (and perhaps the vendor) a "problem"—an emotional term not used until now.	Is finally taking some interest in vendor's conversation.
"We may have a problem meeting the date you specified."	Presents vague, nonspecific message but does lead to the discussion. Reinforces the negative tone set by the buyer by using the word "problem."			"You said in our meeting last week that you could deliver in two weeks. Isn't that this great 'just-in-time delivery' you people claim is so good?"	Uses confrontational language and tone. Uses "you people" reflecting stereotypical attitude that will sabotage open communication.	
"You people just don't quite understand our way of doing things. We can't meet a delivery schedule this tight without a long-term contract. Just-in-time delivery doesn't work that way."	Responds to buyer's stereotyped comment with one of his own.	Recovers and tries to explain just-in-time delivery objectively in terms of the buyer's needs.		"We have to have the order by noon Friday. You understand what I'm saying? Don't beat around the bush; just get the goods here like you said you would."	Cannot control nonverbal reaction to reference to U.S. business executives' inability to understand Japanese business practices. Uses another expression peculiar to U.S. —"beat around the bush." Shows no empathy for vendor; sets forth demands.	Attempts to swallow a stereotyped response: "Well, you're over here now, buddy."

| Sender (Vendor) | | | Channel | Receiver (Buyer) | | |
Message	Breakdown	Breakthrough		Message	Breakdown	Breakthrough
"You see, a just-in-time delivery system puts both of our fine companies on a very strict schedule. We have to protect ourselves because of that. If we enter into long-term, true just-in-time agreement, than we can meet your schedule. But on a one-time order like yours, three weeks is the BEST we can do."	Uses condescending lecturing tone, supporting his opinion that this "tough" female will yield to pressure.			"I know what just-in-time is, but that isn't acceptable. You saw what's happening on the floor. . . Besides, buddy, it's tough to make a profit these days. Of course, you wouldn't know about that would you? Here's the bottom line: Deliver the goods by Friday, or you won't see any kind of contract from us."	Responds to speaker-centered lecture by listing own needs and presents her unyielding position. The result is GRIDLOCK. Makes a subtle "bash" at Japan's recent industrial success. Makes the vendor feel belittled by calling him "buddy"; disrespectful to any person but especially to this Japanese vendor who values politeness. Uses "bottom line," an expression the vendor may not understand.	
"Ok, ok, let's not be too hasty. We are very interested in pursuing a just-in-time contract with your company. . . I'll talk to my production people. Perhaps we can get the order to you by Friday."	Is motivated by his own personal gain—not the interests of the buyer.	Shows first sign of yielding to break gridlock.		"Now we're getting somewhere! Actually, if you could deliver at least half the order by Friday, we could wait a few days for the rest. Will that help you out?"	Vague message— "few days."	Reflects openness to compromise and shows concern for vendor at last.
"That sounds workable, but exactly how many days do you mean?"		Attempts to clarify the message to ensure accuracy.		"By Friday, the 15th. Can we agree on that date?"		Clarifies message and seeks feedback on the decision.
"That sounds good. I'll call the order in right now."		Confirms the agreement.				Sender and receiver are satisfied.

E-mail Style Guidelines

■ Keep line length short (no more than 60 characters).

■ Use upper- and lowercase for easy reading.

■ Do not use special print features that may not be understood by receiving terminal.

Information Ethics Issues

- **Privacy and Accessibility**

- **Property Rights**
  - Software and intellectual property
  - Computer crime and abuse

- **Accuracy**

Minor Concessions Weaken an Ethical Foundation

"Blatant illegalities don't happen overnight. Just like arsenic poisoning, unethical behavior comes in small daily doses. This attitude can grow from pushing to the front of checkout lines to shoplifting to drafting inflated and dishonest resumes to becoming a government contractor taking bribes under the table."

Source: Bates, L. D. (1990). Making the right choices. *Tomorrow's Business Leader*, 22(2), p. 19.

Skating Champion Struggles with Ethical Dilemma

Tonya Harding tried unsuccessfully to prove she was not involved in the attack on rival skater Nancy Kerrigan. Harding avoided a prison sentence but received stiff financial penalties.

Her unethical actions clouded her reputation and has prevented her from becoming a respected world-class skater—the focus of her hard training.

Ethical Messages Disclose Complete and Accurate Information

Ethical Messages Are Expressed Clearly and Understandably

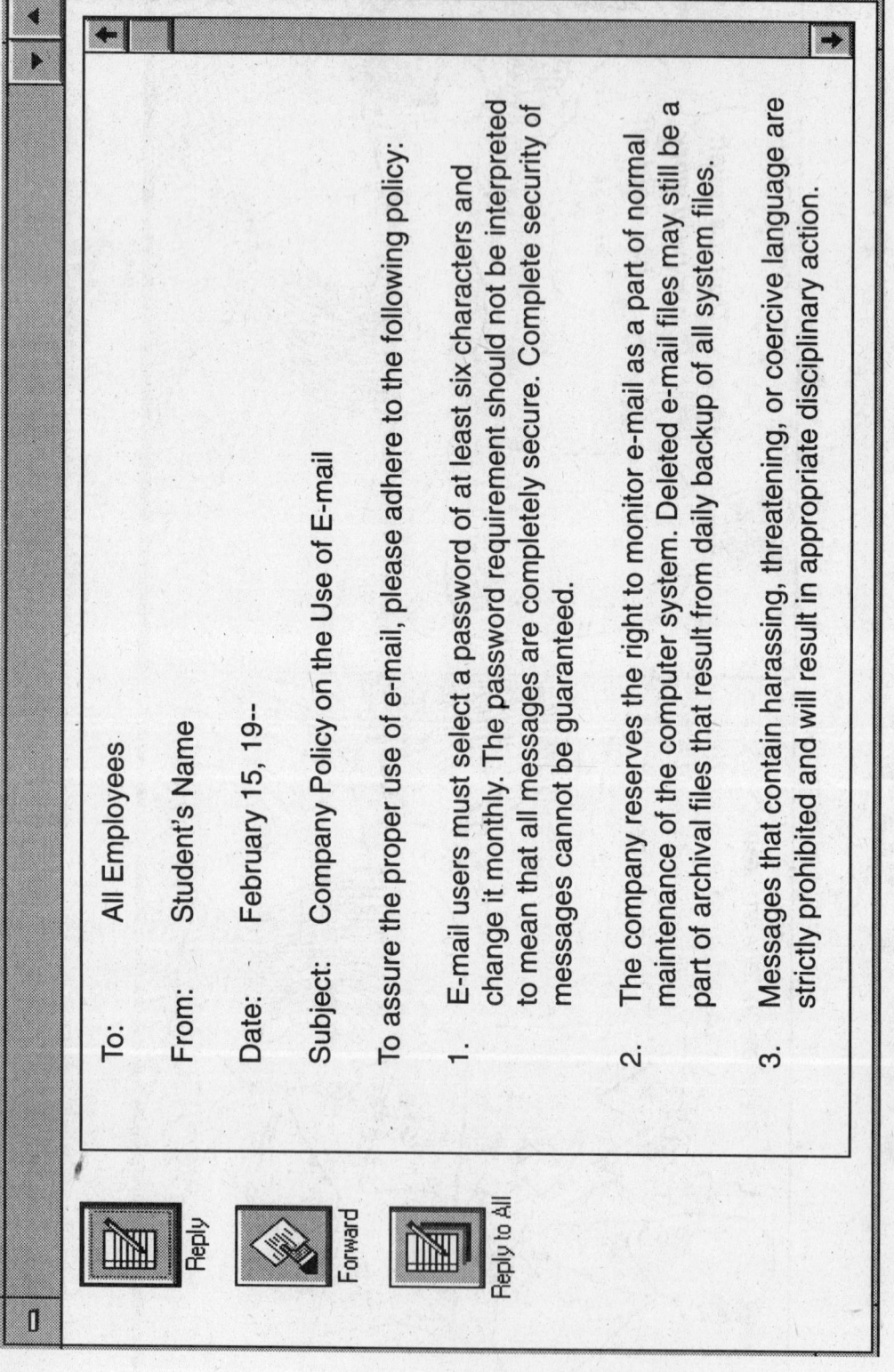

To: All Employees

From: Student's Name

Date: February 15, 19--

Subject: Company Policy on the Use of E-mail

To assure the proper use of e-mail, please adhere to the following policy:

1. E-mail users must select a password of at least six characters and change it monthly. The password requirement should not be interpreted to mean that all messages are completely secure. Complete security of messages cannot be guaranteed.

2. The company reserves the right to monitor e-mail as a part of normal maintenance of the computer system. Deleted e-mail files may still be a part of archival files that result from daily backup of all system files.

3. Messages that contain harassing, threatening, or coercive language are strictly prohibited and will result in appropriate disciplinary action.

Reply

Forward

Reply to All

TO: Carmine Morgan

FROM: Student's Name

DATE: Current

SUBJECT: ANALYSIS OF CURRENT PRACTICE OF HIRING THE HOMELESS

As you requested, I have anlayzed our practice of hiring homeless individuals to purchase tickets. A detailed analysis of the situation will support my formal recommendation about this practice.

The Problem

Because we are hiring homeless individuals to purchase tickets for our firm, we are receiving negative publicity from the media and complaints from record store customers. They allege that this practice is unethical and demand that we stop. Although the practice is legal, the right or wrong of hiring homeless individuals to purchase tickets for our firm is not clearly defined. Therefore, my goal in this report is to analyze the situation and decide if the practice is ethical.

Is it Ethical to Hire the Homeless to Purchase Tickets?

To make this ethical decision, we must analyze the action (hiring the homeless to buy tickets) in terms of costs, benefits, and obligations to each stakeholder. These stakeholders include our brokerage firm, our customers, the record store, its customers, the homeless, and the community. Two theories of ethical analysis will be applied: the utilitarian theory and the theory of duties.

Carmen Morgan

2

The Utilitarian Theory of Ethical Analysis

In this section, I have anlayzed the costs and benefits of hiring the homeless on each of our organization's key stakeholders:

Stakeholder	Cost	Benefit
Omaha Brokerage Firm	Negative publicity; e.g. newspaper articles and record store discontent.	Allows us to maintain profits in competitive market; may allow us to avoid ticket price increases, which in turn could lead to decreased demand.
Firm's Customers		Able to purchase tickets at a reasonable rate; do not have to spend time standing in line.
Record Stores	Homeless people in front of stores may damage store's image.	Possibly higher profits from increased sales.
Record Store Customers	Must stand in long lines with what they describe as "shabby" people; will be dissatisfied when tickets are sold out after they stand in long lines.	

Carmen Morgan

3

Current Date

Stakeholder | **Cost** | **Benefit**

Homeless

Forced to sleep out in cold; may be subjected to ridicule; may do this meaningless task instead of bettering themselves; food is not nutritious.

Receive money and food for purchasing the tickets; may use cash to better themselves.

Community

Shabby people may attract attention and present a negative image.

May help solve the city's problem with the homeless.

The Theory of Duties

The next theory I have applied to analyze this practice is the theory of duties. The following list summarizes the extent to which we meet relevant obligations to each of our stakeholders.

Stakeholder | **Obligation(s)**

Omaha Brokerage Firm

Keeps promise to stockholders to earn profits.

Firm's Customers

Keeps promise to customers to charge fair prices.

Record Stores

May cause harm by hurting their image (shabby people out front).

Could make reparations for harm and show gratitude by involving them in public relations campaign (they are helping the homeless).

Carmen Morgan

Current Date

4

Stakeholder

Stakeholder	Obligation(s)
Record Store Customers	May be harmed by losing opportunity to buy tickets.
	May not be treated justly if we buy all the tickets.
Homeless	Are not harmed since they sleep outside anyway.
	Keeps promise to pay them $50 upon ticket purchase.
	Food shows our gratitude for standing in line.
Community	The action is legal.
	No harm is caused.

The Best Alternative Action: Continue to Hire the Homeless to Purchase Tickets

After carefully analyzing this ethical situation using the utilitarian theory and the theory of duties, I recommend that we continue to hire the homeless to purchase tickets. This policy is best in terms of costs, benefits, and obligations to the stakeholders.

To ensure that the community understands and accepts this decision and to abate the negative publicity our firm is receiving from the media, I suggest we launch a campaign to explain the firm's position. This campaign would entail two actions:

Carmen Morgan

5

1. Hold a press conference immediately to explain that not only are we and the record store profiting, but the community is benefiting because the homeless are being helped. The point needs to be stressed that this practice should be accepted by everyone, since it is vital that the community provide for the homeless.

2. Submit an editorial to the *Omaha Tribune* emphasizing the points presented at the press conference. I don't believe we'll have trouble convincing the newspaper to publish the editorial. Since they published the first news article, they should feel an "ethical" obligation to give us a chance to respond.

Carmen, I am eager to receive your reactions to this analysis of a very difficult ethical situation. Since the next major concert is only four weeks away, let's meet for lunch tomorrow to discuss my recommendation and agree on the direction we should take in purchasing tickets.

Organizing and Composing Messages

- **DETERMINE PURPOSE AND CHANNEL**

- **ENVISION AUDIENCE**

- **ADAPT MESSAGE TO AUDIENCE**

  - Be empathetic

  - Use bias-free language

  - Avoid statements that destroy goodwill

  - Project a positive, tactful tone

ORGANIZE MESSAGE

- Outline for clarity and brevity
- Sequence ideas for desired impact

WRITE FIRST DRAFT

- Powerful sentences
  - ✓ Correct structure
  - ✓ Active voice
  - ✓ Appropriate emphasis
- Coherent paragraphs
  - ✓ Sequence of topic sentence
  - ✓ Linking ideas
  - ✓ Unity and variety

What Would You Think If . . . .

☞ as an employer, you discovered spelling and grammatical errors in an application letter. What conclusions might you draw about the applicant? Would such errors reduce the applicant's chances of being invited to an interview?

☞ as one of a bank's depositors, you noted grammatical and keying errors in the bank's correspondence? Would such errors reduce confidence that the bank processes its numbers correctly?

☞ as an administrative assistant, you discovered that your supervisor's knowledge of grammar, spelling, and punctuation was very weak? Would that weakness have any influence on your evaluation of the supervisor's effectiveness?

☞ as an executive, you recognized your limitations in grammar, spelling, and punctuation? Would you be apprehensive about keyboarding your written messages on your personal computer?

Think It Over

☞ "As an executive, I will have an administrative assistant who will be responsible for the grammar, spelling, and punctuation in my correspondence; therefore, I need not bother with learning."

☞ "If I need to know the answer to a grammatical question, I'll simply use my references."

☞ "I can write without making a mistake because I know my limitations. If I don't know whether a certain word is appropriate or how to punctuate a sentence, I can find another way to express myself and thus avoid a problem."

Punctuating Compound Sentences

Coordinate Conjunctions
AND, BUT, SO
Require only a comma to link independent clauses.

The contract was approved, but the work was not completed. Susan was upset, so she left her job.

Adverbial Conjunctions
THEREFORE, HOWEVER, NEVERTHELESS
Require a semicolon and a comma to link independent clauses.

The contract was approved; however, the work was not completed. Susan was upset; therefore, she left her job.

Omitted Conjunctions
Require a semicolon to link independent clauses.

The contract was approved; the work was not completed. Susan was upset; she left her job.

Editing and Rewriting

■ **CREATE VIVID IMAGES**
- Precise words
- Concrete nouns
- No clichés
- Descriptive modifiers

■ **WRITE CLEARLY**
- Simple, informal words
- Correctly positioned modifiers
- No expletive beginnings
- Parallel construction

■ **WRITE CONCISELY**
- No redundancies
- Active voice
- Necessary details *only*
- Tighten using prefixes, suffixes, compound adjectives, etc.

■ **MONITOR READABILITY**

Factors Affecting Readability

- Difficulty of words
- Sentence length

Use *Grammatik* to calculate readability index.

Fog Index   8–11 grade

Desirable index for business writing

Systematic Revision Procedures

Proofread using an electronic spellcheck to locate keying errors and repeated words.

Content, Organization, and Style

Proofread to be certain document.

- Presents main idea appropriately based on receiver's likely reaction.

- Presents ideas in a logical order.

- Presents accurate, complete information—reader can take needed action.

- Is concise and written at an appropriate level.

- Reflects a considerate, caring attitude and is focused on the receiver's needs.

- Treats the receiver honestly and ethically.

Grammar

Proofread a second time to locate these errors:

- ✎ **Keyboarding**
- ✎ **Grammatical**
- ✎ **Punctuation**
- ✎ **Incomplete sentences**
- ✎ **Omitted and repeated words**
- ✎ **Word substitutions (*you* and *your*) and words that sound alike (*there* or *their*)**

Format and Layout

Proofread a third time to check that document.

- ✎ **Follows conventional business format. Refer to Appendix A.**
- ✎ **Contains no errors in any letter parts.**
- ✎ **Includes all needed special letter parts.**
- ✎ **Places numbered items in the correct order.**
- ✎ **Has the visual impact—headings, enumerations, typestyles (size and appearance), and graphics.**

Proofread a final time using an electronic spellcheck.

Directions: Revise for conciseness, eliminating needless ideas.

Sample 1

Just three days ago you asked us to investigate the problem you had with your air conditioning equipment. We have completed the investigation. As you probably know, your building is steam heated.

Too low humidity is apparently the cause of the trouble. Your solution is to . . . .

Sample 2

You asked us to let you know when the new shipment of R-23 film came on the market.

The R-23 is now available.

Check Your Writing:
Pleasant and Routine Messages

CONTENT

☐ Major idea is clearly identified.

☐ Supporting detail is sufficient.

☐ Facts or figures are accurate.

☐ Message is ethical and abides by any legal requirements.

ORGANIZATION

☐ Major idea is in the first sentence.

☐ Supporting details are presented in a logical sequence.

☐ Final paragraph is courteous and indicates a continuing relationship with the receiver; may include sales promotional material.

STYLE

☐ Words will be readily understood.

☐ Syntax is acceptable.

☐ Sentences are relatively short.

☐ Variety appears in sentence length and structure.

☐ Significant words are in emphatic positions.

☐ Significant or positive thoughts are stated in simple sentences or in independent clauses.

☐ Active voice predominates.

☐ First person is used sparingly or not at all.

☐ Ideas cohere (changes in thought are not abrupt).

☐ Expression is original (sentences are not copied directly from the definition of the problem or from sample letters in text; clichés are avoided).

MECHANICS

☐ Keyboarding, spelling, grammar, and punctuation are perfect.

☐ Paragraphs are relatively short.

Check Your Writing:
Pleasant and Routine Messages (continued)

LETTERS

☐ Letter style is acceptable (block, modified block, or simplified).

☐ Letter is balanced on the page.

☐ Letter parts are in appropriate vertical and horizontal position.

☐ Return address (if plain paper is used).

☐ Dateline

☐ Letter address

☐ Salutation (if needed for letter style used)

☐ Subject line (if needed)

☐ Complimentary close (if needed for letter style used)

☐ Keyboarded name (and title)

☐ Letter is signed legibly.

☐ Reference initials (if needed)

☐ Enclosure notation (if needed)

☐ Other special letter parts (if needed)

MEMORANDUMS

☐ *TO, FROM, DATE,* and *SUBJECT* information is included.

☐ Side margins are consistent.

☐ Courtesy titles are omitted on TO and FROM lines.

☐ Lines are single-spaced; blank space appears between paragraphs; paragraphs are not indented.

☐ Tabulated sentences are indented for emphasis (if appropriate for letter style used).

☐ Handwritten initials are placed by the name on the FROM line or signed in the space provided in the simplified format.

September 30, 19--

The Honorable Mary L. Jackson
Mississippi State Senate
State Capitol
P. O. Box 1018
Jackson, MS 39215-1018

Dear Senator Jackson:

Thank you for your visit to Jackson Zoo this past weekend. Support from our legislators is important to us, especially when you also bring your family to enjoy the zoo.

We were pleased that you and your family shared some of your precious leisure time with us. As an indication of our appreciation, please use the enclosed free family pass for another enjoyable visit to the Jackson Zoo.

Sincerely,

Ted Coleman
Ted Coleman
Assistant Director

CONTENTS
Includes an obvious statement ("shipping invoice is enclosed")

STYLE
Uses inappropriate salutation and complimentary close; uses worn expressions in final paragraph.

ORGANIZATION
Uses the inductive approach.

MECHANICS
Includes two misspelled words (*ad* and *convenience*); needs a comma (after *verification*). Omits writer's address and enclosure notation.

March 17, 19--

Heritage Publishers, Inc.
655 Chadron Plaza
Omaha, NE 68106-0655

Gentlemen:

On March 1, I responded to a magazine add by placing an order for a 12-volume set of aviation history books. When they were delivered, Volume 5 was missing.

I trust you will send me Volume 5 as soon as possible. For your convience in verification a copy of the shipping invoice is enclosed.

Thank you,

John Townsend
John Townsend

1890 Donray Street
New Haven, CT 06050-1890
March 17, 19--

Heritage Publishers, Inc.
1890 Donray Street
New Haven, CT 06050-1890

Ladies and Gentlemen

Missing Volume, Order 23854

Please send Volume 5 of the aviation history books listed on the enclosed shipping invoice.

All other volumes of the set were received in good condition on March 16.

Sincerely

John Townsend

John Townsend

Enclosure

March 9, 19--

Mr. David Graves, Owner
Graves Plumbing & Heating Co.
78 Canterbury Street
San Antonio, TX 78205-1337

Dear Mr. Graves:

LARKIN STREET APARTMENTS

Yesterday evening I stopped by the construction site of the apartments you are under contract to build. You appear to be well ahead of schedule.

According to our agreement, all requests and complaints are to be made in writing. I noticed that water heaters had been installed in two of the apartments. The units are 30-gallon heaters, but the specs call for 50-gallon heaters in each of the 12 apartments.

For some families, the smaller size may be sufficient; but others may need the larger size. Because the larger size is specified in the agreement we signed, I respectfully request that the two 30-gallon units be removed and that 50-gallon water heaters be installed in all the apartments.

Thank you for your consideration in this matter.

Sincerely,

Benjamin Fernandez
Benjamin Fernandez
Contractor

March 3, 19--

Mr. David Graves, Owner
Graves Plumbing & Heating Co.
78 Canterbury Street
San Antonio, TX 78205-1337

Dear Mr. Graves:

WATER HEATER SPECIFICATIONS FOR LARKIN
STREET APARTMENTS

Please replace the two 30-gallon heaters (installed last week) with 50-gallon
units.

Large units are essential for families with children. For that reason, the
contract specifies a 50-gallon heater for each of the 12 apartments.

The project appears to be well ahead of schedule. Thanks for your efforts.

Sincerely,

Benjamin Fernandez
Benjamin Fernandez
Contractor

November 30, 19--

Mr. Benjamin Fernandez, Owner
Fernandez Property Management Corp.
750 Lincoln Road
San Antonio, TX 78205-0750

Dear Mr. Fernandez

Thank you for your letter of March 3. It has been referred to me for reply.

Looking to our contract, I see that it does specify 50-gallon water heaters. Therefore, we are complying with your request that the 30-gallon heaters be removed and that the 50-gallon units be placed in all your apartments.

Thank you for calling this matter to our attention.

Sincerely

David Graves
David Graves
Contractor

November 30, 19--

Mr. Benjamin Fernandez, Owner
Fernandez Property Management Corp.
750 Lincoln Road
San Antonio, TX 78205-0750

Dear Mr. Fernandez

Each of your apartments will have a 50-gallon water heater. The two 30-gallon units are being removed today.

Thank you for reporting the problem before additional heaters were installed. Clearly, "50-gallon" appears on the specs; clearly, "30-gallon" was keyed on the warehouse request.

Excellent progress is being made on this project; all plumbing should be complete by the original completion date.

Sincerely

David Graves
David Graves
Contractor

TO: All Employees
FROM: Transportation Department
DATE: June 1, 19--
SUBJECT: New Bus Schedule

For all employees who must travel back and forth between the airport plant and the production plant, we have developed a new bus schedule.

Two buses will operate beginning June 16. One bus will leave the main gate of the airport plant and another will leave the main gate of the production plant at 8:30 each morning. They will leave each plant every 20 minutes thereafter.

The afternoon schedule will begin at 1:20 p.m., and the last bus will leave at 4:20 p.m. Note that no buses will leave between noon and 1 p.m.

TO: All Employees
FROM: Transportation Department
DATE: June 1, 19--
SUBJECT: Bus Service Between Airport Plant and the
           Production Plant

A new bus service between the Airport Plant and the Production Plant will begin on June 16.

Buses leave the main gates of each plant on the following schedule:

Bus Departure Times from Both Gates

Morning	Afternoon
8:30	1:20
8:50	1:40
9:10	2:00
9:30	2:20
9:50	2:40
10:10	3:00
10:30	3:20
10:50	3:40
11:10	4:00
11:30	4:20
11:50	

Current Date

Newton Plastics Corp.
800 New Light Road
Appleton, WI 54911-2703

ADJUSTMENT ON INVOICE #283-93-9

Please credit our account for $159.30, the 2 percent discount on invoice #283-93-9.

To take advantage of your 2 percent discount for payments made within 10 days, we paid the invoice dated November 10 on November 10. Because this invoice was paid within ten days, we appropriately deducted the discount from our payment.

The enclosed copies of the invoice and canceled check support the dates of the events related to this transaction. If you need any additional information to correct our account, please call me at 555-1394.

Jose Moya
Jose Moya
Accounts Payable Clerk

Enclosure

October 15, 19--

Mr. Russell Hollister, Concessions Manager
Carver College, Athletic Department
P.O. Drawer 2193
Topeka, KS 66601-2193

Dear Mr. Hollister

Completing your order for 20-ounce cups is our top priority. You will receive all 20,000 cups by November 1 in time for your upcoming basketball season.

The past two months have been hectic for our plant because of intense demands to meet the basketball season rush. Although our employees take pride in their work, mistakes do happen—especially during these peak production periods.

Please return the original shipment to us to receive a full credit on Invoice #30903. You will also receive a 10 percent discount on your new order as an expression of our genuine appreciation for your continued business.

Mr. Hollister, with the cups, look for our new catalog so you can design customized cups for your baseball season. Good luck to the Carver College Hoopsters as you "soar to new heights."

Sincerely

Student's Name
Claims Manager

Current Date

Purvis Metals Corporation
1985 Northland Road
Chattanooga, TN 37401-1985

Re: Invoice No. 73-31-3444

Ladies and Gentlemen

Please replace the entire shipment of 10,000 ATM A325 connection pad bolts ordered on the enclosed invoice.

In a randomly selected sample of 78 bolts, 5 bolts stripped at a pressure well below the minimum standard of 40,100 pounds per square inch. Because this shipment does not meet the 99 percent confidence level required by our customers, this shipment must be replaced.

We have purchased high-quality products from you for the past three years and are confident that the new shipment will meet your traditional high standards. Please call me at (615) 555-4310 so we can discuss a delivery date.

Sincerely

Student's Name, Manager
Shipping Department

Enclosure

January 30, 19--

Mr. Kendall Ellis, Controller
Gosa Processors, Inc.
9334 Tower Building
Wichita, KS 67202-9334

Dear Kendall:

Our audit staff is eager to begin your annual financial audit beginning March 1. So that our visit will cause a minimum of disruption to your office routine, would you please make the following arrangements:

- A guided tour of the production facilities on the first day of the audit.

- Ample work space for four accountants.

- Direct billing of accountants' hotel accommodations to your company.

Kendall, the audit team looks forward to its annual visit to Gosa Processors. With these prior arrangements and your staff's cooperation, this audit should be completed efficiently with a meaningful cost savings to you.

Sincerely,

Student's Name
Audit Manager

May 25, 19--

Epley Resort
1083 Central Avenue
Winter Haven, FL 32789-1003

ORDER FOR STAFF/ALUMNI RECEPTION

Please prepare a reception for Brooks and Lincoln to be held on Saturday, June 27 from 7 to 9 p.m.:

Qty.	Description	Price
1	International cheese tray with fruit and crackers	$ 125.00
1	Display of fresh garden vegetables served with assorted dips	75.00
1	Iced jumbo gulf shrimp tray with cocktail sauce	160.00
1	Baked Virginia ham tray with rolls and condiments	150.00
1	Assorted gourmet cookie and candy tray	50.00
6	Fancy mixed nuts, $14 per pound	84.00
8	Fruit punch, $18 per gallon	144.00
1	Regular coffee, $22.50 per gallon	22.50
1	Decaffeinated coffee, $22.50 per gallon	22.50
	Subtotal	833.00
	Sales tax	58.31
	Service charge (17 percent)	141.61
	Total	1,032.92

Our alumni and staff are pleased that this year's reception will be held at the Epley Resort known for its excellent food and fine service.

Frank McPherson
Frank McPherson
Administrative Assistant

Current Date

Mr. Paul Caufield
8062 Gonzales Avenue
Houston, TX 70737-8062

Dear Mr. Caufield

Congratulations, because of a recent increase in stock prices, your stock holdings have increased from 50 to 60 percent of your portfolio. To maintain a diverse investment strategy, I recommend you decrease your current holdings by approximately $10,000.

Your investment strategy suggests that long-term financial wealth is best achieved by maintaining an investment portfolio that diversifies among stocks, bonds, and certificates of deposit. As stocks appreciate in value, gains should be transferred into other investments. When stocks decline, additional stock investments take advantage of temporary declines in stock values.

My suggestion is that you sell your Wal-Mart stock. Although this stock has doubled in price, the stock's growth rate has declined. Thus, I believe you could earn a higher return with other investments.

Please call me at 555-3919 to schedule an appointment to discuss this recommendation and other financial planning strategies.

Sincerely

Student's Name
Financial Planner

Current Date

Ms. Shannon Ware
Broker-Owner
South Realty Company
9837 22nd Avenue North
Champlin, MN 55316-9837

Dear Ms. Ware

Richardson Development is pleased to introduce you to our newest innovation, which has the potential to revolutionize the way realtors do business.

Video Real Estate (VRE) will allow you to meet with clients in your office and "show" them homes on a video monitor. The video programs will save you time and money and will expedite the selling process in two ways:

◆ Eliminating the need to transport buyers from location to location for preliminary viewing of numerous sites.

◆ Expediting the decision process because you don't spend excessive time working around the schedules of the sellers who may not want to be interrupted by prospective buyers.

Ms. Shannon Ware
Page 2
Current Date

The final release of VRE is over a year away. However, you should begin planning now to acquire necessary equipment, design viewing areas, and train your sales staff to use this technology effectively. Our support staff is available to assist you in this planning process.

Ms. Ware, VRE can be a cost-effective investment for South Realty Company. Please call our support division at (218) 555-1939 to schedule an appointment or to receive additional information.

Sincerely

Student's Name
Marketing Manager

TO: All Sales Representatives
FROM: Student's Name, Sales Manager
DATE: Current Date
SUBJECT: Results of Sales Service Survey

American Drug is committed to providing its sales representatives with the tools necessary to maximize sales. Increasing your sales raises your personal income while improving the financial condition and reputation of the company. A recent analysis of our sales information and an informal survey of our customers have helped us identify sales methods that will increase your sales.

The analysis shows that 50 percent of telephone/fax contacts result in a sale. In contrast, personal contacts have an 85 percent success rate. Our customers indicated that they prefer talking directly to our sales representatives. Customers especially appreciate a personal visit when making purchase decisions on new drugs.

This feedback has prompted us to re-evaluate our current sales strategy. Several years ago we elected to reduce our travel costs by eliminating

All Sales Representatives
Page 2
Current Date

personal visits and contacting our customers using communication technology. Although this sales strategy reduced selling expenses, it also has led to a decline in sales.

Considering this feedback from our customers, we believe you can increase your sales significantly by using a combination of personal and telephone contacts. Thus, during the next year plan to spend three days each week making personal contacts. You may set your own travel schedules to provide flexibility for balancing professional and personal responsibilities.

The plan will be implemented after you have had an opportunity to develop a proposed plan for visiting your existing customers and making new sales contacts. This new sales strategy can meet your personal needs as well as help us respond to customer needs more effectively.

TO: All Employees
FROM: Student's Name, Human Resources Director
DATE: Current Date
SUBJECT: Wellness Program Is Overwhelming Success

Your personal commitment to our wellness program has helped Erskine's reduce its health care costs by eight percent, a major cost savings for the company and significant benefits to you in improved health and physical fitness.

Over 200 of you have completed various substance-cessation classes with a 90 percent success rate. The physical fitness classes remain full, the walking track has replaced the snack bar as "the place to be" during the lunch hour, and nearly half of you are regulars at the Tampa Wellness Connection. All of these activities convince us of your genuine commitment to improve your health and physical fitness.

To show our appreciation, we have begun to identify ways to enhance your benefits package as we promised we would when the program was initiated two years ago. In the meantime, best wishes as you continue to strive to meet your physical fitness goals.

TO: All Supervisors
FROM: Student's Name
DATE: Current Date
SUBJECT: Installation of Optical Scanners

The optical scanning equipment has arrived. Employees must be trained and ready to use the equipment when the installation and testing is completed at the end of the month.

Orientation and training of the employees using a system are critical components of an effective information system. Our employees must learn how to operate the system and appreciate the efficiencies it brings them and our company. You will have an active role in moving your employees through the transition from our current system to the optical scanning system.

Please attend an orientation session for supervisors on March 2, 1– 4 p.m. in Room 409. You will receive basic information about the new system and the timetable for implementation and training. However, a majority of the time will be spent discussing effective strategies for assisting employees through the transition period and answering your questions about this major change in the way we track production flow.

Each shift manager will introduce employees to the new system on March 9 during the first hour of each shift. Before that meeting, please talk with employees in your unit about the change and encourage them to share their reservations and any recommendations. Submit these concerns to me in writing, so that I can be sure to address them in the meeting.

TO: All Employees
FROM: Student's Name, Director of Human Resources
DATE Current Date
SUBJECT: NEW INSURANCE CARRIER PROVIDES ADDITIONAL BENEFITS

To lower your insurance premiums without reducing coverage, we have changed the company insurance carrier to Foster Insurance Company.

This change in carrier also signals several changes in procedures. Specifically, the new policy

• Requires pre-approval for nonemergency hospital stays at least three days in advance.

• Reduces annual deductible from $500 to $250 for the policyholder and each dependent.

You can read a detailed explanation of these changes in a brochure to be distributed with your next paycheck. As always, Marc Lowell at extension 259 will be happy to answer any questions about your insurance coverage and these changes.

This solution can be prepared as an e-mail message to expedite the delivery of this routine message. A printed memo will likely serve as a transmittal document for the brochure sent later.

January 20, 19--

Mr. David Crenshaw
Royal Charters
4029 Beach Drive
Gulfport, MS 39507-0234

Dear Mr. Crenshaw:

I have an idea I think you will like.

Later this month, our firm will be host to some of the most influential business leaders in the Southeast. These executives represent names such as Disney and Turner Broadcasting. A lineup of guests like this represents a unique opportunity to promote the Gulf as an area for investment and tourism development.

Several of these executives are boating enthusiasts, and they will be in Tampa during the time that *The Princess* is scheduled for a layover. Although Royal Charters does not normally provide charters during a scheduled layover, Captain Perez suggested that your company may make an exception in this case to take advantage of this unique chance to establish contacts for future business.

Please let me know your decision by the end of the week so that final plans can be made for this charter.

Sincerely,

Student's Name
Account Executive

TO: Martin Sinclair, Manager
FROM: Student's Name, Account Executive
DATE: Current Date
SUBJECT: Pending Approval to Charter *The Princess*

After my initial inquiries to Royal Charters about chartering *The Princess*, some details have evolved of which you should be aware.

After speaking with the captain of *The Princess*, an issue arose about the requested charter. He informed me that all charters must be scheduled in advance with permission of the owner. However, the captain offered to provide an unscheduled charter at a reduced rate. He assured me he would submit the money to Royal Charters and explain the charter to the owner upon the vessel's arrival at home port.

Accepting the captain's offer may expose our company to several potential negative consequences:

1. Risk of the captain's cancellation without notice should the owner learn of the unscheduled charter or make other plans for the vessel.

2. Possibility of the public's (particularly current and prospective clients) being offended if this questionable action were disclosed.

Martin Sinclair
Page 2
Current Date

3. Questionable liability coverage in the event of an accident.

4. Legality of deducting the rate as a business expense if sufficient documentation is not provided.

I have written a letter to the owner requesting approval to charter *The Princess* for the weekend of April 22–25 and will telephone you as soon as he responds. Even though this action may risk our securing the charter, the firm's sound reputation is not at risk.

TO: Jennifer Williams
FROM: Student's Name
DATE: Current Date
SUBJECT: Strategies for Improving Sales Rep Morale

You asked me to research employee motivation and develop a workable plan to help raise productivity among the sales personnel. Based on my knowledge of participative employee-employer relationships, I believe we can develop a plan to improve the performance and morale of the sales force.

The proposed plan is based on the concept of team-directed workforce (TDWF), a management process that emphasizes business performance without subordinating employees. Management's trust in the employees and employees' trust in management are vital to the success of the plan (Versteeg, 1990).

Procedures for Developing a Team-Directed Sales Force

1. Schedule a retreat of the sales force with the objective of identifying problems as they see them. Allow them adequate time to develop workable solutions for the current problems, including their own work procedures. The request to talk honestly about their problems must be sincere if management is to receive an articulate answer that adequately addresses the situation. Allowing sales reps to implement a group-generated solution will show sales reps that the company believes in their ability (Straub, 1991).

Jennifer Williams
Page 2
Current Date

2. Schedule biannual meeting of the sales force to review the plan of action and to solve any new problems.

3. Allow the sales reps to set their own market quotas. These employees are in daily touch with the actual market trends basis. If sales reps are involved in goal-setting, goals will be more realistic than those set exclusively by management, and sales reps will be more committed to achieving them (Versteeg, 1990).

4. Revise the performance appraisal system to allow sales reps to rate one another's sales performance.

Organizational Changes

1. The plan requires mutual trust between management and the sales force and long-term commitment from both groups.

2. Management must regain the trust of the sales reps, damaged by the increased sales quotas.

3. Change in management style from control to direction could result in the

Jennifer Williams
Page 3
Current Date

resignation of the sales manager due to fear of change and loss of control (Versteeg, 1990).

4. Some managerial and stress-reduction training may be necessary to adjust the sales reps to working together as opposed to working independently (Versteeg, 1990).

Benefits to Other Companies

After implementing a total TDWF approach, Northern Telecom Canada Limited, a telecommunications company in Mississavga, Ontario, has reported a 63 percent increase in revenue, 26 percent increase in sales, 46 percent increase in earnings, and 60 percent increase in productivity per employee. Refer to the Versteeg (1990) article for additional information about this company's success with TDWF.

Jennifer, complete bibliographic references are provided in the event you wish to study this management concept further. If you would like to discuss the proposed plan or possible changes, call me at extension 215.

The references page is not included; refer to the *Instructor's Resource Manual* for a list of references used in this solution.

Transparency 9-24 (3 of 3)

Check Your Writing: Unpleasant Messages

CONTENT

☐ Major idea is clearly identified.

☐ Supporting detail is sufficient.

☐ Facts or figures are accurate.

☐ Message is ethical and abides by any legal requirements.

ORGANIZATION

☐ First sentence introduces the general subject

- without stating the bad news.
- without making such an obvious statement as "I am replying to your letter" or "Your letter has been received."

☐ Main idea (unpleasant idea emerges from preceding discussion).

☐ Closing sentences are about something positive (an alternative, resale, or sales promotion).

STYLE

☐ Words will be readily understood.

☐ Sentences are relatively short.

☐ Sentences vary in length and structure.

☐ Principal idea (the unpleasant idea or the refusal) is sufficiently clear.

☐ Some techniques of subordination are used to keep the bad news from emerging with unnecessary vividness. For example, bad news

- appears in a dependent voice.
- is stated in passive voice.
- is revealed through indirect statement.
- is revealed through the use of subjunctive mood.

☐ First person is used sparingly or not at all.

☐ Ideas cohere (changes in thought are not abrupt).

☐ Expression is original (sentences are not copied directly from the definition of the problem or from sample letters in the text); clichés are omitted.

Check Your Writing: Unpleasant Messages (continued)

MECHANICS

☐ Keyboarding, spelling, grammar, and punctuation are perfect.

☐ Paragraphs are relatively short.

LETTERS

☐ Letter style is acceptable (block, modified block, or simplified).

☐ Letter is balanced on the page.

☐ Letter parts are in appropriate vertical and horizontal position.

- Return address (if plain paper is used).
- Dateline.
- Letter address.
- Salutation (if needed).
- Subject line (if needed).
- Complimentary close (if needed).
- Letter is signed legibly.

- Keyboard name (and title).
- Reference initials (if needed).
- Enclosure notation (if needed).
- Other special letter parts (if needed).

MEMORANDUMS

☐ *TO, FROM, DATE,* and *SUBJECT* lines completed.

☐ Side margins are consistent.

☐ Courtesy titles are omitted in *TO* and *FROM* lines.

☐ Lines are single-spaced; blank space appears between paragraphs; paragraphs are not indented.

☐ Tabulated items are indented for emphasis (if appropriate letter style used).

☐ Handwritten initials are placed by name on the FROM line (or signed in the space provided in the simplified format).

March 3, 19--

Mr. George Brandt
981 Hickory Lane
Scottsdale, Arizona 85143-9081

Dear Mr. Brandt

Our trained technicians can probably repair your PC 11 but we will have to charge you for the service.

The reason for the charge is because terms of the warranty were violated. Screwdriver marks on the cover clearly indicate that repair had been attempted by an untrained person. This violates the provision on page 2 of your manual, which clearly states "Do not remove cover; only factory-trained specialists are authorized to do repair work."

Clearly, free repair is unjustified under terms of the warranty.

Our trained technicians will be glad to examine the unit, give you an estimate of costs, and repair it if you choose to do so.

Sincerely

Student's Name
Repair Manager

March 3, 19--

Mr. George Brandt
981 Hickory Lane
Scottsdale, AZ 85143-9081

Dear Mr. Brandt

From your letter, I am convinced that your personal computer is definitely in need of repair.

According to your retailer, repair has been attempted by a person not trained and authorized to do such work. Because such attempts can severely damage a machine and greatly complicate repairs when attempted later by well-trained technicians, purchasers are emphatically cautioned against even removing the cover.

If such cautions (given in the manual and on the tutorial) had been heeded, the seller would have inspected and repaired your computer under terms of the warranty. Under the circumstances, his decision to charge for the service was justified.

Mr. George Brandt
Page 2
March 3, 19--

We have some specialists here at the center. After inspecting your machine, they can give you a fairly accurate estimate of the charges. If the problem is minor, the charges will be small. You could be using your PC 11 in a very short time.

Sincerely

Student's Name
Repair Manager

September 14, 19--

Charlotte Steele
403 North Jackson St.
Gulfport, Mississippi 39501-1403

Dear Ms. Charlotte Steele

Your request for a $144 reimbursement has been received, and I am sorry to say it cannot be made. Clearly, the charge is for import duties.

In the discussion that preceded the purchase and in the documents you signed at the time, it was clearly pointed out that you would be responsible for import duties. Duties are not collected at the time of sale because they cannot be accurately predicted.

I am sure you can understand my position in this matter. Thank you for doing business with us; and if you have any further questions, do not hesitate to call or write.

Sincerely,

Ruben Lopez
Ruben Lopez
Manager

September 14, 19--

Ms. Charlotte Steele
403 North Jackson **Street**
Gulfport, **MS** 39501-1403

Dear **Ms. Steele:**

Your hand-carved, monkey-wood chest was delivered about a month sooner than we had predicted when purchase papers were signed. The invoice you received with the chest shows prepayment of cost and transportation.

Because the import duty can only be calculated on the shipping date, the tax is paid when shipment is delivered. Before sales contracts are written, buyers are told of their responsibility to pay import tax; this information also appears on the sales ticket.

Ms. Steele, by ordering directly from the overseas manufacturer rather than regional markets, you saved about 40 percent on your beautiful, exquisitely hand-carved chest.

Sincerely,

Ruben Lopez
Ruben Lopez
Manager

August 31, 19--

Mr. Jim Read
Read Construction Co.
203 Woolbright Road
Whitehall, OH 43213-2987

Dear Mr. Read:

Your six-year credit history with us and past excellent credit rating make you one of our most valued customers. Your company has stayed with J. J. Ferguson during some tough economic times.

In our company's 53 years of existence, we have been successful by maintaining excellent credit ratings with customers. We follow sound financial practice by extending credit up to 60 days. To show our appreciation for you, we have recently extended your credit to 90 days. We will gladly extend credit to you again when we receive cash payments against these previous credit extensions.

Because of your loyalty to our business, we wish to continue doing business with you in the future.

Sincerely,

T. Bryce Abraham

T. Bryce Abraham
Credit Manager

March 3, 19--

Ms. Arlene Collins
34 South Clanton Street
Lincoln, NE 68501-8730

Dear Ms. Collins

No two cakes prepared by expert chefs are exactly the same. Even the slightest variations in ingredients, oven heat, and humidity can cause visible differences.

The same variations occur in the dying process for our wallpaper patterns. The dyes are mixed precisely, and the same meticulous process is used to produce each run of wallpaper. However, slight variations in the dyes and acid content of the paper can cause differences in the colors of different runs of a pattern.

Because of these uncontrollable variations among runs, customer orders for additional rolls of a pattern are shipped from the same production run as the first order. The sample you viewed at Marlon's Interiors was taken from a run produced solely for product samples.

Ms. Arlene Collins
Page 2
March 3, 19--

Ms. Collins, consult your interior designer for ideas on incorporating your pattern into a different decorating scheme. You might
consider selecting one of our coordinating wallpaper borders that
would harmonize the colors in your wallpaper and ceiling. You can
order these lovely borders for a 50-percent discount until May 15.

Sincerely

Student's Name
Claims Manager

October 28, 19--

Ms. Tandi McRae, Head
Accounting and Budget
SRM Industries
7821 South Third Street
Conway, AR 72032-7839

Dear Ms. McRae

PartyTime Limited was pleased to be part of your staff/alumni banquet and appreciated your staff's compliments on the quality of the food, service, and decorations.

You are correct that the amount of the invoice is more than the price specified by the contract. The contract price was based on the 250-guest estimate provided by your administrative assistant. The estimate considered the amount of food to be served and the number of servers required to serve 250 guests, as well as the cost of decorating the banquet hall.

Your invoice includes an additional $200 for the cost of food served to the 25 unexpected guests of your alumni. Although we typically prepare extra food for large, formal affairs such as yours, we did not anticipate

Ms. Tandi McRae, Head
Page 2
October 28, 19--

the large number of additional guests that arrived that evening. I was relieved our staff was able to obtain additional food from our warehouse to serve these guests.

Had these 25 guests been included in the original estimate, we would have added $200 to the food cost estimate. We would also have included $80 for the cost of two additional servers. Although we were short handed, our staff provided your guests with quality service. Your invoice does not include any additional charges for service.

Ms. McRae, as you begin planning festivities for the upcoming holidays, keep our famous specialty desserts in mind for an extraordinary change from the traditional catered turkey lunch.

Sincerely

Student's Name
Manager

June 29, 19--

Mr. and Mrs. Bart Harris
103 Pinebrook Lane
Bowling Green, KY 42101-0876

Dear Mr. and Mrs. Harris:

With interest rates at their lowest level in 20 years, you chose a very good time to buy your first house.

Choosing a fixed mortgage rate allowed you to "lock in" your 8-percent interest rate, protecting you from potential increases in interest rates before your closing. Had you selected a variable rate mortgage, you could have taken advantage of the recent drop in interest rates. However, you would have been subject to subsequent increases in interest rates.

If interest rates continue to decline, you may want to consider refinancing your fixed rate mortgage. Refinancing is typically cost effective when interest rates are 1½ percent below your current mortgage rate.

Again, we are glad we could be of service in your recent home purchase. Please call me if I can provide information about other financing needs.

Sincerely,

Student's Name
Loan Officer

March 12, 19--

Kim Flaunt
Snowcap Limited
905 Southhaven Street
Boise, ID 83707-7313

Restocking of Returned Merchandise

The HighFly skis you stocked this past season are skillfully crafted and made from the most innovative materials available. Maintaining a wide selection of quality skiing products is an excellent strategy for developing customer loyalty and maximizing your sales.

Our refund policies provide you the opportunity to keep a fully-stocked inventory at the lowest possible cost. You receive full refunds for merchandise returned within 10 days of receipt. For unsold merchandise returned after the primary selling season, a modest 15-percent restocking fee is charged to cover our costs of holding this merchandise until next season. The enclosed check for $2,069.76 covers merchandise you returned at the end of February.

Kim Flaunt
Page 2
March 12, 19--

While relaxing from another great skiing season, take a look at our new HighFly skis and other items available in the enclosed catalog for the 19-- season. You can save 10 percent by ordering premium ski products before May 10.

Student's Name
Credit Manager

Enclosures: Check and catalog

Simplified block format is appropriate because the writer does not know the gender of the receiver. The courtesy title is omitted to avoid possible embarrassment.

Current Date

Mr. and Mrs. Charles Moore
873 North Spruce Lane
Davenport, IA 52802-8510

Dear Mr. and Mrs. Moore:

Ensuring that your home furnishings were delivered to your new home in Davenport in excellent condition was a top priority of our dependable, highly trained workers. Providing this quality service at an affordable price is also important to both of us.

One way of keeping insurance affordable is to use a standard insurance policy that insures personal property for its replacement cost. Separate insurance policies are available to insure heirlooms, such as your family painting, for their sentimental values. Our representative explained these insurance options before you signed our standard insurance policy. The enclosed check for $250 is based on our insurance estimates of the cost to purchase a similar painting.

Best of luck to you and your children as you settle into your new home in Davenport. If we can assist you in future moves, please call us at 555-MOVE.

Sincerely,

Student's Name
Claims Manager

Current Date

Mr. Stephen Shook, Manager
Edgewood Golf Club
957 Edgewood Boulevard
Springfield, IL 62701-3498

Dear Mr. Shook

The design specifications for your new clubhouse reveal that you have spared no expense to provide members with spacious, multi-purpose rooms complete with exquisite Williamsburg furnishings. Clearly, a sprinkler system designed to protect this valuable investment is one of your top priorities.

Currently your specifications include a traditional wet sprinkler system that carries water in the pipes to be used in case of fire. Over the years, our experience has been that pipes often freeze when exposed to subfreezing temperatures over extended periods, a common condition here in Illinois. The water in the pipes freezes and causes the pipes to break, which results in extensive damage to the structure and its furnishings.

Mr. Stephen Shook, Manager
Page 2
Current Date

Based on our experience, we believe that a dry sprinkler system is preferable in our cold climate, especially for structures with exquisite furnishings such as yours. In the dry system, pressurized air in the pipes releases a valve that pumps water into the pipes *only* when a fire is detected.

Although the dry system carries additional installation costs, you save money in the long run by preventing the unnecessary costs of structural repair, replacement of expensive furnishings, and the inconvenience caused by a burst water pipe. Please take a look at the enclosed brochure that illustrates the operation of the dry sprinkler system.

Mr. Shook, we will gladly consult with your architect to redesign the blueprints to include the dry system or a wet system with a heat source in the attic to warm the pipes during subfreezing temperatures. Just call us at 555-9760 to give us your instructions.

Sincerely

Student's Name, Owner

Current Date

FACSIMILE

Mr. Tom Delancy
Laird and Associates
411 McDowell Road
Charleston, IN 47011-0411

Dear Mr. Delancy:

Six months ago we agreed to participate in a "Partnership with Russia" program to help Russian businesses improve their accounting systems. Today we learned that a change in the group's schedule requires them to tour our MIS department next week—exactly when your audit staff is scheduled to arrive.

May we discuss how we can resolve this conflict? We would prefer that the audit be rescheduled to a later date. Because the tour only affects the MIS department, perhaps you could rearrange the timing of your audit procedures to avoid testing the MIS department during that week?

Can you check your audit schedule while I set up the itinerary for our guests and call me so that we can discuss an acceptable solution? I will appreciate your flexibility. Once our visitors have returned to Russia, we can focus on assisting you in completing the audit efficiently.

Sincerely,

Student's Name
Controller

April 25, 19--

Dear Tim

Thanks for trying out for the 12-year-old competitive baseball team this year. The effort you put into the tryouts shows your love for the game.

Almost 150 talented and determined young boys tried out to fill the 12 positions on the 8 teams. The players selected had to show their ability to throw, catch, and hit. Although your batting skills need improvement, your ability to throw and catch is excellent. With improvements in your hitting, you will have an excellent chance of being accepted next year.

Tim, so you can stay involved in the game and work on your basic skills, consider playing on one of the church league junior teams. With your strong arm and eagerness to play, you would be a welcome addition to any of these teams. Let's play ball!

Sincerely

Ron Sims
Ron Sims

Gene Rankin
Gene Rankin

Current Date

Ms. Lisa Aultman
Financial Manager
WRMW Television
P.O. Drawer 93001
Salem, OR 97301-8461

Dear Lisa

You can take pride in the major role you and others at WRMW have played in the recent five percent rise in adult literacy. We were pleased to read the complimentary article in the Salem Daily News about your program, Oregon's Lost People.

Petrol Corporation, which has recently purchased ChemCon Engineering, has redefined its corporate goals, resulting in a number of changes in our day-to-day operations and commitments. Affecting WRMW is the new advertising focus; advertising dollars will no longer be allocated to support educational programming.

Lisa, we are proud to have been a partner with WRMW in the campaign for adult literacy and expect to see future improvements in adult literacy as a result of the outstanding programming at WRMW.

Sincerely

Student's Name
Public Relations Director

Current Date

Dunn/Malcolm Construction
9831 Downing Street
Minneapolis, MN 55440-9831

BID ON ROCHESTER COMMUNITY CENTER

Thank you for submitting a bid on the proposed Rochester Community Center. The 10 bids received on the project have been reviewed carefully.

Because all bids were above our architect's cost estimate, we are revising the blueprints to eliminate several high-cost areas. Would you resubmit your bid incorporating these changes? You should receive the revised blueprints in a couple of weeks and must submit your new bid by February 28. The contract will be awarded to the low-bid company with work to begin as soon as possible.

We appreciate your involvement in such a worthy community project. A May 19-- grand opening is still possible—perfect timing for a summer filled with enriching, fun activities for Rochester's "young" people of all ages.

Student's Name
Chair, Building Committee

Current Date

Mr. Stan Martin
Mitchell Savings and Loan
8324 Randall Street
Cheyenne, WY 82009-8324

Dear Mr. Martin:

Your new RSL local area network will improve your interoffice communication significantly and provide your employees instant access to bank records. Your system can be installed as soon as you authorize us to begin.

The technology in your RSL system remains state of the art. The manufacturer's recent 15 percent discount reflects the increased demand for this powerful computer technology. Our contract with you was based on the manufacturer's price at that time. Assuming immediate installation, we ordered and received the hardware before these price reductions were announced.

Your RSL local area network can be expanded easily as your business grows and new technology becomes available. Once your system is online, our service technicians will be ready to provide routine maintenance and 24-hour emergency service.

Sincerely,

Student's Name
Sales Representative

Current Date

Mr. Julian Robbins
Robbins Construction Corp.
P.O. Box 9408
Eau Claire, WI 54703-9408

Dear Mr. Robbins:

Thank you for submitting your loan proposal to Colonial National. We are quite interested in supporting the development of a shopping center to service the Westside community.

The recent declining real estate market has required many lending institutions including Colonial National to modify their lending guidelines for real estate loans. A borrower must now show how the loan can be repaid from assets other than the development itself. This new policy is designed to assure that the loan can be repaid regardless of the success of the proposed development.

Mr. Robbins, if you can revise your loan proposal to show that the loan can be repaid from other investments, Colonial National will approve the $14 million loan. Please review the enclosed pamphlet for additional assistance in preparing a successful proposal.

Sincerely,

Student's Name
Loan Manager

Enclosure

TO: All Supervisors
FROM: Student's Name, Director, Human Resources
DATE: Current Date
SUBJECT: Company Personnel Plan Needs Feedback and Discussion

A thorough study of rising business costs and our financial condition is completed, and we are ready to begin implementing solutions generated by this research. Among these ideas are upgrading computer systems, changing insurance carriers, and streamlining our personnel selection and training methods.

Even with these cost-cutting measures in place, some downsizing of our workforce is necessary. Normal turnover and retirement should account for a projected 10 percent reduction in the next three years. All departments will need to be cut another 10 percent over the same time period rather than the 30 percent projected at the beginning of this process.

These reductions will also necessitate some changes in responsibilities, especially among upper-level personnel. For example, architects will be given supervisory control over all phases of a project, rather than separate

All Supervisors
Page 2
Current Date

personnel handling each aspect (i.e., as budget, bidding, and work crew assignments). Also, managers will assume additional support-staff functions such as originating and producing correspondence on their own personal computers.

Your role in preparing the employees for this transition is vital. Please begin talking with the employees in your unit about these changes. Assure them that the change will be gradual; they will receive advanced notice of changes affecting them. Solicit their preferences related to severance pay, continuation of benefits, and some type of outplacement service.

Send a brief summary of the employees' suggestions and major concerns to Tina Stewart in Human Resources by September 30. Later this month a meeting of all employees will be held to discuss the planned reorganization and respond to these employee concerns and preferences. With your help, we can achieve our downsizing objective while maintaining a positive relationship with our employees.

TO: All Sales Representatives
FROM: Student's Name, Sales Manager
DATE: Current Date
SUBJECT: Results of Sales Service Survey

American Drug is committed to providing its sales representatives with the tools necessary to maximize sales. Increasing your sales raises your personal income while improving the financial condition and reputation of the company. A recent analysis of our sales information and an informal survey of our customers have helped us identify sales methods that will increase your sales.

The analysis shows that 50 percent of telephone/fax contacts result in a sale. In contrast, personal contacts have an 85 percent success rate. Our customers indicated that they prefer talking directly to our sales representatives. Customers especially appreciate a personal visit when making purchase decisions on new drugs.

This feedback has prompted us to re-evaluate our current sales strategy. Several years ago we elected to reduce our travel costs by eliminating personal visits and contacting our customers using

All Sales Representatives
Page 2
Current Date

communication technology. Although this sales strategy reduced selling expenses, it also has led to a decline in sales.

Considering this feedback from our customers, we believe you can increase your sales significantly by using a combination of personal and telephone contacts. Thus, during the next year plan to spend three days each week making personal contacts. You may set your own travel schedules to provide flexibility for balancing professional and personal responsibilities.

The plan will be implemented after you have had an opportunity to develop a proposed plan for visiting your existing customers and making new sales contacts. This new sales strategy can meet your personal needs as well as help us respond to customer needs more effectively.

TO: Jill Ainsworth
FROM: Student's Name, Controller
DATE: Current Date
SUBJECT: Recommended Disciplinary Actions for Will Mallory

A customer recently called stating her order had not been received even though her check had been returned with her bank statement. While investigating this order, I discovered that Customer Service has received similar complaints during the year.

After auditing our accounting records, I suspected that a mail clerk, Will Mallory, was cashing checks received in the mail. When confronted with the allegation, Will confessed that he stole the money to pay for gambling losses. Will has been very cooperative in providing documentation that indicates he embezzled $20,590 during the past year. Will appears repentant that he took advantage of his position to steal from the company and understands he has broken the law.

The procedures for handling mailed payments have already been changed to assure that he will not embezzle funds again. We must now determine whether to retain Will as an employee, file civil and/or criminal charges, and attempt recovery of the stolen funds.

Jill Ainsworth
Page 2
Current Date

Recovering the stolen funds will be difficult since Will has no financial resources. His attitude suggests that we may be able to recover the money by transferring him into a non-accounting position and setting up a repayment plan. No civil or criminal charges would be filed as long as Will cooperates and enrolls in a counseling program.

I believe this action will send a strong yet compassionate message to our employees. The plan would prevent any negative publicity and return the largest amount of the stolen funds over time. Please call me with your comments so that I can schedule a disciplinary conference.

Current Date

File

FORMAL DISCIPLINARY CONFERENCE WITH WILL MALLORY ABOUT EMBEZZLEMENT

I met with Will Mallory on Monday, May 19, to discuss disciplinary actions to be taken as a result of his embezzlement of $20,590 from the company.

During the past year, Will has periodically taken and cashed checks received by mail. The thefts were discovered when the accounting department investigated a complaint by a customer who alleged she had not received her order even though the check had been returned with her bank statement. When Will was confronted with the allegation he confessed that he had stolen the money to pay for gambling losses. Will has provided copies of the customer orders that accompanied these checks.

After discussing various options with Jill Ainsworth, I decided to transfer Will to a nonmanagerial position in the Maintenance Department. We also agreed on a repayment plan that authorizes us to withhold 5 percent of his gross salary each month until the stolen money is repaid. Will will also be

File
Page 2
Current Date

required to attend counseling sessions approved by Human Resources.

No criminal or civil charges will be filed as long as Will complies with this plan. This plan should make Will accountable for his actions, minimize any negative publicity to the company, help ensure repayment of the stolen funds, and give Will a chance to redeem himself and continue supporting his family.

During the disciplinary conference, I discussed the full nature of these actions, and Will stated that he understood why these actions were being taken. Will Mallory's transfer is effective immediately.

TO: Mark Rackley, President
FROM: Student's Name, Plant Manager
DATE: Current Date
SUBJECT: Crisis Communication Guidelines

Mark, as you requested, I have reviewed the research about communicating crisis information to employees and have developed guidelines for improved communication. I located the following predominant ideas from an extensive search of current business periodicals.

1. Release the news as soon as possible to prevent misinformation and to reduce employee anxiety (Alessandra & Davidson, 1989).

2. Give employees as much information as possible on a regular basis. Balance any bad news with positive information (Scollard, 1990).

3. Encourage questions and concerns about the plant from employees. In dealing with concerned employees, no questions are "dumb" ("Meeting the Challenge," 1991).

4. Keep in mind what you would want to know if you were in the employee's position. Tailor the method and content of the communication with that attitude in mind (Grove, 1988).

These guidelines have worked for banks, chemical corporations, and software manufacturers; I believe they can work for Janata. Please refer to the attached bibliography if you wish to read about these concepts in greater depth.

Attachment

TO: Robyn Coblentz, Tax Partner
FROM: Student's Name
DATE: Current Date
SUBJECT: Approval to Resign as Accountants for Bradley Ford

A matter has recently surfaced with Bradley Ford, a tax client for the past eight years. Because of the potentially litigious nature of the matter, your approval is needed.

Recently, Bradley asked us to prepare a business plan to secure a bank loan for his business. The income statement he provided for preparing the business plan showed twice the amount of net income provided to us for preparing his 19-- tax return. His reply to my questions about the discrepancy was evasive, and he has refused to discuss filing a Form 1040 amended return. These actions seem to indicate that the understatement of net income was intentional.

Of course, maintaining accountant-client confidentiality (Rule 301 of the *AICPA Code of Professional Conduct*) prevents us from reporting his actions to the IRS. However, the AICPA's *Statements on Responsibilities in Tax Practices* states if the CPA believes that the IRS relies on him or her as corroborating significant information which is known to be false, the CPA is under duty to disassociate from the engagement.

Robyn Coblentz, Tax Partner
Page 2
Current Date

Continuing to act as Bradley's accountants would constitute an implicit conspiracy in his fraud, leaving us open to prosecution. We also have an obligation to our stockholders to maintain an untarnished image; this duty requires us to avoid costly legal entanglements and to keep our integrity intact. Thus, I recommend that we

• Withdraw from our engagement with Bradley Ford.

• Notify our board of directors of this action in writing.

• Notify our legal counsel of our decision.

Because of the sensitive nature of this situation, please send me your response within the next couple of days. With your approval, I will draft the resignation letter to Bradley Ford for your signature.

August 11, 19--

Ms. Allison Murrell
Route 3, Box 14
Webster, OK 71331-7909

Dear Ms. Murrell

The Waldheim piano you purchased on March 15 seemed to be ideal for your needs.

In addition, terms seemed to be ideal ($150 each month, payable by the 15th). We have not received your July payment. Because the August payment will be due four days from now, we need an explanation.

Please send it in the enclosed envelope or send a $300 check to cover the July and August payments on your sustained-sound Waldheim.

Sincerely

Sydney Franke
Sydney Franke
Credit Manager

Enclosure

August 25, 19--

Ms. Allison Murrell
Route 3, Box 14
Webster, OK 71331-7909

Dear Ms. Murrell

Because you were interested in a piano with the utmost in sustained-sound vibration, we introduced you to the Waldheim.

When you agreed to pay $150 by the 15th of each month, we agreed to make quick delivery and provide in-the-home tuning by an expert. Having fulfilled our part of the agreement, we are confident of your desire to fulfill your part.

Please use the enclosed envelope to send a check for the July and August payments ($300).

Sincerely

Sydney Franke
Sydney Franke
Credit Manager

Enclosure

September 8, 19--

Ms. Allison Murrell
Route 3, Box 14
Webster, OK 71331-7909

Dear Ms. Murrell

Noting that your July and August payments are yet to be received, we have two concerns: our money and your credit rating.

To us, a good credit rating means (1) the ability to purchase at the most appropriate time, (2) less need for building up large amounts to pay for purchases, and (3) a feeling that merchants have confidence in you. Surely, a good credit rating has similar meanings for you.

Because your credit rating is so important to you, please send a $300 check to cover your July and August payments.

Sincerely

Sydney Franke
Sydney Franke
Credit Manager

September 22, 19--

Ms. Allison Murrell
Route 3, Box 14
Webster, OK 71331-7909

Dear Ms. Murrell

From our credit department, I have learned about the status of your account. It shows an unpaid balance of $450, the last payment having been received on June 21.

The promptness with which you made the first payments seemed to confirm your satisfaction with your sustained-sound Waldheim and the contractual credit agreement. Under that agreement, we do have alternatives if payments are not made. But we prefer that you send a check for $450, continue to enjoy your Waldheim, and protect your credit rating.

Ms. Murrell, I urge you to do so.

Sincerely

Kim Lopez
Kim Lopez
General Manager

September 30, 19--

Ms. Allison Murrell
Route 3, Box 14
Webster, OK 71331-7909

Dear Ms. Murrell

A date has been set for action on your account—October 9, 19--, at 4:30 p.m.

If $450 is received by that time, you may retain possession of the piano and make plans to make the next payment ($150) on or before October 15 as scheduled.

If payment is not received by that time, legal steps (as described in the credit contract) will begin immediately.

Sincerely

Kim Lopez
Kim Lopez
General Manager

TO: Cyndi Johnson, Senior Distribution Manager
FROM: Ted Coleman, Transportation Manager *TC*
DATE: October 10, 19--
SUBJECT: Modifying Current Distribution System to Increase Customer
           Satisfaction

A change in our distribution system will enable us to meet customer demands for home delivery. Delivering products directly to customers' doors will save their time and improve our service.

In a recent survey of over 1,000 customers in the Milwaukee area, 85 percent of the respondents indicated high to very high interest in home deliveries. Because of significant improvements in our product catalog this year, customers may order products directly from their homes. Home deliveries will build a broader customer base and increased customer loyalty. The present system limits customer demands for direct service.

To implement a home delivery system on a test basis in Milwaukee, we must add two local carriers. These carriers will transport products in small vans to individual homes. Please review the attachment itemizing the added costs and personnel requirements. The projected increase in sales resulting from home deliveries is shown in Table 1.

After you have considered this change, including the increased sales and customer satisfaction, please let me know whether you will approve this change in our distribution.

Attachment

TO: All Employees
FROM: Student's Name, Director of Human Resources
DATE: April 14, 19--
SUBJECT: Information Session about 403(b) Plan

Everyone at Northwest College is aware of our excellent employee benefits package, especially the more common features, such as health care and state retirement. However, many of you may not be aware of the 403(b) plan.

Although the plan has been available for several years, only a few have taken advantage of this opportunity to invest up to 25 percent of their income in a tax-deferred annuity. Participants do not pay taxes on either the funds invested or the investment income until the funds are withdrawn at retirement.

Some of you may feel that you don't have the extra cash to start an investment plan, but Northwest makes investing possible for all employees. From 1 to 15 percent of your gross income may be deducted automatically from your paycheck and the funds placed into this tax-deferred annuity. This plan is a virtually painless way to save for your future while reducing your current taxes.

All Employees
Page 2
April 14, 19--

Because retirement plan requirements can seem confusing, an information session about the 403(b) plan will be held next Wednesday in the conference room from 1:00 to 2:30 p.m. A representative from the Human Resources Division will be on hand to answer questions and explain in detail the advantages of this investment opportunity and to enroll employees in the 403(b) plan.

Please stop by to see how Northwest can help you start saving for retirement now.

Current Date

Mr. Glenn Marshall
1103 Commerce Street
Denton, TX 76205-2955

Dear Glenn:

On my last trip to the U.K., I uncovered an excellent set of stamps to begin your son's collection: a sheet of 100 Winston Churchill commemorative stamps issued as a part of the British Statesmen Series. Only 20,000 stamps of each historical figure were printed and sold ten years ago; the market value has risen fourfold from the original issue price for a set in mint condition.

I inspected these stamps myself, and they are in mint condition. None of the original 100 stamps were ever used; the glue on the back has no paper scraps attached nor any retouching glue used to cover such flaws. The dyes and inks are authentic and distinctive; the British Statesmen Series innovated the modern use of painted images rather than printed dyes.

Mr. Glenn Marshall
Page 2
Current Date

The seller bought the commemorative set when it was issued for $96.50 and is willing to sell the 100 stamps for $315. This well-preserved exhibit of Winston Churchill could be your son's for only $346.98 (includes my normal 10-percent finder's fee).

Glenn, please call me at (713) 555-9890 to set up a meeting where you and your son could examine these stamps and finalize the details. Beginning with such a premier commemorative set is certain to cultivate your son's interest in stamp collecting as well as his interest in one of the world's most celebrated leaders.

Sincerely,

Student's Name
Broker

Selling price = 200 pounds/currency rate x 1.10

April 11, 19--

Ms. Carmen Costello
Ole Tyme Deli
1405 McKee Boulevard
Tacoma, WA 98413-1405

Dear Ms. Costello:

Welcome to the Seattle/Tacoma area and best wishes for the success of Ole Tyme Deli.

Since your arrival, we hope you have had a chance to tune your radio in to WLOX and listen to our usual fare of classic rock—the music of the 25–40 age group. A recent survey indicated that approximately 9,900 households, each consisting of 3.7 persons, listen to WLOX regularly—that's 36,630 people! We believe that Ole Tyme Deli would benefit from an appeal to this large demographic group that regularly tunes in to WLOX.

Because of the magnitude of the competition in the restaurant business, particularly from the fast-food franchises, Ole Tyme Deli could benefit from advertising during "drive time" (7:30 to 8:30 a.m. and 4:00 to

Ms. Carmen Costello
Page 2
April 11, 19--

6:00 p.m.) to attract lunch and dinner customers who might otherwise drive elsewhere. Advertising on WLOX will ensure that nearly 40,000 potential customers hear about Ole Tyme Deli. When these listeners know where you are, chances are they will become loyal customers.

WLOX can offer you a "grand opening" package of 40 thirty-second advertising spots at $150 a spot to be run during "drive time" during the week of your grand opening. You can furnish the ad script if you like, or we can write the advertisements and submit them for your approval.

Ms. Costello, I will call you in a few days to discuss scheduling an appointment to develop an advertising strategy for your grand opening. Please call me at (206) 555-WLOX if you have questions. Again, best wishes in your new business venture.

Sincerely,

Student's Name
Sales Manager

April 14, 19--

Mr. and Mrs. David R. Denson
373 Joline Avenue
Sacramento, CA 95813-0373

Dear Mr. and Mrs. Denson:

You are cordially invited to enjoy 18 holes of golf on our signature golf course followed by complimentary appetizers and beverages in our luxurious clubhouse inspired by the elegance of colonial Williamsburg.

Crystal Stream *is* one of the premier golf courses in northern California! We are willing to back up this statement by inviting guests like you whom we believe will appreciate what we have to offer—a challenging golf course inspired by the world's famous golf courses, a well-equipped pro shop and luxurious clubhouse, and facilities for business meetings, luncheons, and private parties. The enclosed brochure illustrates our facilities, but we believe that you must visit Crystal Stream to get a truly accurate picture.

Golf is only one of the activities you may enjoy at Crystal Stream. You can swim in our indoor and outdoor Olympic-size swimming pools and work out in a gym complete with Nautilus, Nordic-Track, and an assortment

Mr. and Mrs. David R. Denson
Page 2
April 14, 19--

of free weights, exercise cycles, and other premium equipment. The gym is staffed by certified fitness trainers who offer aerobics classes and exercise routines designed specifically to meet your fitness needs. You can end your workout with a relaxing sauna or whirlpool.

If Crystal Stream appeals to your active lifestyle, please call the pro shop at (916) 555-GOLF to schedule a tee time for your complimentary 18 holes of golf and plan on enjoying dinner in our clubhouse afterward. When you arrive, present the enclosed invitation certificate to the pro shop manager. Our staff is waiting to provide you with a memorable recreational experience.

Sincerely,

Student's Name
Public Relations Director

Enclosures

March 25, 19--

Mr. Jose Fuentes
General Manager
Crystal Stream
P.O. Box 2383
Long Beach, CA 90810-2393

Dear Mr. Fuentes:

Crystal Stream has been dedicated to community involvement activities in the Long Beach area for as long as I can remember. Last year, I worked with my friend Dr. Janet Robbins when Crystal Stream hosted the Long Beach Medical Association's AIDS Project Golf-a-thon. The children benefited from the money that was raised, and everyone appreciated Crystal Stream's support of the community.

Gamma Alpha Epsilon sorority is also a loyal supporter of our community. Our members frequently participate in nonprofit/civic projects. Most of us hold part-time jobs in the community, and we are recognized as one of the most responsible groups on campus.

As the president of Gamma Alpha Epsilon, I am planning the sorority's annual spring formal. Because this formal will commemorate the sorority's fiftieth anniversary at State University, over 100 alumni and members of the national

Mr. Jose Fuentes
Page 2
March 25, 19--

staff in addition to our 75 members are expected to attend. To ensure a memorable occasion for our seniors and to showcase the community's exclusive social and recreational community, we believe Crystal Stream is the perfect location for Gamma Alpha Epsilon's 19-- Spring Formal.

The enclosed recommendation letters from Dr. LaRue, President of State University, and Dr. Matthews, Dean of Students, confirm my statements about our impeccable reputation. Additionally, the enclosed financial statement and other information about Gamma Alpha Epsilon should help you understand that Gamma Alpha Epsilon is an organization of young women committed to community involvement and personal development.

Mr. Fuentes, please call me by April 15 to confirm that Crystal Stream will be the site of Gamma Alpha Epsilon's formal and to initiate the preliminary planning for this event.

Sincerely,

Student's Name, President

Enclosures

March 15, 19--

Mrs. Louise Cox
976 Thompson Road
Mena, AR 71953-0976

Dear Mrs. Cox:

Meeting you and touring the building on your property last week was a pleasure. That little building provided me with a fascinating glimpse of the past. You must have found it convenient using the building as a big "attic," storing all your canned goods and old farm implements over the years.

As the manager of the Down-Home Barbeque in Mena, I am constantly looking for items to build and display in our restaurants. Our restaurants are constructed of weathered wood to create a genuine rustic atmosphere, which we think complements our "down-home" menu.

As I toured your building, I couldn't help but notice some of the unique items inside and the old weathered boards hanging outside. The wood from the building and its contents would enable us to build and furnish a new restaurant in Mountain View and refurbish our Jackson location. Marc Lane, owner of Down-Home Restaurants, has asked me to extend you the offer explained in the enclosed proposal.

Naturally, the building holds many memories for you, for which no amount

Mrs. Louise Cox
Page 2
March 15, 19--

of money could compensate. However, we would be happy to purchase the entire contents of the building, excluding any special items of sentimental value that you may want to keep.

Although the thought of selling the building may sadden you, think of the "second life" that the old farm equipment, dishes, washboards, seed bags, and weathered boards would have in our restaurants. People who would otherwise never see such Americana will have the opportunity to learn a little about its rich past.

After you have reviewed the proposal, please call me at 555-3253 to discuss our offer to display your treasures in our restaurants.

Sincerely

Student's Name
Manager, Mena Store

Enclosure

April 30, 19--

Mr. Tom McHann
1239 McDowell Road
Indianapolis, IN 46206-1239

Dear Mr. McHann:

Meeting you a few weeks ago at our annual fund-raising kick-off meeting was a pleasure. I enjoyed talking with you and learning about your business. McHann Electronic Service is a dynamic member of our business community, and we at HomeBuilders are pleased that you made the decision to join us in our efforts to see that hard-working citizens become homeowners.

When you agreed to serve as an executive volunteer, you received a packet of information about the fund-raising drive. If you will refer to that packet, you will see that the conclusion of this year's effort,

Mr. Tom McHann
Page 2
April 30, 19--

May 15, is only two weeks away. Yet, as of today only five of your fifty pledge cards have been submitted. Most of your colleagues in the executive volunteer program have completed at least 80 percent of their solicitations.

Please let us know if our staff can assist you in completing your solicitations before May 15. Just a little more work and we can all celebrate the success of this year's fund-raising drive at our annual victory dinner and begin plans to build homes for many more of our community's citizens.

Sincerely,

Student's Name
Executive Director

TO: Patrick Williams, President
FROM: Student's Name, Data Processing Manager
DATE: November 30, 19--
SUBJECT: Advertisements During *Lifestyles of Mob Heroes*

Williams Department Store has been a respected business in Maplesville for as long as I can remember. I was pleased when I could return to Maplesville as data processing manager and could work in such a wholesome environment. Although Metropolis was exciting and educational, I always knew that I wanted to settle down in Maplesville, away from the crime and danger that abound in some of our cities.

This week I was surprised when I saw a Williams Department Store advertisement featured during an episode of *Lifestyles of Mob Heroes*. This television program, although critically acclaimed, glorifies violence and drug use. Surely Williams Department Store does not want to endorse the dangerous life styles portrayed on this show.

Patrick Williams
Page 2
November 30, 19--

Over the years, Williams Department Store and the Williams family have been actively involved in community affairs and church activities. Additionally, your involvement with Rehab, Inc., shows that the company believes that drug abuse and violence should not be condoned. However, advertising on a television program that carries parental discretion notices sends a very different and negative message to current and potential customers.

Please consider discontinuing advertisements on *Lifestyles of Mob Heroes.* Other excellent television programs that reinforce themes consistent with the Williams corporate culture are available and would be much more suitable for Williams' advertisements.

May 20, 19--

Harrelson Producers
3674 Elmhurst Avenue
Los Angeles, CA 90052-3674

Ladies and Gentlemen:

When Thunderbolt negotiated with Harrelson to produce our first music video, we were impressed with the clips of other Harrelson videos and your proven performance record. Like you, we strive to satisfy our customers with innovative and exciting new approaches in entertainment.

When we viewed your video of the Indigos, we were intrigued with the subtle use of symbolism in the graphic images along with creative shots of the musicians. This tape was no "garage job" or simplistic concert tape; it was art—exactly what we wanted for the Thunderbolt video.

After viewing the first draft of our video, we were disappointed to see very little symbolism and no evidence of innovative ideas when we specifically asked for graphic symbolism juxtaposed with shots of the band.

Harrelson Producers
Page 2
May 20, 19--

The video closely resembles a concert tape, focusing primarily on live-concert footage of the band. Although we believe our band is exciting, this video will not sell Thunderbolt to the MTV set.

With Harrelson's reputation for excellence and fairness, we are confident the video can be revised to meet our expectations. The band will do its part to assist in re-shooting footage and will meet with the creative director at his convenience to discuss the kind of graphic imagery appropriate for interpreting our music and its message. Please call me at 555-3920 to schedule this meeting.

Sincerely,

Student's Name
General Manager

TO: Bart Kegel, President
FROM: Student's Name, Assistant Accountant
DATE: January 6, 19--
SUBJECT: Seminar on Online Services

In previous meetings, we have expressed interest in going online and have discussed how the information superhighway could help Kegel, Inc., operate more productively and generate more revenue. However, none of us yet has the expertise to implement an online system.

While completing other research on information technology recently, I noticed an advertisement for a seminar designed to help small businesses get online. This seminar, entitled "Making Online Services Work for You," will be held May 15–17 on the campus of Oakland Technical College and will be taught by Barry Wise, a nationally recognized authority on the Internet and other computer network technologies.

Because I've already begun to research online services and have become the unofficial "organizer" of these efforts, I believe that

Bart Kegel, President
Page 2
January 6, 19--

sponsoring my attendance at this three-day seminar could benefit the company. The intensive training would provide me with the knowledge we need to develop our strategy to implement this rapidly growing and changing technology.

Let me know if you need more information about the seminar and wish to discuss a strategy for pursuing an online connection to expand our business.

Attachment

TO: Gordon Zaharias, Manager
FROM: Student's Name
DATE: May 2, 19--
SUBJECT: Serving More Customers Without Expanding Facilities

Over the past few weeks, I have noticed an opportunity to expand our sales volume. As you know, many lunch hour customers are turned away because of the typically long waiting line for a table. I believe we can serve these customers without adding to our facility.

Implementing a FaxFood Line is, I believe, an excellent, low-cost means of increasing revenue and customer service while maintaining our low overhead. We could install a fax machine through which we would send advertisements and order forms to local business (see attachments). We would then deliver food to these businesses for a nominal fee above the menu price.

Maintaining our reputation for quality food and service would require the delivery service to be organized slightly different from current operations. Only those menu items that can be delivered effectively would be offered on the delivery menu; note the selected items included on the preliminary delivery form I've drafted. To limit the number of small-dollar deliveries, a delivery fee would be charged for orders less than a certain dollar amount.

Gordon Zaharias, Manager
Page 2
May 2, 19--

Although new delivery personnel would be needed during the lunch period, I believe the current kitchen staff could handle the increased orders effectively.

The delivery service could be introduced to businesses with the attached sales letter. Copies of the delivery menu and order forms would be attached or periodically faxed to interested customers and available at the cash register. The attached draft of the order form allows groups to submit one order while having totals for each individual. Our delivery personnel could carry sufficient cash to make change for each customer.

Implementing a delivery service will allow us to serve our customers more effectively, lead the restaurant business in technology, and demonstrate our creativity to the community. After you have reviewed the draft of the sales letter and order form, I would welcome the chance to talk with you further about this idea.

Attachments

May 2, 19--

Ms. Gabrielle LeBlanc, Manager
Designer Publications, Inc.
8181 High Street
Atlanta, GA 30305-8181

Dear Ms. LeBlanc

As a busy manager, you appreciate the importance of meeting deadlines; customers demand prompt service. On the other hand, you are sensitive to your employees' needs. When the day is too hectic for an hour away for lunch, employee performance can suffer. Gordon's Deli has a solution that will serve your needs.

Gordon's is proud to introduce our FaxFood Line. Your employees can choose from our special "FaxFood Menu" and fax their order using the attached order form. Within forty minutes of receiving your order, fresh sandwiches or salads will be delivered right to your place of business. Forget the hassle of collecting correct change—our delivery staff will provide everyone with an individual bill and assist with making change. Delivery is free for orders over $25.

Ms. Gabrielle LeBlanc, Manager
Page 2
May 2, 19--

With Gordon's delivery service, your employees can spend more of their lunch hour relaxing rather than fighting lunch hour traffic. For employees working to meet tight deadlines, our delivery service will provide them with precious extra time.

Be among the first to discover our quality food and fast, friendly service by faxing an order today. Just select from the items on the enclosed FaxFood Order Form, write the item number(s) in the order section and your name and address at the top, and fax to us. To receive a 15-percent introductory discount, send this letter along with your first order. Keep taking care of your business and leave lunch to us!

Sincerely

Student's Name, Manager

Enclosure

TO: All Employees
FROM: Student's Name, MIS Manager
DATE: January 2, 19--
SUBJECT: Computer Security Measures

Our company has seen rapid growth in the use of electronic mail during the past year. The ease at which we can send messages across the office and the country has encouraged us to use e-mail instead of other forms of communication, such as letters and telephone calls. Like many forms of new technology, however, unintentional problems can occur when users are not completely familiar with the technology.

Please take a moment to review the computer security policies outlined on pp. 24–26 of your *Employees' Handbook*. Take the time to discuss with your supervisor any policy you do not understand fully. Two extremely important policies deserve your attention.

First, many of us assume that e-mail is completely confidential: that is not true. Although your right to privacy is important to us, selected employees in the Information Systems Department must have access to your e-mail files to maintain the computer networks. To safeguard your privacy, then, use discretion when writing e-mail messages because others *can* read what you write.

All Employees
Page 2
January 2, 19--

Second, the security of your e-mail account is a potential problem. Recently, a university professor was almost indicted on federal charges as a result of inadequate computer security. Because the professor did not log off his terminal when leaving his office, a disgruntled student was able to use the professor's e-mail account to send a threatening message to the President of the United States.

For your own security and the security of confidential company records, be sure to log out each time you leave your terminal—regardless of the length of time. If the nature of your job makes it difficult for you to perform the log-off procedures every time you leave your computer, we can program your computer to log off the system automatically if the computer is not used for a certain length of time.

As we grow together and learn more about how new technologies can help our business, please follow these policies to protect your own security and the company's. No one wants the indignity of having one's "confidential" messages read or their accounts used to send inappropriate messages. Please call me if you have any questions or experience any problems following these policies.

Current Date

Mr. and Mrs. Curtis Alford
4211 Main Street
Memphis, TN 38115-4211

Dear Mr. and Mrs. Alford

During the WBRO news coverage of the Beale Street Blues Fest, I saw a film of you and your family arriving at the festival in your brand-new Star Blaze minivan.

Your children's obvious excitement not only aroused my interest in blues, but my professional interest as well. As advertising manager for Minivans Unlimited here in Memphis, I am always looking for owners who are pleased with the minivan's features and usefulness. Such satisfied customers are our best advertisers!

One of the most effective selling points of the Star Blaze is its convenience for families with children. If you would allow Minivans Unlimited to use the WBRO film in a commercial, it would be a background scene in an end-of-season special promotion. Only the

Mr. and Mrs. Curtis Alford
Page 2
Current Date

scene of your family arriving at the festival and getting out of the Star Blaze would be shown. You would not be required to give a testimonial, and we *will not* alter the film in any way.

Mr. and Mrs. Alford, as an expression of our gratitude for use of the film, we will send you $150 and coupons for three oil changes/routine service checkups at our dealership. If you wish to allow your family to appear in our commercial, simply sign and mail the enclosed permission card by (*specify date*). Then tell the children to look for themselves on television!

Sincerely

Student's Name
Advertising Manager

Enclosure

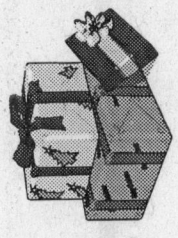

The Holiday Store Brings Jobs to Community Children

"Peace on earth and goodwill toward all people."

This familiar phrase reminds us that the holiday season is a time of sharing. Being a part of the Thirteenth Annual Holiday Store will provide two very special opportunities to share this season.

First, you can share joy with parents and children by donating toys to stock the Holiday Store. Festive boxes for depositing toys will be placed throughout the community. Please make your deposit by 5 p.m. November 30.

The parents of approximately 400 needy children will come to the Holiday Store to select toys for their children. The store will be located in the lobby of the Main Street Fire Station on December 6-8 from 3 to 6 p.m.

Second, volunteers are needed to set up the Holiday Store and to assist parents in selecting and wrapping gifts. Indicate your willingness to be a part of this important community project by completing and returning the form below. Be sure to check the date you will be available to help.

Experience the real gift of the holiday by sharing with others.

The Holiday Store Volunteer Form

Name _____   Telephone _____

Check the day you are available to work:

☐ December 5   ☐ December 7
☐ December 6   ☐ December 8

Return the completed form by November 30, 19-- to

Mari Cooper, 3771 Abilene Street, Cambridge, MA 02140-3771 (555-1043)
or Frances Kuhnle, 101 Mangrove Drive, Boston, MA 02184-0101 (555-9031).

November 14, 19--

Ms. Jolene Forrest
250 Hampton Circle
Jackson, MS 39288-0250

Dear Ms. Forrest:

Your concern about the state insurance plan for teachers and loss of the deductible will be investigated. You deserve to be treated fairly and equitably by the state insurance plan.

As chair of the Senate Education Committee, I can knowledgeably address this issue for you. My staff and I will research the applicable law related to your insurance deductible. In addition, the current insurance administrator of your plan will be asked to clarify the wording of your policy.

Ms. Forrest, thank you again for bringing this concern to my attention. You will receive a response as promptly as possible.

Sincerely,

Ronnie Musgrove

Ronnie Musgrove
Mississippi Senate

TO: Dennis Pierce, Sales Representative
FROM: Stephanie Royston, President *SR*
DATE: Current Date
SUBJECT: Congratulations on Completion of Spanish Course

Congratulations on your recent completion of the conversational Spanish course. By taking this course on your own initiative, you have shown you are self-motivated and deserve recognition for your accomplishments.

Your new skill will be extremely helpful in relating to our growing number of Spanish-speaking customers. Dennis, by increasing your ability to communicate with our clients, you have set an outstanding example for the rest of the staff. Thanks for your outstanding work and for your ambition to go beyond typical expectations.

TO: All Employees

FROM: Student's Name, President

DATE: Current Date

SUBJECT: Peak Performance During the Harvest Sale

Congratulations on your excellent performance during our recent Harvest Sale.

Although the crowds were large and the days were long and hectic, your expertise and endless patience contributed to a profitable, safe, and service-oriented sales season. In fact, we had higher sales and fewer customer complaints than last year, and no reported accidents. Each of you is to be commended for the extra effort you put forth and the consistency with which you graciously served our customers.

We sincerely believe that your commitment makes Wolcott an outstanding store. Thanks for being such an important part of the team; we truly appreciate your excellent work.

CONTENTS

Vague; uses overly complex words that may be perceived as intended to impress.

Is not specific about what is appreciated.

STYLE

Includes cliché, which is overly exaggerated.

Closes commendably with a German thank-you learned from Anna.

ORGANIZATION
Uses the deductive approach.

MECHANICS
Misspells *vielen Danke*.

Current Date

Ms. Anna Herpfer
Bahnhofstr. 9
7000 Weinstadt 2
Germany

Dear Anna:

Thank you very much for your facilitation of procedures during my recent excursion to Germany. I simply don't know what I would have done without you.

Vilen danlee, again!

Sincerely,

Sheila Leigh
Sheila Leigh

Current Date

Ms. Anna Herpfer
Bahnhofstr. 9
7000 Weinstadt 2
Germany

Dear Anna:

Thank you so much for helping me during my stay in Germany.

Your quick reactions helped me get my luggage in just a couple of days and my traveler's checks the next day. Because I could rely on you to solve these "unnerving problems," I was able to concentrate on the seminar and on touring the country.

Anna, courteous and supportive people like you are what makes life enjoyable. I really appreciate the time and effort you spent to make my trip so memorable.

Sincerely,

Sheila Leigh
Sheila Leigh

2594 Woodland Drive
Portland, ME 04101-3408
Current Date

Mr. Donald Keller
Human Resources Director
Southside Manufacturing, Inc.
189 South 29th Avenue
Portland, ME 04101-1897

Dear Mr. Keller:

Thank you for taking the time from your busy schedule to talk to our Business Communication class at West State University last week. Your suggestions on resume writing have proven quite helpful to me and the rest of the class.

Resume writing had posed a particular challenge to me until I revised my resume using the four-step plan you suggested for writing a "sure-fire resume." I was pleased with the finished product, but I was delighted when our Career Services director and several recruiters complimented me for having such an informative, concise, and attractive resume—just as you predicted. Dr. Cox also told me that several other students who heard your talk have had similar experiences. Many of them have landed strong job offers.

Mr. Keller, I sincerely appreciate your sharing this information so vital to getting an edge in today's competitive job market.

Complimentary close and signature block are omitted.

Current Date

Mr. Leonard Tomlinson
12 Main Boulevard
Downingtown, PA 19335-8100

Dear Leonard:

Thank you for recommending me to Angela and Michael Nelson. Their wedding was beautiful and a joy to photograph. Wedding photographs have been only a small part of my bookings, but this event has changed that.

The Nelsons were so impressed with the photographs that they have recommended me to several other couples. Because of your thoughtfulness, I have been able to make weddings a regular part of my business.

Leonard, I really miss having you in the studio, but I continue to wish you the best in your new work. Please let me know if I can reciprocate your kindness in any way.

Sincerely,

Student's Name

391 Meadowview Circle
Bloomington, IN 47401-4391
Current Date

Ms. Victoria Sanchez
Manager, Heartbeats
715 McAdams Avenue
Thomasville, NC 27360-8601

Dear Victoria:

Thank you for helping me secure the position with American Greetings that would allow me to relocate near my sister. Without your outstanding recommendation, I could not have found a similar job so quickly.

Already my supervisor has commented on my knowledge of both the creative and the marketing phases of the card industry. I told her about the rewarding work experience at Heartbeats, a company that involved me in almost all phases of the operation.

Victoria, I sincerely appreciate your genuine, sincere concern for me and my sister. Please let me know when I can return the favor in some way. Today I learned that I'm scheduled to attend the April card show in your region; perhaps we could meet for dinner.

Sincerely,

Student's Name

TO: Larry Pruitt, Chair
           Planning Committee

FROM: Student's Name
DATE: Current Date
SUBJECT: Tax Report Available for Planning Committee's
           Next Meeting

Please accept my apology for missing yesterday's meeting of the Planning Committee. If the plane from Denver had arrived on schedule, I could have attended.

The report on tax considerations for the proposed site of the Windermere Apartments is ready. Let me know if you plan to include it on next week's agenda.

TO: U.S. Managers in Mexico Less than One Year
FROM: Student's Name, Partner
DATE: Current Date
SUBJECT: Major Differences in Culture and Business Practices in
          Mexico and U.S.

Recently miscommunication between our managers and Mexican business partners has occurred primarily because of lack of knowledge of Mexican culture, customs, and language. Being sensitive to their culture and practices is an important *first* step toward communicating and building strong relationships with the Mexican business leaders on whom we rely.

To increase your managerial effectiveness, please study carefully the following guidelines for conducting business in Mexico. These guidelines are related to time, interpersonal relationships, family and religious ties, and language.

Time

Mexicans view time as being for them instead of against them. Therefore, they place less importance on adherence to schedules and appointment times than U.S. managers do (Himstreet, Baty & Lehman, 1993). Thus, when a meeting or an appointment is scheduled, allow a grace period of fifteen to twenty minutes for Mexican business associates. Try to avoid holding important meetings between 11:30 a.m. and 2:00 p.m. to allow for the Mexicans' longer lunch periods. Likewise, do not be offended if Mexican managers do not start meetings promptly.

Interpersonal Relationships

Trust and compatibility are much more important to Mexicans than are bureaucratic

U.S. Managers in Mexico Less than One Year
Page 2
Current Date

regulations and norms of conduct (Copeland & Griggs, 1985). Mexicans tend to consider a person as a friend first and a business associate second, so act accordingly.

Always be sincere and cultivate a personal relationship. Remember names and pronunciations, give each member of a group personal attention, and shake hands when meeting someone and when departing. Mexicans also show respect for rank and proper placing in the hierarchy, even extending to the language. Spanish has two forms of *you*: formal used with new acquaintances and informal used with friends and family (Himstreet, Baty & Lehman, 1993).

Family and Religious Ties

Mexicans place more importance on family, personal, and church-related activities than on business activities. Accordingly, they have longer lunches, more holidays, and no work whatsoever on holidays. Because 97 percent of Mexicans are Roman Catholic (Hoffman, 1992), be sure to note religious (Catholic) holidays and schedule around them when scheduling meetings.

Language

If your Mexican associates speak to you in English, they have obviously taken the time to learn it. Extending them the same courtesy of learning Spanish, the official language of Mexico, will also help you better understand what is being said around

U.S. Managers in Mexico Less than One Year
Page 3
Current Date

you (Copeland & Griggs, 1985). Learn the fundamentals of the language. The company offers biweekly language lessons in several offices in Mexico. If your branch does not offer the classes, you may find listening to language tapes an excellent way to master the basics. For example, learn how to say pleasantries, basic questions, and phrases in Spanish.

Summary

To build business relations with your Mexican counterparts, please incorporate these basic suggestions in your business and personal dealings: slow down, establish friendships first and conduct business second, remember that courtesies take priority, and show respect for the Mexican culture and system. To obtain an in-depth understanding of the Mexican culture, refer to the attached bibliography as a starting point for your study.

If you need additional information, please call Ana Maria Silva, director of International Assignments Division, who is located in the home office. She will be happy to direct you to other resources or arrange customized training sessions.

Attachment

Current Date

Community Leaders of Monroeville
Monroeville, AL 36460-6732

Dear Community Leaders:

Would you lend support to a project that could

• Attract new industry to Monroeville?

• Avoid increases in city taxes caused by excessive garbage disposal?

• Reduce litter and assorted garbage and preserve the environment?

Your support of the Monroeville Plastics Recycling Plan can help accomplish these goals.

Many items that we and our children throw away every day can be made useful again through plastic recycling. Broken plastic toys, used and leftover picnic items, and empty milk and soft drink bottles can become fiberfill for children's coats, plastic lumber for city park furniture, and wastebaskets to store your recyclables in until they are carried to the recycling center. The Plastics Recycling Plan can make it convenient for us to reduce waste, recycle plastics, and help keep our city beautiful!

Community Leaders of Monroeville
Page 2
Current Date

Many companies making these plastic products are now looking for recycled materials. Monroeville can better attract those industries by having a ready supply available without shipping expenses. In addition, citywide support of the plastic recycling plant will eliminate the need for new landfills and incinerators. All Monroeville citizens benefit if the city is not forced to increase taxes to defray the cost of exorbitant garbage disposal.

Your support of the Plastics Recycling Plan represents a commitment to preserving our environment and an investment in the economic development of Monroeville. You can pledge your support by organizing plastic collection competitions in your local civic clubs, educating your employees and children about recycling, and setting up a collection area in your workplace. For additional information on organizing drives or educational programs, call me at 555-4319. Let's all work together to improve our community by preserving our environment.

Sincerely,

Student's Name, Chair
Environmental Preservation Task Force

DANA W. HOWARD
587 Birchwood Road
Clinton, MS 39056-0587
(601) 555-4977

CAREER OBJECTIVE To obtain a secondary teaching position in business computer applications.

EDUCATION **Bachelor of Science.** Fulgham College, Jackson, Mississippi. To be conferred May 16, 19--.
Major: Business technology
Grade Point Average: 3.39/4.00
Honors: Graduated Cum Laude
Initiated, Phi Delta Kappa
Recipient, Mitchell Academic Scholarship
Computer Competencies: *WordPerfect for Windows, Microsoft Word, Lotus 1-2-3, Paradox, PageMaker, PowerPoint, and PaintBrush*

EXPERIENCE Editorial assistant, Synic Printing Services, Pearl, Mississippi. August 19-- to May 19--.
• Refined computer competencies while completing on-the-job applications; software operated included *PageMaker, WordPerfect for Windows,* and *Adobe Illustrator.*.
• Keyed, proofread, and edited materials for publication.
• Refined management and interpersonal skills while supervising four printing clerks.

HONORS AND AWARDS Phi Delta Kappa, honorary education fraternity
Phi Beta Lambda, national business organization
First place national and second-place state winner, Information Management Competitive Event, 19--
Lincoln Achievement Award, 19--

INTERESTS Walking, swimming, and historical sightseeing.

REFERENCES Available on request.

Checklist for a Winning Resume

☑ *Be sure resume represents your best work.*

- Include no typographical or grammatical errors.

☑ *Format for outstanding first impression*

- Prepare resume/envelope on high-quality (24-pound, 100-percent bond), standard size, neutral-colored paper.

- Print with clear, sharp type—preferably use a laser printer.

- Balance on page; use ample white space.

- Exploit special enhancements (typestyles and graphics) to ensure a positive impression. *Keep the resume clean and simple to read.*

- Be consistent throughout document; i.e. headings, parallelism, similar information in parallel items.

☑ *Provide reader at-a-glance comprehension*

- Use a format that (a) emphasizes key qualifications, (b) is acceptable in the job field sought, and (c) reflects your personality.

- Use crisp phrases with subject-understood sentences; do **not** use *I, me,* or *my.*

- Give reader bite-size pieces—easier to read and can be remembered more easily. Use bullets (■ , ✓ , ●) to make achievements "glitter like diamonds."

- Allow for plenty of white space even if two pages are required. Put your name and the page number on subsequent pages.

☑ *Highlight (sell) your qualifications in terms of the employer's needs*

- Include only job-related information (gained from self- and job analysis).

- Stress what you have accomplished on the job—don't just list obvious job duties.

- Set yourself apart from other applicants whose resumes look like job descriptions.

- Provide deeper insight into your ambition, capability, and personality.

- Omit information that could lead to discriminatory hiring (gender, religion, age, marital status, disability, or national origin).

- Include objective references to confirm your statements.

☑ *Present qualifications honestly and ethically; do not inflate qualifications to increase chances of getting a job.*

Kevin Rueter
8901 Brookdale Road
Pueblo, CO 81002-8901
(405) 555-3920

OBJECTIVE: To obtain a supervisory position in commercial lending.

EXPERIENCE: **Commercial loan officer**, Baker Mortgage Corporation, June 1978–November 1995.

- Managed a $25 million loan portfolio, including international and domestic clients.

- Made final decisions on substantial loans averaging $800,000.

Intern, Sunbelt Bank, Ft. Collins, September–December 1977.

- Selected as result of intense competition; earned three hours' college credit.

- Approved small commercial loans and assisted the branch manager.

EDUCATION: **B.S., Finance and Real Estate,** Westbrook University, May 1978.
GPA: 3.6 (4.0 scale).

- Held leadership positions in professional organizations, received academic honors and scholarship.

INTERESTS: Golf, racquetball, and weightlifting.

REFERENCES: Available on request.

Effective Interviewing Techniques for Interviewers

Good interviewers

- Create a nonthreatening climate:

  - Friendly tone and positive nonverbal signal.

  - Advanced preparation with attention directed at the interviewee.

  - Introductory comment that puts interviewee at ease.

  - Clear explanation of the purpose of the interview.

- Work from a logical plan.

- Ask open-ended questions that generate in-depth discussion about qualifications.

- Do not ask questions that could lead to discriminatory hiring.

- Keep the interview moving.

- Are good listeners.

Guidelines for Effective Performance Appraisals

As an employee, you should

■ Seek frequent informal feedback on your performance.

■ Request an informal performance review near the mid-point of the period.

■ Be actively involved in your evaluation:

● Learn to evaluate your performance honestly.

● Suggest strategies for improving performance.

● Help supervisor set specific, measurable goals.

As a supervisor, you should

■ Actively involve employees identifying ways to improve and in setting realistic goals.

■ Create a nonthreatening climate.

■ Be prepared and highly organized.

■ Avoid generalizations, broad statements, and opinions; discuss only two or three weaknesses.

■ Offer specific, job-related comments.

Primary and Secondary Sources of Data

Primary Sources

- Customer surveys
- Market research
- Operational research
- Historical research
- Performance observation
- Product development
- Financial reports/forecasts
- Employee surveys

Secondary Sources

- Newspapers
- Magazines
- Journals
- Abstracts
- Almanacs/fact books
- Books
- Government documents
- Online sources

Sampling Methods

Simple random sampling:

The "fish bowl" sampling technique that ensures that each entity has an equal, known chance of being selected.

Selecting a door prize from among the 50 persons who placed their names in a basket.

Stratified random sampling:

Ensures that some characteristic of the population is proportionally represented in the sample.

Selecting a sample of 100 students for a survey with freshmen, sophomores, juniors, seniors, and graduate students represented in the same percentage as the total student body.

Systematic random sampling:

Taking every "nth" item from a list to produce the desired number of subjects.

Taking every 10th name from a telephone directory list of 500 to produce a sample of 50.

Convenience sampling:

A non-scientific sampling method in which the researcher selects subjects that are "convenient" to him/her, thus producing a sample that may not be representative of the population.

Using student responses from one particular class as representative of the entire campus's opinion on the cafeteria food.

Guidelines for Designing Effective Questionnaires

■ Arrange items in a logical sequence.

■ Ask for factual information that can be recalled readily.

■ Write clear questions that respondents can interpret consistently and answer easily.

• Brief, easy-to-follow directions
• Words with precise meanings
• Short items related to *one* idea
• No "skip-and-jump" instructions

■ Avoid threatening and awkward questions; provide ranges if possible.

■ Design for easy tabulation.

■ Do *not* force respondents to choose an answer that does not apply to them.

• Provide all possible answers
• Add "Undecided" or "other" category

■ Pilot test the questionnaire and revise based on feedback.

■ Create an appealing, easy-to-answer design.

Common Item Types for Questionnaires

Open Question

What will you do to combat inflation?

Forced Choice

What is the one most important problem you . . . .

Checklists

Check all that apply to you:

☐ Male   ☐ Married
☐ Female   ☐ Single

Rating Scale

Circle the number indicating how you feel about each statement:

Disagree				Agree			Strongly Agree
1	2	3	4	5	6	7	8

Ranking Scale

Please rank the following problems in order of importance. Use a 1 for most important, 2 for second most important, and continue until all are ranked.

_____ World Peace   _____ Unemployment
_____ Inflation   _____ Drug Abuse

Statement of the Problem:

The purpose of this study is to examine the problem of inadequate parking on campus.

Research Method and Sources of Information:

A normative survey by questionnaire to a random sample of students will be conducted.

Nature of Data to Be Gathered and Analyzed:

Data will be gathered on student perceptions of the severity of the parking problem, areas of campus with parking problems, and times of day/night when parking is a problem.

Hypothesis or Hypotheses to Be Proved or Disproved:

Inadequate parking is a problem that plagues the campus.

Parking Survey

Answer each of the following items by checking the appropriate option.

1. Your classification:

   ☐ Freshman ☐ Sophomore

   ☐ Junior   ☐ Senior

   ☐ Graduate ☐ Other

2. Residence Status

   ☐ Live on campus

   ☐ Live off campus

3. Attendance Status

   ☐ Day student only

   ☐ Night student only

   ☐ Attend day and night

4. Parking on campus is

   ☐ grossly inadequate

   ☐ somewhat inadequate

   ☐ generally inadequate

   ☐ more than adequate

5. Overall, how serious a problem is parking on campus? (Circle the number)

   Not a problem   A very serious problem

   1   2   3   4   5   6   7   8

6. What comments do you have concerning the parking on campus?

   Comments: _____

   _____

   _____

Jennas Yogurt Questionnaire

Answer each of the following items by checking the appropriate option.

1. Sex

   ☐ Female
   ☐ Male

2. Age

   ☐ Under 20   ☐ 41-45
   ☐ 20-25   ☐ 46-50
   ☐ 26-30   ☐ 51-55
   ☐ 31-35   ☐ 56-60
   ☐ 36-40   ☐ 61-65

3. Annual household income

   ☐ Under $15,000
   ☐ $15,001–$25,000
   ☐ $25,001–$35,000
   ☐ $35,001–$45,000
   ☐ $45,001–$50,000
   ☐ over $50,000

4. Have you purchased packaged yogurt in the last six months?

   ☐ Yes (continue with items)
   ☐ No (end interview)

5. What brands of yogurt that your household eats have you purchased in the last six months?

   ☐ Breyer's   ☐ Yoplait
   ☐ Brennan   ☐ Store brand
   ☐ Jennas   ☐ Other _____

6. Which of the brands just mentioned have you bought most often in the last six months?

   _____

Jennas Yogurt, Questionnaire, page 2

7. Who in your household eats yogurt?

   ☐ Self

   ☐ Spouse

   ☐ Other adult(s)

   ☐ Teen(s)

   ☐ Child(ren)

8. Rank the following factors in terms of the order in which they influence your yogurt purchase decisions. (1 is the most important factor.)

   ☐ Taste

   ☐ Healthy ingredients

   ☐ Price

   ☐ Brand confidence

   ☐ Other _____

Note: Questionnaire items should be logical and advance from simple to complex.

Lot Pricing Comparison

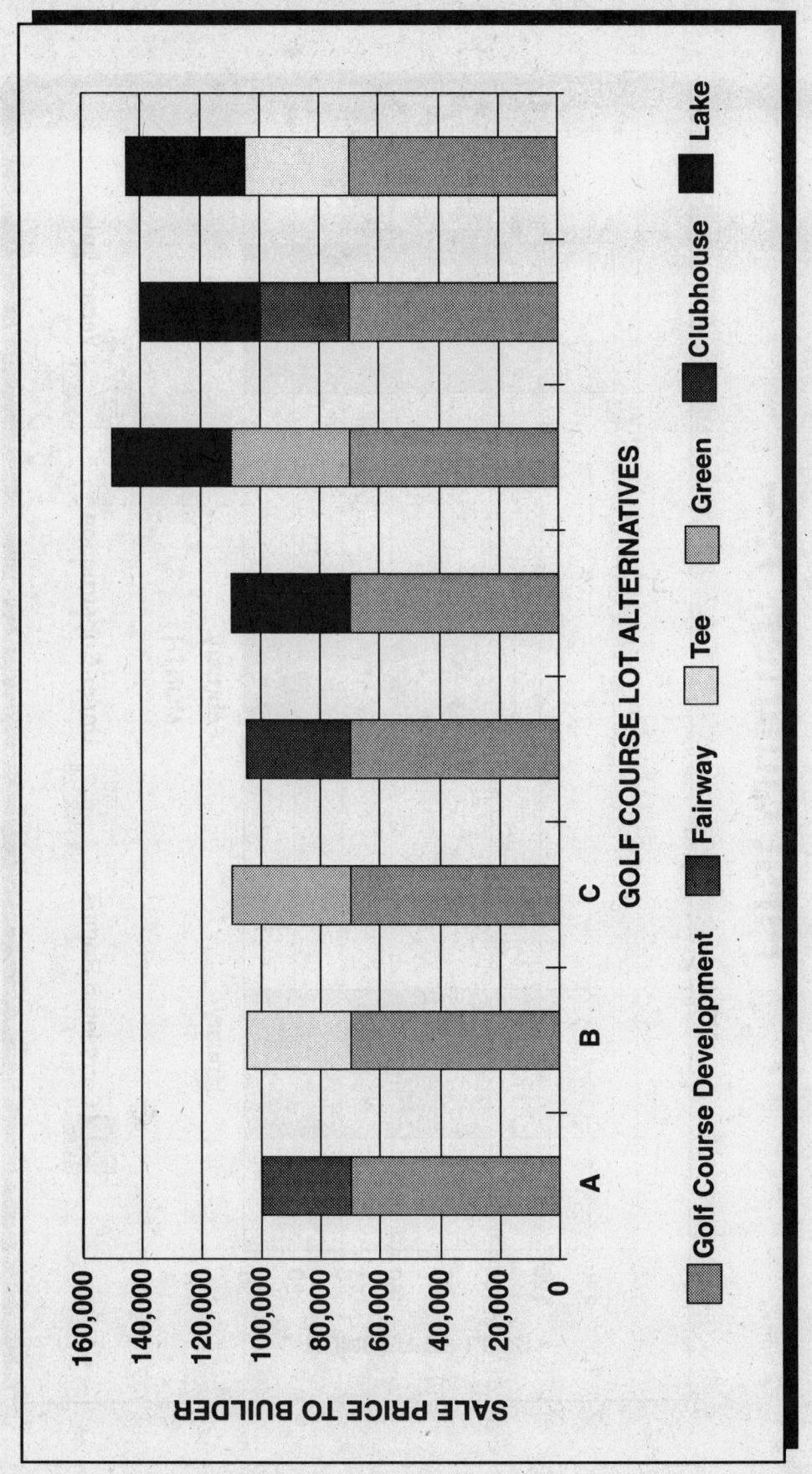

Lot Analysis for Gill Construction First Quarter, 19--

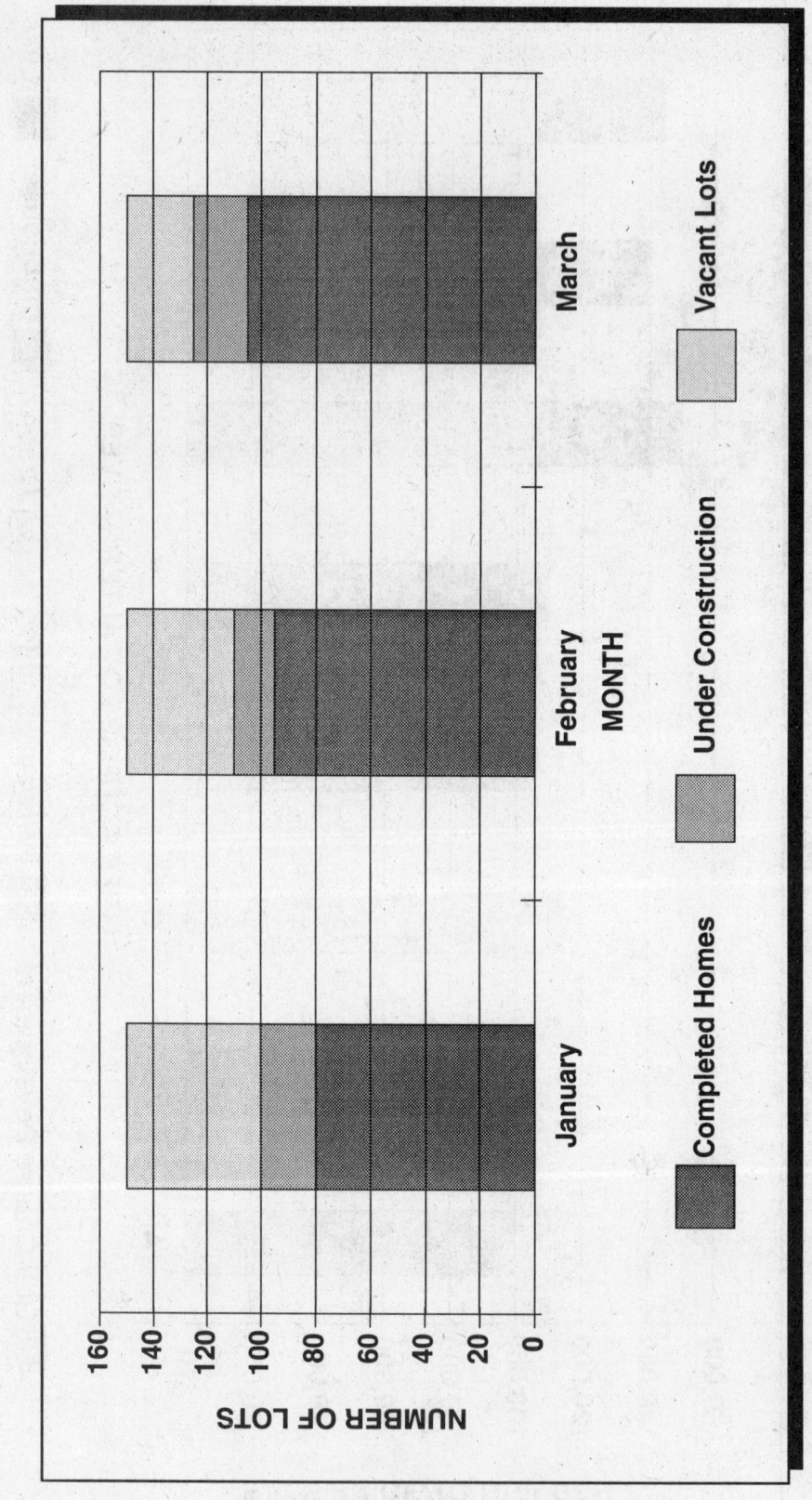

SALARIES	NUMBER	NO. X MIDPOINT
90–99	3	283.5
80–89	4	338.0
70–79	6	447.0
60–69	3	193.5
50–59	2	109.0
40–49	4	178.0
30–39	3	103.5
	25	1,652.5/25 = 66.1 (Mean)

Salaries of Chief Financial Officers in 25 Firms

SALARIES (000)	NO. OF EXECUTIVES	PERCENTAGES
90–99	3	12
80–89	4	16
70–79	6	24
60–69	3	24
50–59	2	12
40–49	4	8
30–39	3	12
	25	100

Southport Manufacturing Frequency of Injuries by Plant, 19--

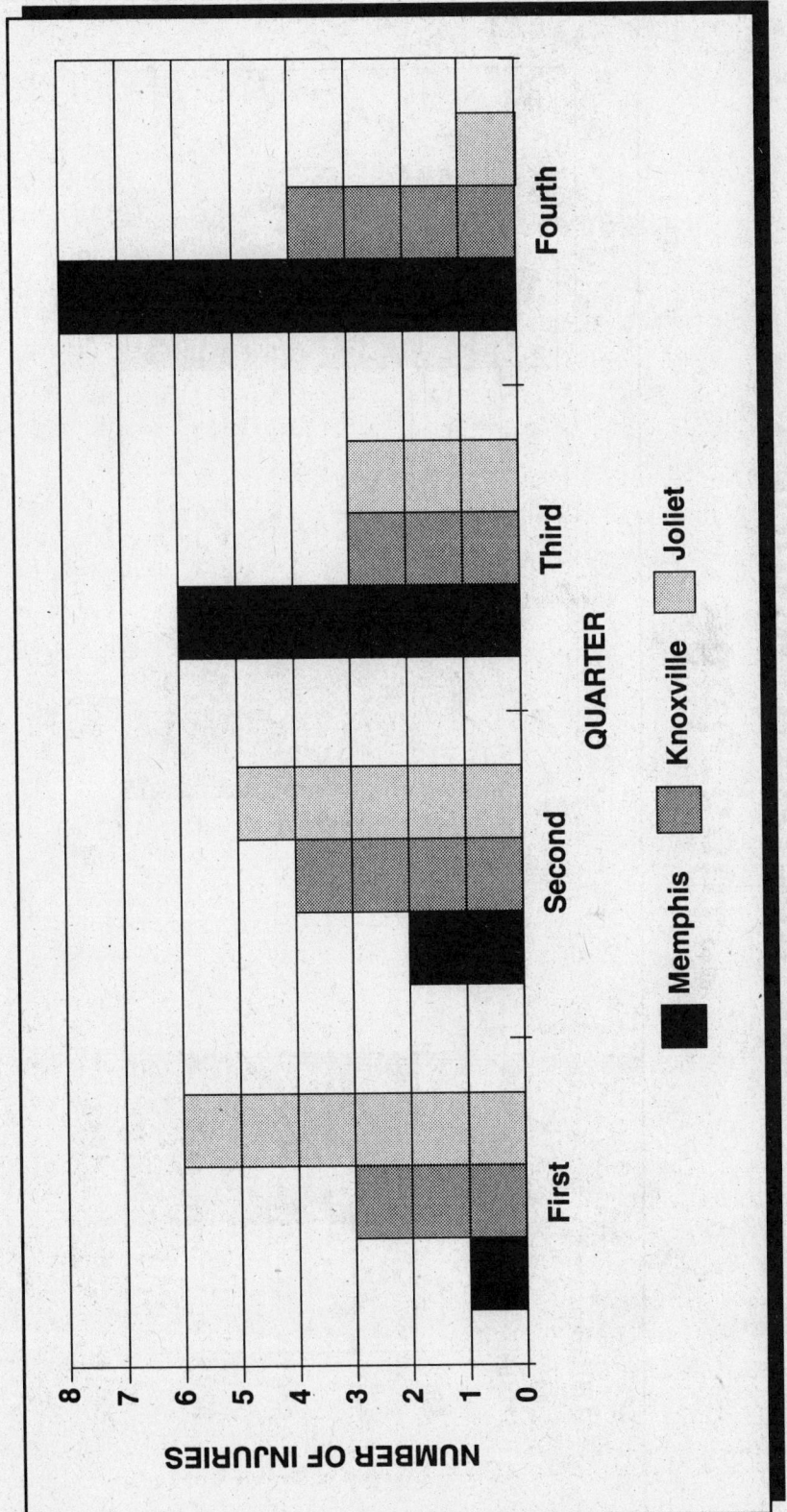

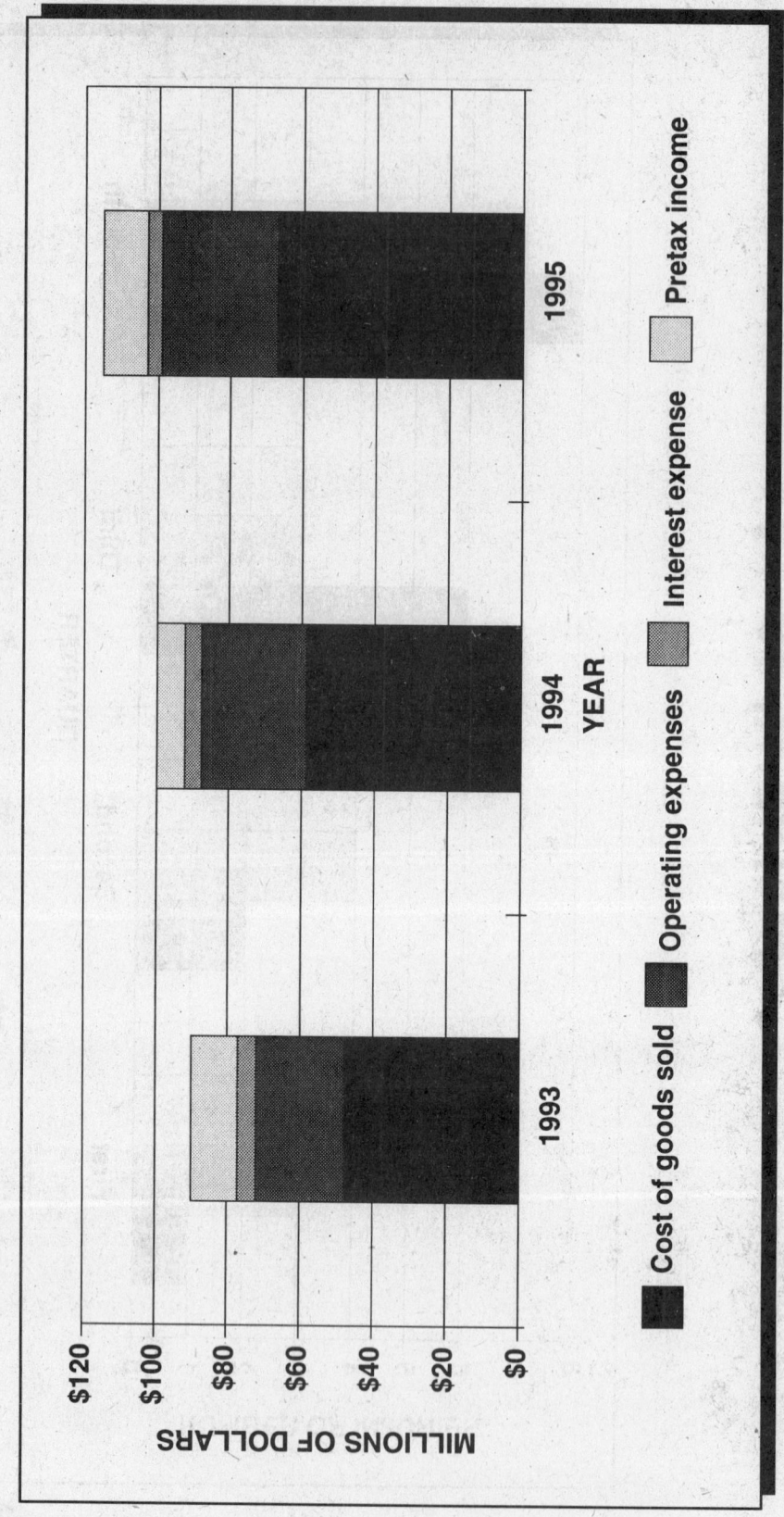

Arlington Fitness Connection
Results of Operations
1993–1995

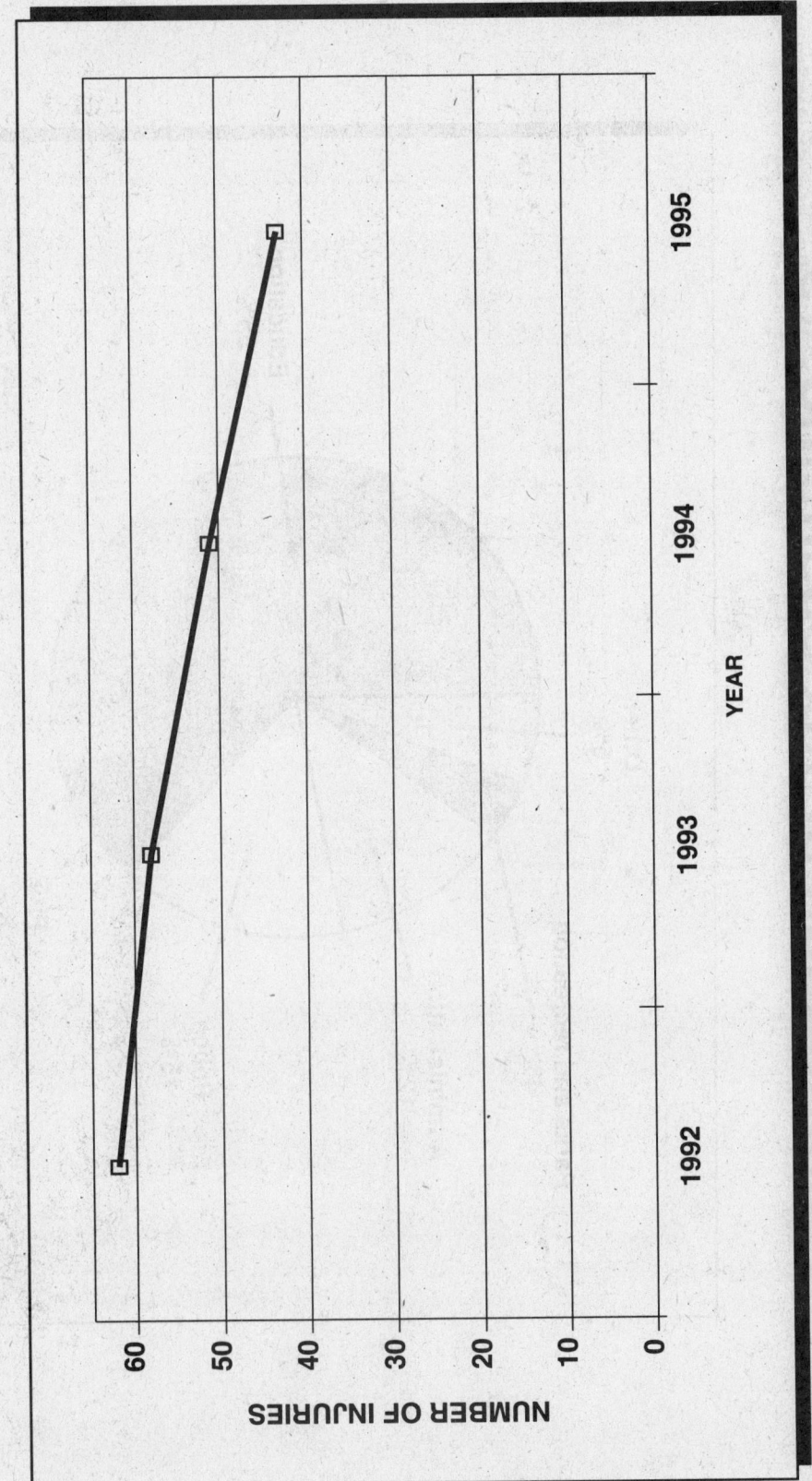

Southport Manufacturing
Total Work-related Injuries
1992–1995

Distribution of Tax Spending, 19--

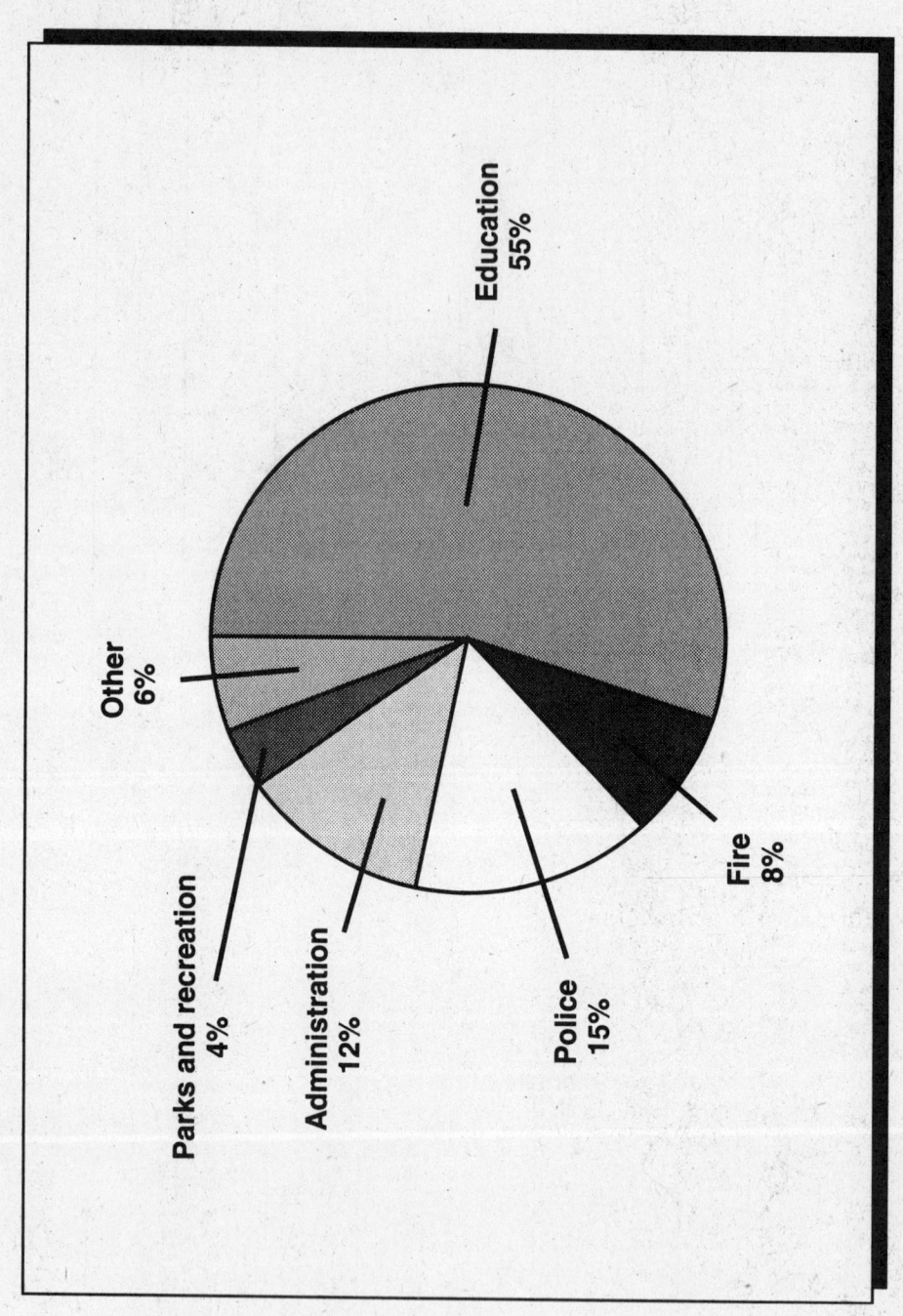

Education
55%

Other
6%

Parks and recreation
4%

Administration
12%

Police
15%

Fire
8%

Express Printing
Total Employer Health
Insurance Contribution
January 1–March 31, 19--

INSURED	NO. OF EMPLOYEES	PREMIUM PER EMPLOYEE	TOTAL AMOUNT
Employee / 0 dependents	32	$45	$1,440
Employee / 1 dependent	26	54	1,404
Employee / 2 dependents	18	60	1,080
Employee / 3 dependents	29	72	2,088
Total Contribution			$6,012

TOTAL CONSUMER CREDIT
MARCH 19—
(in billions)

	Total	Percentage
Noninstallment credit	$32.8	17.8
Personal loans	51.6	28.0
Automobiles	50.5	27.4
Consumer goods	49.4	26.8

Writing Techniques for Short Reports

- Use a personal writing style (first or second person) and contractions that contribute to a natural style.

- Use graphics to reinforce text.

- Use headings to partition text and reflect organization.

- Use letter format for external reports and memorandum format for internal reports.

September 1, 19--

Mr. Jason L. Moore
Attorney at Law
1535 Main Street
Providence, RI 01010-1535

Dear Mr. Moore

I have examined the inventory and visited the property included in the estate of Helen G. Smith. The services to be provided, as discussed in our recent conference, and the approximate amount are summarized below:

Specifications of Service

1. Preparation of a thorough analysis and documentation of the market value of each property listed in the inventory as of the valuation date, September 12, 19--.

2. Presentation of the results of the investigation at a conference to be held immediately upon completion of the analysis.

3. Preparation of a report outlining my conclusions about the value of the individual properties, including a summary of the method of analysis and limiting conditions.

Mr. Jason L. Moore
Page 2
September 1, 19--

4. Conference discussions with representatives of the Internal Revenue
    Service, if required and authorized.

Approximate Cost

My firm is prepared to furnish these services on the basis of $50 an hour
for each hour of appraiser time required. Based on a preliminary analysis
of the properties, I estimate the total project cost at approximately $8,200.

The services can be provided within sixty days from the date of authorization. If you wish to proceed, please sign and return one copy
of the enclosed agreement.

Sincerely

John H. Kelly
John H. Kelly, M.A.I.

Enclosure

TO: Professor's Name
FROM: Student's Name
DATE: November 18, 19--
SUBJECT: Change in Value of Stock Portfolio, November 11 – 15

After purchasing 100 shares of common stock in each of ten companies, as reported in my memo of November 11, I followed their progress for five trading days. The total invested was $59,450. At the close of the market on Friday, November 15, the value of the stocks was $60,100. The $650 gain represents a 1-percent growth during the week.

During the same one-week period, the Dow Jones Industrial Average decreased 1 percent from 2640 to 2614. Therefore, my selections, as shown in the following table, outperformed the Dow Jones:

Performance of Ten Selected Stocks, November 11 – 15

Stock	11/11 Price & Total*	11/15 Value & Total
Atlantic Richfield	$102½ – $10,250	$104 – $10,400
Citicorp	31 – 3,100	30½ – 3,050
General Mills	68½ – 6,850	70 – 7,000
Houston Industries	34 – 3,400	33 – 3,300
Lilly	103 – 10,300	106 – 10,600
NIPSCO	18 – 1,800	18½ – 1,850
Pitney Bowes	52 – 5,200	51 – 5,100
Ralston Purina	88 – 8,800	90 – 9,000
Snap-on Tools	34½ – 3,400	34 – 3,400
Xerox	63 – 6,300	64 – 6,400
TOTAL	$59,450	$61,000

*Total is price per share x 100.

Cannon Engineering, Inc.
Impact of Cellular Phones on Gross Profit
Second Quarter, 19--

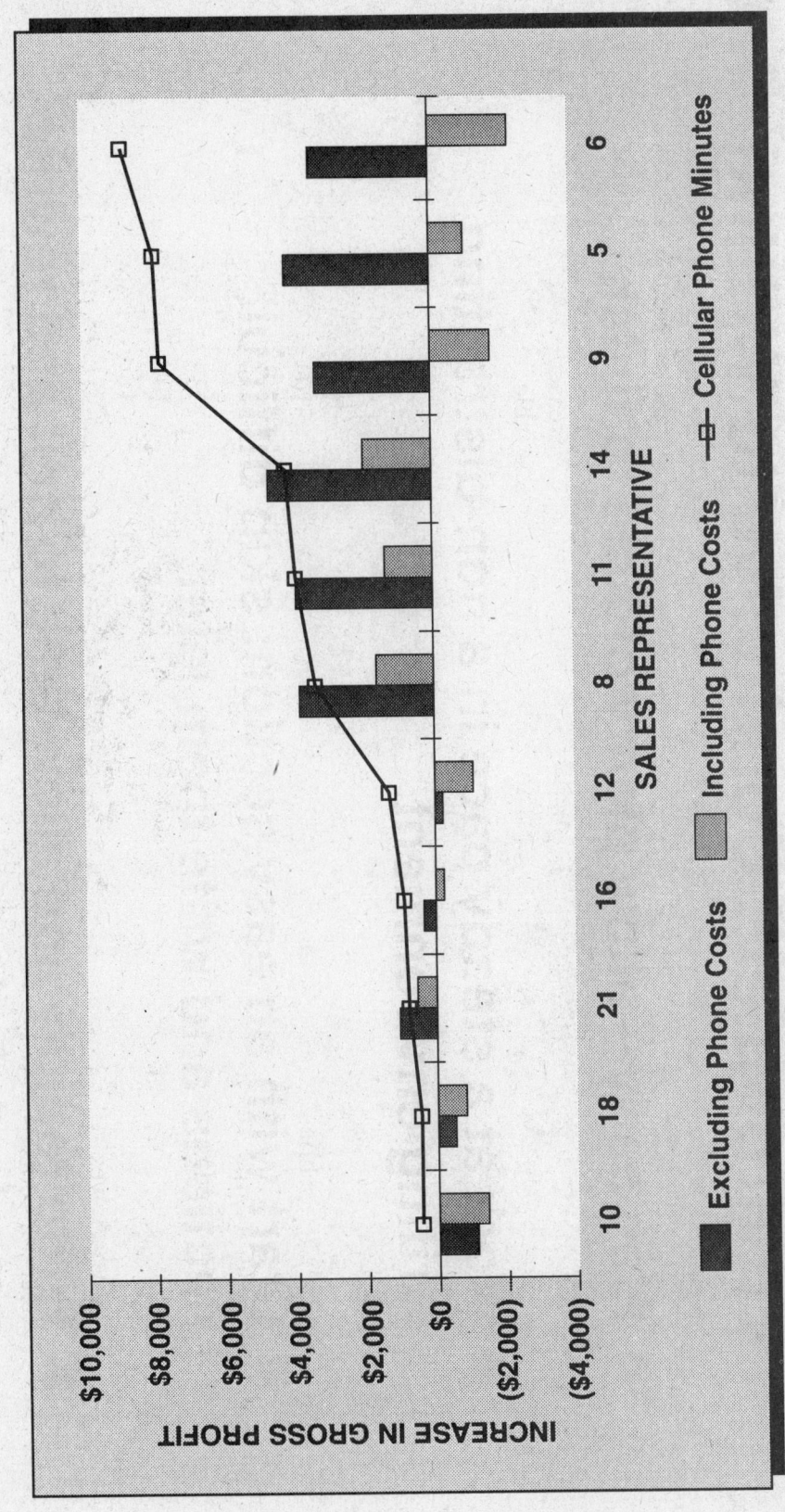

Cellular phones were installed at the beginning of the second quarter. Sales representatives are listed in order of cellular telephone usage.

Suggestions for Creating an Environment Conducive to Writing

■ Plan early—allow plenty of time to finish.

■ Work at a steady pace in a non-distracting writing environment.

■ Start with an easy section; skip difficult sections and write them later.

■ Write rapidly and allow time to edit and rewrite your first draft.

Current Date

Mr. James Becker
Riverside Cafe
151 Riverside Road
Little Rock, AR 72204-0151

Dear Mr. Becker

We are pleased to submit our analysis of Riverside Cafe. Despite intentions to attract young singles, you are attracting a mixed clientele of young families and singles. Identifying effective strategies for attracting a specific target market will result in a higher return on your investment.

Three alternative solutions are available:

- Convert exclusively to a singles' bar.

- Renovate the cafe into a moderately elegant seafood restaurant that will attract a broad range of patrons.

- Remodel the building to separate the bar from the restaurant. This change serve the needs of both the young singles and the families.

Singles' Bar Format Is the Best Alternative

We recommend that you convert the cafe to a singles' bar format. Our recommendation is based on the following factors: (1) profitability, (2) capital investment, and (3) owner's preference.

Mr. James Becker
Page 2
Current Date

Profitability. Converting to a singles' bar is the most profitable of the alternatives according to the attached financial projections. The singles' bar format is projected to increase profitability by 37 percent; the seafood restaurant, 23 percent; and the cafe with separate seating, 20 percent.

Capital requirements. The singles' bar format will require the least amount of capital to implement. A relatively small investment will be required to renovate the existing facility to support the singles' bar format. According to our estimates, this alternative would require approximately 80 percent less than the other alternatives.

Owner preference. Because your original goal was to attract young singles, we assume that you are interested in targeting this particular market. Consequently, we believe your interest will result in greater levels of energy and commitment.

Recommendations

The following changes are recommended to attract the singles' crowd:

Atmosphere. Easy listening music and a warm, cozy setting will encourage patrons to relax and enjoy the food and conversation with fellow patrons. Recessed, accent lights will contribute to this desired mood. Construct an outdoor deck on the river side of the restaurant with a bar, benches, and a dimly lighted walkway along the river.

Mr. James Becker
Page 3
Current Date

Menu. Add more appetizers and desserts and limit the number of entrees to encourage patrons to order throughout the evening rather than to order one large entree and then leave early in the evening. Provide a larger variety of drinks. Design an attractive menu giving your foods catchy, appealing titles.

Advertising. Specifically target your advertising to radio stations that young singles listen to, such as WJAM, and to the local MTV cable network. Plan a special advertising campaign to emphasize to the public that Riverside Cafe has undergone significant changes.

Mr. Becker, implementing these changes in atmosphere, menu, and advertising will allow you to target the singles' crowd more effectively and, therefore, should result in your earning a higher rate of return. If you wish to discuss these recommendations, please call me at (501) 555-9309.

Sincerely

Student's Name
Consultant

Current Date

Mr. James Becker
Riverside Cafe
151 Riverside Road
Little Rock, AR 72204-0151

Dear Mr. Becker

We are delighted you are pleased with the recommended changes that will allow you to implement the singles' bar format at Riverside Cafe.

Please review carefully the enclosed materials, which will help you implement these recommendations. These materials include:

- Form letter sent to five construction companies requesting an estimate to construct the outdoor deck.

- Routine request letter and news release sent to WJAM radio station.

- Sign designed using PrintMaster, which will be displayed at the front entrance and on each table to announce the appetizer of the day.

Mr. James Becker
Page 2
Current Date

- Menu designed using desktop publishing (or PrintMaster and word processing).

Mr. Becker, we appreciate the opportunity to help you develop effective strategies for reaching your target market. One of our staff will call on you in a couple of weeks. Best of luck in creating a new image for Riverside Cafe.

Sincerely

Student's Name
Consultant

Enclosures

Special Letter Parts

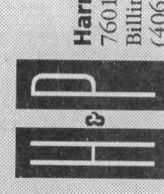

Harrison & Pearson, LTD, CPAs
7601 Faulkner Building, Suite 350
Billings, MT 59101-7601
(406)555-3400   Fax (406)555-6874

January 19, 19--   DS

FACSIMILE
DS

Attention Ms. Margaret Daniel
Communications Systems, Inc.
Mitchell Building, Suite 250
Atlanta, GA 30311-5309
DS

Re: Engagement No. 39-29-3773   DS

Ladies and Gentlemen:
DS

ENGAGEMENT AGREEMENT FOR COMMUNICATIONS SYSTEMS, INC.
DS

Harrison & Pearson is pleased to confirm arrangements to audit the
financial statements of Communication Systems, Inc., for the year
ended June 30, 19--.

MAILING NOTATION

ATTENTION LINE

REFERENCE LINE

SUBJECT LINE

Special Letter Parts (continued)

SECOND-PAGE HEADING

Communications Systems, Inc.   1-inch   (Line 6)
Page 2
January 19, 19--   **DS**

Sharon Hampton has been assigned as the audit manager in charge of your audit examination. Please review the enclosed preliminary time schedule she has developed and direct your questions to her at 555-3095, extension 25.

We at Harrison & Pearson look forward to providing these and other quality professional services to you.   **DS**

Sincerely,   **DS**

COMPANY NAME

HARRISON & PEARSON, LTD., CPAs   **QS**

Jerome S. Fuja

Jerome S. Fuja
Audit Partner

REFERENCE INITIALS

ek   **DS**

ENCLOSURE NOTATION

Enclosure: Audit Agreement   **DS**

COPY NOTATION

c Mr. David Banks   **DS**

POSTSCRIPT

Our annual tax update has been scheduled for March 5-6, 19--. You will receive an agenda from the tax department just as soon as all details have been finalized.